The Complete Book of BABY and CHILD CARE for Christian Parents

BY Grace H. Ketterman, M.D.

Teenage Rebellion (with Truman E. Dollar)
How to Teach Your Child About Sex
*The Complete Book of Baby and Child Care for Christian
Parents* (with Herbert L. Ketterman, M.D.)

The Complete Book of BABY and CHILD CARE for Christian Parents

Grace H. Ketterman M.D. and Herbert L. Ketterman M.D.

Fleming H. Revell Company
Old Tappan, New Jersey

Scriptures in this volume, unless otherwise identified, are from the King James Version of the Bible.

Scripture quotation identified TLB is from The Living Bible, copyright © 1971 by Tyndale House Publishers, Wheaton, IL. Used by permission.

Special thanks to Ginny McDermott for providing the diagrams used in this book.

Grace H. Ketterman received her M.D. from University of Kansas School of Medicine. She practiced pediatrics at the Hickman Mills Clinic before taking a fellowship in Child Psychology at Western Missouri Mental Health Center. She is presently Medical Director of the Crittenton Center, Kansas City, Missouri.

Herbert L. Ketterman received his M.D. from University of Kansas School of Medicine. He served an internship at Bethany Hospital in Kansas. Dr. Ketterman is now on the staff of the Hickman Mills Clinic, Kansas City, Missouri.

Library of Congress Cataloging in Publication Data

Ketterman, Grace H.
 The complete book of baby and child care for Christian parents.

   Bibliography: p.
   Includes index.
   1. Children—Care and hygiene.   2. Child
rearing.   3. Christian education of children.
I. Ketterman, Herbert L.   II. Title.
RJ61.K44   649'.1   81-17871
ISBN 0-8007-1280-3   AACR2

TO our children
  Kathy
  Lyndon
    and
  Wendy
who have taught us much of
what we know about children.

And to our grandson,
  Andy,
who reminds us!

Contents

Part I

Preparing to Have a Child

1
Having a Child—
Are You Ready?

In all of our combined fifty-five years of busy medical practices, we have shared a wealth of emotional experiences and agree upon many concepts. There is one incomparable drama, however, that we believe transcends all the rest. That is the birth of a child. The repetition of the miracle of all creation is breathtakingly focused for the moment on that tiny, new human being.

A BABY IS BORN

Trying to capture in words the awesomeness of that sacred event is impossible. At one moment there is a tired, disheveled woman who has shared her very existence with a growing fetus. She has endured the pain and stress of labor and the difficult processes of birth. In the next moment, that woman is transformed by the radiant expression of incredulity at the person to whom she has given existence.

As the baby's reassuring cry rings out, we have seen tears of relief and joy spill unashamedly from the tender eyes of the mother and father alike. Their gratitude to the doctors and nurses is exceeded only by their intimate love and pride in each other. For those moments, the entire world and the hope for its future seems to rest in the three of them—father, mother, and baby—in their sense of joy and fulfillment.

Surely no other human experience is so intense or profound as the bonding together of mother to father to child—and all to the Great Creator and Father. The ecstasy of this experience must even out in the days to come, or it would exhaust the family!

But many times, as we have examined babies in the nursery,

we have caught the echo of that excitement. Mothers' noses are flattened by their pressure against the glass, as they anxiously scan our faces during the physical evaluation of their babies. As soon as our smiles have reassured them of the baby's perfection, the early glow of pride is restored and all is well.

The Contrast Later

How tragic, then, is the contrast to such radiant joy in a new-born life to the jaded disappointment of some parents later on. The number of parents who wish they had never had children is certainly not an accurate count, but it seems to be alarmingly high.

There is an undercurrent of parental discontent, and more than a little suggestion that children are often in the way—a bother to be shifted as much as possible. As Christians, we believe that such attitudes are wrong. We hope in this book to help you accept the realities of parenthood and to prevent most of the disenchantment of later years.

CHILDREN IN SCRIPTURE

Certainly it is not easy or convenient to be a parent, and there are sacrifices to be made if you become mothers and fathers. These, however, are of the quality of a farmer who labors to sow and cultivate his grain because the harvest will enrich him and provide for his old age. Children are eulogized throughout the Scriptures. They are described as wealth, as protection, as a source of pride and honor, as well as joy. It was cause for real grief in biblical times for a woman to be unable to bear a child.

Jesus Himself paid the highest compliment to children when He said, "Whosoever shall not receive the kingdom of God as a little child, he shall not enter therein" (Mark 10:15).

Our children have enriched our lives immeasurably. The memories of their illnesses, as well as their exciting growth and development, are treasures. We still laugh together over their funny expressions as they learned to talk, and are amazed at the simple profoundness of their childish wisdoms. We have wept together over the pain each of us has unknowingly inflicted on the other, and we have gratefully rejoiced at being forgiven.

During the writing of this book, Dr. Herbert Ketterman's

eighty-nine-year-old mother suffered a heart attack, and then a stroke that took her life. The attention of her children was an inspiration. They traveled across the country to take up a vigil by her side, not as a duty, but in the loving concern that she not be alone. She had stood by them in all of their illnesses and the struggles of their growing up. It was their turn to stand by her. This is the blessed cycle of birth, and life, and death.

FUNDAMENTALS OF PARENTHOOD

In thinking about readiness for becoming parents, let us look at the fundamental functions of parents. What is it that you must do to create an environment in which your children can grow up to bless you, rather than hurt and worry you?

Creation of New Lives

We believe that a major purpose in marriage and the development of a home is the *creation* of new lives. It is instinctive (and therefore God-given) to reproduce one's own life in that of a baby. Having grown up in rural and small-town areas, we, the authors, are especially aware of the biologically normal function that this process is in all of nature.

In the birth of each of our children, we felt a rare and special kinship with God the Creator. He had given us the ability to form, out of invisible cells, a brand-new human being. *We, too, were creators.*

Bond to God and Each Other. Not only does a child represent a kinship with the heavenly Father, but it also is symbolic of the union of husband and wife. As you learn to work through your differences, you achieve a close interpersonal relationship. As you grow in your trust of each other, you develop an intimate emotional life. The sharing of your lives and experiences can produce an amazingly beautiful unity that enhances each one, while bonding you together.

We believe children are an evidence of that bond. They begin from unique half-cells that are useless alone. But in their joining together, they become a new life, part of each of you and all of your ancestors before you. Each child is a reminder of your love for each other and your families, and he will soon wedge himself into your hearts for his own share of love.

Christian parents, especially, have a right to rejoice in the opportunity to bear children. The chance to teach your children to become part of God's family, as well as your own, is eternal in its implications.

Dream of the Future. The Jewish ritual of circumcision is an ancient and dignified ceremony. It is an occasion for feasting and celebration that we have been honored to attend. We shall never forget the solemnity of the greeting by devout Jews to the parents of a baby boy: "Another son is born to Israel!" The deep feeling wrapped in those simple words was the hope of the Jewish future.

And perhaps that is, in a simple way, the hope of every parent. Each new child represents our dreams and hopes for the future. He will brighten our home and enrich our world. Even heaven will be made better by the eternal life of this, our child!

Nurturing

If the advent of a new child is to have such beneficial results, however, the second function of parents must go into effect. That is the role of *nurturing.* We will discuss the feeding of your children at length later on in this book. Proper nutrition is essential to the physical growth and health of your children.

There is an equally vital role that nurturing plays in the spiritual and emotional life of your child. You need to be mature in your own lives, in order to provide that nurturing.

Prayers. It was my [Grace's] parents' prayers and exemplary lives that were the nutritional elements of my spiritual life. Every single day of our lives was begun with prayers. We all shared in petitions or praise for rain, the fruitfulness of the crops, the health and safety of our lives, and any conceivable needs or joys we experienced. The Bible's promises were our insurance, and we truly lived by them. Mother even prayed over the purchase of new shoes in those anxious years of the depression of the 1930s.

Sharing. Our emotional lives were richly fed by those same unusual parents. The teasing and laughter we shared lightened the drudgery of long days of hard work. The worries, indignation, and hopes of the troubled years of World War II and its aftermath were shared openly within our family. The grief of one was pain to all, and we shared our successes, as well.

Intellectual Stimulation. Intellectually we were challenged by the games that occupied long winter evenings. Dad read aloud to us, entire books full of humor and pathos, and always, he managed to clarify the basic philosophy of an honest, godly life. Mealtimes were often a chance to discuss some current issue, and I relate the ability to be accepting and tolerant of others to those very conversations.

In your own way, you need to plan to provide a climate of emotional warmth, honesty, and openness, as well as intellectual stimulation. Children thrive and develop well in such surroundings.

Protection

Parents obviously must be able to protect their child if he is to survive. This protection needs to include physical aspects of preventing diseases, avoiding the hazards of Nature, and the attacks of an increasingly violent society. To be ready for parenting, be sure that you are aware of the many subtle (as well as apparent) dangers to your children.

Spiritual dangers are especially frightening in their implications. The risk of secular, atheistic humanism is of growing concern to Christians in nearly all churches in the United States. Other Christians, equally sincere, are worried about the possible development of a rigid legalism that can stifle the growth of healthy spiritual freedom.

Providing protection from both extremes demands your awareness, parents. You must read, listen, and think deeply. In fact, it demands the superhuman wisdom and guidance of God's Spirit. You must step ahead of your children, if you would adequately guard them.

A Wonderful Memory. When I was only nine, my older sister and I had to walk alone to our country school. On the plains, there was little protection against the force of the cold north winds, and temperatures often fell below zero. On one particularly cold morning, not a single farm vehicle would start, so we could not drive to school. It was, of course, unthinkable that we should miss school, but our father did not want to risk our safety. Frostbite was a real and dreaded danger.

As long as I live, I will not forget Dad's solution to our predicament. Both of us children bundled up as warmly as we could.

But our warmth was best provided by our father. He walked before us up the frozen dirt roads, facing the winds. As he felt the intense cold, he unbuttoned his own overcoat and held it wide open, so that we could be sheltered. How he survived that bitter cold, I don't know—but his loving protection, I'll never forget!

We hope you will devise your own unique patterns for the protection of your children. As you consider having children, think about the dangers of life and plan for your walk before your children to be one that will guard them in every way!

Training and Education

Another significant function of parents is that of training and educating their children. While few parents are equipped to teach academic skills, you are the best experts on giving your children the values and self-discipline they will need to become productive adults.

Our experience has shown that it is in the area of training that many mothers and fathers lose their children. In the intensity of their desire to force conformity on their son or daughter, their disapproval and anger transcend their love, approval, and enjoyment of this child. The very fact of their disciplinary actions evidences deep caring, but a child who receives much harsh discipline in her training simply cannot feel the love.

In considering the arrival of a child, you need to know that you can do these two things:

1.   *Consistently feel loving toward your child, and communicate that honestly.*
2.   *Respond just as intensely to all of your child's strengths as you do to her problems. Never take a child's assets for granted.*

If or when your scolding and disapproval outweigh your pride and love—you can count on it—you will lose your effectiveness with that child.

Judging Yourself. How can you know, early on in your deliberations about having children, how you will be later on? We believe you can have some idea by the way you treat each other as husband and wife. If you remember to compliment each other and express your love in sincere and creative ways, you will no doubt do this for your child. In the same way you work through disagreements, restoring your fundamental love to ever stronger bases, so you will almost surely deal with your child. Furthermore, if you love your own selves as you love your neighbor, (as Jesus Christ taught), your love will automatically spill over onto the child who will one day live with you.

The Pillow Top. One experience from my childhood shows the lifelong value of good training. I was nine years old when my mother decided I was old enough to learn to do fine needlework. I was excited about the bright fabric and colorful thread that I would transform into a beautiful pillow top. For about an hour I toiled industriously, and proudly worked several inches in the corner of the big square. Laying it aside, I ran out to play, and may well have left it forever unfinished.

But my mother knew better than to let that happen. Later, she reintroduced the needlework and made me complete still more of the design. The threads became tangled and sweaty, the stitches were monotonous, and I came to detest the project. I hid it and my mother found it. I deliberately made mistakes in the pattern, and Mother fixed it. I pouted, cried, yelled, and rebelled. But Mother firmly and tenaciously required me to finish that pillow top.

That was a long, tiresome summer for me; it must have been unbearable to Mother. When I came home from school one day in early autumn, there on the sofa was my summer's discipline. Mother had stuffed it with a pillow, added a bright pink ruffle, and told everyone who visited that Grace had made that. I must admit that I felt quite guilty every time she bragged about it, for I never would have finished it without her "help"!

A dozen years later, that pillow top was again to be significant in my life. I had just started medical school. How exciting it was to find myself in one of those coveted positions, learning so many new and intriguing things! Like the pillow top, however, the glamour soon was gone and the stark reality of the indescribable discipline of the medical student's life was undeniable. I wanted to quit. I was newly in love and I thought it would be fine to get married and put my husband through school. He could do the hard work!

The lesson of the pillow top, however, held firm in my being—any project worth beginning should be finished. There was help and hope, and finish, I did. So, parents, don't minimize the training of childhood. Its fruits are far-reaching and well worth all of your efforts.

Discipline Yourselves. Perhaps you were not blessed with parents who taught you this lesson. Begin now to discipline yourselves. You can learn from their mistakes and by knowing the importance of follow-through, you can develop that quality and be prepared to teach your children.

Letting Go

For us, the hardest job of parenting has been the letting go of our children. Even in planning on your children's birth, we suggest you do so with the awareness that they are not yours forever—only yours to hold in trust until they are ready to function alone. Perhaps that is why God inspired David to write, "As arrows are in the hand of a mighty man, so are children of the youth. Happy is the man who hath his quiver full of them . . ." (Psalms 127:4, 5). Arrows are useless unless they are sent out to a target. And each child has his own unique aim and goal in life. Your job is to be sure your children are straight and balanced, so they can reach their target.

Knowing and planning toward that end can help you let go when the time is right. In your dreams and plans, keep your awareness clear: "This child will leave us; he has a purpose in life. And we are only to serve as guides to help him fulfill that plan."

As you teach your children well and include in that instruction a meaningful trust in the heavenly Father, you can more easily let go. The transfer of a child's hand from mother to father is not too difficult; and as you give your children over to God's hand, letting go is possible.

Home Base

The last function of good parenting is that of becoming a base for your child's returning. His bearings in life's journey will be easier to keep if he can return to you for an anchoring place now and then. During times of stress, I could revisit that old farmhouse. The wisdom and comfort of the parents who always loved me was instantly available. Every visit was a recapitulation of the beginning of life, its nurturing, protection, guidance, and freedom. Even in memory, those qualities are there whenever I need to draw on their strength.

PRACTICAL CONSIDERATIONS

A Matter of Inconvenience

There are some practical concerns you need to face before deciding to have a child. Let us emphasize a profoundly simple fact: *It is entirely inconvenient to be a parent!* You can count on that fact for sure! The nice part, however, is this: If you accept that fact and expect the inconvenience, you will be remarkably able to handle it. It is in striving for everything to be easy and finding it otherwise, that we are frustrated and disillusioned. A great deal of energy can be spent in this sort of struggle.

Our Western culture, unfortunately, has held up as ideal the qualities of ease and pleasure. Pain and hardship are to be avoided at all costs, and pleasure is the goal of life for many people.

One family I know illustrates the tragic deceptiveness of that concept. The parents loved their own busy social world. They also loved children and believed they could have both children and a continual social life outside the home. Missing hardly a single event, they sailed through the births of six children. At first they left them with sitters and grandparents. But soon they left the older children in charge of the younger ones; they were alone most evenings and several weekends out of each month. The children developed serious personal problems, because they lacked even the minimum time they needed to feel their parents' caring—genuine though it was.

Quality, Not Quantity

In general, we adhere to the belief that it is the *quality* of a parent's time with a child that counts more than the *quantity*. In families like this one mentioned above, however, or where work consumes a disproportionate amount of time and energy, a child cannot help feeling unimportant.

As a busy pediatrician, I had to spend long hours away from home or attached to a telephone. While I sincerely devoted the time I did have to our wonderful children, there were many times that I was unable to give them enough. One day our oldest child, perceptive and painfully honest, asked, "Mom, who is more important—me, or your patients?" *I* knew the answer, but she couldn't know, for my actions and feelings were not consistent.

Arranging Priorities. A part of the inconvenience of parenthood (and, paradoxically, part of the answer) lies in your need to organize and discipline your way of life. If you are to have the energy and the time it takes to be a good parent, you will need to arrange your priorities. Perhaps you value a meticulously kept house or attractive and well-balanced meals. Be sure that when your baby is small, you will rarely be able to achieve those goals and still have time to attend to his needs. Will you allow the baby to cry too long, while you finish chasing the last specks of dust? Or will you attend to the infant halfheartedly, or even irritably, because of your frustration over a dirty house? In either event, yours and the baby's joy and contentment will be marred unless you rearrange your priorities.

After some thirty years as a busy wife and mother, I can assure you that dirt will last. It simply waits for your convenience. A baby does neither. She grows with incredible rapidity to the point of not needing you and, if she has to wait too long, she will either give up and withdraw, or become an angry person. So ask for some help; learn to pick up and keep the surface clean; know that you can survive admirably on soup and sandwiches until your first priority is old enough to need less of your attention.

Role of Husbands. In case you husbands feel we are writing this to your wives, let us clarify that this philosophy includes you, too. Fathers have been horribly left out of modern, urban parenting roles. The medical profession and society have unwittingly joined to exclude you until recently. Many fathers are afraid of the fragility of a tiny baby. Superefficient moms, with all their modern conveniences, may not seem to need you. But they do—and the baby does. Most of all, you fathers need the incomparable feeling of intimacy with your own child. You need to help in his care, help about the house, and give encouragement and help to your wife. It is true that much of your time together as husband and wife must be sacrificed in serving the needs of your child. What you will lose in your freedom and privacy while a baby is tiny, will be more than compensated by the joy of sharing together in the training and loving of this tiny person, who is part of both of you!

Being an intern when I was just out of medical school was a grueling job. It demanded long hours, anxiety, little sleep, and great responsibility. It was, therefore, with special admiration that I shared the stories of another intern. He and his wife had their first baby during that year. No matter how tired he might be, he would invariably give their baby boy his evening bath and bottle. He really wanted to be his son's dad and not just his breadwinner. It's that sort of effort, even self-sacrifice, that it takes to be a parent. It's not convenient and certainly not easy, but for sure, it's rewarding when it's done gladly.

Relatively Speaking

Another important point in determining your readiness for parenthood relates to the way you feel about each other and your in-laws. What if your child became the "spitting" image of your spouse? Or what if he looked and acted exactly like your father-in-law? When there are hidden dislikes or resentments toward relatives, they may have to come right out in the open if your child resembles one of them. Failure to genuinely respect, as well as love, your spouse, may create many hazards in your interactions as a family later on.

As you search out your heart and mind on these issues, be honest. Then be energetic. Set about understanding each other and choose to respect and accept each other *and* your relatives. That isn't too difficult if you really do understand them. Learn to give up some of your selfish interests for the good of others. Get your priorities straight. Discipline yourself to follow through with your decisions and responsibilities. Not only will you be on your way to readiness as a parent, but you will be a much happier and more lovable person.

This book is an effort to help you achieve a positive balance in your anticipated role as parents. By considering your new responsibilities, you can prepare yourselves for them beforehand.

Through accepting and loving yourselves and each other, you will be ready to love and accept your child.

SUMMING UP

Nurturing your child is a big job—one that encompasses his mind, emotions, and spirit, as well as his body.

Protection of your child is not likely to demand walking into a freezing north wind on the plains. It is, however, a very cold world into which your children will be born. The selfish, humanistic environment of our culture is an even more deadly threat than frostbite. You must become strong to protect your children from this.

Training and guidance are, first of all, and most importantly of all, your responsibility. Training today for the child's future is awesome, but it is exciting to know that doing it right now will bear good fruit later.

Even before you have them, planning to let them go can help you gain perspective in your child rearing. Holding on too long can cause rebellion. Letting go too soon can cause dangerous uncertainty. Finding the balance is an ongoing challenge in parenting.

Once you have let go of your children, be prepared for their need to return to you. That is their great respect for you, and yet you need to handle that carefully. You are not to overprotect or pamper them, but offer your wisdom and counsel, your confidence in them, and your love.

In all of these functions, with their infinite range of details, be sure you remember your own heavenly Father. As you walk momently with Him, your resources are assured. His energy, love, and wisdom will empower and guide you. Don't try to go alone!

2
Getting Pregnant—
What You Need to Know

Having discovered that you are ready for parenthood—even though you are not perfect, but you are aware and growing—your next decision may well be "When?" With the birth-control measures that are so safe and available, today's parents have the special privilege and responsibility of choosing when they want to have a child.

Many couples sail through such a decision with ease, but for others, it is much more complicated. It is possible, for example, for one or the other to have some lurking old fears or unconscious resistance to giving up freedom for such a responsibility. Once those are discovered, talked about, and the decision really firmed up, they may have no difficulty achieving conception. (We will discuss later the few cases, however, where there is serious difficulty in becoming pregnant.)

PRACTICAL CONSIDERATIONS

Some practical issues to consider before you stop all contraceptive measures are these:

Financial Security

Do you have reasonable financial security? Having an income that will support a family without the mother's working for a while, at least, is certainly essential. A small savings account for emergencies and an insurance plan in the unlikely event of a tragedy certainly are good planning.

Adequate Housing

Do you have housing that will accommodate a baby? An apartment complex may not allow children; or neighbors in adjoining apartments may resent the sounds of a noisy child. Will the presence of a child, with his necessary equipment, make life uncomfortable for you? Perhaps you could find an old house that you could enjoy restoring or a small, newer one that you would find more private and cozy for your family. Be certain that you do not wait for elaborate or expensive quarters or furnishings. In today's world, that could delay things past the childbearing years! Sturdy used furniture can be refinished and made uniquely your very own creation. This is especially true of baby furniture that is used for a short time anyway.

Medical and Hospital Insurance

Be very sure that you have medical and hospital insurance, if at all possible! The cost of some complications could ruin your budget, at the present costs of medical care. If this is not possible, you may save carefully, and by explaining your limitations to your physician, arrange for a payment plan. In most larger cities, there are very fine low-cost clinics where good maternity care is based realistically on a couple's income and ability to pay.

Importance of Teamwork

It is extremely wise to have developed a meaningful communications system and a spirit of teamwork. Being truly willing to divide responsibilities and help each other during times of stress can tide you through many difficult times. During our years in medical school, my husband and I had to wear white uniforms. When I had a paper to write or needed to study for an examination, he would iron my uniforms. Through thirty years of marriage, that support (being a job he disliked) has endeared him to me!

Solve Personal Problems First

Any serious personal problems that you may not have solved should be worked through before you start a family. This is especially true if those issues involve severe misunderstandings with your parents or fits of depression. The feelings you have toward your parents or your in-laws will not only influence your attitude toward each other, but toward your child as well.

My own mother was very loving, writes Dr. Grace, but she did have a habit of yelling at and scolding us that frightened and angered me as a child. I recall vowing at such times that I would never yell at my children! And I rarely did. When our oldest child reached the teen years and did some early rebelling, she hit me on target one day by saying, "Mother, why don't you ever yell at me? I think I need it sometimes!" Had I known that some scolding was useful, I could have yelled at her, when she deserved it, in a constructive way.

One young wife went through several months of counseling before getting pregnant, in order to be free of some old resentments toward her parents. She wisely has avoided taking those destructive old feelings out on her son.

Strong Personal Faith

Be sure that you have a meaningful relationship with the heavenly Father. This needs to be individually yours and not someone else's rigidly prescribed code. There will be many times when your choosing to ask God's guidance and draw on His love and energy will see you successfully through some tense situations. As you walk with God, He will enable you to be a parent who will make it easy for your child to trust in Him as he grows.

Falling short, however, may seriously hinder the development of your child's own faith. A personal reading of the Bible will give you a good idea of God's ways with people and can guide you well. There are many clear commands about child rearing as well that will help. The Book of Proverbs in the Old Testament is full of wisdom that fits well with good child psychiatry of today. In Galatians and Ephesians in the New Testament, there are some extremely wise admonitions.

Reliable Physician and Special "Backup"

Have a reliable person or persons on whom you may call for help when it is needed. Be sure to have a family doctor or pediatrician whom you can trust and who will be available to you. A special friend or relatives (when they are near) may be like an insurance policy—knowing they are there may be so reassuring that you won't need to call on them. But arrange that ahead of time. You may return the favor of their help later.

Importance of Your Own Health

Be sure that you both are in as good health as possible. Recent studies are revealing evidence that excessive caffeine, smoking, and, of course, drug or alcohol abuse do affect the health and development of a child. So take care of yourself. Having a baby will be a great favor to you if this helps you to develop good habits of eating, resting, and exercise. Now don't become a food faddist or a "health nut." Just practice good common sense and listen to your own body. It will tell you when to rest and eat and even how much—if your wishes don't block out its messages.

While it certainly is not necessary, you, the wife, may want to consult your doctor before you try to become pregnant. This is especially true when you have been using the Pill or an I.U.D. to prevent pregnancy. The latter, he obviously will need to remove before you can carry a child. He may be able to give you some advice that will make the timing of your pregnancy easier and help you to be more relaxed.

OVERCOMING INFERTILITY

Recently I spoke to a group of twins' mothers and was greeted by a woman whom I knew. She had attended some classes I taught and asked if I could help her find out why she had not been able to get pregnant with a third child. Her first two had been timed just as she and her husband had planned. After talking with her, I suggested that she not worry so much, but just relax and enjoy lovemaking with her husband. If that didn't work, I assured her that her gynecologist could do several things to help them. My first advice, however, worked. But while struggling with one-year-old twins, this mother was not at all sure I had done her a favor!

Possible Causes

Unfortunately, there are some couples in the childbearing years who have great difficulty in conceiving a baby. If having your own child is very important to you, visit a clinic or an obstetrician who can diagnose your problem and, perhaps, cure it. A blocked Fallopian tube in a wife or seminiferous tubules in a husband may be the problem. Microsurgery can correct some of these. A hormonal imbalance may prevent ovulation, or perhaps the husband's sperm count is low. It may be that the wife's time of ovulation is very short and the timing of their sexual intercourse can be adjusted by watching her basal temperature.

Fertility medication is now available to help many couples have their own children. And I use that plural term deliberately because a fairly high number of women on fertility medication do have multiple births—twins or even triplets. So be prepared!

Artificial Insemination

In our world, it is increasingly difficult for people to accept limits and *nos*. Medical scientists now may borrow semen from another man and artificially inseminate a woman. This must be carefully discussed and agreed upon by both husband and wife. Some men feel inadequate or unmanly because they are unable to biologically father a child. Living with a baby whose father was someone else could be very painful to him. Some women feel this is actually a sort of adultery. Only the two of you can decide. We hope you will think unselfishly of each other as well as of yourselves, seek expert medical advice, and ask sincerely for God's guidance before you decide.

Surrogate Mothering

Television is currently bringing to every layman's attention the possibility of "surrogate mothering." This is the opposite side of artificial insemination. A husband's sperm are implanted into the womb of a volunteer mother. She provides the ovum, of course, and agrees to give the baby to the couple as soon as it is born. When a wife is sterile, she may prefer to have a child who is at least half her husband's to an adoptive child, or none at all.

Test-Tube Babies

Then there is the case of the baby born to an English couple who started her life in a test tube. An egg from a woman and sperm from a man were able to be joined and nurtured for a time in special laboratory conditions! The fertilized embryo was then implanted in the wife's uterus, where it grew and was born to her. This was an amazing event. Many doctors feel strongly against such a procedure, due to the risk of damage and the possibility of a deformed baby. The one in England is said to be doing well as a toddler.

You may see any or all of these procedures as heroic, sinful, or somewhere between. They are, however, possible, and they offer you some choices.

Seek God's Will

There are times when one simply cannot have one's way. We cannot (and I think) ought not have everything we wish. Just where to draw lines, however, is hard to know. There are many families today enriched by the life of a child conceived by artificial insemination. Had they blandly assumed their sterility to be God's will, they would have missed this joy and the opportunity to bear and train up a child—one who could better his world, as he brought happiness to them. Again, let me remind you *to seek God's will,* and then do as you feel personally guided to do.

One study showed that it was the ability of a couple to take time to work through their inability to have a child together that helped them most. In talking out their grief, understanding came to each for themselves and the other, and a mutually agreeable choice was possible. When a decision was hurried, however, and one or both failed to reveal their real feelings to the other, the decision for insemination, adoption, or no children, later resulted in misunderstandings and even divorces.

In counseling with and reading about infertile couples, we have observed the following issues to be most common:

VARYING VIEWS OF INFERTILITY

1. The one who is sterile often feels inadequate and unwomanly (or unmanly). The truth is, manliness and womanliness are qualities of being and have nothing whatever to do with bearing children.

2.   Inability to conceive or bear a child is often seen as punishment for some past sin or misdeed. This is rarely true, although venereal disease (usually the result of sexual promiscuity) can cause sterility. In most cases, however, no one knows why the sterility exists, so it is not logical to assume it is God's punishment. It is simply a fact—a problem to be overcome if possible—accepted and lived with, if it is not curable.

3.   Being unable to have a child may cause disapproval or some degree of rejection by others. One spouse may blame the other. Would-be grandparents may react in frustration or seem condemning. It is important to be somewhat vulnerable if such interpersonal hurts are to be healed. The sterile person may admit his or her own sense of failure and grief with a simple explanation and statement of the heartache this has created. With honesty and dignity, a request for understanding and support may be made. In most cases, such a plea will result in just that.

Most of this chapter has dealt with the decision about when to have a first child and what to do if it is difficult or impossible to conceive a child at all. It is also helpful to discuss the spacing of children and how many children to have.

Even with today's birth-control accuracy, there are some so-called accidents, and a child may come along who was not precisely planned at a given time. We respect the maturity of parents who can love and accept this child just as sincerely as if they had planned each detail.

THREE YEARS IDEAL SPACING

Given a choice, however, there are some facts that may help you decide when to have a second or later child. It is our experience, as a family physician and former pediatrician, that about three years between children is ideal. Here are the reasons we observed and experienced that convinced us that waiting at least three years is wise:

1.   By three, a child is usually toilet-trained, removing a large burden of care from the parents. Parents who have had

two or more children in diapers at a time have told us this is a harrowing experience, filling life with a nightmare of changing, laundering, and feeding babies. It spoils much of the joy of both parents and children.

2. The "terrible twos" are notoriously difficult for parents and child. By three, the older child has finally accepted certain limits with much less testing, knows some of his own powers, and has moved on to a more enjoyable period of creativity.

3. Most sleep disturbances are resolved by three, and parents are able to cope with a new baby's nighttime demands without total exhaustion.

4. Language is usually fairly well developed in the three-year-old. This makes explanations easier and enables more reassurance of the older child, who will feel threatened by the new baby. A three-year-old can help the parents with a baby in many ways and may feel more important to the family instead of being a nuisance.

Perhaps you may wait longer than three years. In some ways this is easier on parents since the more independent an older child is, the easier it will be for parents to cope with a baby. An older child can also play with and enjoy a baby even more safely than a three-year-old. It is usually true, however, that when a child is much older than four at the birth of a baby, his interests are elsewhere, and he may never develop a real closeness with the younger brother or sister.

Whatever you decide (or Nature decides for you!) let us urge you to prepare your older child for the arrival of the new baby.

PREPARING THE OLDER CHILD

As long as I live, I will never forget a May morning when I was five and a half years old, writes Dr. Grace. It was unseasonably chilly and the old heater in the living room felt comforting and warm. But there was an air of something different about the house on this special morning. I felt disquieted, and soon I knew why. My father gently escorted me to a big basket sitting beside the heating stove and showed to me the surprise of my life—a baby!

Perhaps the greatest thrill of my life, up to now, had been that of experiencing new babies on the farm where we lived. From baby chicks, to piglets, calves, and colts, a new baby was a shared joy between Daddy and me. But this baby was different somehow, and I didn't know why at first. It was a girl, my sister! She had gorgeous brown ringlets and a pink, round face that was perfect in every fine detail. The problem was that I had not expected her, and yet here she was—usurping the throne on which I had sat unchallenged, as the youngest child, for over five glorious years. It took many years for me to learn to accept this beautiful little sister.

No matter how hard you try, it may be impossible to help an older child accept completely the arrival of a new baby. But there are some things you can do to make it easier.

1.   Tell your older child (or children) that you are expecting a new baby. We believe it's wise to wait at least until the midterm of the pregnancy. There is much less danger of a miscarriage then, and the waiting time won't seem quite so endless to your child.

2.   In telling your child, let him feel your loving pleasure in him, and tell him that you believe another baby will bring even more love and joy into your family. We hope this will help your child to feel a part of the welcoming committee, rather than the ousted prince or princess!

3.   Talk over with your child the plans for a new brother or sister. If he will need to give up a bed or other equipment, prepare him for that, and try to transfer him to some bigger furniture long before the baby's birth. If it is possible to provide a separate room for the baby, there are advantages in that. A new baby will sleep better in his own quarters, and the older child will feel less threatened in his old room.

When such space is not available, however, it's not a big problem. Just find a creative way to help the older child to feel generous and loving toward the new baby. The best way is to make your love and pleasure in the child you have so genuine that he will have no cause for jealousy.

4.   Prepare your child for the size and helplessness of the new baby. Some children conceive of the new sibling as a playmate ready to have a go at swinging or building blocks. If

he can see a new baby who lives up the block or attends your church, it will help him picture his own baby realistically.

5.   Help your child understand the needs of the new baby. He will resent the time and energy that are taken away from him, but he can tolerate that loss better if he is fore-warned.

Our oldest daughter was four when her baby brother arrived. We tried very hard to prepare her for his birth and to help her enjoy him as a tiny baby. We had given Kathy a doll to feed, while her brother took his bottle. Sitting on her little rocking chair as I (the mother) sat on my big one, she was chatting away, but I was focusing intently on the wonder of our new son. Suddenly I became aware of Big Sister's annoyance as she said, "Mommy, you're not paying any 'tenshun to me!" There will be times when that's exactly how your older child will feel—left out and displaced!

Try hard to understand that. While your baby sleeps, give extra attention to the older one. Let her know how special she still is and will always be. And encourage her to help with the new baby, so she will feel he belongs to her, too. When Kathy could make her growing brother giggle by playing with him, she found, along with us, that her total love was increased by his fondness for her.

6.   Help your friends and relatives to consider the feelings of your older child. When they see the baby, remind them tactfully of the older child's presence. One way to do that is to ask your child to escort the visitors to the baby's bed, or have him hold the baby for a minute to display his tenderness—if he is old enough. You do need to supervise an older child's handling of a baby and help him support the back and head. But a bit of handling goes a long way. Older children get bored with it, but they also enjoy it at special times, and feel closer to a baby they can cuddle.

It can be hard to balance the development of an older child's sense of involvement and closeness with the baby, with his need for freedom to live his own life. Try to watch for the times of real interest and curiosity, and encourage that. Bath time, feeding time, and playtimes may interest an older brother or sister.

Ask your older child for help when you really need it, and be sure to let him know your genuine appreciation for that help. This may involve being handed a diaper or a blanket by a young child, or it may mean an older child's entertaining a baby for some time while you are busy. Be aware of the capability of your child, and ask no more than that. Then let him know his importance to you in doing this special bit of helping.

We believe by such careful preparation before the baby's birth, and by gentle sensitivity to your child's needs afterward, you can prevent much of the sibling rivalry that otherwise develops. Your whole family can grow in love with the addition of each new member!

Sex Education

Many parents use the occasion of the arrival of a baby to teach the older children some practical lessons about sex. Allowing the older child to feel and see a baby's movements in the mother's abdomen is an exciting experience. Simple explanations about conception and birth are very natural at this time. We suggest you discuss these issues even if your child doesn't ask. You will find some helpful suggestions in my book *How to Teach Your Child About Sex* (Revell, 1981).

DETERMINING FAMILY SIZE

How many children should you have? This is a question that is both easy and difficult to answer. According to extensive studies, the only way to avoid serious overpopulation of this world is to limit each family to 2.2 children. Since we know of no way to have two-tenths of a child, this means some families may have two, and only two out of ten may have three children.

Many thoughtful and concerned people today have a high degree of awareness of overpopulation and its burdens. Such parents are extremely careful to limit the number of children they have. While this is commendable, they may need to face the ultimate consequences of such a decision.

Many other parents are less informed. They may not be able, through personal limitations, to understand and practice birth control. Unfortunately, many families functioning on a poverty level are among this group. Thus there could develop in our world a large, dependent population with too few taxpayers to support welfare needs.

As with many issues, we cannot decide for you how many children to have, but you need to decide with the best information you can collect and with the most honest search for real wisdom you can conduct.

Unfortunately, some people find that they cannot have a child of their own. Even with the best of modern medical intervention, conception may be impossible. Here are some possible resources for you to use in achieving parenthood.

ADOPTION?

First let's discuss the possibility of adoption as an answer to your desire to have children. Adoption has made a marvelously happy family life possible for many childless people in times past. It may answer certain questions or doubts some of you experience about having children. For example, some couples who have a serious sense of responsibility about overpopulation, believe they can help other children in need of a home and parents, and fulfill their need for children at one and the same time.

The availability of children for adoption, however, has decreased dramatically in the past decade. Due to freely available contraceptives and the legalization of abortions, but mainly due to the removal of social stigma against unwed parenthood, there are few babies to be found for adoption. To be sure, there are some and, tragically, "black-marketing" (selling babies) has become all too common. But the average waiting time in this country for adopting an infant is about three and a half years.

Older Children

More easily found, however, are older children. Many of these were children of unwed mothers who desperately tried to care for them and couldn't. They had to give them up. Some of these babies, due to the immense stress and inexperience of their young mothers, received a less-than-ideal start in life, and thus present special needs and handicaps. Many times these can be overcome. But the first eighteen months are crucial ones in a child's habit patterning and development. We may wish that a toddler were just as easy to accept, love, and raise as an infant,

but that simply is not so, especially when he has been neglected
or abused. We may empathize and care about the heroic young
mothers, too, but that doesn't change the facts, either. In many
large cities, one out of every five births is to a teenage
mother (often unmarried). Rarely have they gained the maturity and experience it takes to successfully parent a child.
Every community needs to take action about such a deplorable
situation.

Handicapped Children

But that is not the purpose of this book. There are many
adoptable children of two or three years. There are also a number who have various physical or emotional handicaps who may
be adopted. Many of these require costly medical attention and
certainly need parents who can manage to honestly accept and
love them as they are. They demand a fine balance in empathy
and concern, but firmness and consistency in expecting them to
help overcome the handicap as fully as possible.

Children From Overseas

There also are children from other countries who need parents. After the Korean War, there were many Korean children,
fathered by American servicemen, who were brought to
America for adoption. This has continued with full-blooded Ko-
reans, half-American Vietnamese, as well as children from various other countries. The death rates in some impoverished
countries leave a disproportionate number of orphans, and
there are several adoption agencies which can help you find
such children. There is, unfortunately, a great length of red tape
to untangle in bringing such a child to this country.

Children of Other Races

In many communities, there is still some racial prejudice.
This is tragic but true. So before you decide on adopting a child
of another race, be careful that you are doing him a favor.
Sound out your friends, neighbors, schools, and church. See if
they will accept, love, and help you raise this special child with
sincerity. If not, you may even move to a community that is

more democratic. A child may be better off in poverty in his own country than to live in prosperity yet suffer the rejection of prejudice.

CONSIDERATIONS IN ADOPTION

Telling the Child He's Adopted

If you decide to adopt a child, there are several ideas you must consider. First, how and when should you tell him he is adopted? If he is older or of another nationality, he may well know from the start that he is adopted. If not, you will want to tell him before he hears from someone else. For some reason, it is shocking to a child to learn that his parents did not give birth to him.

In a well-meant effort to save children from such a shock, adoptive parents many years ago tried very hard to keep children from finding out that they had been adopted. Fortunately, that practice gave way to a better one (in our opinion). Adoptive parents started, when the child was one year of age, to have a biological birthday celebration and an adoptive anniversary party. They would explain to this small child about their search for him and how very much they loved and wanted him. This helped the child to view his adoption as a happy event. It is likely that some parents overplayed this, and perhaps a more ideal plan is to simply begin to explain as soon as the parents wish.

Have Information About Biological Parents

Adoptive parents need to understand their feelings about not having a child of their own. They must get over any sense of failure, inferiority, or guilt if they are to be free to be really confident parents. In the case of adoption, *it is also urgent that adoptive parents know something and feel comfortable about the child's biological parents.* Sooner or later, many adoptive children become curious about their background. They will want to know how their mothers or fathers looked, what they did for a living, what their interests were, and rarely spoken, but extremely important: *Why did they give me away?*

Curiosity Not Rejection

When adoptive parents see such interest as a rejection of themselves, they will be hurt. Often they unconsciously bristle defensively and create an unnecessary chasm between themselves and their child. This is understandable, since such questions often begin during adolescence when there will be some rebelling in any family. Please understand, however, that such curiosity is natural. You need not take it as a wish to replace you. Discuss their concerns openly, and tell them all you can about their biological parents. Tell them especially of the heroic love that prompted them to release the child to a family who could provide what they could not. Let us assure you that starting early to give as much information as is desired and appropriate can prevent problems later. You need to find out as much as you can about the biological parents without identifying them. Any condemnation or judgment on your part—no matter how bad their behavior may have been—will be subtly but definitely conveyed to your child. And he is likely, with time, to feel that he may have inherited or acquired some of that badness. Find a way to feel loving and grateful to those people for giving you your special child. You will just as certainly convey that positive feeling to him, and he can grow in the self-esteem that is so important to healthy personality development.

Search for "Birth" Parents

Another important issue involves the fact that it is becoming increasingly possible for adoptive children to find their "birth" parents. Courts are often willing to open records and even help trace parents once the child has reached a legal age. We believe this decision bears careful consideration. Such a search is often an outgrowth of the philosophy that one should have the right to anything he wants. We personally disagree with this idea. Having worked with several hundreds of unwed mothers and their families, Dr. Grace understands the pain they experienced through conceiving, bearing, and releasing the child. Laboriously, most of them worked through profound pain and grief and only slowly put it to rest. To be reminded of that period of their lives is not necessarily a useful thing or a happy ending. Marital problems and resentments and confusion by later children may result from the sudden appearance of an earlier child.

Perhaps a trusted intermediary could find out if the "birth" parents wish to rediscover the child. At any rate, it seems, they need a vote in the matter. If they choose to remain unknown, the adopted child and his parents will need to respect that choice and resolve their grief. It may be that this will draw them even closer to each other.

The glamorized television depiction of happily reunited families may be extremely deceptive. American people have become quite gullible and they may believe, even unconsciously, that every case will have such a happy ending. That is not true. If you were adopted and cannot find your biological parents, remember that it is not life threatening to grieve, and accept limits over which you have no power.

Adoptive Children and Emotional Problems

Still another consideration regarding the adoption of children demands a look at statistics. Significantly more adoptive children have serious emotional problems than do biological children. There are several theories but no proven facts about why this is true. It seems logical to assume that some of it comes from what we've just discussed—the unconscious rivalry of adoptive parents with the biological parents—even when the latter are unknown. Children, so prone to manipulate adults in favor of their own wishes in all circumstances, may (knowingly or not), encourage such competition and then become the victims of the outcome. Perhaps they just feel that something must have been wrong with them to make their birth parents give them away, or they may feel that they were an undue burden upon those parents. In some cases with which I have worked, all of the above factors played a role.

If you have an adopted child or plan to have one, do remember such issues. Don't worry over them, but if your child seems sad or preoccupied regarding his background, invite him to discuss it openly. Accept his feelings; comfort and reassure him. It may be useful to have a few visits with a counselor to be sure things are right, or to set them right if your own help doesn't seem to be doing the job with your adopted child.

An adoption by loving and secure parents can create a delightful family. Children need parents and a home, and if you need and want children, I hope you can find each other and live happily ever after!

3

Carrying Baby— A Word for Expectant Mothers

By Herbert L. Ketterman, M.D.

COMMONSENSE RULES

The excitement of pregnancy and the eventual birth of your child is often tempered somewhat by the fact that every woman knows during pregnancy she is going to lose some of the physical qualities which have made her attractive to her husband. The beauty of this is that, even though you will have obvious changes in your figure during the pregnancy, if you will follow a few simple instructions from the doctor and a few commonsense rules, those physical changes during pregnancy, and those subsequent to delivery, can be kept to a minimum.

Weight Control

There are a few complications of pregnancy over which one might not have any control, just as there are many diseases over which one might not have any control. However, just as some illnesses are brought about by carelessness, neglect, or by an attitude of taking a chance by pursuing habits that could be health hazards, so can complications of pregnancy be brought about by one's not paying careful attention to well-established prenatal care. The most important, of course, of all of these things is the total amount of weight gained during the pregnancy. Most doctors will not want their patients to gain more than twenty pounds during the nine months of pregnancy. This allows you about two pounds per month. Since you may not gain this much in the first trimester, it is easy to become careless. Do not be deceived, however, because from that point on, it will be more difficult to keep it at the two-pound-per-month gain. For those women who are able to discipline themselves in such a fashion as to keep their total weight gain at twenty pounds, the rewards will be great. They will not have as severely stretched skin and the subsequent stria associated with that excessive weight gain; they are less likely to have the complications of pregnancy such as hypertension and edema; and they are more likely to have an uncomplicated course at the time of labor and delivery. Therefore I cannot recommend strongly enough that, of all of the disciplines so necessary during the prenatal course, that which requires your greatest attention will be your *diet.*

Another reward for limiting your weight gain to this twenty-pound maximum will be the fact that you will continue to look attractive, not only to your husband but also to your friends, during the prenatal course. I have always felt that pregnant women show on their countenances a certain radiant glow. If you combine this with the maintenance of good physical condition, then the state of pregnancy can be even more attractive than one would expect or hope for.

Exercise

The role of exercise in pregnancy is also extremely important. I suppose the most satisfactory and the easiest type of exercise is that of simple walking. However, most physicians will recommend other forms of exercise as well in the prenatal months.

Grooming

In my twenty-five-year experience of taking care of mothers during their prenatal course, I never ceased to be amazed at the fact that there were those mothers who maintained immaculate grooming during the total time of their pregnancy.

Other women, it seemed, took the pregnancy as a license to become less careful about their personal appearance. This manifested itself not only in their total weight gain, but also in their manner of dress, the manner in which they maintained their hair, and the manner in which they maintained their makeup.

Attractive Appearance

Every husband wants to be proud of his wife and he wants her to look the very best that she can at all times. This applies not only to how she appears to him when he arrives home from work, if she is a housewife, but also to how she looks when he is with her in public, either at a social gathering or in casual public appearances, such as routine shopping trips. His concept and expectations of his wife do not really change even though she is pregnant. Therefore, it behooves her to try to maintain her best personal appearance all of the time. This is not to say that sometimes you can't just wear shorts and tennis shoes or even go barefoot, but it does mean that the physical changes of pregnancy should not allow you the liberty to become careless in your personal appearance.

Helpmate

Unfortunately most husbands are not really very well oriented to normal household chores and duties. For some reason our culture has pretty much programmed the male to the concept that he is the wage earner and that the woman is the housekeeper. In spite of the fact that large numbers of our women are working mothers, this has not yet changed the concept in the mind of the husband. He feels that his role as provider for the family ends when his working day is over. Household duties, however, become more burdensome during pregnancy because of the way you feel and because of the purely mechanical problems that you have simply because of the changes in your body. It would be well for you to spend some time explaining to your husband how much more difficult many of these tasks have become, and it would be perfectly all right to ask him to share some of the responsibilities. If your husband does this without asking, count yourself among the fortunate few. If your husband is one who doesn't help, recognize that this is a part of our cultural background and that a little nudging (not nagging!) on your part may be all he needs to recognize how much easier he can make things for you.

By the same token, you must be careful not to use the pregnancy as a tool by which you seek to get attention. Some of the symptoms which you might experience in the first trimester are the long-familiar morning sickness, the vomiting which may accompany it, and the drowsiness of early pregnancy. These miseries may be enough to make you seek some compensatory attention which you didn't have prior to the pregnancy. You may very well feel the need for that now! On the other hand, your husband should be aware of the fact that you are having this discomfort, and be supportive and understanding of you. Even though he does not have to share in the physical discomforts of your pregnancy, he must recognize that these are a part of your pregnancy, and that he shares half the responsibility for your being in this state.

Breathing Space

Every person needs room to move about and room to create and room to think. The need begins at birth and can be demonstrated by the response of frustration when a small child is held too tightly for a prolonged time. The need continues throughout life in varying degrees. Couples need time apart from each other to be creative, or to do the things which they enjoy individually but which are not enjoyed by the other spouse. A major problem arises when a spouse feels that he or she must share everything with the mate to make the marriage complete. Actually, the ability of each to have some of his needs met, apart from the other, may make the marriage stronger. If either feels threatened by such a need for freedom on the part of the other, the relationship is not on the strongest basis.

Prior to marriage, both parties have been free and independent persons, able to come and go as they wanted. When a spouse is willing, early in a marriage, to recognize that sudden confinement—after so many years of independence and freedom—is sometimes difficult to handle, there may be a willingness to make allowances permitting the mate to have time for those things which he might find enjoyable. The one who has this need for freedom can make it easier on the other, if he or she will explain this need. It can avoid a sense of rejection and loneliness!

Once the parents have learned to allow each other "room to breathe," they will be able to permit the child similar freedom. Unlike the parents, the child, of course, must have some perimeters set, rules established, and guidance at every move to develop the responsible character which is the aim of every parent. It is essential for Mother and Dad to resolve their mis-understandings and establish a healthy basis for their relation-ship *before* a baby arrives.

Expect Inconveniences

Another issue you need to work on, mothers, is that of ex-pecting many inconveniences in your life. They are a fact of par-enting, but if you resent them and rebel against them, your problems will be compounded. If, however, you learn to submit to the temporary hardships, you will work your way through them more easily and graciously. Fighting consumes a great deal of energy—even when the fight is a silent, internal conflict.

ALWAYS TIRED?

Being chronically tired tends to create a mood of depression or grouchiness that hinders the healthy development of chil-dren. Let's think about the issue of fatigue and how you may overcome it.

One of the very common complaints that physicians hear from mothers is the complaint that they are "always tired." This symptom is a discouraging one when it has no physical basis, and I am convinced (from watching different generations of families) that these mothers probably learned that way of life from their own mothers or fathers. Therefore, it is important to get some insight as to why some people are always tired, if you hope to prevent passing on to your children this same concept.

Medical or Psychological?

Of course there are some medical reasons for always being tired, and these should be given consideration before one makes a final judgment in attributing this particular problem to the realm of a psychological attitude. The common things that must be ruled out in such a complaint would be anemia, hypo-thyroidism, and hypoglycemia. There are several other less-common entities which may cause one to be tired a great deal of the time. It would, however, be the experience of most physi-cians that when a patient presents this complaint, the problem is on a psychological basis.

In the case of a housewife, the most likely explanation for being tired is the fact that, even though she finds her role as a full-time mother a satisfying life, there is nonetheless a certain monotony about her work. To begin with, she has spent her day with small children, who obviously do not communicate in the stimulating way in which adults communicate. She also has repeated a task of the previous day and the previous week insofar as washing, ironing, mending, preparing meals, changing diapers, disciplining, comforting, and the many other tasks that a mother does every day. Unfortunately, unlike her husband, whose role as a provider brings him in contact with adult people every day and gives him the opportunity for daily rewards in his striving for success, she finds that her reward is actually many years away. Her attempt is to raise healthy, well-adjusted, happy children, but this will not finally be known to her for many, many years.

The Working Mother

The problem is complicated somewhat when the young mother is also a working mother. Not only does she work her forty-hour week, but she also must come home and often do all of the things that many other mothers do in the course of the day. Too often the husband is not very understanding of this, and again feels that his time is his own—that he does not have responsibility toward the menial tasks of daily household maintenance. This mother becomes even more frustrated in her attempt to accomplish everything she has to do. She actually is serving two careers and she perhaps has every reason, on occasion, to have actual physical fatigue. Such fatigue is certain to be accented by her resentment of her husband's failure to help and care about her needs.

Obviously, if the mother is always tired and conveys this impression to her children either by direct expression of this feeling or by attitudes, actions, or sighs, she is indelibly impressing on the child that this is the way life often is. Since the child learns so readily from the mother, it is not surprising that this child will pick up from that mother the same type of attitude, and likely, in the child's adult life, will give expression to this same unnecessary fatigue.

Such chronic fatigue causes serious problems for children.

They do, indeed, learn to be tired or bored. But children have a great need to be enjoyed, played with, and taken care of. The tired mother, usually mildly or seriously depressed, cannot give to her children what they need emotionally or spiritually.

Geraldine was so depressed as a young mother that she had to seek psychiatric help. As she reviewed her own experiences as a child, she discovered an important fact. She could not recall a single time that her mother had given her a hug. While there had been affectionate exchanges, it remained in Gerry's mind a one-way flow of love from her, a child, to her lonely, tired mother. No wonder she was depressed! Her own childhood had been drab and draining of her energies. As a mother, she had little left to give!

OVERCOMING FATIGUE

Be sure that your doctor does rule out a physical problem as noted above, then try the advice in this section.

Some of the answers to the problem are, of course, fairly obvious. The first thing the mother can do is make sure that she has some type of adult companionship. When I was delivering babies, I instructed the mother, when she took her baby home, that she should have one-half day a week away from the home and away from her children. Hopefully she could find some type of baby-sitting facility which could give her this time away by herself. This would allow her to have some adult interaction or give her time to do whatever she might find pleasurable for herself. Hopefully, the husband who has any insight into this dilemma will also make an attempt to give his wife some time away from the children, when he himself can do the household chores. This can be in the evening or on the weekends. Husbands have to be instructed in this because most of them feel that since they have worked a full forty-hour week, their free time should be leisure time. They don't recognize that the forty-hour week is not known to the housewife.

Remember some of the dreams and wishes of your childhood and think of ways to make some of them come true. Perhaps that means learning to paint or developing some other creative skill. There are many inexpensive ways to start to develop these skills. Look around you and take some action.

Enter into the creative play of your children. They usually

have delightful ways of enjoying life. Many parents enrich their lives in this way to the point of having enough resources to give back to their children.

If you simply don't know what to do to overcome the fatigue, go to a play area where parents and children congregate. See how they interact and have fun. Use all your willpower and make yourself practice what you see or think of. You will be surprised at the speed with which you will lose your fatigue and find your life full of joy.

One young wife who worked found her housework simply too much for her. The children and home suffered from her fatigue. One evening she returned from work to find a clever card propped on the dirty kitchen table. Inside her husband had penned, YOU ARE BEAUTIFUL, AND I LOVE YOU! Miraculously, she reported that she felt a surge of energy and cleaned her entire kitchen as it had never been cleaned!

One of the attributes of God as revealed in Jesus was limitless energy. As you depend on Him and learn to listen to Him for guidance and wisdom, you will have found the ultimate answer to being "always tired."

4

Sharing Responsibility—
A Word for Expectant Fathers

By Grace H. Ketterman, M.D.

UNDERSTANDING THE EXPERIENCE

Creating a brand-new life is no laughing matter, but it certainly is one of the most exciting experiences one can ever know—perhaps *the* most exciting. I have always felt a bit sorry for men in general, and my husband in particular, because they can never know all the feelings—good and painful—that are involved in those nine months and their climax in that ancient miracle of childbirth.

Since this is such a profound experience, I want you husbands to understand as much about it as you can. You wives may read this, too, but you will be experiencing it anyway, so let your husband read it first.

Somehow your lovemaking becomes even more meaningful when you have decided to have a child. There is a special purpose in it that will reach completely into eternity, and that is awesomely wonderful. Once that one little sperm has found the ovum, fertilized it, and the new life has started, you, the father, are pretty much outside of things, but here are some events your wife will go through.

THE GROWTH OF THE BABY

The two half-cells that have become one in the Fallopian tube (usually) move into the womb. There, the egg settles into the soft uterine lining that is full of tiny blood vessels and nurturing fluids. Around this potential baby a protective and nourishing cover called the *placenta* is formed. Through this the developing baby is fed and its waste products are carried away. The mother's body has to work overtime to provide these processes.

Morning Sickness

At first the womb and its tiny occupant lies in the mother's pelvis, protected and confined by the pelvic bone. During this time (about three months), the pressure of the enlarging uterus creates a sense of discomfort. Your wife will need to urinate more frequently and will find her sleep disturbed. In some women this pressure, or some other factors, causes a feeling of nausea. This is especially common when getting up in the morning and is called *morning sickness.* A mother may have to vomit and, in some cases, this may take place repeatedly throughout the day. Your wife may feel really miserable during these weeks, and she will need all the encouragement and support you can give her.

Be careful, however, not to pity her or feel so sorry for her that she feels even worse. Your doctor will tell her what to do to relieve this discomfort to some extent, so just reassure her that you care, and remember that it will pass. Helping her with food preparation is especially beneficial, because the odors of certain foods may make her feel even worse. Ask her what she needs from you without hovering over her or babying her too much.

Second Trimester

In the second three months (called a trimester), the uterus rises out of the pelvis, and usually the nausea and vomiting stop as abruptly as they began. During these months the uterus enlarges quite rapidly, and this makes necessary an entirely new wardrobe.

Now let me tell you something very important. Women in today's society are considered beautiful only if they are tiny-waisted and slender. Your wife will be anything but slender for the last five or six months of her pregnancy. She may feel fat and ugly. It is extremely important, therefore, that you help her select an attractive wardrobe. It need not be large or expensive, but a few new items from time to time, over these often tedious weeks, will encourage her and can help her feel pretty and valued by you. Your interest in her body's changes will help her to feel special and it will also help you to feel more a part of this process.

Movements of the Baby

Some time during the fourth or fifth month, a mother first feels her baby move! She may not even recognize this at first. It feels a bit like a gas bubble. But as the baby grows and its very tiny arms and legs move, she will recognize the feeling for what it is. This is usually an experience of profound joy. The fact of the presence of a life within her becomes a reality. For most mothers this is intensely moving, and helps to compensate for the earlier discomforts.

It will be late in the fifth or early in the sixth month before you, the waiting dad, can feel the movements of the baby. But that, too, will come in due time, and most fathers find excitement similar to the mother's in the early acquaintance with their awaited baby. The more you involve yourself in the early growth of your baby, the more you will feel a part of this process of becoming a parent. Do be sensitive, however, to your wife's moods and her need for some privacy. If you are honest and kind in your interest—not idly curious or demanding—you may expect your wife to enjoy sharing this developing baby with you.

Let me urge you, as an expectant father, to visit the doctor who will deliver your baby. Getting to know each other will be another step in your really becoming a father.

Lamaze Method

The wonderful practice of including dads in the actual birth of the baby is relatively new and I strongly encourage your doing so. This procedure, called the Lamaze Method, involves a series of classes during the last three months (or last trimester) of pregnancy. The process of labor and delivery is explained, and fathers are taught how to "coach" the mother through this somewhat difficult experience. The dad helps the mother to relax and breathe properly with her contractions and thus hasten delivery. Mothers seem to feel safer, do not resist the muscular contractions, and avoid some of the difficulties of delivery. Many young fathers have personally expressed to us the deeply emotional—almost spiritual—experience this has been for them.

Last Trimester Discomforts

Back to the last trimester of pregnancy. Fathers, let me prepare you for a somewhat trying period. In shorter mothers especially, the enlarging uterus climbs relentlessly to the mother's rib cage. The active baby's motions kick her stomach and ribs and cause real discomfort. At night the baby may be so active, he disturbs her sleep. Her urinary bladder, more comfortable during the second trimester, is crowded again, and the regular nightly trips to the bathroom resume. Often the pressure of the uterus against her stomach causes some of the bitter contents of the stomach to be regurgitated into her esophagus and mouth. This is called heartburn, and is especially likely to happen at night. It is miserable for her, and she is likely to disturb your sleep. Try to be patient and sympathetic with her. A gentle touch and encouraging word, or a small drink of milk, will help her to endure these traumatic nights. I know you have to work the next day, but so do many pregnant wives. At least you don't have to feel the discomfort!

During this trimester, your wife's enlarging abdomen will create pressure on the large blood vessels in her pelvis. This will cause swelling of her feet and legs. Her doctor will watch this and will probably require her to elevate her feet and lie down more. He will also restrict her salt and will want her to watch her diet. Gaining too much weight at this time is very risky for her and the baby. Again, your understanding and support will help. Please believe she is not getting lazy or spoiled, but do go out for walks with her and encourage her to do whatever exercises her doctor recommends.

By the sixth month, most mothers develop purple lines over their hips, lower abdomen, and often the breasts. These are called *striae* and are permanent. Their color will fade, but they are lasting marks, and most women hate them. They don't look good in a bikini! Your consolation and love will help. Let your wife know that it is her inner beauty that is most important to you. Remind her that the baby will bring more joy to her than these marks bring disfigurement. You may even get her a one-piece swimsuit that is especially attractive, but be sure it can be returned!

With all of these painful or uneasy feelings, you must be wondering why I described becoming a parent as such a marvelous event, but you will understand that, as soon as your baby is born.

GETTING READY

You and your wife will need to be prepared for that momentous occasion. She will have her bag packed and ready for her hospital stay. You need to help her prepare everything for the baby's arrival before leaving the house for the hospital. A special surprise for her (such as a bottle of her special perfume or a single flower) during labor, or as soon as she is in her room, would be especially appreciated.

Before the birth of our first baby, my husband and I thought we had everything possible ready for her. She was a tiny baby—only five pounds when we took her home—and I'll never forget how excited and nervous we were. Of course, she began to cry as soon as we reached the house, and I was sure she was hungry. Feeling tired and weak, I asked my husband to bring her bottle—only to discover that we had totally forgotten that life-sustaining item! I managed to quiet and comfort the baby while my husband went in search of the prescribed formula. All three of us survived and have laughed together over that historic oversight. You will have them, too, and you also will work creatively through or around them. I hope you will learn to laugh together over them and not accuse or blame yourselves or each other.

The television caricature of the calm expectant mother, in labor, driving herself to the hospital, while her nervous husband is frantically hunting the left shoe he holds in his hand, is unfortunate. I, for one, believe you fathers have been the brunt of bad jokes long enough. Your image has faltered and failed at the hands of media people searching for a laugh.

"The Dry Run"

You will, of course, feel worried and nervous when your wife goes into labor. There are too many cases of taxicab deliveries for you to feel perfectly calm, but you will make it. In her last prenatal visits, your doctor will have prepared your wife (and hopefully you) for the procedure of getting admitted to the hospital. If you have been taking the Lamaze classes, the other people there will be discussing such matters. Nevertheless, I strongly suggest that you both do a "dry run." Find the best route to the hospital, and an alternative one, in case you must drive in rush-hour traffic. Ask for the way to the admitting office of your hospital, and be sure you carry your health-insurance identification with you. Hospitals are costly to run, and they really do need prompt payment for their services if they are to maintain the quality of care you want for your family.

Some hospitals conduct tours through the labor rooms and delivery area, and explain what to expect there. Most doctors and hospitals now encourage the presence of the father and his help all the way through delivery. The old fears that fathers will faint, fall, and suffer a cerebral concussion are found to be groundless, although it does happen occasionally. You men are much tougher than we thought. Your involvement in the birth process, as well as that of holding and giving bottles to your own infant and learning to change diapers, is now part of all good hospital routines.

Alternatives for the Squeamish

There are people, men and women alike, who are squeamish about medical situations. Having a finger pricked for a blood count can cause our daughter to faint. If you are one of those people, you may find that you simply cannot go through with all this labor and delivery coaching, but perhaps you can do parts of it. Be assured that this does not mean you are a coward, or that you don't love your wife, and emphatically explain that to her. It has, in fact, happened that a waiting father has fainted and fallen, taking away medical staff who were needed to assist at the baby's birth, in order to help him. So know yourself and have an alternative plan.

One young couple borrowed a woman friend of the mother to coach her through labor. They all shared in the birth of a beautiful boy, and this helpful friend has continued to give both parents support and love as their baby grows. Such a person is especially wonderful if you are far away from relatives.

AFTER THE DELIVERY

Please spend as much time as you possibly can with your wife and new baby in the hospital. I know her big tummy (that you thought would deflate like a balloon), painful stitches, and engorged breasts may all be a letdown to both of you. The image of an immediate return to a trim figure, "people" clothes, and a burst of good feelings and energy rarely, if ever, is a reality. Your wife will still need your encouragement. Let me tell you a secret! If you allow the real thrill of fatherhood to penetrate your very soul, you will find it easy to adore your wife and be grateful to her for enduring such rigors in the interest of creating your child—and hers.

Babies, like mothers' figures after delivery, may be a colossal disappointment in the looks department. They may be swollen or even bruised at first. The nose may be huge or almost left out, and the ears may look just like Uncle Harry's, but don't be too alarmed. In a few hours (or days at the longest), the child will miraculously become beautiful. The amazing perfection in such a miniature human being will hook you, and you will even be able to distinguish your baby's cry from that of all the others in the nursery.

Selecting a Name

I hope you and your wife will have a name picked out that means something special. A friend of mine has mourned over the name he was given—*Quentin Delmar*—which means "fifth born by the sea." He was the sixth child and only saw the sea twenty years later. His parents no doubt liked that name, but you do need to consider how a certain name may—or may not—fit a child later. Giving a name that could fit either male or female like *Francis* or *Marian* may be a handicap to a child seeking his sexual identity in our unisexual world!

PREPARATION FOR CHANGE OF LIFE-STYLE

Now I want to forewarn you about an extremely important concept that I have only recently understood. Perhaps it needs its own chapter, but it's too brief, so just recognize its significance, think it over, and it will help you and your wife immensely!

In all the major changes in life there is joy, excitement, and anticipation. You have been experiencing each of these as you awaited the arrival of your child. What we often do not allow ourselves to experience is the fact of grief, as well. Grief is painful, so we tend to deny it, push it aside, or turn it into some kind of anger.

At the lovely wedding of my niece sat our three-year-old child. The church, beautifully decorated, the bridesmaids, and the radiant bride, had held her enraptured. We had visited in the home of my brother and his wife and shared in the excitement of the wedding preparations. As we finally sat awaiting the ceremony itself, Wendy grew quiet. She whispered over the organ music, "Mommy, isn't Karen ever coming back to Uncle Orville's house to live again?" I explained that she and Mike had their own home now, and they would be living there instead of in her old home. In the incomparable honesty and awareness of childhood, Wendy wept aloud. The loss and its attendant grief of an era of time and an old, familiar relationship, were quite clear, even to this child.

Deal With Your Loss

In having a baby, too, there is a major loss. And you need to recognize it. You will lose a major share of your wife's time and energy to this new arrival. Furthermore, you will lose much of your own free time and energy, if you are a responsible dad. You will incur financial burdens for many years to come, and you may realize other uniquely personal losses. Whatever they are, face them. Think about them, and cry or yell about them, if that is your mode of expression. You may or may not need to share this awareness with a trusted friend or relative. But if you fail to deal with this loss and grief, they will spoil your enjoyment of your new baby in some degree.

Processes of Grief

The processes of grief are simple though painful—denial of the whole thing, anger about it, then a certain preoccupation with the loss itself (that is, you will find your thoughts—unbidden—reverting to this loss); a deep sadness will accompany this, but as you submit to the inevitability of your loss, a miraculous healing will gradually take place. It is this healing that sets you free to feel the pure joy of what you will gain.

Postpartum Blues

I have never seen this concept used to explain what we call the "postpartum blues" or depression in mothers. But I personally believe that this grief is exactly what such depression is all about. Mothers, unfortunately, aren't told about it, and when it hits them they try to hide it. It seems selfish, unnatural, or unmotherly to feel sad at the presence of a new baby that you both wanted, but a mother loses even more freedom, and carries an even heavier load of responsibility for this child than you do as the father. She usually has to quit work, is housebound, loses her glamour, has to feed, change, bathe, and do laundry for a baby who shows his love and gratitude only by making more demands of her—for a long time.

So perhaps you will want to talk with your wife, before the baby is born, about this idea of loss and grief. As you share this deep feeling, neither of you need feel selfish or guilty—just normal and human. And as you comfort each other, you will be comforted. It is then you will be ready for the joy of parenting.

P.S. BY DR. HERB

Life-style Changes

When a new baby arrives in a home, the life-style of that family changes. The most dramatic change occurs when the first child arrives, but with any subsequent child there is a further change in the life-style of the parents. The newborn baby requires so much attention, and the demands of that infant from the first weeks into the early years of life require so much of the mother's physical and emotional energy that a husband may find himself displaced somewhat in his relationship with his wife. Obviously, the man who anticipates that this will happen will handle it in a much more acceptable fashion than the man who has not given it much thought prior to the event.

The Considerate Father

Unfortunately, there are men who do not recognize this extra burden upon their wives and who continue to demand (or at least expect) the same type of attention and care which they received prior to the arrival of the new child. It is physically as well as emotionally impossible for the new mother to meet the needs of the new arrival, along with the demands of her husband. The considerate father will recognize from the very beginning that he must not only expect less from his wife, but that he also must be in a position to give more of himself in order to lessen her responsibilities. Fortunately, most new fathers do get caught up in the excitement of the new child and are willing to take their turn in some of the routine chores associated with child care. The main problem in my experience with fathers is that the newness soon wears off, and the monotony of the routine fails to continue to elicit their willingness to share in these routine tasks.

Moments Alone

Although we mentioned it elsewhere in this book, this is a good time to remind fathers that there are some really important needs which the new mother has. One of these primary needs is the fact that she has the urge to be able to get away from the confinement in which she has suddenly found herself, because of the constant demands of a newborn child. Therefore we have recommended for years that arrangements be made for the young mother to have one-half day a week of her own free time away from home to be used in any manner which she desires. We also have long recommended that, as the husband, you arrange to take her out either for dinner or for some other enjoyable event in the evening every week or so, so that she may look forward to some time alone with you away from the child. The rewards to both parents from such action can be immeasurable.

In the next chapter we will discuss the first days and weeks of your baby's life, and how to make his adjustment in your family a happy one—for both you, your baby, and your wife.

5
Giving Birth—
An Experience to Treasure

There are few, if any, experiences in life that can compare with creating a baby. The union of those two tiny cells, so symbolic of the union of the hearts and bodies of the parents, results in the forming of a whole new human being. To the mother is entrusted the privilege of protecting and nurturing that developing new life. And to the father is given the opportunity of providing for both mother and child some of their special needs through the long wait for birth.

THE WAITING GAME

And the waiting does seem long. The discomfort of the nausea of the first three months gives way to the enlarging abdomen of the next trimester, and in the last few months there is considerable pain, as the developing baby takes over more and more room in that abdomen.

While there is discomfort, there also is great excitement. Surely, no mother will forget that first faint flutter of the tiny baby's motions. As these become more pronounced, it is fun to imagine the little body and miniature fingers and toes that are developing.

Sharing the baby's movements with the husband adds to the excitement. The baby must be fairly large before Daddy can feel those kicks and thrusts of the baby's feet and hands. About that time in a pregnancy, mothers need a dad's excitement.

One good thing about the discomfort of the last couple of

months is the readiness that it creates to get the pregnancy over with. Most expectant mothers have some dread (and even fear) of the birth process itself. And the discomfort does effectively overcome that apprehension.

We hope you have both attended Lamaze classes or similar ones and plan to share in the wonderful process of the birth of your child. Such classes teach both of you what to expect and how to help each other through the labor and delivery of your baby. Fathers who have been involved with the birth of their baby, in our experience, are much closer to their child as he grows.

Are You in Labor?

Just about the time that you have every closet cleaned, every floor scrubbed, and have decided this is one baby who will never be born, an amazing thing happens. When you least expect it, there comes a different sort of hardening of the womb inside of you. There have been some feelings similar to this for several weeks, but this one is definitely different.

Almost every expectant mother asks, "How will I know when I'm really in labor?" And we've both tried to explain it to them, leaving them just as puzzled as ever. I can tell you this—ever since the dawn of creation, women have known when that birth was beginning. And so will you.

There is a slow, gradual buildup of the muscular contraction of the womb that is painful for a few seconds at its peak, before it relaxes and stops. After some minutes (usually five to seven) the same thing happens—squeeze, pain, and rest—lasting about one-half to one minute. You can set the clock by the regularity of these contractions. If you have attended classes, you'll know that this is examination time, so get to work. Dad can practice coaching your breathing and relaxing, while you watch the clock, until it's time to go to the hospital.

Off to the Hospital

You should have your bag packed, take a turn around the nursery to be sure everything is in order for the new family member, and when those contractions are about three minutes apart, call your doctor. He'll probably meet you at the hospital.

Take time, as you leave the house, to say a special good-bye to life-as-it-was, because it will never be that way again! Even though you are excited about your baby-to-be, you will miss some of your old freedom and privacy. This is especially true when it is your first child, but there is a bit of this feeling with each birth. It is normal and won't bother you a lot unless you try to pretend it away. Just feel it, share it with each other if you can, and then let go of it. I believe this will help you to enjoy your baby even more, later on.

At the hospital, there is quite a ceremony to checking in, but with a lady-in-labor, they usually cut that short. They'll need to know you are financially responsible, and that's understandable since hospitals have bills, too.

LABOR

In the delivery area, nurses usually whisk Mama away to be enemaed, cleaned, and made ready. Usually, they shave the pubic hair to make it easier to keep everything very clean, as your body heals after delivery. They will then return her to you, Dad, in the labor area. The contractions will increase in frequency and intensity after the enema, so you will be busy breathing, relaxing, and reassuring each other for a while.

Bag of Waters

Sometime in the course of all this, Mother, there will be a gush of water from your body. You will think you have regressed to the "wetting" stage, but you haven't. This is just the breaking of your bag of waters. You probably already know this, but I'll remind you. Around the baby, inside the uterus, there is a sac containing fluid (amniotic fluid) that cushions and protects the tiny one. As the womb tightens and pushes, that sac breaks and the fluid flows out. Depending on the position and movement of the baby, it may come in small spurts, or one or two bigger gushes. Sometimes that happens early and you have to clean up the mess at home. But usually it takes place later on in the hospital.

Checking the Cervix

The process of labor is followed by the timing of the contractions, but it also is done by checking the opening of the womb (or cervix). In the last week or so of pregnancy, the cervix is dilated about one-half inch just from the pressure of the baby. During labor, however, the contractions push the baby slowly into the birth canal. That pressure stretches the cervix until it is big enough for the baby to slip through—about four or more inches across. When it is completely dilated, the nurses will move you into the delivery room. That's an exciting move, because it means the many hours of labor are about over. By now, you're both tired and about ready for a rest.

Anesthesia

Your doctor will have talked with you about using a little anesthesia at this stage to lessen the pain, and it does get a bit intense at this point. Usually he will recommend a local anesthetic that numbs the pain in the birth canal, but lets you be alert enough to know every detail of this wonderful process. We suggest you accept a little anesthesia because you will be able to relax and work better with the doctor. Most of us reflexly tighten up with pain, and that may slow down the actual delivery.

Not only does the cervix have to dilate, but so does the skin around the outlet of the vagina. If your baby is very big or comes too fast, this opening may tear, and that tearing can cause serious problems, so your doctor will do an episiotomy. That is a small incision on one side of the birth canal's outlet. That relieves the pressure on the baby as well as on the mother, and will make the birth easier.

Bearing Down

As the baby moves slowly out of the womb, into the birth canal, you will feel an urge to strain or bear down. It feels as though you are having a bowel movement. Sometimes the doctor will want you to go ahead and bear down, but sometimes he can see the baby is not quite ready, or the outlet needs to stretch a little more, and he will ask you to hold back. Be sure to trust him and work closely with him.

Dad, you will really have divided attention during the delivery process. You will be all eyes to see this new life arriving, and you will also want to attend to your wife. You'll just have to take turns. By watching the baby, though, you can tell your wife exactly what is happening and share what she can't see in the mirrors that have been set up for her convenience.

First Appearances

The first glimpse of the baby is a bit confusing. You probably have a mental picture of the latest disposable-diaper ad. He won't look like that! So be ready for it—he will be covered with the white coating that protected his skin before birth—the *vernix caseosa*. There will be some blood on his body from the episiotomy, and his head may appear deformed from the birth process. Furthermore, the cord looks weird and he may be having his first bowel movement of that greenish black meconium stool! Babies simply do not dress for the occasion.

Take heart! He'll never look worse, and if you look with your new-parent eyes, he will soon begin to appear beautiful, in spite of it all. Be assured that most honest parents need some time to begin to love a new baby. We don't make friends with anyone instantaneously, and babies are no exception.

God gave you the instincts to be good parents. Wait for them and listen to them. You'll be fine parents!

TYPES OF DELIVERIES

Not Always Headfirst

Usually, babies are born headfirst. That makes things easier in some ways. Now and then the buttocks come first, or rarely, the feet. The problem with this is that these parts of the body are soft and the mother's openings don't always fit the later birth of the head, so it takes a bit of a beating. The doctor may have to reach in with instruments and help that head be delivered safely. Doctors use instruments only when they have to.

Caesarean Section

Before labor, many doctors do special tests to be sure of the baby's size as compared with the mother's. If your doctor feels that you may have serious trouble delivering the baby, he may decide to do a Caesarean section. That is a surgical procedure that opens the abdomen, then the womb, and delivers the baby through that surgical opening. Such operations have been so well perfected that the risks are very small. We feel that vaginal deliveries are better whenever possible. But when there is serious doubt, the Caesarean surely can save the life of a baby.

Home Delivery?

We hear of some young couples wanting to have their babies born at home. While that sounds very nice, let us warn you that there is danger in it. Fifty years ago, most babies were born at home, and quite a few died because of complications. Your baby's life is priceless. Why take a chance on losing it, when the best of safe care is available?

GOING HOME AND AFTERWARD

If all goes well, you may want to return home soon after delivery. Some mothers go home the first or second day, but most wait until the third day. Please let your doctor advise you. Taking a little extra care of your body now may come in handy after you get home with the new baby, if you can afford it. An extra day or two in the hospital will allow you to regain the strength you will need when you get home.

Making plans for taking the baby home may not be as simple as it sounds. You will tend to get too many things together for your first child's homegoing. All you will need are the clothes, an extra diaper or so, and a blanket or two, depending on the climate and the time of year. Most new mothers love to dress up the baby in some of the gifts they have already received. Do so, if you like. But if you prefer to keep it simple, dress the baby in a knit shirt or one of the lovely and practical sleep-wear items. Then when you get home, a bit nervous and tired, with a baby who also is nervous, and perhaps crying about the strangeness of his new world, you can put him right to bed.

Your Figure

Speaking of dressing, Mother, you are in for a big shock, if you're like most of us. You probably couldn't wait to get back into "people" clothes. I'll bet you even put a cute dress into your bag before going to the hospital. After your baby's birth, you could lie on your back and actually see your toes! But when you stand up, you look like you're still pregnant and none of your "people" clothes will fit. So plan on something to wear home that will be loose and comfortable.

This problem will not be so great if you have watched your weight well, so do that. But most of it is due to the great stretching of those poor tummy muscles and to the fluids that accumulated in your tissues during the last few weeks. Your doctor will give you some exercises to do when you feel better, but I devised some simple ones of my own that didn't hurt those "episiotomy" stitches. As you lie in the hospital or walk about the halls, or stand admiring that most beautiful child in the nursery, practice tightening up those stomach muscles. Pull in and relax, twist your upper body around to the right and then to the left as far as you can go. These are not fatiguing and you'll be surprised at the way they help flatten your tummy and get your waist size back.

Help!

Most new mothers need some help after they get home. I was twenty-six years old and a graduate from college and medical school when our first baby was born. But I was more nervous than a teenager on her first date over giving that tiny baby girl her first bath! It was really nice to have a friend there to help. You may be more relaxed than I was, but don't be afraid to admit that you need help if you do, in fact, need it. Sometimes fathers are all the help you could ever ask for, but often new dads are also nervous.

The time-honored source of help has been the baby's grandmother. We looked forward to enjoying both the grandchild, our child (now a parent), and the wonderful memories of when that child was born. I know families, however, in which a grandmother's presence has brought far more tears than joy. Some grandmas are controlling and even dictatorial. Others talk too much or too little, and one or both of you may feel tense around her. Frankly, we believe you parents need most of all to get comfortable and relaxed about your new roles and your new baby. So you decide what is best and who is best. You can think of a kind way to announce your decision and work things out with the grandparents.

Having someone come in for a few hours a day during your first week at home seems like a good idea. You can get some rest, catch up on some work, or just share your excitement or your worries about being a new parent. This plan will give you both the opportunity for privacy. You can be as silly or senti-mental as you like about this special event! Some companies now have plans for a paid "paternity" leave, which we think is a wonderful idea. Having shared so closely in the birth of your baby, you dads can now help in the adjustment of your new child into your own life, as well. Babies need to feel close and secure with both parents, so if you can, dads, do be there to help and enjoy this experience.

It's surprising how quickly you will establish a routine and forget how it used to be. The kaleidoscope of the baby's ever-changing behavior and looks is a joy and often a challenge. One thing you can count on—your lives will not be monotonous for a long time, if ever again.

Part II

Nurturing a
Newborn Child

6

Getting Acquainted— The First Thirty Days

Before going into a discussion of this wonderfully made stranger who has come into your home, we want you to take note of a styling to attract your attention—one which will be used throughout this book. This is a notation of when to call your doctor or go to the emergency room. Such a reminder will be set in boldface, small capital letters, and will give you information about symptoms that warrant a phone call and probably an office visit. Also in the same typeface, we have listed symptoms that demand you see your doctor at once; or it may be that a hospital emergency room is nearer. Important (but not emergency) situations appear in italics.

You will note that we have repeatedly urged you to ask your doctors any and all questions you have. This reminder comes about because of the frequent complaints we hear from our patients that doctors do not answer their concerns. We know doctors who are busy and may seem abrupt. Most of them will, however, respond if you will be assertive about your needs and questions. Do not be afraid, *but speak up!* If you should be the victim of a truly rude and unkind doctor, we recommend that you consider finding a different physician. Rudeness is never justified.

Once your baby actually is here you will have some getting acquainted to do. While the prenatal movements made his existence evident, and may have given both of you some parental feelings, it takes time to really be a mother and father. Knowing this can be a relief to you because many mothers have confided in us that they felt something was wrong with them. They had heard of the "glow of motherhood" that allegedly suffused a woman when she first saw her new baby, and they didn't experience that. What they may have felt was simply relief at having an empty stomach and no more heartburn!

PHYSICAL APPEARANCE OF THE NEWBORN

A newborn, still covered with his thick, protective shield of white *vernix caseosa,* with his head a bit (or a lot) misshapen, and some bruise marks, does not look exactly like the Gerber baby! Even when he has been cleaned up and comes to visit in your room properly attired in a hospital shirt and diaper, he may not look so good. You will almost certainly be afraid to unwrap and inspect him—especially with a highly efficient nurse standing by to see your ineptness! If you are like I was, you'll wait for the nurse to leave, and do your exploring gingerly—but privately. It's so great that in most hospitals, new fathers can now put on a gown and share this discovery with you.

Swelling of the Head

You will undoubtedly see your baby's head and face first. Often there is some "molding" of the head that is caused by the pressure of the passage through the birth canal. This may make the head look pointed or flat in certain areas. Occasionally there is some swelling of the scalp called *caput succedaneum.* Don't try to pronounce that, but do understand that it is not serious. This swelling will go away in a few days.

There is another type of swelling that is limited to one or two of the bones of the scalp. It is actually a bruise that causes some bleeding under the covering (*periosteum*) of a certain bone. It causes no apparent pain but it does look a bit alarming. And it will take two or three months to heal. Your doctor will discuss this with you and give you more reassurance. But be certain that we have never seen a complication or a problem from a *cephalhematoma,* the scientific name of this condition.

Hands and Feet

Your baby's hands are a joy to explore. The fingers and nails are so tiny and perfect, they are amazing. When you place your finger in that miniature hand, it will automatically close around it. That grasp will make most parents aware of a baby's need for protection, and may be one of your first sensations of the thrill of parenthood.

The dimpled wrists, elbows, knees, and ankles are also delightful demonstrations of God's handiwork. The baby's feet and toes will also be fun to touch. As you stroke the soles of the feet, the toes will curl or stretch and you may be reassured of your baby's healthy nerves, muscles, and bones.

It truly is a miracle that all of a baby's body is so remarkably developed and coordinated!

The Navel

You will probably be a bit nauseated by the appearance of your baby's navel. It will have a couple of inches of the umbilical cord attached. It will be clamped or tied and it really isn't pretty. But remember, that used to be his lifeline through which you nurtured him so he could grow. Understanding its purpose helps, somehow, so you won't even mind dressing and caring for it. Your doctor will explain how to look after it, but it mainly needs to stay dry. So keep the diaper folded below it and lay the baby on his side or back until that bit of tissue dries and falls off. It will do that by itself when your baby is a week or ten days old. You will find a healthy navel underneath, though it may be a bit moist and pink. Good drying and an alcohol wipe with a cotton swab will take care of that in a few more days.

Genitals

Your baby's genitals will look as disproportionately large as the head. And they are. Babies—both boys and girls—may even have a little breast enlargement and secretion from the nipples. It is not uncommon for infant girls to have a slightly blood-tinged vaginal discharge for several days. Don't worry at all about these happenings. They are due to the collection in your baby's system of some female hormones from your own body. The baby will soon excrete this, and these signs will disappear.

Circumcision

If you have a boy, you will face a decision about circumcision. In case you don't know, that is a very minor surgical procedure that removes the bit of foreskin that covers the head of the penis. It is difficult to understand why God made men with that piece of skin and then, thousands of years ago, told the Jewish people to remove it. But He did. We do know that adult men who have been circumcised have almost no incidence of cancer of the head of the penis, and their wives are less likely to have cancer of the cervix. Recent studies raise a question as to whether this is true any longer, but at any rate, it is easier to keep a boy's penis clean when he has been circumcised. You and your doctor may decide for or against this procedure. But if done, it should be on the first day when your blood serum is still present in the baby's blood (some doctors do it immediately after delivery), or after the third day. This is because your baby's own blood-clotting mechanism is not mature until the third day. If the circumcision was done at birth, it will be nearly healed by the time you take him home. If it is done later, you will be instructed to keep a petroleum-jelly dressing on it until it is well healed. This simply keeps it from sticking to his diaper and bleeding when you change him.

Heat Treatment

We found it useful for the care of both navel and circumcision to use an ordinary 40-watt light bulb in a dresser lamp or goose-neck lamp. Holding this about ten or twelve inches away from the navel or circumcision is very soothing and dries the areas nicely. Perhaps thinking of how good a heat lamp feels on the area of the episiotomy stitches makes it seem right for a baby, too. Hold the lamp carefully and watch the baby, so the lamp doesn't touch that tender skin. About ten minutes or less will dry and soothe the irritated tissues.

Scrotum

If your baby is a boy, explore the scrotum and see if there are two tiny testicles in it. They will be about the size of a bean and when you touch them they may retract a bit. Occasionally, a baby boy has an "undescended testicle," and that will need your doctor's attention. He will, of course, check your baby completely, but you will understand what he is talking about if you discover this, too. The only important fact about this condition is that if the testicle does not come down into the scrotum by the time your son is four or five (and most do), it may need to be brought down by a simple surgical procedure. Otherwise, that testicle probably would become sterile.

Labia

If your baby is a girl, the labia that protect her vagina may seem large. Sometimes they are stuck together. Neither of these is any cause for alarm. As she grows and moves, they will separate, or your doctor can do that for her without significant pain. The size will even out in a few weeks.

Be sure to ask your doctor or nurse anything about which you have questions. They will not think you are dumb. We both feel good about parents' interest in the baby's anatomy, functioning, and appearance. The more comfortable and sure you are about your child, the more you will enjoy him, and frankly, the more at ease you feel, the fewer telephone calls you'll need to make later!

POSTPARTUM CARE

Stitches

Now let's turn our attention back to you, Mother, because you need to understand your own body and its return to normality. To your disappointment, perhaps, this will take some time. Very likely your doctor will have made an incision, or cut, at the outlet of the birth canal. As mentioned previously, this is called an episiotomy, and usually prevents a jagged tear during the birth process—one that would be slower to heal and could be dangerous. This incision will not be felt at the time, thanks to a mild anesthetic, but the stitches, as they heal, will be felt by you! Usually they have healed by the end of a week. Your doctor will suggest various measures to insure faster healing and less discomfort. Be sure you follow them.

Returning to Routine

Usually your doctor recommends few stairs, no driving, and lifting nothing heavier than your baby for ten days to two weeks. Sometimes it may require even longer before you are ready for your usual routine. Don't rush this process, but don't overpamper yourself. Your strength will return faster if you keep active every day and balance that with plenty of rest.

Contracting of Uterus and Bleeding

After the birth of your baby and the afterbirth (discharge of the placenta), your uterus begins to contract. You can easily feel it through your now-flabby abdominal wall. The medical staff will massage it and may ask you to do so. That is to keep it small and contracted, so you will not bleed as much. Even though this is mildly uncomfortable, go along with it. The less bleeding you have, the faster you will recover your strength. You will have some vaginal bleeding that may last from one to several weeks. After that stops, there will usually be several months of no menstruation or very irregular periods before you return to your normal cycle. If you nurse your baby, you may have no menstrual periods for some months, or even until you stop nursing.

Postpone Intercourse

Your doctor will recommend that you do not make love for several weeks. That is not because he wants to frustrate either one of you. It is just to be certain you have healed, that your tender tissues don't get infected, and to give your muscles a chance to return to normal. While many people get by with none of those complications after the third week, you will have an easier and more comfortable return to happy lovemaking if you wait. Many doctors no longer require this period of sexual abstinence, but we find that most new mothers are pretty uncomfortable and find intercourse painful for several weeks.

BREAST-FEEDING

A new mother's breasts automatically prepare her to feed her baby. Whether to breast- or bottle-feed is another big question. You should decide this some time before your baby's birth. Perhaps you did decide but now you want to change your mind. Here are some facts to help you decide.

Mother's milk was made for babies. It is automatically warm and germ-free. It is easily digestible, usually gives babies fewer, less irritating bowel movements, less colic, and is always instantly available. It also contains certain antibodies that help prevent illness in your baby.

Some mothers, however, simply cannot breast-feed. They may have to return to work. Their bodies may not produce enough milk; their nipples may be inverted and make it hard for baby to nurse (though this is not an insurmountable problem). The skin may be tender and an abscess could develop. Perhaps psychologically they just cannot feel right about nursing. Each mother is different.

Nursing may cause some breakdown of breast tissue and later figure changes may disappoint the wife and husband. In today's breast-conscious society, many couples do seriously consider this fact.

The La Leche League has promoted breast-feeding of infants zealously. And many mothers, having tried it, find it a highly enjoyable experience. Mother and baby find an intimacy that is special, and that is fine. Contacting a local La Leche League chapter through a telephone directory will provide a wealth of information and support.

If, for any reason, a mother decides not to breast-feed her baby or tries it unsuccessfully, she need not feel guilty, or think she is an inadequate mother. The bond of intimacy encouraged in breast-feeding can be just as strong between the bottle-fed baby and mother as the breast-fed one. It is important, however, that a baby be held while he is fed. The warmth and cuddling feed his soul, as the milk does his body. He also needs adequate sucking time. The nipple holes can be adjusted in size to fit each baby's sucking strength and needs—and that is one advantage over breast-feeding.

You, the mother and father, must decide what method of feeding is best for all of you, and then rest in that decision without further doubts or negative feelings. If you choose to bottle-feed, it is a great idea and wonderful experience for father to feed at least one bottle per day. The baby needs to feel warm and cuddled by you, Dad, just as much as by his mother, and this is one way that can be accomplished. Though fathers often feel a little awkward at first, practice will quickly change that. Father's helping with a baby amazingly knits an entire family together as a real unit. Mothers will usually have extra-tender feelings toward fathers who help them in such ways.

BOTTLE-FEEDING

Formulas

There are many formulas available today that are chemically identical to mother's milk. The baby's doctor will recommend one that he feels will best suit your baby's needs. The same holds true for bottles and nipples. The ones with collapsible plastic sacks have some advantage in preventing the swallowing of air, but if a baby burps readily, that is not necessarily a factor.

Bottles

Ordinary Pyrex bottles are just fine for feeding your baby. They are cheaper than the disposable plastic-sack type. *But they do need to be sterilized.* You may use a big kitchen pan with a rack on the bottom to prevent breakage, or you may buy a sterilizer. Your doctor will advise you about "terminal sterilization," or just sterilizing the bottles, nipples, and water, and then adding the concentrated formula.

Many child manuals go into great detail on feeding equipment and the mechanical aspects of child rearing. Do look at them if these concerns are important to you. We believe that babies are endowed with great resources by their Creator. And as you learn to relax, watch your baby's signals, and respond to them, you will become good parents. *The equipment is not as important as the people involved.*

Milk Temperature

The temperature of mother's milk, of course, is just right. Bottles should be warmed slightly, so that a drop of milk shaken on your wrist feels lukewarm, or just as warm as your skin. It's better to have the formula a shade too cool than too hot. Many mothers give cold milk, and we see nothing wrong with that. Your baby will thrive on it just as well as warm milk.

STARTING THE BREAST-FED BABY

Feeding is an instinctive function for all babies. Just put a nipple in their mouths, and they know what to do with it. At first, however (only a feeding or two), they may need help in getting started. For breast-fed babies, hunger will usually cause them to open their mouths and search for the mother's nipple. It is called the "rooting reflex." If your baby is slow about this, stroke the side of his face nearest the breast. This will encourage the baby's readiness to nurse. At first he should nurse only four or five minutes on each side, so the mother's nipples do not become tender. There is little nourishment for the first several days in the mother's milk (called *colostrum* when it is still thin and watery). As the nipple and areola (pigmented area around the nipple) become tougher, and the real milk comes in, the baby may nurse as long as he likes—usually fifteen minutes on one side, and five or ten minutes on the other. Mothers get to know when a breast is empty. The next feeding should start with the breast last used to keep the milk supply balanced, and hence mothers more comfortable.

Care of Breasts

For support and comfort, nursing mothers should wear a special nursing bra. Usually it is necessary to wear a small pad over the nipple to avoid the leaking of milk onto the clothing. It is important, however, to keep the skin dry to prevent irritation and infection.

Rarely such an infection may develop. If you become aware of pain in a local area of a breast, unusual tenderness under the arm, and any fever, call your doctor. This may mean that an abscess is forming. It will need to be promptly treated with antibiotics, and the baby should not nurse from that breast until it is well.

Breast Pump

A breast pump may be used to relieve the pressure in that breast and keep the milk supply ready for nursing, when the infection is well. A breast pump is a special type of a rubber-bulb syringe attached to a container. It fits firmly around the nipple and gently withdraws the milk which goes into the container. If you have an infection, you will want to discard this milk.

Water or Formula

If you are a nursing mother, offer your baby a bottle of water occasionally through the day. Also teach your baby to take formula at times. This frees you a bit more for an occasional time out alone or, hopefully, with your husband. It is important that the two of you keep your relationship close and happy. If your baby refuses formula, you may pump your own breast milk and leave it in a sterile bottle for the sitter to feed the baby while you are gone.

STARTING THE BOTTLE-FED BABY

Feeding a bottle to a baby is as easy as the breast, but again, at first, it is necessary to get the sucking started. Touching the baby's mouth on the side of his cheek with your finger will trigger his rooting reflex and make his mouth fly open if he is awake and hungry. Stroking his tongue gently with the nipple will start the sucking. Let him take as little or as much as he wants. In newborns this is usually less than three ounces. Do not try to get him to empty the bottle. If there is milk left, it is wonderful to use in cooking, so it needn't be wasted. Forcing babies to take more formula than they want can cause spitting up, and it may make your baby too fat. And too fat is not healthy. The baby's doctor will tell you if he's gaining too much or too little, so let him worry about that.

If He Won't Take the Bottle

If your baby tires out before he has a reasonable amount of milk, it may be due to being too tired before feeding. He may have cried too hard or waited too long; or the nipple holes may be too small. The only way we found to enlarge the holes in a rubber nipple was to heat a needle red-hot over a stove burner. Hold it firmly with a pair of pliers. Then insert it into one of the existing holes in the nipple and burn it larger. Test the nipple with milk in it. If it is the right size, the milk will drip slowly and steadily out. If it runs out, the hole is too big and that nipple will have to be discarded. Most new-nipple holes are far too small, and the baby will be worn out too soon. It takes only a little time and patience to get it just right.

Burping

After a baby has nursed for some ten or fifteen minutes, gently withdraw the nipple and burp him. Burping is the ancient custom of helping an infant expel the air he has swallowed while he was nursing. Breast as well as collapsible-bottle-fed infants swallow less air, but they usually need to rest a bit and may need to burp, too. Putting the baby over the shoulder so the upper abdomen rests on the firm part of the shoulder, and patting him on the lower part of his back, usually will press and jostle the air bubble out—sometimes loudly and sometimes quietly. Another method we found helpful with a hard-to-burp baby is to hold him with the heel of one hand pressing gently into his tummy, while the tumb and forefinger support the head. Firmly but gently rubbing and patting the back should do the trick. It's fine to try different ways. *It is important to take time.* Babies are good for parents—though trying at times—because they don't know how to hurry. If you will listen to them, you will learn to slow down, too, and may develop calmness and patience you never thought possible.

By the time you burp your baby, he may feel quite content and be nearly asleep. The more relaxed he is, the harder it is to burp, so you may need to stimulate him a little. Then allow him to nurse again to the point of contented fullness. One final burping and a diaper change later, with good fortune, he is ready for his next three- or four-hour nap.

In the hospital, due to necessary routines, a baby must be brought to the mother at scheduled intervals. He may have been awake and hungry earlier, but perhaps has fallen asleep by the time you get him. Don't worry about that. As soon as you get home, you and the baby will establish his own schedule, and he can be fed when he is hungry.

SIGNS OF TROUBLE

The importance of feeding and burping is, of course, to nourish a baby and help him be comfortable. Air bubbles, hunger, and cramping due to milk that doesn't agree with a particular baby's digestive system, may all make a baby miserable. And when he is miserable he will cry, as he should, for how else will you know something is wrong? Be careful that every time your baby cries, however, you don't think he is hungry and feed him too much.

Formula Problems

Signs that something is wrong with a new baby's formula include vomiting (not just spitting up, but actual regurgitating of all the stomach contents), diarrhea (watery or mucus-filled stools that irritate baby's skin and may even contain blood flecks), and a failure to thrive or gain weight. Now it may be that a nursing mother has eaten too many onions, or some food that makes her milk unpleasant. You will discover what these foods are and may easily avoid them while you are nursing.

Formulas may simply be too rich. Diluting them more may help; or the baby may be allergic to cow's milk and may need another type of formula. Be sure to ask your doctor before you change and *don't* change too quickly. It will take several days to get all of the last formula out of a baby's system, before you can evaluate the new one.

MENTAL OUTLOOK

One important point we cannot emphasize enough is your own sense of *calmness*. Babies are one large bundle of receptor nerves. They sense the least bit of tension on your part. Now that won't damage them, but your shakiness may feed into a vicious cycle of baby's tension and crying, your reaction of anxiety about his crying, and more tension. It is at such points that you really need another person to take over, while you rest.

During my [Dr. Grace's] residency in pediatrics I had an emergency call one afternoon. It was to check a newborn who was rooming-in with her mother. When I reached their room, both mother and baby were sobbing, and I immediately rechecked the infant for any possible illness or some defect. Even as I checked her skin, ears, throat, and rectal area, the baby relaxed. As soon as she was dressed again, I cooed at her and rocked her for a minute, and she fell gratefully asleep. There was nothing wrong but an overly anxious, tired mother. My strength and calmer handling were all the baby needed!

Rooming-in

"Rooming-in" is the practice, well intentioned, of having a newborn stay in the mother's room in the hospital, so they can get acquainted and set up their individual schedule even before going home. It is intended to encourage the "bonding" of mother to child that creates the environment for baby's security. Our personal belief is that both mother and baby are tired after birth and labor. Both need much rest and time to reestablish their normal physiology. Perhaps a modified system, in which the mother could have her infant for longer periods of time (but not around the clock), might serve both purposes.

You Make the Decision

At any rate you, the mother, can choose. That power of choice is most valuable to you. So use it now, regarding the mode of feeding, whether you want to room-in or not, and how you will take care of yourself and your new baby. Take time in choosing, get all the information you need, and find a reliable person for a "sounding board." But do develop that special God-given authority. You will need it more and more in days and months ahead. You don't always have to be right, and new information may give you cause to make newer and better decisions. But practicing this strength will enhance your own confidence and will encourage your baby's developing sense of trust.

Establishing Authority

My father, in my memories, practiced that sort of decisive authority. I'm sure now that he was wrong sometimes. But I'm equally sure he never knew it. Consequently, as a child, I didn't know it and I felt totally safe with him.

More recently, our daughter and son-in-law related an experience with their baby. At three months, he was fussy, wouldn't sleep, wouldn't take his bottle, and was fast creating bedlam. After checking, they found no sign of illness such as fever, sniffles, vomiting, or diarrhea. One parent finally said to the other,

"Are we going to let this tiny child get the best of both of us intelligent, healthy adults?" With that awareness, the strength of their healthy authority returned. Kathy firmly marched Andy to bed, and with some final cuddling, he was asleep. Their indecisiveness and fatigue were feeding his tenseness and preventing his rest.

WHY YOU SHOULDN'T WORRY

We are aware in writing as well as in reading many other child-care books, of saying and seeing these words: "Don't worry about it!" Every time we write them, we feel the reader's reaction, which is likely to be, "How can I help worrying? *She's* a pediatrician and a psychiatrist, and *he's* a physician! What do they know about a mother's anxiety?"

Let me tell you! Until I, as a mother, learned how not to worry, I worried even more than the average parent. When my first baby cried excessively, I didn't even think about colic or constipation. I feared she had an intussusception, or some anomaly of her central nervous system, when she trembled during her crying (as all normal babies do at times!).

Trust in God and Your Instinct

What I learned that helped me to stop worrying was really a growth in my trust in God the Creator. There are rarely certain developmental abnormalities, and these are readily identified by the doctor who checks the baby at birth and in later examinations. Other than those, each baby is a perfectly functioning, amazingly tough, though tiny, human being. He will survive all sorts of parental mistakes because God's breath of life, breathed into mankind, intends him to live and enjoy life. As a parent you mainly need to allow the baby's normal physiological processes to function unhindered. You need to love and nurture, clean, protect, and warm that life. You need to observe and be sensitive to it, and be aware of the mysterious parenting instinct in yourself—and then enjoy the rest.

Regular Checkups

When that instinct hints that something is wrong, you need the objective help of a doctor. His advice and guidance will prevent the mistakes your anxiety could make. And he will pick up any clues of a problem that could be serious. So don't rely on your instincts alone. Do have regular checkups with your doctor. And do chat with other parents. Sharing parenting enhances the fun.

Pitfalls of Comparing

There are pitfalls, however, in such sharing. Babies are so uniquely individual that even identical twins are not exactly alike. In hearing of another child's activities or development, you may feel yours is either retarded or a genius. Such comparisons may cause needless worry, or maybe you will be tempted to hurry your baby's creeping, standing, or talking. In this, there is potential danger. By rushing a baby's development, he may go through certain stages too quickly, and this can weaken later functioning. We believe, for example, that babies who do not crawl enough, may have trouble distinguishing right from left later on, or even have learning disabilities. So enjoy your friends' success stories and compliment their precocious youngsters. But accept and cherish your baby exactly as he is. Play with him, teach him all you can, but don't shove. He's far too little to shove back, and such pressure may only stunt him. When you are tempted to worry, reread this section, then relax and enjoy your baby!

MORE ON FEEDING THE NEWBORN

Solid Foods?

Comparing babies brings us back to feeding. Let's finish this and move on. In the first weeks of life, babies do not need food other than milk. Even vitamins are present in mother's milk and most formulas. A number of years ago, it was common to start babies on cereal by four to six weeks of age, adding fruits, vegetables, and meats fairly soon after that. While that was intended to make more satisfied babies who would sleep all night very early, we did not realize it could overload a baby's digestive and urinary tract. Too much protein of the wrong kind, or certain other foods, we now know can increase allergic tendencies and cause extra work for a baby's kidneys. Now we don't know of a single baby who was really damaged by those feeding practices. But this is an example of new information inviting better choices. Why take a chance? Wait to give solid foods until your doctor advises you—usually about five or six months of age. The money you would have spent on those foods can pay a sitter now and then so you can get out!

POSSIBLE PROBLEMS

Bowel Movements

The other end of feeding babies, obviously, is their bowel functioning. Babies' bowel movements vary as much as every other thing about them. Breast-fed babies and some others may have a small, soft, yellowish stool every other day or less. Some babies have a small one after every feeding. The first few days after birth the baby's stools contain *meconium,* which is composed of bile from the liver, some tissue cells, and fluids. This is black or dark green in color, it is sticky in texture, and will continue for three or four days. After milk is taken and digested, the stools become yellowish or light brown and may contain some white pieces of curdled, undigested milk. The presence of milk curds only means your baby has an active digestive system. There may be a watery fluid mixed with more formed stools. While this may be an early sign that the baby is eating too much, or the formula is too rich, it usually means nothing. So watch it, and if it continues or worsens, let your doctor know when you go in for the baby's three- or four-week checkup.

Civilized countries, for some reason, become excessively "bowel conscious." Some mothers, and even doctors, observe and describe every detail of a baby's bowel movement. If there is one more than the day before, we have known mothers to call the doctor, even in the middle of the night. Let us assure you his bowel movements will be perfectly normal if you feed your baby right and protect him from sickness. As you get to know your baby, you will discover what his normal bowel habits are.

Constipation

Babies may pass stools without evidence of straining, or they may strain for some time. If they seem to have much difficulty in a bowel movement, insert a rectal thermometer about one inch into the rectum. This helps stimulate the rectum and allows the movement to begin. Hold the baby's feet together in one hand and bend his knees up over his abdomen. This holds him and helps open the tight rectal muscles. After a few days, you probably can stop this. If the stool is really dry and hard, the chances are the formula needs just a bit of enrichment, or the baby may need a little syrup in some water. Your doctor's nurse will be able to advise you, but we suggest one-half teaspoon of white syrup to four ounces of sterile water. The baby won't take all of this, but offer it once a day. If the light syrup won't work, try dark syrup. *Do not give a laxative to a baby.* But there are infant rectal suppositories that can be used. Let us remind you, resort to such a practice only in severe constipation, and then only on your doctor's advice.

Irritated Rectum

It is not uncommon for a baby's rectum to become irritated from either loose stools or hard ones. There may even be a tiny scratch in the rectal tissue called a "fissure" which may bleed a bit during a movement. Now don't panic. Babies do not have hemorrhoids, and this is not one of the seven signs of cancer. It simply means the baby's tissues are tender, and his bowel movement a bit large or hard. Here's a very easy and successful remedy. Get a rubber or plastic finger covering; cut your fingernail short and put the covering over your smallest finger. Place a small bit of a lubricant, such as petroleum jelly (Vaseline), or a vitamin ointment (A & D Ointment), on the end of your finger. Very gently and slowly, but firmly, insert your finger just to the first joint. Turn it a bit to massage the ointment into the folds, and remove it. After this, when you have cleansed the rectum after a stool, spread the buttocks a bit, place a dab of the ointment in the opening, then press the buttocks together. This will heal the irritation and be very soothing to your baby. We have seen infants with raw and weeping rectums evidence no pain, while others scream in pain with a fairly minor irritation. If you have had rectal pain, however, you will know how this must feel, and you will find this simple treatment comforting to your own feelings as well as to the baby's bottom!

Vomiting

If your baby vomits, wait a while, and offer an ounce or two of boiled water. Later, refeed him and usually he will be fine. If he has been exposed to people who have stomach flu, or if he vomits more than two or three times, call your doctor. He will want to know if the vomiting was just a gentle rolling-out of the stomach's contents, if the baby acted nauseated or "retched," if he looks or acts sick, or is contented after the vomiting. He will especially need to know if the vomiting was "projectile" or forceful enough to hit the sides of the crib or partway across the room if you are holding him. He may need to see the baby and may prescribe medication by mouth or a suppository.

Projectile vomiting may be due to enlargement of the muscles at the outlet of the stomach. This is called *pyloric stenosis* and may be a serious problem. Most doctors will examine the baby, and may feel the "knot" that is symptomatic of this diagnosis. If there is any question, he will recommend X-ray studies. If such a diagnosis is made, the doctor may give your baby medicated drops. Sometimes these relax the tightness, and after a few weeks the baby outgrows this tendency.

Possible Surgery

In a few babies, however, the tightness will not relax and the baby's vomiting becomes so severe that surgery is necessary. You will be anxious and will find it difficult to believe that such a tiny human being can survive surgery. Actually, this type of operation is fairly simple and in the hands of a good surgeon, your baby will recover in only a day or two. It is important during a time of stress like this to trust the Lord and know He will guide your doctors.

SIGNS OF DEHYDRATION

Babies under a month, and even later, can become dehydrated if they vomit for very long, or have severe diarrhea, so you need to know these signs of dehydration:

1. *The baby is lethargic but irritable and restless and really looks sick.*

2. *The mouth and tongue are somewhat dry and fuzzy; there is little saliva in the mouth.*
3. *The baby does not urinate for some hours.*
4. *The eyes appear sunken.*
5. *The fontanel or soft spot will be sunken in a bit.*
6. *When you pinch his skin up gently, it returns to position slowly.*

This poor "turgor" is evidence of a loss of water from the skin and is a sign of impending dehydration.

DO NOT WAIT FOR ALL OF THESE SIGNS TO DEVELOP. IF YOU SEE TWO OR MORE OF THEM, GO AT ONCE TO YOUR DOCTOR'S OFFICE OR TO ANY HOSPITAL EMERGENCY ROOM. THE EARLIER SUCH A CONDITION IS DIAGNOSED THE MORE QUICKLY AND UNEVENTFULLY YOUR BABY WILL RECOVER. WE HAVE SEEN BABIES RETURN FROM LOOKING EXTREMELY ILL TO SEEMING QUITE NORMAL IN A FEW HOURS.

TRUST YOUR DOCTOR

With every magazine offering medical opinions and advice, many young parents question the use of medication and the need for hospital care. Let us tell you that a little knowledge can indeed be a dangerous thing. Do feel free to question your doctor and even to change doctors if you do not trust one. *But do put your trust in your doctor, pray for him, and follow his instructions to the letter*. It may save your baby's life. Few doctors we know overmedicate or rush to hospitalize. Neither will they withhold medicine if your baby needs it. When you find a doctor you can trust, stick with him. As you get to know each other, it will help both of you to provide the best medical care for your child.

Be Frank With Your Doctor

Be open and honest with your doctor about money, his charges, your fears—no matter how ridiculous they may seem—and your feelings about medications. If in your questioning, however, you quote an article from a magazine to him, please don't act as though that article is a greater authority than he is. Your doctor has spent a minimum of five and up to nine or more years beyond college in becoming a physician and a specialist. Few lay journalists, no matter how bright, can challenge that. Furthermore, your doctor's daily experiences and postgraduate study keep him learning as long as he is in practice. So make him take time to listen to you and answer you. Have your questions ready and clear, and then trust him, unless he evidences real stupidity or discourtesy. In such an instance, please do find a better doctor!

Baby's Kidneys

So much for your medical practitioner and your relationship with him. Let's move on to getting acquainted with all of your baby's functions. A baby's kidneys usually function extremely well. He will be wet much of the time, but you usually need to change him only about as often as you feed him. Then wipe his skin carefully with a damp cloth or cotton ball to remove the irritating urine, dry the skin well, apply a soothing lotion or cream if the skin is tender, redress the circumcision (if it is not well healed), and rediaper him.

P.K.U.

Every hospital now routinely tests babies' urine to detect the presence of phenylketones. When this chemical is present in a baby's urine soon after birth, it is diagnostic of an abnormality of protein digestion (or metabolism). When untreated, this chemical causes severe brain damage that results in marked mental retardation. With early diagnosis, however, your doctor can prevent this problem by dietary regulation.

It is most heartening to realize the breakthrough this discovery represents in preventing a tragic birth defect and its consequences.

DIAPERS

Cloth diapers are certainly the cheapest, but not so convenient. They need to be folded so that they are not bunched uncomfortably between baby's legs, and so that the greatest thickness is there to absorb the wetness best. The usual rectangular diaper can be folded into an elongated triangle, the tip folded in twice and placed over the baby's front, while his backside rests on the long end of the diaper. Bring those corners frontward, over the thick part, and with your own fingers underneath, carefully pin the corners. One pinprick of your baby due to hurrying and failing to protect his stomach, will cure you. His yelp of pain is real, and you will feel like a criminal. You won't be, of course, and the wound will heal. But you probably will not do it again.

Proper Laundering

Laundering your baby's diapers and other linens is most important. Improper washing can cause more skin rashes than you can clear in a month. At least during the first month, when baby's skin is especially tender, use special care. Here's what we recommend from experience with our own children and our busy medical practices.

Soak and rinse the diapers in the toilet at once, when they are soiled. Place them in a plastic-lined container until you have a washing machine full.

For any stains from bowel movements or upchucked milk, soak clothes in an enzyme preparation. These come under many trade names. You will find them in the laundry section of your grocery store. They help keep diapers beautifully white and soft.

After soaking according to the directions on the package, wash thoroughly in a gentle soap—not a detergent. The best one, after all these years, is still Ivory Snow, according to our experience. Do *not* use a bleach. With the enzyme you won't need one, and bleaches can be counted on to cause skin rashes.

Rinse the laundry thoroughly through an extra rinse cycle and dry well. If you prefer a clothesline and sunshine for drying, that's fine, but very time-consuming. We hope you have the convenience of an automatic dryer, but be sure it is not so hot it scorches the delicate fabrics.

Refold the diapers when dry, and have them ready for the next round.

Diaper Service and Disposables

If you can afford a diaper service or disposable diapers, you are fortunate indeed. This will save over an hour a day. Be sure to get the size suited to your baby's weight and needs. The plastic outer shield protects the linens and baby's other clothes from soaking, and if you change often enough, the extra wetness it encloses won't hurt the baby's skin.

Plastic Covers and Diaper Liners

Plastic diaper covers are helpful with cloth diapers, in spite of some opinions to the contrary. Having urine soak into sheets and bed covers by unprotected diapers makes a foul odor and much more laundry. Just keep the diaper changed often enough so that the baby won't stay too wet for too long. Diaper liners are available in some stores to protect babies with extrasensitive skin. They magically let the wetness through into the absorbent cloth, but stay fairly dry and protective of baby's skin. Disposable diaper advertisements make a great deal of this fact, and there is some advantage to it.

SKIN, HAIR, AND NAILS

Now let's discuss your baby's skin, hair, and nails. Proper information about these can save you much worry, and enable you to prevent many problems.

Babies may be born needing a haircut, or they may be almost bald. Their bodies may be covered with fine hair, light or dark, depending on the complexion, called *lanugo* hair. This usually is lost in a few weeks and will grow back only at puberty. Many babies show little if any body hair.

Their skin will be fair or darker, depending on their parents' coloring. Boys tend to have darker skin in the genital area, especially the scrotum, and in girls, the labia may be darker. Over the lower back, there may be a very dark area of pigmentation. These are called "mongolian spots" and occur in babies whose ancestry includes Spanish, Indian, oriental, or negroid nationalities. These pigmented areas are not disfiguring, and in our experience, may tend to fade but do not get darker.

Jaundice and Rh Factors

Baby's skin may turn yellow (or jaundiced) in the first day or two of life. This discoloration may be due to the rapid breakdown of red blood cells. In Rh-negative mothers, a baby was most likely to have such a problem due to antibodies that the mother's body formed, which then returned to the baby's circulation. Such a problem was life threatening, and only a total exchange of the blood of such a baby would save its life, in many instances. There is now a vaccine that may be given to mothers who are Rh-negative. By testing such women during and after their first pregnancy (which rarely is complicated with any problems), doctors can tell if they have formed any antibodies. If so, the vaccine called Rhogam is given to prevent such problems in later pregnancies. Problems with Rh-negative mothers' pregnancies are now extremely rare.

Other Jaundice Causes

Sometimes, however, newborn babies become jaundiced for reasons other than Rh incompatibilities. Usually this sort of jaundice is related to the improper function of certain enzyme systems in the liver. The jaundice needs to be measured carefully by blood studies, to be certain it does not become severe enough to cause brain damage. This form of jaundice, interestingly, is treated by placing the baby under a special lamp for periods of time. Almost always, this clears up the condition and the baby will be fine.

Birthmarks

Over the bridge of the nose, forehead, and at the nape of the neck, there are often areas of reddish discoloration. They become quite noticeable when the baby cries and then fade some when he sleeps. These are not true birthmarks and are definitely not a cause for alarm. They require no treatment and will disappear by about eighteen months of age.

True birthmarks are of three kinds: 1) *the "strawberry" nevus* that is usually small, raised, and looks bright red; 2) *the purple nevus or port-wine stain* that may be fairly large, is dark purple in color, and usually is flat; 3) *the brown nevus* that is dark brown, may have some hair growth over it, and usually is flat.

The *strawberry nevus* tends to go away by itself and needs only to be watched for the failure to do so by three or four years of age. Since it contains many little capillaries, an injury to it may make it bleed a bit more than other skin. Gentle but firm pressure, however, will stop that, so no special care is needed. If it continues to bother you or the child, ask your doctor about treatment. He will advise you or ask for a consultation with another doctor.

The *purple marks* (*hemangioma*) *and the brown ones,* are quite disfiguring and parents will feel some grief if their child is born with one of these in an obvious place. Some of these can be treated surgically, and with plastic surgery excellent results have been obtained. It is advisable to have a plastic surgeon see your child if he has such a problem, and he can tell you if and when surgery can or should be done. There are good masking cosmetics that may be safely used, if you like.

Parental Attitude Toward Defects

Fortunately such defects are rare, and many people have learned to overcome their feeling of being ugly or different. Your attitude, as parents, will encourage your child's adjustment to it. Be assured that nothing either of you did caused this or any birth defect your child might have. It is only amazing that so few things go wrong when one considers the countless cells and tissues of the baby's many systems. Any external abnormality can remind you to focus on the real, inner beauty of your child and encourage its development, along with his courage to achieve healthy self-esteem. In my experience, parents' love of a baby with some sort of problem is a bit more deep and thoughtful than their feeling toward a normal child. Be careful to avoid the extremes of hiding and overprotecting or "flaunting" to provide an acceptance that is truly hard to achieve.

Those Annoying Freckles

Small brown spots or "freckles" may be present at birth on some part of the body. These are not disfiguring, though they do not disappear. Babies born with these tend to develop freckles as they grow older and are in the sun. Strangely, everyone seems to think freckles are charming, except those of us who have them! I recall, as a child, going through every fad that came along, from buttermilk to lemon juice—anything that offered any hope of fading my freckles. But I still have them!

SCALP

Your baby's scalp at birth is notable for its tendency to be soft and pulsating over the soft spots or fontanels. There are two of these—front (anterior) and back (posterior)—and they are spaces God intended to allow for your baby's head to grow as his brain does. All the skull bones are separate at birth, but they grow shut by about eighteen months to two years, the back soft spot closing first, and finally the front one. You need not be squeamish about this. That scalp is thick and tough and you won't hurt the baby's brain by washing his head. We sometimes see babies spic and span everywhere but dirty over that soft spot because mothers are afraid of it.

Cleaning the Scalp

Here's what you need to do to keep your baby's scalp clean, his hair healthy, and to prevent "cradle cap." The latter is a scaly or crusty condition of the scalp, due to oil secretions that dry and stick to the skin.

1. Have a soft but effective brush that will brush out scales and dried oil without scratching or hurting the baby. Use this brush thoroughly at least once a day.

2. Whenever you bathe your baby, wash his scalp with warm water and a washcloth. Two or three times a week, use a mild baby soap or shampoo. Scrub gently but thoroughly into his scalp, rinse it off well, rub it dry, and brush it. If his skin is dry, rub a bit of baby oil into his scalp and leave it until his next bath.

3. Comb his hair with a blunt-toothed comb—and he will be gorgeous!

Other Skin Care

Tear Ducts. The rest of the skin needs some special care. The eyes, nose, and ears may be washed with a soft cloth and warm water. Until the baby's tear glands start functioning, there may be slight crusting of his eyelids. The tear ducts that lead from the corners of the eyes into the nose may take some time to function, and when they do, the crusting will clear up quickly. Your doctor will tell you whether or not you need a prescription for this—usually you will not.

Nose and Ears. Do not use a cotton swab in the nose or ears. The body has a built-in mechanism for cleaning itself inside. All you need to do is wipe off crusts around the nostrils and wax at the opening of the ear canals. Do avoid getting soap into the ears, as it may harden the wax. Simply use a moist washcloth for such cleansing.

Neck. Babies' necks do have a tendency to get dirty—especially if they are fat. Lay the baby down and move his head from side to side to stretch out the rolls of skin and fat, and wash it clean. Warm water is usually the best cleanser, but a mild baby soap now and then may be needed. Under his arms, in his groin, around the genitals and diaper area, you will need soap occasionally, but do not use too much soap. It will dry your baby's skin and make it more susceptible to rashes and infections.

BATHING THE BABY

As soon as the navel and circumcision are healed, you may put your baby in a small tub or the kitchen sink for the bath. Before that, lay him on a large towel on a flat surface and sponge bathe him. A tiny baby may seem frightened and cry when he is totally undressed. Since he will outgrow this, don't feel you have to teach him bravery at this tender age! Just cover him with a blanket or towel and wash one area at a time. Dry it carefully, and move on to the next place. Be sure the water is warm, not hot.

Warnings

Usually a baby likes being immersed in warm water. Test the water temperature on the inside of your wrist to be sure it is not too hot. Since he is quite squirmy and slippery, however, have a towel in the bottom of the tub or sink, and *be sure to have all of your equipment very handy.* You will need one hand to support the baby's head and neck and the other to wash, rinse, and reach for items. *Never, even for five seconds, leave a baby alone in water or on a high surface.* He can move with remarkable speed when you least expect it, and may fall.

Cleaning the Vagina

The care of the rectum and genitals has been described. Let us only add that cleansing a little girl's vaginal area is like cleaning her eyes and nose—best left to a minimum. Wipe between the vulva (or lips) occasionally with a moist cotton ball. Do not use cotton-tip swabs and do not use soap. Her own mucous glands will tend to keep her clean.

Oil Baths Not Recommended

Some people used to recommend oil baths for new babies. We hope that practice has been put to rest. Baby oil is a refined vegetable oil and is an excellent medium on which bacteria thrive. One of the worst skin rashes we have ever seen on a baby was the result of the use of oil. Keep oil just for the scalp for the first several weeks. Antiseptic baby creams or lotions are perfectly fine. They are sold under many trade names and a variety of smells. Choose one that appeals to you, or one that your doctor recommends, and use it after the bath or on the days when you may not give a complete bath. It's fun to have a soft, sweet-smelling baby.

When our first baby was born, I was twenty-six years old and a graduate of medical school. Nevertheless, I was petrified at giving her that first bath. Perhaps too much knowledge made it worse. But I was afraid of getting water in her eyes or nose. I was sure I would damage that gruesome cord and navel. And none of those things happened. She shook a bit with the strangeness of the water and cried at being cold, but snuggled up so delightfully when I dried her and held her close. I hope you and your baby will learn to love bath time as I did!

Oil and Sweat Glands

At about three weeks of age, your baby's oil and sweat glands start functioning. His tears will start coming about the same time. When the tiny pores are covered with scales of epidermis (outer layer of skin), the oil and sweat build up inside and form whitish bumps called *miliaria* because they look like tiny rice grains. You will think your tiny one has reached a very early adolescence. But he hasn't. Just rub the skin a bit more vigorously, keep it extra soft with lotion, and in a few days those bumps will disappear. You will need to use a little more soap after this, but do be sure to keep the skin soft and prevent drying.

SKIN IRRITATIONS

Prickly Heat

Getting too warm will cause a fine, rough, red rash called "prickly heat rash." You can prevent this by keeping your baby cool. As strange as it seems, babies do not need temperatures warmer than you do. So keep his room as cool as yours, unless you have temperatures below sixty-eight degrees or seventy degrees Fahrenheit—and cover him lightly. To treat heat rash, wash the baby with lukewarm water, dry him well—but gently—and rub him all over with cornstarch. The starch is soothing and absorbs the irritating perspiration. The rash will usually disappear as quickly as it came.

Other skin rashes you need to know about are chemical and bacterial and require special care.

Special-Care Rashes

First, let's discuss *ammonia dermatitis*. This is caused by bacterial action upon the baby's urine, breaking it down into ammonia. You will immediately recognize it by its unmistakable odor. The skin will be fiery red and quite tender. We recommend immersing the baby in warm water—not hot—and soaking for several minutes. Dry her well with a soft towel. A few minutes under a low-intensity light bulb will prove soothing.

An old and still-good remedy is dusting the diaper and skin with baking soda. This is alkaline and will neutralize the more acid ammonia as it forms. Be sure the baby drinks some extra water to dilute the urine. Use a diaper liner or disposable diapers for a few days. Over-the-counter items we have used and recommend freely are the antibiotic ointments such as Neosporin, Neomycin, and Bacitracin. Applied to the diaper area, they help kill the bacteria that cause the ammonia to form. Leaving the diaper off for some time each day is also helpful. You will need to stand by to catch the spray of a boy's urinary fountain or lay a girl on a well-folded diaper to avoid having the urine spread everywhere.

A *monilia dermatitis* (or skin irritation) is rarer than the ammonia type. It is caused by a microscopic organism commonly called yeast. This is a fairly frequent inhabitant of a mother's vagina, where it causes monilial vaginitis. Babies may have such organisms in their mouths, where a condition known as "thrush" results, as well as in the diaper area.

Thrush is manifested by whitish patches that stick to the tongue or the insides of the cheeks. Brushing these patches with a cotton-tipped swab will not easily remove it, and if it does, it leaves a raw, reddish area beneath. In the diaper area the rash is red, raw looking, and may have a faintly sweetish odor. You'd better call your doctor if you suspect thrush or yeast dermatitis. He can give a medication to cure it quickly. If untreated, it will spread, and the mouth will hurt enough to hinder baby's sucking. Breast-feeding mothers especially need to be careful to avoid yeast infections around or in the nipple. Yeast and other microorganisms grow well in warm, moist areas.

Keep your baby's diaper area extra dry, and you will prevent or cure almost all rashes there.

Strep and Staph Infections

If you, or anyone in the family who handles your baby, has a strep throat or a staph infection, such as a boil or pimple, be extra careful. Tiny babies rarely get strep throats, but they may get skin or gastrointestinal infections. This may cause vomiting and diarrhea, which your doctor will need to treat. On a baby's skin, strep germs may cause a red, weepy, flat sore called *impetigo*. A crust will form over this, but it does not heal well. As it slowly heals in the center, it spreads outwardly. While this is rarely very painful, any strep infection may result in complications. Your doctor needs to be notified about such a sore, and he will probably prescribe an antibiotic as both an ointment to the sore and medication by mouth.

A staph infection may cause pustules or little boils even in a small baby. They are more localized than the strep and develop a golden yellow point. As this breaks, bacteria may spread, causing more pustules. These, too, need to be treated by your doctor. Since many of these bacteria are now resistant to treatment by antibiotics, he may want to take a test and see exactly what sort of medication will cure it.

Sunburn

Your little baby may be outside as soon as you are, but be careful to avoid extreme heat or cold. Sunlight may quickly burn the tender skin of a newborn, so allow only two or three minutes of direct sun at a time. A cap or bonnet, a light wrap or thin shirt, will protect the baby. Watch the skin carefully for redness, but remember that sunburn may show up only later. So do not take a chance. Precaution and prevention are so much better—and easier—than the cure for a fretful, hurting child.

Nail Care

Your baby's fingernails are intriguing. Those fingers are so tiny yet perfect, and the nails are often quite long, even at birth. The white end of a new baby's nails may have sharp corners and she can easily scratch herself fairly painfully with them. They will need cutting. But let me caution you: Feel under the infant's nails very carefully with your own nail or a blunt orange-wood stick from a manicure set. The ends of those nails are stuck to the flesh much farther than they look. If you cut them very short, the finger will bleed.

To cut a baby's nails, it will pay you to invest in a special pair of scissors. Your druggist will carry them. They are curved and have rounded ends, so your baby's jerky, unpredictable motions won't result in a jab. Until you get the feel of it, have someone help hold the baby to avoid jerking.

IRREGULAR BREATHING

Your new baby's breathing may worry you at times. He will be softly, regularly breathing away, and then you may just happen to see him apparently stop breathing. While this will be for just a few seconds, until you get used to it, it will seem like an hour. You'll be tempted to run screaming for the rescue squad, but before you do, wait a few more seconds. The baby will take a deeper breath—and resume his regular breathing.

After a few days or weeks, this will disappear. This phenomenon results from certain physiological processes. Apparently there must be a little buildup of carbon dioxide (the waste product of metabolism eliminated by our lungs), in order to stimulate the breathing center in the brain. As your baby's nervous system and respiratory system mature and coordinate better, the breathing becomes automatic and regular for the rest of his life.

Mucus and Difficulty With Mouth Breathing

You do need to understand, however, that it takes some time for a new baby to learn to breathe through his mouth. This becomes especially important at feeding time. To demonstrate this, pinch your own nose shut, try to suck on a bottle, and swallow—all at the same time—and you will see how frustrating or even frightening that can be. Or just take our word for it and save the trouble. At any rate, have a small nasal bulb syringe handy. If your baby has mucus in his nostrils at feeding time, especially, squeeze the bulb of the syringe shut, insert the tip gently but firmly into the nostril, pointing more downward than up along the nose, and slowly release the bulb. It will suck out the mucus and free the nostrils to take in air. Repeat this process on the other side. The baby may cry, but this is from his frustration at being held still and the tickle as the mucus is withdrawn. At first it is really helpful to have someone else hold the baby's hands and head still. But you will get adept at this and it is so useful in case of colds. Babies are usually past two before they can blow their noses.

Your doctor can tell you of safe nose drops or decongestants for your baby. During the first month of life, few babies catch colds, but if yours does, you'd better call your doctor just to be certain that he doesn't need to see him. As the baby and you get acquainted, and as you and your doctor get to know each other, you may very well get by with phone calls much of the time.

SLEEPING HABITS OF THE NEWBORN

Normally new babies sleep eighteen to twenty hours out of every twenty-four for a week or two. They awaken when they are hungry, wet, or need to move. After getting these needs met, they sleep again. Usually they have a wakeful time of several hours. If you are fortunate, this will be in the daytime, but it usually is in the late evening. Whenever that time is, it may help if you give the bath and skin care during those hours. A bath is soothing (once baby gets used to it), and you won't have to just listen to that offensive crying.

Place the new baby in his own room if you possibly can. The quietness this makes possible will often enable him to sleep longer during the night. When he awakens at night, feed and change him and get him back to bed as quickly as possible to avoid a habit of staying up for attention. Play with him all you like at other times, but even with a new baby, setting good sleeping habits will be helpful later on.

(*See* the section on Sleeping Pattern in chapter 7.)

HANDLING YOUR MISGIVINGS

There will, however, be times when you wonder about your new baby. What in the world will you do with him or her? It may be most frightening to realize that you are stuck with a helpless, needing human being, night and day, for what seems like the rest of your life! Your freedom has vanished, your own needs no longer seem to count in comparison to the constant needs of this little baby-turned-monster. Even your marriage appears to be sacrificed to serve this new little tyrant over your time and energy.

Deal With Your Fears

If and when you become aware of such feelings, find a time to be alone and sit still. If baby is crying, let him cry in the crib. If the phone and doorbell are both ringing, let them. The person will call again. You need to deal with fears and resentments of this order when they hit you. Otherwise, they lurk just beyond your consciousness, ready to pop out of hiding when you least expect them. Fear and anxiety are almost always dispelled by love and knowledge. So think of these facts:

1. God put His love in you through several avenues— through your own friends and family, through His Spirit in your heart, and through certain instincts.

2. Let yourself relax and rest in all these resources of love for yourself, and quietly let that love include your intuitive sense of parenting. Fear blocks that flow, but love restores it. It is not selfish to love yourself first. Jesus said, "Love your neighbor [your own child] *as* yourself."

3. If you need reassurance that you are still important and loved, call a friend or your spouse and simply relate to them that need. Ask for what you want! A wonderful way to replenish your love supply is to picture yourself in the presence of Jesus Christ. Talk with Him and listen to Him. Let yourself feel His special love.

4. Make a plan for your day that is realistic. Let lots of housework and yard work go for a few months. It will wait. I can promise you that! Do a surface job of picking up the house, so your environment won't add to your frustration. But deep cleaning is not needed as often as we think.

5. Do rest when your baby is asleep—at least part of the time. And do some short jobs like putting laundry in the washer, picking up clutter, or quick wipe-ups. This avoids the frustration of interruptions in the midst of longer jobs. Plan for easy, quick meals during the days and weeks when your baby needs you most.

6. Get a friend or two to trade baby-sitting once a week. Keeping two for a few hours won't be too much worse than one, and the free time will be a great relief to you. Parents also need to take turns in caring for baby, so each will feel close to him and neither need feel in bondage to him.

7. Look for the joys of parenting. Lie down on the floor with your baby (if he is older and could roll off the bed). Let yourself just feel close with him and give him the freedom to roll about. Feel the warmth of his always coming back to

you—his security. Much of parenting is not *doing* so much as it is *being*.

8.   Even when baby cries, you are not responsible to make him stop crying! Isn't that comforting? You need to see that he is dry, fed, comfortable, and not in pain. Cuddle and rock him all you like. But then lay him down and let him cry in peace, at least for a while. Babies get their most intense exercise when they are crying, so don't let that be a major threat to your peace of mind. The more anxious you become, the harder it will be for you to transmit your calmness to your baby.

9.   Look for the simple pleasures that your own physical senses will offer you—the softness of your baby's skin, the sweetness of his breath, the small, fine perfection of his eyelashes, the song of a bird outside, the flash of a squirrel, the wind in your face. In a sophisticated and mechanistic world, many people lose contact with these daily small joys that are waiting to satisfy your needs and refill you with the excitement of God's creation. As a new parent, you may share uniquely with Him in the thrill of creation.

CRYING IN THE NEWBORN

One of the worst fears of parents of a new baby is that of being unable to stop his or her crying. Parents instinctively want to soothe and comfort a child, and when they cannot do that, they may feel most inadequate.

Reasons for Crying

There are several reasons for babies to cry: 1) they are hungry; 2) they are uncomfortable due to wetness, gas pains, a bowel movement, or simply needing to turn over; 3) they are bored or lonely; 4) they have learned that crying brings attention from you; 5) they may be sick or have colic. (*See* Colic section at end of this chapter.)

Exercise. Crying creates the most strenuous exercise a baby can do, and it will serve as your alarm clock, letting you know it's time to do something for her. So first of all, be grateful for your baby's cry rather than worried over it.

Checklist. When your baby cries, check her over. If it's been about three hours since the last feeding, offer some nourishment. Change the diaper if it is wet, and check to see if diaper pins (even closed ones) could be pressing into the skin. See if the baby is straining to have a bowel movement. Help her, as described earlier in this chapter, if she needs that.

Soothing Effects. Wrap her snugly in a light blanket. Some babies feel most secure when bundled up. Rocking, soothing music, and walking with a baby may comfort her.

There are records and stuffed toys which repeat the swishing sounds of the mother's circulation before birth. A friend recently described the incredibly soothing effect of that sound on a fussing baby. This could work so well, in fact, that parents may be tempted to soothe even a good baby with such a device, rather than comforting her with their own presence. If you guard against such practices, you may well find the soothing sounds useful.

When All Else Fails

It will not hurt a baby to cry even for fifteen or twenty minutes at a stretch. Stay nearby, but let your baby put herself to sleep now and then. It is not good for a child to grow up tyrannizing a household, and catering to her fussing too much may allow that very thing to happen. So, when all else fails, put baby in bed, and let her cry it out.

COLIC

Still a Puzzle

After all these years of scientific study and discoveries, colic is still a puzzle. We do not know how to cure it, or what causes it. We can describe it, and most people live through it! Colic begins at a few days of age, usually shortly after arrival home from the hospital. Baby cries hard, pulls up his legs as if he has severe abdominal pain, and waves his clenched fists wildly. He usually has excess gas, but it is hard to say this is worse than in a non-colicky child. He may eat frequently but does not seem satisfied or content. He sleeps only fitfully and wakens to cry again. Parents walk the floor, feed the baby, diaper him, give him rectal suppositories to help him expel the gas, and nothing really helps. No medicine or formula change seems to be a magic wand.

Suggestions for Overcoming Colic

So what can you do if you have a baby with colic? Here are some suggestions:

Your Diet. Call your doctor about your diet if you are breast-feeding or a formula change if you use formula. Ask him about any possible medication. The only ones we have are sedatives, and he will usually not want to get your baby "hooked" on them.

Cool It. Work very hard to be calm and soothing. We do know that parents' tensions create tension in babies and feed into a vicious cycle. This may mean that you ask relatives and friends to help out so you can get some sleep.

Act (Sort of) Tough. Set your mind to a bit more calloused attitudes. Once you know your child is well, you really can ignore his crying sometimes. Most parents of colicky babies are always doing something to them. If he's going to cry, why not let him cry in peace and quiet? I have a suspicion that colic would stop sooner with such a practice. Babies can get into a habit of crying over nothing.

Hurrah for Three Months! Count the days until the end of three months. Most colic goes away by then, and you can recover and enjoy him. Rarely it may last until six months, but don't think about that if your child is three weeks and going strong!

A New Discovery. Very recently, researchers have discovered that some babies will stop crying when they hear a tape recording of their own crying. We cannot vouch for this, but it is an intriguing idea. It must be his own crying—not that of any other infant. If you have a tape recorder, you may experiment with recording your baby's crying and playing it back. By gradually reducing the sound level, you may be able to stop your baby's crying!

7

Establishing Relationships— The Next Two Years of Life

There are some worries and joys that are unique to the first two years of your child's life. There are a number of wonderful opportunities, as well. The chance is yours to lay a solid foundation of good health, meaningful discipline, and emotional balance. As Christian parents, take this chance seriously. Your success will influence your child's entire life, and it will make your enjoyment of your child much greater. Don't wait. Start right, start now!

PHYSICAL CONCERNS

Baby Skin

First, let's discuss your baby's skin since that is the wrapping of his body. Not only does the skin protect the body from pain, but it also helps keep the temperature even, along with the lungs, by sweating. Oil glands help keep the skin itself healthy, soft, and elastic. The many nerve endings in the skin bring delight and fun from touching and tickling. They also warn of potential harm from heat or sharp objects.

After the first month, you will need to take continued good care of your baby's scalp, hair, skin, and nails.

Baby's Scalp. A baby's scalp needs shampooing several times a week, depending on its dryness or oiliness. Use a mild soap or shampoo on a washcloth. Rub gently, rinse carefully, and dry.

Brush with a soft brush to remove scales. A nonoily lotion rubbed in gently will prevent scaling and itching from dryness.

Cradle cap is a crusty coating of the scalp due to heavy oil mixing with the ever-shedding cells of the epidermis (outer layer of the skin). Sometimes the skin underneath is pink and irritated. It may itch or sting a bit. The procedure just described will cure it in almost every case. If it doesn't, of course, ask your doctor about it the next time you see him for a checkup. If you want a fancy name for cradle cap, it is *seborrheic dermatitis*. It may occur at any age. We have found that many new mothers allow this condition to develop because they are afraid to be thorough enough in their scalp care.

Please don't worry about the soft spot. The skin and underlying protective coatings are tough, so you needn't be concerned about injuring the child's scalp or head.

Skin Care. Your baby's skin needs to be kept soft and clean. Wash it with warm water and a little bit of mild soap. The skin's own oil and sweat glands will keep it fairly soft after they begin to function at about three weeks of age. You may continue to use lotion, however, as long as you like.

Navel. Your child's navel may cause some concern to you. After the cord falls off, and the navel heals, you will find it usually becomes a little round point with the skin turned in. You can feel a little firm, cartilage ring that surrounds the navel. (Children fondly refer to it later as their "belly button.")

In some children the skin, instead of being inverted, lies even with the rest of the abdomen, or may even stick out. Most of these will return to the usual position later. If not, remind your doctor to watch the navel. Rarely it may allow a loop of intestine to move into the protruding navel. This is like a hernia and bears a small risk of becoming caught or "strangulated." If your doctor sees this as a real danger, he will recommend surgery to correct it.

You may want to explain the different appearance of his navel to your child. Children often see others' navels as they grow up, and may worry needlessly unless you reassure them.

Birthmarks. There are several types of birthmarks you may note on your baby. These are discussed in chapter 6, "The First Thirty Days."

Hair and Scalp Care. The care of your baby's hair and scalp continues to be that described earlier. You may increase or decrease the frequency of shampoos according to your baby's needs. Watch for scaling or crusting and treat it as you did before. It's best to prevent such problems by this routine good care.

The amount, color, and texture of your baby's hair are all decided by his ancestors. It may be that you need to look back a few generations in the typical American family, or in families of mixed nationalities. But you will always find someone with similar coloring or other characteristics of your child. We believe in telling children, as they grow, about their "roots," so you may enjoy finding out, if you can, whom your child resembles. Such information can give him a sense of belonging and fitting into the larger patterns of the generations, as well as your own immediate family.

Nails. Care of your baby's nails continues to be important. Until a child becomes coordinated, after the sixth month, the movement of the hands can scratch the face or even the eyes. So trim the nails regularly and keep them clean.

Bones and Muscles

Your baby will grow very fast during his first two years. By six months he will double his birth weight and triple it by a year. By two he will have reached about half of his adult height! The head grows most rapidly in the first year and will be within an inch or two of the adult size by two. Your doctor will measure the baby's length, weight, and head circumference on each visit during these years. That is not just for your excited reports to the grandparents about baby's growth. It tells your doctor that your baby is developing normally, or it will give him early warning of any trouble that could be developing. It also tells you where your child fits among all the children in this country insofar as being average, above, or below average in size.

Bone Development. A baby's bones are remarkably pliable in the first year of life. He can take surprising tumbles with little or no damage. But don't let that bit of information give you permission to be careless. The soft parts of bones, called cartilage, are especially evident in the ribs, the nose, and small bones of the hands and feet. They harden gradually by calcium being laid down in those tissues. Be sure your baby's diet continues to have enough milk and vitamin D to form strong bones and teeth. (*See* Feeding and Nutrition later in the chapter.)

Muscle Growth. Your baby's muscles grow in size and develop in their skills right along with his bones. In fact, the use of the muscles has something to do with stimulating the formation of strong bones. Most babies will naturally use their muscles with the exuberance of being alive. Holding, bathing, and playing with your child will get his arms and legs going like a tiny windmill. Some parents, usually enthusiastic exercisers themselves, want to do exercises with their babies. We think that is harmless unless:

You try to get the child to support his weight too soon, putting stress on those soft little bones. Now don't hold back the child's own instinct for moving, but don't push him, either. Just trust God's own individual schedule for development.

Or:

You get so eager for your child to walk, that he misses crawling. We believe babies need to go through that stage to properly develop their sense of "handedness." A number of older children with certain learning disabilities have been found to skip the creeping stage of development. These children often have "mixed dominance," which means they may be right-handed and left-footed. Or they may be able to use either hand, but neither is very dexterous. Such confused handedness is what we are referring to here. Much of the time this problem can be prevented by the slow, steady progression of a child in the musculoskeletal development. Now someone may find later that is just a theory, but until then, encourage your baby to *crawl before he walks,* and even afterward.

Development of Bones and Muscles

Your baby's motor development, with great variations, should follow a pattern about like this:

From Birth. He will turn his head from side to side, move his arms and legs, and grasp by reflex any object placed in his hand.

By About Three Months. He will be holding his head up, sometimes by himself. This will be very jerky, however, so have your hand ready to give support. He may hold on to rattles if they have a small handle, and he will reach for and hit at objects. A jungle gym is a delightful toy at this age. You can make your own by stringing some of the many rattles you probably were given at a baby shower, and tying them across the baby's crib.

By Six Months. Some babies are sitting alone, though only briefly. They are beginning to creep along a smooth floor, or scoot backwards, or sideways. They reach for and grasp toys for a longer time and chew on anything that will get close to their mouths.

Six months is a joyful age for most babies and parents. They are happy, responsive, and love to have you jostle and toss them. Their laughter can brighten your days!

About the Eighth or Ninth Month. Your child will be crawling on hands and knees, or rarely, hands and toes. (That takes some skill, by the way!) He will love to move toys about, needs plenty of them, and still will be responsive and delighted with your attention.

(We watch young parents get down on the floor and play with their babies, and we wonder why we rarely did. Being physically close is so important in creating emotional closeness. Babies can't fall far when they are on the floor, so feel free to roll about and play with them. Stay on a child's eye level or bring him to yours, to keep one important avenue of communication open— eye contact.)

At About a Year. Walking is the big event of this period of time. Usually it is begun by twelve to thirteen months of age. Most parents encourage this, but your child will walk when he is ready. Early walking does not mean a child is going to be smarter or better than a late-walking child. Some doctors recommend firm shoes that support the ankles. Personally, we've seen babies do as well barefoot or in soft shoes. If you or your doctor have a preference, follow it, unless there are some special problems. We'll discuss those in a few paragraphs.

By Two. You'll wonder why you were so eager for your child to walk! He'll be running, climbing, and exploring every area he can. Be especially watchful that he not explore out of his own control or your observation. A child should be out of an adult's sight or hearing only when he is asleep, in these first years. He simply does not know enough to stay out of danger. He still needs your protection.

Birth Defects of Bones and Muscles

There are several possible birth defects that may affect a child's bones and muscles. We wish none of you had the need to know these, but by the law of averages, some of you will.

Foot Problems

The commonest of such problems are those affecting feet. These are probably due to the position of a developing baby in the womb, though there may be inherited weakness. These range from mild "toeing in" or out, to severe turning in or out of the feet, causing a child to walk on the ankles unless this is corrected.

Treatment may be as simple as turning the toes out or in and laying a small sandbag over them to hold them in an exaggerated position of correction during sleep. Or your child may need special shoes, sometimes with a metal bar to hold them in the corrective position most of the time. Rarely, corrective surgery is necessary. Fortunately, these procedures will work. Catching the problem early usually will mean it can be remedied in time to walk normally.

Flatfoot. This is also a common congenital defect, especially in boys. For some reason, the usual arch of the bones in the foot literally becomes flattened. This condition can be diagnosed at home by looking at your child's wet footprint on a sheet of blotting paper. Normally, there is a concave curve on the inside of the footprint. In a flat-footed child, the curve is absent, or it may actually bulge out. A child with this problem should be fitted with shoes which have arch supports.

Exercises for Flat-footedness. There is an exercise your child can do when he is old enough to cooperate. Try it yourself and teach your child:

1. *Stand on tiptoe with the feet bare.*
2. *Rotate the feet so the weight rests on the small toes.*

3. *Shift the weight back to the larger toes.*
4. *Rest on the whole foot.*

Do these maneuvers five times the first day and gradually build up to twenty times daily. You may expect some improvement in about three weeks, if this helps at all.

Flat feet are not a real handicap, but they become painful as one grows older. They may prevent a child's becoming truly proficient in athletic performances.

Dislocated Hip

A much rarer defect is called a *dislocated hip.* No one knows why, but the socket in which the long bone in the thigh (the femur) should fit, is too shallow. This allows the femur to slip out of joint and fall somewhat outside this socket. People can walk if such a defect is not found, but the affected leg is shorter and the motion is limited, causing a waddling gait on that side. Very rarely does this affect both sides.

Diagnosis and Treatment. While this may be diagnosed at birth, it may not show up until later. The signs you may notice are the shortness of one leg, and the unevenness of the creases of the buttocks where they meet the baby's thigh. Be sure to ask your doctor about such signs if you should suspect them.

An X ray is necessary to be certain of this diagnosis. And the treatment, though cumbersome, is highly effective. Basically, it involves keeping the leg turned outward like that of a little frog, so the ball of the femur's end lies in the socket of the pelvic bone. The socket then tends to grow around this until it is normal. Sometimes extra diaper thickness will create enough pressure to accomplish this. In more severe cases, a brace or a cast may be necessary. While this is extra care and a nuisance as well as expensive, you may rejoice that your child need not be crippled for life.

Spina Bifida

A still more rare, but more serious birth defect is called *spina bifida.* The lower part of the spinal bones do not form properly, allowing the spinal cord and nerves to be poorly formed or damaged. This may be so mild it can be detected only when the child starts to walk, or it may be severe and extensively involve the spinal cord.

The child with such a defect will have trouble with bowel and bladder control and will have trouble walking.

Help Available. There is much that medical science can do to improve and correct some of the problems involved with this birth defect. Your doctor will send you to specialists for surgery, braces, special exercises, and therapy. Be sure to work very closely with them to insure the greatest help possible for your child.

Try to get through your own grief, so you may help your child accept the limitations with dignity and compensate for them in other areas. Both parents need to support each other, comfort, and relieve each other of the extra work and time such a situation involves. Be careful to avoid the neglect of any other children while focusing on the handicap.

Cleft Lip and Cleft Palate

These are other defects of the bones and muscles that are fairly common. Most of us know someone who was born with this. A cleft lip involves a separation of the lip on one or both sides just under a nostril. When this defect is more extensive, it will involve an opening of the hard palate, or roof of the mouth. The size of such an opening will vary a great deal.

Feeding Problems. The immediate problem at birth involves feeding. A nipple must be pressed against a firm surface to express the milk. Without the palate, such a surface, of course, is missing. Your doctor will help you with this problem. It may mean you will need to cup-feed the baby, though sometimes an artificial appliance may be fitted. Babies with a cleft palate choke easily, since the milk may go into the nose.

Correction of Condition. A cleft lip may be nicely repaired by a plastic surgeon quite early. A cleft palate, while it may need temporary surgery early, cannot be really repaired until the child's bones have begun to reach adult proportions at about age two. Surgery is, however, the answer, and remarkable results are often possible.

Other defects of the bones and muscles are so rare, we need not even worry you with them.

RESPIRATORY SYSTEM

Makeup of the System

Your baby's respiratory system—the nose, throat, voice box, windpipe, and bronchial tubes, is like an upside-down tree. Air goes through the nose, normally, where tiny hairs (*cilia*) catch particles of dust or pollen and push them back outside. A sneeze helps this process. With the push and pull of the muscles of the chest, the air is pulled through the opening in the voice box (*larynx*) into the windpipe. The vocal cords and other structures were ingeniously devised by our Creator to protect the breathing tubes from being bothered by food or foreign bodies. Rarely, these structures fail, and all of us have choked as a result.

Once in the windpipe (*trachea*), air flows into the bronchial tubes which branch and rebranch to the tiniest of tubules which end in air sacs called *alveoli*. These are lined with a special membrane that performs an amazing function. It allows oxygen from the air to be admitted into the bloodstream through tiny capillaries. At almost the same time, it also allows carbon dioxide, a waste gas from the body's metabolism, to be excreted, or pushed out. Every breath we breathe involves this process. The carbon dioxide, by the way, is food for the green plants, which help purify our air.

The windpipe and bronchial tubes are lined with tiny hairs (*cilia*) similar in function to those in the nose. They also help trap particles of material dangerous to the lungs and move them back outside. A cough helps get rid of such material.

Defects of Respiratory System

Birth defects of the respiratory system are rare.

Blockage. There may be a blockage at some point throughout the bronchial tree due to abnormal development or mucous plugs. Such blockage causes a section of lung tissue to collapse. An X ray will reveal this and surgery may be necessary to correct it.

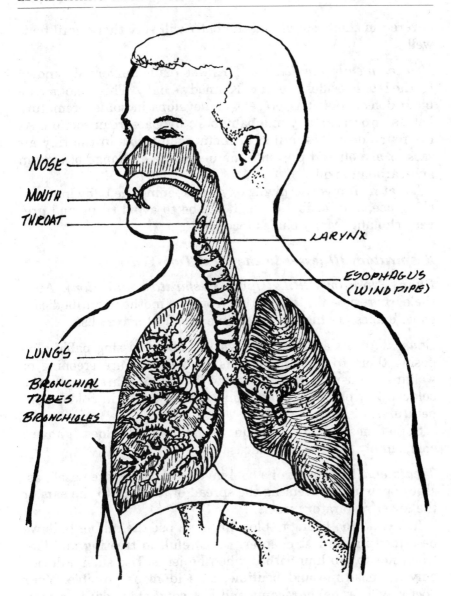

NOSE

MOUTH

THROAT

LARYNX

ESOPHAGUS
(WINDPIPE)

LUNGS

BRONCHIAL
TUBES
BRONCHIOLES

RESPIRATORY SYSTEM

Small Opening. Rarely a baby is born with a small opening between the trachea (windpipe) and the esophagus (tube leading from the throat to the stomach). Such an opening will allow milk or other foods to get into the trachea, causing severe coughing and choking. This is called a *tracheo-esophageal fistula.* It requires that a baby be fed through a stomach tube until surgery can correct the problem. Almost always, this will be discovered in the hospital and the baby will stay there until he is well.

Hyaline membrane disease. This was made universally known by the late President John F. Kennedy's baby. This is not a true birth defect, but it is present or develops in some premature babies or occasionally in a baby born by Caesarean section. As the name describes, a film or membrane forms in the tiny air sacs or alveoli and prevents the necessary exchange of oxygen and carbon dioxide.

Treatment involves giving oxygen, keeping the baby in a special place, and feeding through a tube to avoid tiring and prevent choking. Many babies recover.

Respiratory Illnesses in the First Two Years

Runny Nose or U.R.I. (Upper Respiratory Infection). After the early resistance to infection from the mother's antibodies is gone, babies are highly susceptible to colds or U.R.I.s.

Causes. Adults are often thoughtless about kissing babies, exposing them to their mild colds. Babies who are creeping or walking are usually near or on the floor. Floors are usually the coldest part of a room and many viruses thrive in colder temperatures.

Sometimes a child's nose runs even though she doesn't have a cold, simply from excess mucus.

Treatment. Treatment of a cold involves keeping the nasal passages open and preventing the spread of the cold to the ears or the lower respiratory tract.

In a child too young to blow his nose, use the rubber bulb we described in the last chapter. Be careful, in treating an older child, not to jab him with it when he jerks. Use such a device only at mealtime and bedtime, as seldom as possible. Your doctor will probably recommend a decongestant with an antihistamine or ephedrine in it, if the symptoms are severe. Antihistamines usually make a child drowsy, though at times the reverse is true. Ephedrine stimulates the heart and rate of breathing, so it may disturb sleep. You simply have to try these out to see how your special child reacts. A vaporizer is usually soothing. We recommend one that makes a cool mist rather than steam. It is easy to make a room too warm and uncomfortable.

Nose drops are very helpful in getting some sleep for your child and yourself. You will probably want to talk with your doctor about them. We often recommend them for the acute phase of a cold. A type such as ¼ percent Neo-Synephrine is available from your druggist. Do not use them more than three or four times daily, and never more than three or four days in succession. To use them most effectively, clean out the mucus with your bulb syringe. Hold the child with his head hanging backward over your lap or a bed. Gently administer three or four drops and let them soak in. This allows them to reach the tissues that need them and prevents them from running down the throat where they do no good and only cause choking.

A mentholated ointment may soothe irritated noses and chapped lips, though it does sting a bit when first applied. Parents have applied such ointments, as well as mustard plasters, over babies' chests to help colds and coughs ever since such preparations were first made. We do not see how they can realistically penetrate the chest to help a lower respiratory infection. The fumes do help open a stuffy nose, and if you feel better using them, they do no harm.

COMPLICATIONS: AN EARACHE MAY DEVELOP IN THE COURSE OF A COLD DUE TO THE TYPE OF OPENING BETWEEN THE MIDDLE EAR AND THROAT. YOU WILL SUSPECT AN EARACHE IF YOUR CHILD KEEPS YOU UP ALL NIGHT WITH PAIN AND CRYING. TOUCHING THE EAR USUALLY ELICITS A HOWL OF PAIN. BE SURE TO CALL YOUR DOCTOR IF YOU SUSPECT SUCH A COMPLICATION. HE WILL PROBABLY SEE YOUR BABY AND PRESCRIBE ANTIBIOTICS.

Infections in the Lower Respiratory Tract. These are a common complication of a U.R.I. These are discussed in some detail in chapter 10 in the section on illnesses of children. But some information is needed regarding a younger child.

Tracheobronchitis. This affects only the larger tubes. The child's breathing sounds frightening. If there is fever, usually it is mild. Call your doctor for advice and reassurance. He will probably recommend fluids, aspirin, and cough syrup. If the baby is under six months, he probably will want to see him.

Croup or Bronchiolitis. These are often more serious. Be sure to call your doctor if you suspect these. (*See* chapter 10.)

Pneumonia. This is an infection of the lung tissue itself, the alveoli or air sacs, and not just the bronchial tubes. Usually only one lobe or less is affected. The breathing sounds better than in bronchitis, but that is because there is swelling that holds the mucus and it cannot be coughed up. Usually there is high fever, rapid, labored breathing, and a dry, painful cough. There is usually a low-grade fever in viral pneumonia.

IF YOUR CHILD SHOWS SUCH SIGNS, BE SURE HE IS SEEN BY A DOCTOR THAT DAY. PNEUMONIA IS STILL A SERIOUS DISEASE, BUT IT IS ALMOST ENTIRELY CURABLE WITH EARLY AND APPROPRIATE TREATMENT. YOUR DOCTOR MAY NEED TO HOSPITALIZE YOUR CHILD, BUT HE WILL NOT DO SO UNLESS IT IS ABSOLUTELY NECESSARY.

The older your children, the more relaxed you may be about respiratory problems. Their ability to cough and sneeze improves and you can better sense the seriousness of the condition. *Never be hesitant* to call or visit your doctor with such illnesses. You and he would rather you did this needlessly than to let an infection become severe.

LYMPHATIC SYSTEM

Your child's lymph glands are generously scattered throughout his body. They are connected by channels through which a fluid called *lymph* is conducted. Part of their function is to catch and localize any bacteria or viruses that may enter your child's body.

The lymphatic system develops well and early, so it is ready to help keep your child well.

Sometimes, however, these glands themselves become infected and may even need to be drained or removed. An infected sore of little notice on a toe or hand may result in a seriously infected gland in the groin or armpit.

IF YOU FEEL OR SEE A TENDER, SWOLLEN LUMP WHICH MAY LOOK RED AND FEEL HOT, DO NOT WAIT. CALL YOUR

DOCTOR. THIS RARELY WILL HAPPEN BEFORE YOUR CHILD IS CREEPING OR WALKING, BUT BY THEN SUCH INFEC- TIONS ARE NOT UNCOMMON. HE WILL PROBABLY SEE YOUR CHILD AND MAY VERY WELL ADMINISTER ANTIBIOT- ICS.

Other well-known lymph glands are called *tonsils* and *ade- noids*. They are in the throat and back of the nose. At one time they were often removed after a few infections. We now know they are needed to help prevent lower respiratory or other in- fections. We now recommend the removal of these glands *only* if a child has frequent ear infections, or if the tonsils are so in- fected they do not really clear up with antibiotics. In such cases, these chronically infected glands may seed new infections in- stead of localizing them. Your doctor must advise you about this.

There are no common birth defects of the lymph glands.

GASTROINTESTINAL SYSTEM

The stomach and intestinal tract is composed of the mouth and throat, esophagus (tube leading from the throat to the stomach), the stomach, small and large intestines, and the rec- tum. Attached to this long canal are the liver and pancreas, as well as the salivary glands. All of these organs secrete various chemicals and enzymes that help break down and digest the food, so it can be absorbed into the body to feed the tissues and keep them healthy.

Liver

This amazingly complex system is well formed at birth and develops very little afterward. The one exception to this in- volves the liver. In a number of babies, certain enzyme systems are not efficient enough at birth, and this allows some waste products to accumulate in the bloodstream. The result of such a problem is a yellowish color of the baby's skin called *jaundice*. The chemical that builds up is called *bilirubin*. Hospital staffs are trained to observe and test the levels of this substance. If it reaches a concentration that could be dangerous, a special treatment will be used. Usually this involves placing the baby under a certain kind of light. Very rarely, it may require an exchange blood transfusion such as we once used in babies with Rh-negative mothers.

Birth Defects

A few birth defects are known in the digestive system.

Blockage of Some Level of the Digestive Tract. This may occur in the esophagus, or at some point in the intestinal tract, or rectum. While these blockages are extremely rare, they can almost always be cured with surgery. They will be discovered in the hospital, so you are not likely to worry about finding them yourself.

Blockage From Liver. Rarely there is a blocking of the ducts or tubes leading from the liver. A baby who becomes yellow or jaundiced after a week or two of age should be seen by your doctor to check out such a rare possibility.

Pyloric Stenosis. This was mentioned in the last chapter and needs to be explained a bit more. It usually shows up at one to three weeks of age with projectile vomiting that occurs a few minutes, or as long as an hour, after feeding. The muscular outlet from the stomach becomes enlarged and simply traps the food in the stomach, finally resulting in the tired muscles of the stomach itself throwing the food out. Babies with this problem cannot gain well depending, of course, on how severe the condition is. They may not even be able to hold down water, and could become dehydrated.

IF YOU SUSPECT YOUR BABY MAY HAVE PYLORIC STENOSIS, CALL YOUR DOCTOR. HE WILL SEE THE CHILD, WHO MAY NEED AN X RAY. IF THE DIAGNOSIS IS CONFIRMED, AND THE SYMPTOMS ARE SEVERE, SURGERY MAY BE NECESSARY. THE CURE IS ALMOST 100 PERCENT AND RECOVERY REMARKABLY RAPID. OCCASIONALLY, IN MILDER CASES, YOUR DOCTOR MAY TRY THE BABY ON SOME MEDICATION TO TRY TO RELAX THAT MUSCLE.

TEETH

Teeth are obviously necessary for breaking down solid foods so they can be swallowed. Until your child needs solid food, he really doesn't need teeth. So if your baby is slow to get his, don't worry.

Myths

Some teeth may be present at birth, but usually the time to cut the front, or incisor teeth, is between four to eight months. There are several myths about teething that you can disregard. And some of them are dangerous.

Fever. One such misconception is that babies often run a fever while teething. Only rarely is this true, and then it is usually a low-grade temperature of less than 100 degrees F. The temperature would not be elevated unless there is an abscessed gum where the tooth has started to grow. *So do not blame a child's fever on teething.*

> **CALL YOUR DOCTOR IF YOUR BABY RUNS A HIGH FEVER. TEETHING BABIES ARE LIKELY TO GET INFECTIONS THAT REQUIRE TREATMENT.**

"Pushing" Teeth. Another myth is that teeth may be "helped" through the gums by rubbing with a spoon. Rarely this is true when the gums are hardened or swollen. Sometimes, however, such pressure will bruise the gums and cause more pain, swelling, and even infections in the mouth.

The first teeth to come in are usually the lower front incisors; later the upper four incisors; then two more bottom ones. Between eighteen and twenty-four months come the molars, or grinding teeth, and the canine, or sharp, pointed teeth, beside the incisors. These sixteen teeth are not followed until age three with the rest of the molars.

Treatment of Teething Pain

The earlier teeth are cut, in our experience, the less pain there is. At three months, you will be surprised to see those teeth grinning out at you. Later, however, as a child's biting and nursing go on, those gums become pretty tough, and even the sharpest tooth may have trouble erupting. There are many lotions advertised to numb a child's pain. Some of them help, but only temporarily.

The best and time-honored treatments are cold pacifiers, teething biscuits (which are very messy), and gentle massage with your own clean finger. Be sure that you do not attribute to teething, symptoms of a cold or other illness. Your doctor may need to help determine that fact.

FEEDING AND NUTRITION IN THE FIRST TWO YEARS

Feeding recommendations change from time to time and could be an interesting study of their own. Two or three decades ago, it was the thing to do to start babies on cereals and strained foods as early as three or four weeks of age. In the last five or ten years, however, doctors are reversing this trend. They now believe that all the nutrition a child needs is present in the milk. To make this true, that milk needs to be mother's milk or a modified formula. Only iron and vitamins need to be added to that food to keep the child growing and healthy.

Cereal

We recommend starting cereal at about five or six months. To avoid possible grain allergies, we suggest rice cereal first. It rarely if ever causes an allergic reaction. Make a soft gruel out of it, using some warm formula, and feed it to the child with a spoon. Usually, at six months, a baby is willing to cooperate and especially likes to put things in his mouth. A small spoon with smooth edges is safe and easy. If the baby eats it willingly at the first sitting, that's fine. If he is doubtful, or resistive, do not be too pushy. Give him a few bites and try again the next day. Dry infant's cereal is cheaper than canned and keeps well. It's best not to teach your baby to love sweets. He doesn't know any better now, so don't add sugar. Fix only a teaspoonful at a time; try it with varying consistency—and discard any he doesn't want. More may be prepared if baby seems to want it.

Forming Food Habits

Now is the time to watch yourself, so that you do not form habits of deciding how much food baby should have, and then make her eat it all. Her own system knows how much she needs. She will thank you forever for not making her fat! Do recall that your baby's growth rate slows down drastically after the first eighteen months, and she will need less food then than she does before her first birthday. Many parents fear the opposite—that baby has suddenly stopped growing because she is eating less.

By a baby's second birthday, she has reached about half of her adult stature. If this growth rate continued, she'd be a giant by the time of her sixth birthday. As a Christian parent, we encourage you to avoid battles over physical issues that are quite normal. God made our bodies to function well with very little push or interference. It is not being permissive to go along with your child's body. We believe the real battleground is that of teaching moral, social, and spiritual issues. Save your energy for that.

Introducing New Foods

Gradually increase the solid foods you offer your child. By that, I mean introduce one new food only every four or five days. Thus, you will know which food, if any, may cause some untoward reaction. Increase the quantity very slowly, as your child's appetite increases. Restrain yourself from forcing down that "last bite for Mommy"!

We suggest *introducing foods* somewhat in this *order:* 1) rice cereal; 2) applesauce or bananas; 3) carrots or peas. Avoid any mixtures until your child has had most foods separately. After the above list, gradually add: 4) chicken or veal; 5) egg yolk; 6) whole egg; 7) pudding. Branch out to a variety of simple cereals, fruits, vegetables, and meats, and then, if your child has not shown any problems such as spitting up, loose stools, or skin rashes, try any and all foods.

Blending Your Own

You need not buy canned baby foods, which are becoming very expensive. If you have a food blender, use it to grind up a serving or two of any table food. Put it in sealable plastic bags, or clean old baby food jars, and freeze the food. After thawing and heating, discard what is left. Babies like to eat finger foods by eight or nine months, so green beans, carrot sticks, and strips of tender, lean meat may be served from the family's table.

Eating Binges

Many young children go on *eating "binges"* of sorts. When we found our oldest (at eighteen months) wolfing down fingers full of shortening and margarine, we were concerned. And then we learned of very reliable studies that proved children's bodies crave certain foods at specific times. So we let her eat all she wanted. After only a few days, that craving subsided. In any one day, children do not have to have every basic food element. Over a period of two or more weeks, however, if they are offered the basics, they will choose an adequate amount. These studies reminded me once again of God's incredible creativity!

Eating Habits

Scooping Technique. Babies are a mess! By now you know that's the name of the game of child rearing! And eating is no exception. They are messy when they spit up formula, and they are messy when you spoon-feed them. Their tongues are used to sucking, so they press the food against their lips and palate, pushing most of it out. Be ready with the empty spoon, scoop it up, and push it in again. Then touch the next bite to the lips, tip it in, and repeat the scooping! After a few endless feedings, the baby will catch on, and it becomes, fairly quickly, a lot neater process—though not yet *really* neat.

Self-feeding. About the time baby is good at eating what you feed him, you will be starting him on self-feedings—and the mess will begin all over again. You may help him get the idea more quickly by holding his hand in yours, as you feed him. He will only do so now and then, but it will help. We used a spoon with a curved handle for our children because it seemed easier to hold, and put the hand close to the bowl of the spoon. It may have lessened spills a bit, but the sort of spoon really isn't a big issue. Gently guide baby's hand whenever he cooperates, so he won't flip the food out. Give finger foods that are soft enough to "gum" but firm enough to take a little handling. These, too, teach the hand-to-mouth coordination that will speed better self-feeding skills.

Using a Cup. Drinking from a cup can be started by six or seven months if you hold the cup. Only by nine or ten months can a baby hold his own cup or glass. It needs to be one he can hold with both hands, and best of all are the small, plastic juice glasses. There are many fancy cups with one or two handles, lids with holes, and lids with spouts. Try them if you like, but we think you'll prefer a plastic glass. After spilling milk and cold water down the fronts of our babies, I learned they do better at tipping it themselves as soon as they can possibly hold on to it. (By the way, stay nearby to grab it, because baby will let go suddenly, until he learns how to set it down.)

Coordination Lacking. Baby does not throw food and eating utensils around because he is bad. He may or may not be bad, but he is prone to spills and dropping because he is not coordinated, and doesn't know how to handle things. If you are right-handed, and suddenly have to do things with your left hand, you will know how baby feels. Patience, guidance, and time will see you through.

When a child is full, however, he may find that squeezing mashed potatoes and gravy through his fingers, rubbing it in his hair, and dropping it on the floor, feels good. Food is not for playing in, so it's best to remove it when he is through eating. Replace it with a toy, or better still, put him in another safe place.

"Drop the Spoon." As soon as babies sit in a high chair, they have a special game they've just been waiting to play. It's called "Drop the Spoon." After a child bangs a spoon, so he can blink at his own loud noise, he accidentally drops it. The next move is to fuss at the boredom of having no banging tool. To keep the peace, you will instinctively bend down and retrieve the spoon. Baby's turn is next. He smiles adoringly at you and resumes a few beats, but much more quickly, drops the spoon again. He's delighted with your attention and his power. And it all happened so smoothly. Now it's a harmless and happy game unless you become weary. You may stop the game, but it seems a bit unfair to get angry before you do so. Just keep a ribbon on the chair and tie a toy to it. Baby can retrieve it himself, and you won't be breaking your back to pacify the little tyrant!

Weaning

When and how do you do it? As with so many other issues, do it when baby is ready. He will usually show you when that is. Often, the time will coincide with cutting some teeth, when sucking hurts. With all three of ours, the time was about seven or eight months of age. I particularly loved rocking and feeding the baby at naptime and bedtime, so I was sad when each, in turn, wanted no more of it at that early age. We did, reluctantly, put the bottles away, but I continued the rocking! I suspect many parents, like me, do not like baby to give up the bottle, rather than it being baby's idea! Don't give in to the temptation to keep the bottle-feeding going, because later, it may be quite difficult to stop.

If you do not find that easy time to quit, don't worry. Some babies seem to need more sucking for a longer time. Frankly, we think it's better to allow them to have a bottle longer, and maybe avoid thumb-sucking. If your child hasn't voluntarily discarded the bottle by eighteen to twenty-four months, you may encourage him to do so by being sure he is not hungry and is good and tired at bedtime. Distract him by rocking and singing to him, telling him he is too big for a bottle, and offering him a drink from a glass. Wait for a time to do this that is advantageous. A cold, for example, may make sucking harder. Or watch for a day when your baby will fall asleep from sheer fatigue. We do not believe in fighting over a bottle any more than over eating or toilet training. We'll get to the battles later!

Be careful that your child does not use demands for drinks as an excuse for delaying sleep time. You decide when the bedtime drink is, give it, then tuck the baby in and leave. (*See* Sleeping Pattern—this chapter's end.)

BOWEL TRAINING

Often bowel control is easier to achieve than bladder control. There are at least two reasons for this. 1) There is a reflex action between eating and emptying the rectum called the *gastrocolic reflex*. When your child is ready to use a training chair, watch him for signs of wanting to move his bowels after meals. This may occur with only one meal or after every meal in a day; or it may happen only every few days. 2) The movement of the bowels is usually accompanied by some preliminary straining, a red face, and becoming otherwise quiet.

Explaining the Process

Catching your child at such a point, putting him on the chair, and waiting with him, may well get the point across. We suggest that you explain the process to him, in a gentle manner, so that you avoid fear or tenseness that may make him lose that reflex. Children who are secure and relaxed can cooperate much better in an atmosphere of warmth, calmness, and encouragement.

Once your child understands the use of the potty chair, there remains his willingness and remembering to use it. Without nagging or exaggeration, remind him at the time he usually has a bowel movement to go to the bathroom. Take him if you need to, wipe him afterward, gently, and praise him warmly.

Some people make much of the child's possessiveness about his bowel movements. Perhaps he feels that way. If so, wait to empty the potty until he is back at play. Frankly, we believe some of the struggle about both bowel and bladder control, and the disposing of the movements, has more to do with power struggles. It's a big deal for a child to give up carefree babyhood in favor of growing responsibilities. Be sure to compensate for such efforts with your honest pride and love.

VOMITING AND DIARRHEA

We discussed vomiting and diarrhea in the newborn in chapter 6, "The First Thirty Days." In a tiny baby, this can quickly become a serious problem. In older children, however, it is rarely serious, but it is worrisome.

Various Causes of Vomiting

Stomach trouble in a child under two is always a matter of concern, but rarely panic. Vomiting may signal the onset of a cold or sore throat. Usually, however, it is the result of some viral infection of the stomach or intestinal tract. True vomiting needs to be distinguished from simple spitting up of an overfull stomach or the process of regurgitation. In some babies, the opening to the stomach is exceptionally relaxed. The normal movement of the stomach muscles intended to push the milk or food through the stomach into the intestinal tract may push some of it back through the esophagus and out the mouth. Moving such a baby or his rolling over onto his stomach may also squeeze out some food. Normally babies will outgrow this by six to nine months. Propping up the head of the bed with blocks two to three inches higher than the foot will cut down this annoying problem somewhat. It is not serious, there is no treatment, and the sour smell and frequent laundry will end when he is able to sit or stand up.

What to Do

Vomiting is the forceful emptying of the contents of the stomach by a reverse motion of the stomach muscles. Usually it is preceded by a sense of nausea, paleness of the face or about the mouth, and a "sick" look and feel. Often a young child does not want to eat or drink, and this is Nature's way of letting you know the stomach needs to be at rest. After a bout of vomiting, wait until the child acts thirsty, and offer a small amount of a clear carbonated drink such as ginger ale or 7-Up, diluted half-and-half with water. Only one-half ounce at a time is enough. If the child keeps this down, wait twenty to thirty minutes, and try another half-ounce or ounce. Increase the amount as the child wants more and keeps it down. We have seen babies actually made worse by overanxious parents who gave too much too soon to a sick child.

> IF THE VOMITING LASTS LONGER THAN TWO FEEDINGS, OR IF THE BABY CANNOT KEEP DOWN THE CLEAR LIQUID AFTER SEVERAL HOURS, CALL YOUR DOCTOR. HE WILL PROBABLY RECOMMEND A SPECIAL FORMULA CALLED PEDILYTE. THIS IS ESPECIALLY PREPARED TO REPLACE THE SALT AND OTHER ELEMENTS SO IMPORTANT IN PREVENTING THE COMPLICATIONS OF STOMACH UPSETS. EVEN IN CHILDREN WHO ARE OFF THE BOTTLE, THIS SOLUTION MAY BE GIVEN IN A CUP.

Feeding the Sick Child

Other liquids that may appeal to a sick child and are easily tolerated are liquid fruit-flavored gelatin, weak tea, diluted fruit juice, such as apple juice, and clear carbonated bottled drinks.

Avoid solid foods and milk for a day or two. Avoid ice cream and any rich or fat-containing foods. These are hard to digest and may prolong the illness. Gradually return your child's diet to its normal routine, starting with weakened formula and adding starchy foods, applesauce, or apples, bananas, cereals, and other foods, slowly. Watch for the return of his appetite and general sense of well-being.

Causes of Diarrhea

Diarrhea is the excretion of bowel movements that are "loose" or watery and frequent. Usually there is cramping and pain with such movements and between them. This may be due to some food intolerance, but more commonly it is due to an infection of the lining of the intestinal tract. In temperate climates, the usual cause is a virus, and the duration is a few days or less. In warmer climates, especially when sanitary conditions are poor, bacteria may be the cause. Bacterial infections are more serious and usually require antibiotics.

FOR MILDER INFECTIONS, THE CLEAR LIQUID DIET LISTED ABOVE WILL USUALLY BE ENOUGH. SHOULD THE PROBLEM LAST MORE THAN TWO DAYS, HOWEVER, OR IF THE CHILD SHOWS EVIDENCE OF DEHYDRATION, BE SURE TO SEE YOUR DOCTOR.

The signs of dehydration are these:

1. *Scanty urine output—baby's diapers are dry for longer periods of time than usual.*
2. *The mouth is not moist and the tongue is dry.*
3. *The skin is not as elastic and soft as normal. It feels "doughy."*
4. *The eyes appear sunken a bit.*

DO NOT WAIT FOR THESE SIGNS TO BECOME MARKED. IF YOU SEE ONE OR MORE OF THEM IN THE COURSE OF PROLONGED OR SEVERE VOMITING OR DIARRHEA, GO AT ONCE TO YOUR DOCTOR'S OFFICE OR AN EMERGENCY ROOM.

After several days of treatment with antibiotics for an infection, it is common to have some diarrhea. This is due to the destruction of the normal, healthy, bacteria in the intestinal tract. Usually this will correct itself in a few days. Giving a child a concentrate of such healthy bacteria in cultured buttermilk, yogurt, or cheese will often help reestablish normal "flora" or bacterial growth and the diarrhea will stop.

IF THIS CONTINUES, HOWEVER, BE SURE TO CALL YOUR PHYSICIAN.

CYSTIC FIBROSIS

There is another serious illness that involves the stomach and intestinal tract, as well as other parts of the body. Unfortunately, this disease is always fatal, though life expectancy has increased. It is *cystic fibrosis*—an inherited disease that affects the mucous glands of the body, the sweat glands, the lungs, and the pancreas. The pancreas is an organ of digestion that manufactures enzymes or chemicals that act on fats, proteins, and carbohydrates (sugars and starches) and helps prepare them to be used by the body to create energy and maintain health.

The fat-digesting enzymes are especially lacking in cystic fibrosis. The sweat glands put out more than the usual amount of salt in manufacturing sweat, and mucous glands create secretions that are thick and stringy. This is especially harmful in the lungs where mucous plugs may block the bronchial tubes.

Diagnosis

Usually this disease is diagnosed by the character of the baby's stools—unusually hard and dry at birth and unusually bulky and greasy-looking later on, due to the undigested fats. Collecting a few drops of a baby's sweat and testing its content of salt is helpful in the diagnosis. And the early increase in the number of attacks of bronchitis and colds also helps your doctor make this diagnosis. A family history of any relatives having cystic fibrosis is useful, though this is so rare that you may not have such information.

Treatment of Cystic Fibrosis

The treatment of this disease is complex and very technical. You will need a physician who is experienced in its treatment and supportive of you. You will also need friends who understand the constant worry, frustration, fatigue, and even despair you may feel. It occurs in one out of one thousand or more babies, so in any larger city, you will find other parents with the same concerns. Do contact them and help build a mutually supportive group of people to see one another through the rough times. The National Cystic Fibrosis Research Foundation has helpful information for parents, teachers, and older children. Their address is: National Cystic Fibrosis Research Foundation, 3379 Peachtree Road, N.E., Atlanta, Georgia 30326.

THE URINARY SYSTEM

The urinary tract includes the kidneys; ureters (tubes) leading from the kidneys to the bladder; the bladder itself; and the urethra or channel leading from the bladder to the outside. The kidneys are very efficient purifiers of the bloodstream. As the blood circulates through this filtering system, waste products are removed along with water to flush them into the urinary bladder. The blood normally stays in the blood vessels and returns through the body to collect more waste materials. The kidneys are located in the small of the back on either side of the backbone.

Urinary Bladder

In the lowest part of the abdomen, under the pubic bone, is the urinary bladder. Its cells are especially made to be stretchable, so it can hold amazingly large amounts of urine. Normally, children will hold about half a cup or less as newborns, before the bladder automatically empties it. As they grow, however, and when they are ready for toilet training, that amount will increase to a cupful and, later, even more.

Normal operations of this system are in full swing at birth, and your baby's wet diapers will reassure you of its effectiveness.

Birth Defects of Urinary System

There are some birth defects of this system, but they are rare. They include some variations in the size and shape of the kidneys themselves, some variations in the placement of the three tubes and, very rarely, a tumor involving the kidneys that is called a *Wilms tumor*. This is a cancerous tumor of a kidney that is usually present at birth. When it is found early, it can often be cured by the surgical removal of the affected kidney. Abnormalities of the ureters or urethra may allow infections to occur in the bladder or kidneys. (*See* the section in chapter 10 on the illnesses of children.) If your child has repeated infections, do ask your doctor for any studies he feels might be helpful to reassure you.

TOILET TRAINING

The only part of your baby's waterworks that is *not* developed at birth, is the control mechanism for the bladder. It empties purely by reflex at birth and until about two years of age. If you are an exceptionally aware parent, you may "catch" your child when his bladder is about to empty itself, even at a year of age. This is not really toilet training but parental alertness. It does, nevertheless, save lots of diapers and does no harm unless your child resists the potty chair.

Don't Rush It

Toilet control, like eating and sleeping, is partially a natural process. Please do not create needless battles by starting too early, being too rigid, or punishing. You will know your child is ready for training when he stays dry for longer periods of time, such as during a nap. Rarely is this before two or two and a half years of age.

Introducing the Training Chair

Introduce the child to the training chair at this time. Even though he may not have a complete vocabulary, he will understand much of your explanation. Tell him what the chair is for, and help him sit on it. Some children may fear falling down into it. If your child is a bit anxious, you may let him sit on it with his diaper on. Frankly, we think that is confusing to both child and parent, but some authorities advise it.

Chair Types. We prefer the small training chair that sits on the floor. There are child seats that fit over a regular toilet, but children will need a stool for their feet, and often are truly afraid of falling into the water, or down from that height. It really is not too hard to help a child graduate to the big toilet when he is larger and really trained. The little deflector for boys on a potty chair may be helpful, but we find boys may injure the penis on it, so just teach them to hold the penis down or even to stand up for urinating.

Toilet Training Suggestions

Watching parents or older brothers and sisters may give many children the idea of toilet use easily. Others will be slow no matter what you do. Here is a suggested system you may try.

1. When you believe your child is ready, plan your week's schedule, so you can focus on helping him learn control.
2. Keep the training chair in the bathroom and plan to spend some time there!
3. When you catch him dry for over an hour, put him on the training chair (with or without a diaper) and sit with him. Do not strap him into the chair. Do not make this a play area.
4. Offer him a drink of water, turn on a faucet, even spill a bit of warm water over the lower abdomen. Wait five to ten minutes.
5. If such attempts work, praise him generously and honestly. Put his diaper back on and watch for dryness again.
6. When such attempts do not work (and they rarely do at first), let the child play about in the bathroom for a few minutes without a diaper. Many times, he will find the urge to go after leaving the chair. Without scaring him, quickly put him back on it, and then praise him. Some authorities insist a child who is physically ready may be taught control in a day or two *if* you are willing to spend those days in the bathroom!
7. When none of the above work, put the whole process to rest for a month or two and try again. Think through your

approach. If you have been too nervous or harsh, practice patience. If you are too lenient, try a firmer approach.

8. During warm weather, put your child in training pants. They are quicker to get off, easy to wash, and help the child feel more grown up.

9. Comfort yourself when the process is slow! Neither of us has seen a college graduate wetting his pants unless there is a physical problem.

Nighttime dryness. This normally follows daytime control within a few months. When your child is doing well during the day, tell him it is time to stay dry at night. Put a mattress protector on his bed, well-padded training pants on, leave a night-light on, and expect him to stay dry. Be sure he empties his bladder before retiring, and limit his evening fluids a bit. Do not allow any cola drinks or tea as these contain caffeine, which stimulates the output of urine. If he is nervous or fearful about getting up to go to the bathroom, ask him to call you for help.

Sound Sleeper. Some children sleep so soundly they do not awaken, even with the discomfort of a full bladder. They may dream they have gone to the bathroom, only to awaken in a flooded bed. Such children may need to go to bed earlier to avoid extreme fatigue; rarely a medication may help break the old habits, and occasionally a firm command helps a child assume the responsibility for his own dryness. This responsibility rests with the child eventually, anyway, and we believe many parents delay a child's control by assuming responsibility for him.

A seven-year-old girl was brought to me because of consistent bed-wetting. A thorough examination revealed no physical reason for this. I sat down with Janie and told her my findings. I then said that I'd like her to make up her own mind, really firmly, not to wet her bed again. She looked surprised at first, but said she would do that. Her mother reported a miraculous cure. This won't work with every child, but some authorities find it will work very often.

Anger and punishment have cured some bed-wetting, but usually at the price of fear or hatred from the child. Find that important balance between permissiveness and abusiveness, which is a fair, gentle, but firm approach. Once you achieve that, many problems will disappear.

THE REPRODUCTIVE SYSTEM
(Genital)—FEMALES

The reproductive organs are present but tiny at birth. They do not function until puberty, so their real development occurs later. The most concerns about the genital area are those at birth. (Refer to chapter 6, "The First Thirty Days.")

Birth Defects

These are not common in girls' genital areas. Rarely there are deformities of the uterus (womb) such as a *bicornate uterus*. In this condition the womb is partially divided into two chambers. This creates no symptoms until the time of trying to become pregnant. It is then likely to cause miscarriages.

Even more rarely, the ovaries may be absent. This is called *primary ovarian agenesis* or Turner's syndrome. It has other problems associated with it, mainly involving hormone imbalances in the endocrine system. It is often associated with some degree of mental retardation and various abnormalities of the heart and circulatory system.

Infections and Injuries

These are very rare in little girls' genital systems. Usually, they are the result of straddle-type falls or tragically commonly are due to sexual abuse or incest. (*See* section on Child Abuse in chapter 16.)

Incest

This is the practice of sexual activity of one type or another among near relatives. Commonest is that between brother and sister, but all too often it is practiced between fathers and daughters. Grandfathers, uncles, and cousins are all on the list. It is extremely rare between mothers and sons.

In cases of incest, mothers are often guilty of negligence and failure to respond to the signs of, or even confessed information, about such situations. Dr. Grace has worked with many guilt-ridden adolescents and adults whose problems go directly back to incestual attacks in childhood.

When incest is suspected, Mother, please get professional counsel at once. While it is horrifying to admit and painful to deal with, it is unthinkable to ignore or wish it away! Good psychotherapy will be able to stop such practices, enable emotional healing to take place through understanding, and prevent the scars of incest from damaging your child's eventual physical and mental health.

IF A SEXUAL ENCOUNTER CAUSES PHYSICAL DAMAGE, DO NOT HESITATE, EVEN THOUGH YOU MAY FEEL ASHAMED AND AFRAID. TAKE YOUR CHILD AT ONCE TO YOUR DOCTOR OR AN EMERGENCY ROOM. THERE HAVE BEEN DEATHS FROM BLEEDING OR INFECTIONS DUE TO THE NEGLECT OF SUCH INJURIES. WHATEVER THE EMBARRASSMENT TO AN ADULT, A CHILD'S LIFE IS WORTH INFINITELY MORE. THINK AHEAD TO THE TIME OF RESTORATION AND HEALING. DO NOT GIVE IN TO THE TEMPTATION TO AVOID DEALING WITH THE ISSUE!

REPRODUCTIVE SYSTEM—MALES

Male genitalia are formed at birth, but small. The parts of this system include the scrotum and testicles, the spermatic cords, seminal vesicles, prostate gland, and penis.

Birth Defects

Undescended Testicles (*Cryptorchidism*). This was discussed in the last chapter. Undescended testicles are quite common but are easily watched. Most of them move down into the scrotum by themselves. If this has not happened by the age of five, your doctor will almost certainly recommend surgery that will bring the missing item into the scrotum. When such a placement is not achieved by puberty, that testicle will almost certainly be sterile.

Now do not confuse an undescended testicle with the reflex ascent of a testicle into the area in the groin. Such events happen often in some boys. It always returns to its proper place when he relaxes. If in doubt, ask your doctor.

Hypospadias. This is a condition of baby boys in which the end of the penis is open for some distance along the urethra. It may be only a few millimeters but even such a small space can cause trouble. The urinary stream will be a bit harder to guide when your son is learning to use the toilet. Plastic surgery can correct this defect in some cases.

Hydrocele. This is a little sac of fluid that normally surrounds and protects the testes. In some cases, for reasons we do not understand, this sac enlarges and fills with excess fluid. It may become quite large but it rarely hurts. Many times, especially in earlier childhood, it goes away as unexplainedly as it came.

IN CASE YOUR SON HAS SUCH A PROBLEM AND IT DOES NOT DISAPPEAR, PLEASE DO NOT HESITATE TO ASK YOUR DOCTOR ABOUT IT. HE CAN TELL IF IT IS LIKELY TO NEED SURGICAL CORRECTION.

Hernias. These are problems that may be birth defects or may result from an injury. They involve some abnormality of the abdominal muscles. Though they occur in the area of the spermatic cord, hernias are not actually part of the genital system.

Due to a weakness in the muscle fibers in the area where the abdominal muscles attach to the pubic bone, those fibers may split and allow a loop of intestine to protrude from the abdominal cavity just under the skin. Hard crying or active movement may make this swelling become quite large. It is possible for such an intestinal mass to become trapped in the tissues and swell enough to cut off its blood supply.

SUCH A CONDITION IS CALLED A "STRANGULATED HERNIA." AN ORDINARY HERNIA NEEDS TO BE REPAIRED AT SOME TIME, USUALLY AT YOUR CONVENIENCE. A STRANGULATED HERNIA BECOMES AN EMERGENCY AND MUST BE REPAIRED AT ONCE. THESE ARE THE SIGNS OF A STRANGULATED HERNIA:

1. *The hernia cannot be reduced—or pushed back up into the abdomen.*
2. *The child is fretful and in obvious pain.*
3. *The abdomen may become distended and cause shortness of breath.*

4. *The loop of intestine present in the hernia sac may become firm and tender.*

DO NOT WAIT. CALL YOUR DOCTOR AND SEE HIM AT ONCE, OR GO TO YOUR HOSPITAL EMERGENCY ROOM. THIS IS AN EMERGENCY.

Masturbation

This is of concern to some parents of both male and female children. Infantile masturbation is harmless. It is significant only in that your baby would be abnormal if he did not discover his penis and she, her vagina. They also find their ears, fingers, toes, noses, and chins! Only when parents treat the handling of the genitalia differently from the rest of the body does it become different. Such curiosity will subside in favor of rattles, music boxes, and blocks. Don't worry about it.

THE HEART AND BLOOD VESSELS
(Circulatory System)

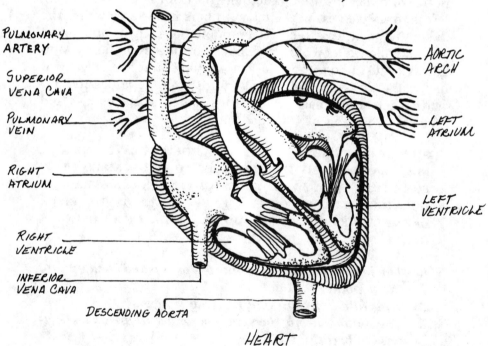

Parts of Circulatory System

The kidneys and liver are a purification plant for the blood, and the heart is its pumping system. Blood vessels going away from the heart are called *arteries,* and those going to the heart are called *veins.* Arteries from the right side of the heart go to the lungs, where the blood they conduct exchanges the waste material, carbon dioxide, for oxygen. The blood returns through various valves, ending up in the left side of the heart. There it is pumped out to the rest of the body through a branching system of increasingly tiny blood vessels until, in the capillaries, the arterial blood flows into the veins. The veins, returning blood to the heart, become larger and larger until they become one large vein emptying into the right heart. All along the way, these systems of arteries and veins are delivering nutrients and picking up waste products.

Blood in the Bible

Someone has said it is not by accident that the Bible speaks of the blood as being symbolic of cleansing. In Old Testament sacrifices and in the New Testament account of the sacrifice of Jesus Christ, this marvelous pattern is used.

Blood Cells

We now know that the exact size and shape of the blood cells makes them uniquely able to destroy quantities of toxic-waste products many times their own volume. Red blood cells exchange carbon dioxide and oxygen, and a variety of white blood cells engulf bacteria and tiny specks of other poisonous materials and destroy them.

Supplements

You child's body needs proper nutrition, rest, and protection to keep the blood cells healthy. Chapter 8 on feeding and nutrition discusses this topic in greater depth. You need to remember to give younger children enough iron and vitamins, as well as milk. From three weeks of age until about six months, when they are on solid foods, they need some iron supplement. Please ask your doctor how much to give. Babies vary in their needs and their ability to absorb iron. It is just as dangerous to give too much as too little.

Birth Defects

These are not uncommon in the heart. The usual ones involve defects of the valves controlling the blood flow between the chambers of the heart, and between the heart and large arteries and veins. Occasionally there are holes in the walls that separate the various chambers.

Symptoms. Most heart defects cause symptoms that are found soon after birth. Usually there is a murmur, an abnormal sound your doctor will hear when he first examines your new baby. Sometimes the murmur will not appear until a few weeks or months later. You will not be able to hear a murmur without a stethoscope. You may, however, detect that your child's color is pale, or sometimes dusky (called cyanosis). Your child may have trouble breathing; the heart may beat very hard or rapidly.

Fortunately, many testing procedures are now available that can quickly, accurately, and safely diagnose the sort of problem a baby may have. A great many serious heart abnormalities can now be corrected surgically, many of them even before your baby goes home.

Treat Child Normally

If you do take a child home knowing he has a congenital heart problem, treat him as normally as possible. Your doctor will tell you any danger signals. Except for being alert to these, allow your child to live normally. Use necessary disciplinary measures because handicapped children need to learn obedience in order to cooperate with medical care. Allow the child as much activity as he wants. Babies do a remarkable job of living within their limits and learn to push these only much later in childhood. (*See* The Handicapped Child in chapter 19).

Birth Defects of Blood Cells

Hemophilia. Other birth defects involve the blood cells. *Hemophilia* is an example of this. Very rarely, a boy may be born with the failure of his blood to clot properly. This disease is inherited from ancestors and is transmitted through the genes and chromosomes of the mother. Girls are never afflicted with hemophilia, but they do pass it on to their sons. The problem lies in the failure of the clot to contract and seal off the blood vessels and capillaries that may be injured. Even a slight bruise may cause internal bleeding, and a cut of any severity may actually threaten the life of a child. While this is rare, you may need to help your child understand another child who suffers such a problem. Teach him to be gentle and supportive, but also natural and accepting of him.

Sickle-cell Anemia. This is an inherited disease affecting the red blood cells. It occurs only in children and adults who are black or dark-skinned. In this condition, the red cells, under certain conditions, change from their normal round shape to a roughly semicircular or sickle shape. This change in shape makes the cells less effective in their job of carrying oxygen and removing carbon dioxide. The children may also become anemic due to the fact that such abnormal cells break down much faster than normal cells. Other symptoms include pain in the joints, severe muscle cramps or aching, and heart enlargement and murmurs. The liver and spleen often enlarge.

Treatment must be done in a hospital and may involve blood transfusions, as well as special medication. As children grow older, these severe episodes tend to decrease and may nearly disappear.

Iron-deficiency Anemia. This is a disease of the red blood cells in which there is not enough iron. The hemoglobin, or red-colored material, in the red cells is not able to carry enough oxygen, and the child tires easily. When this becomes especially severe, a child looks pale. Usually an anemic child does not eat enough iron-containing foods such as green, leafy vegetables and meats, and often drinks too much milk.

The treatment of simple anemia is the administration of iron. This needs to be given in concentrated form to correct the deficiency. A good diet, however, should keep the blood healthy. In babies who are on special formulas or breast milk, iron-deficiency anemia should not occur. If it does, or if, in spite of taking extra iron, the blood does not improve, special tests may need to be done.

In some cases, babies do not absorb iron well from the intestinal tract. An injection can be given to such children. This works effectively and usually builds up those red blood cells in a hurry.

Leukemia. This is a malignant disease of the white blood cells, which function as protectors of the body against infections. In leukemia, the body usually manufactures large numbers of one or more kinds of white blood cells, but some of them are unhealthy or abnormal cells. They do not fight off infections, as they normally do, but allow them to spread. Eventually the red cells are destroyed and the patient becomes severely anemic. A less common form of leukemia is one in which there are few, if any, white blood cells formed.

Leukemia is a form of cancer and once was inevitably fatal, though some children lived several years before death. It still is serious, but new forms of chemotherapy are now bringing about hopeful results. A five-year arrest or remission of leukemia may bring hope of a permanent cure.

There is great controversy over the use of *Laetrile,* a chemical derived from fruit pits, to treat all sorts of cancer. While we can't blame any parent for trying any possible cure for such a tragic illness, we strongly urge you to stick with reliable cancer specialists if your child ever should develop this dreaded disease.

THE BRAIN AND NERVES
(Neurological System)

How the System Works

The brain and spinal cord, with their many branching nerves, are well formed at birth. But there is much development that takes place as these nerves are stimulated. Some nerves take messages to the brain carrying information, much as a telephone does to its central computer system. The brain then sends messages back out over the specific network in response to that original information. For example, a finger touches a glowing light bulb. The message the finger sends is "That hurts!" The brain instantly sends an impulse to the finger say-ing, "You're right. So move!" Such an exchange of information and action is almost instantaneous.

The process of learning begins with just such simple neuro-logical interactions. These become even more complex and re-sult in recognition, memories, the ability to·think and apply facts to life situations; even some of the ability to love and feel a range of emotions are involved in the brain and nervous system.

Major Senses

There are five major senses our bodies are capable of inter-preting to us.

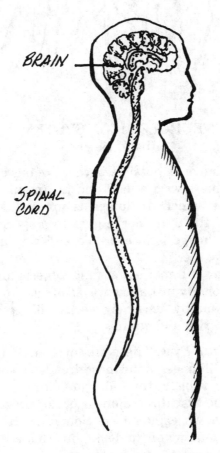

BRAIN

SPINAL CORD

NEUROLOGICAL SYSTEM
(side view)

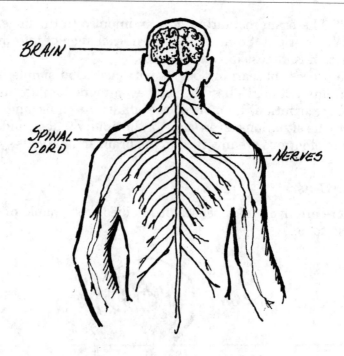

NEUROLOGICAL SYSTEM
(back view)

Sight. This, of course, is possible because of our eyes. Each eye is a lot like a camera with a light shutter (pupil), a lens, and a sensitive area on which an image is imprinted (the retina). From the retina, the optic nerve goes to a special area of the brain where the image is interpreted and we understand and can label what we see.

In babies, vision is imperfect at first. Objects are blurred and there is little color. By just a few weeks of age, however, a child can focus more, and by five or six weeks will respond to smiles and cooing with grins and gurgles.

Birth Defects of the Eyes. These are fortunately fairly rare but may be serious. Blindness is the most dreaded visual problem. It may be caused by rubella (three-day or German measles) in the mother during the first three months of her pregnancy. It may occur with no known explanation. Sometimes a child is born with cataracts (clouding of the lens), but this can be corrected surgically in many cases.

More common are defects affecting the muscles that move the eyes. These may be weak on one side or the other, allowing one or both eyes to turn inward or outward. Such problems are highly correctible with surgery. Since babies' eyes do not focus really well until several months of age, your doctor will not usually refer you to a specialist until six to nine months of age, or later.

A *lazy eye* is the common term given to an eye that for some reason simply has not been used by a child. Doctors may discover this, or you may suspect it if your child bumps into things on that side but not the other. One treatment is to place a patch over the good eye, requiring a child to use the weak eye. When such a defect is diagnosed early, the correction may be nearly perfect. Later on, correction is likely to be more limited. Sometimes glasses can be fitted that may improve this problem.

Nearsightedness is one of the most common eye defects. It is inherited, and usually affects both eyes. The eyes see objects that are close clearly but visualize distant sights as fuzzy. Usually nearsightedness (myopia) cannot be diagnosed until the child is able to cooperate by pointing the direction of an arrow, for example, or identifying some letters. Glasses can correct most myopia, but it is important to keep your child under good eye care. Some encouraging new possibilities are being explored that may improve vision for the severely myopic.

Farsightedness is the opposite of nearsightedness. It generally does not affect children and usually need not be of concern to parents, except when their own arms become too short!

Hearing. This is the function of the ears and the brain. As sound waves are collected by the outer ear, they are neatly funneled into the canal, where they hit the eardrum. The eardrum transmits the sound waves through three tiny, loosely connected bones to the inner ear. There the nerve endings collect the sounds and transmit them through the auditory nerve to a special area on the surface of the brain that translates them into recognizable voices or other sounds. The memory files them and uses them to understand the auditory part of the world.

Birth Defects of the Auditory System. These are usually limited to impairment of hearing. This may occur through: 1) conductive damage involving the absence of the outer ear, or some problem with the bones in the middle ear; 2) nerve damage in which even the loudest sounds simply cannot be sent through the auditory nerve because it has been hurt or destroyed. One of the commonest causes of nerve deafness at birth is rubella in the mother during the first three months of her pregnancy. As immunity is acquired to this disease through shots in childhood, many cases of deafness will be eliminated.

A Sense of Smell. This is the contribution of the nose to the joy of living. Tiny nerves in the mucous membranes of the nose pick up the scent of roses or the spicy odor of food. Through a nerve called the *olfactory* nerve, the impulses of smell are sent to the brain. There they are interpreted in a fashion similar to sight and hearing. Much of the enjoyment of food comes from the sense of smell. Remember when you had a severe head cold? Food probably tasted flat. If so, it was largely due to the impairment of your sense of smell from the irritation of the cold.

Birth defects affecting the sense of smell are so rare, we do not know of any.

Taste. This is limited to the tongue, though we have just discussed the fact that taste and smell are intertwined. Amazingly, taste itself is limited to four sensations. They are *sweet, sour, salty,* and *bitter.* If you doubt this, close off your nostrils and taste anything you like. It will be bland and tasteless, or it will taste like one of the above. Tastes are transmitted to the brain to be learned, identified, and remembered.

At birth, babies have very sensitive taste buds. As they grow, according to authorities, the acuteness of the taste very slowly deteriorates. In old age, people often yearn for a food they enjoyed as children. All too often, that treat is disappointing due to the loss of some of the sense of taste.

We know of no birth defects directly affecting taste.

Touch. This is made possible by numberless nerve endings all over the body. They register cold, heat, pain, and itching, in all their varying degrees of strength. The nerves also go to the brain for interpretation and appropriate reactions. Touch in the American culture (and everywhere, in various forms) becomes symbolic of affection and interpersonal regard. Hitting, the touch of anger, usually symbolizes ill will and hatred, unless it is the "tough love" of discipline!

There are no known birth defects affecting the sense of touch except severe, total brain damage.

Neurological development is fairly complete by the age of two. Babies need an opportunity to see a variety of colors, hear a range of sounds, and smell, taste, and touch as many different things as they safely can. We know such stimulation of these senses does several wonderful things.

It teaches children the pure joy of their own little bodies. I see many troubled, hardened young people. Few of them can find a feeling of well-being from their own senses and seek escape in a sophisticated, heavily exciting life-style and a sensation of being "high." Teach your child the simple, profound joy of wind, sun, bird songs, and tickles. She will be less likely to need a high on drugs later.

Extensive studies indicate that early stimulation of a baby's senses actually increases the child's intelligence. Such stimulation, when it is also loving, will increase a child's security and enhance her own potential to be loving.

Birth Defects of the Brain and Nervous System. These are not, unfortunately, uncommon. *Cerebral palsy* is an affliction that still brings frustrating limits to children and heartache to parents.

Cerebral palsy is a neurological defect that is present at birth. Even after years of study, we do not know what causes it. It is the failure of muscles to relax, so that voluntary control of the muscles simply is not possible. It may be mild or severe; it may affect a few muscles or nearly all of them; and it may be associated with other neurological problems, and even mental retardation, or there may be no other such defects. Many cerebral palsy victims are exceptionally bright.

Treatment includes physical therapy to improve voluntary function and relaxation of the spastic or rigid muscles. Braces may help in the control, and some medication might aid a bit. Treatment, however, is discouraging at best. Children afflicted with cerebral palsy should be encouraged to live as normally as possible. They need help to accept the rude stares and curiosity of others, and they especially need help to overcome the pity others may show. (*See* The Handicapped Child, chapter 19.)

Muscular Dystrophy or Atrophy. There are many variations and forms of this affliction. It may be present before birth or it may show up as late as in adolescence. The cause is unknown but may be inherited. The nerves that stimulate the muscles to move slowly stop functioning. The muscles in parts, or all of the body from the neck down, become increasingly weakened and eventually fail. When the weakness becomes severe, it may paralyze the respiratory muscles, and death will occur due to the inability to breathe.

There are other neurological defects that are much more rare. *Hydrocephalus* is one such rare birth defect. In this condition the brain is often normal at birth, but the channel that drains the spinal fluid as it is secreted to protect the central nervous system does not work. The spinal fluid accumulates, stretching the child's head to grotesque proportions. Surgery is now possible to create a drainage system, and many such children may lead relatively normal lives.

Microcephaly is a condition in which the brain and head are very small. Such a child is usually severely mentally and physically retarded. We have no remedy for a condition such as this, but research goes on to try to prevent such birth defects.

Normal Reflexes. There are several normal reflexes that will help you know that your child is neurologically healthy at birth.

One of the first reflexes you will notice is the *startle reflex* (Moro reflex). With a sudden motion or loud noise, the baby extends his arms and legs, looks surprised, may shiver, and often cries. Another is reflex grasping. Many parents have felt strong emotion as a baby's tiny hand gripped their fingers. Please continue to feel good about that gesture of trust. It also means his nerves and muscles are coordinated and strong.

Babies also have a reflex that causes them to pull away from painful stimulation. This helps to protect them from burns or other injuries.

The firm touch or soothing motion of a parent often quiets a fussing child. This also is a reflex response, though it quickly becomes learned as a pleasure, too.

In determining handedness, the *tonic neck reflex* is interesting. Babies' heads usually tend to rest on a side rather than the back. The hand on the side toward which the face is turned flexes upward, so the child can see it, and the leg also flexes. The opposite arm and leg extend. Most babies automatically turn to the right. This reflex tends to disappear at sixteen weeks of age, though turning a child's head in an exaggerated position will often cause a repeat of this reflex for many months or years.

The *rooting* and *sucking reflexes* were described earlier. They certainly can be seen as the forerunners of eating and drinking in all the ways these can be enjoyed.

Babies of a few days or weeks can make crawling, stepping, and swimming motions. In fact, it has become quite popular to teach babies to swim at a very early age. Watch your baby for a readiness to swim or crawl, but do not rush him into such complex activities.

THE ENDOCRINE SYSTEM

This is a highly complex system with actions and reactions of each on the other. Medical science has learned much about the endocrine glands and the hormones they secrete, but there is still much more to know. Hormones affect a baby's birth, growth, energy level, digestion, and eventually reproduction and aging.

Endocrine Glands

The most commonly known endocrine glands are these:

Pituitary Gland. This master gland is known to strongly influence the other glands and the growth rate. It is located at the base of the brain, carefully protected in a special case within the skull.

Thyroid Gland. There are two major lobes connected by a narrower band of tissue. It is located in the neck on the level of the voice box or larynx. It regulates the rate with which the body burns fuel to provide energy.

Adrenal Glands. They are located near the upper area of each kidney, protected by the lower ribs in the back. Their hormones include cortisone, hydrocortisone, and adrenalin. We are learning much about these and know they are needed during stress of all kinds.

Sex Glands. In males, these are the testes, and are located in the scrotum. In the female, they are ovaries, and lie in the pelvic area. They secrete testosterone and estrogen, among other hormones that have much to do with sexual function and reproduction.

Thymus Gland. Located lower in the neck than the thyroid, this gland is still a mystery. It is thought to have some function in the physiology of nerves and muscles.

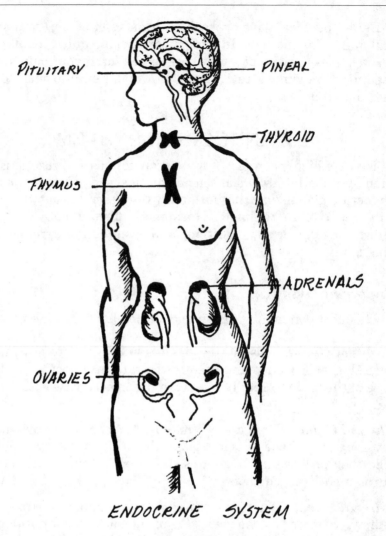

PITUITARY —— PINEAL

—— THYROID

THYMUS ——

—— ADRENALS

OVARIES ——

ENDOCRINE SYSTEM

Birth Defects. Among the endocrine glands these are rare. A very low *thyroid* output is the only one of any degree of frequency. This condition is called *cretinism* and needs to be diagnosed to differentiate it from Down's syndrome (Mongolism).

A test of thyroid function can readily be made on the child's blood. Giving thyroid extract cures this condition quickly.

Down's syndrome is a condition that is all too common in babies born to women over thirty-five; it may, however, occur in younger mothers, too. It is due to chromosomal abnormalities, but no one yet knows why. Since such babies are more common in older mothers, it may be due to some hormonal or other factor related to older age groups.

At any rate, Down's syndrome children have characteristic physical signs:

1. *The skin is a bit "doughy" feeling.*
2. *The upper eyelids are prominent, causing the eyes to look somewhat oriental.*
3. *Noses are usually short and have a flat bridge.*
4. *The fingers and toes are short, and the little finger curves out at the middle joint and back in. There is an unusually big space between the great and second toe.*
5. *The lines on the palms lack the usual curves and tend to be quite evenly horizontal.*
6. *These babies are mildly to markedly retarded, though early stimulation and teaching are believed to improve a child's capacity to learn.*
7. *Often there are severe congenital heart defects.*
8. *Usually the ultimate height is shorter than normal.*

Encouraging work is being done with early and extensive stimulation of all of the senses discussed above. With such efforts, many of these children are able to attend and function within regular classrooms. They still have limited abilities to learn, but indicate greater potential than most people have thought.

THE INFANT'S SLEEPING PATTERN

During the first two or three months of life, a baby will sleep from fifteen to twenty hours a day. Some mothers will be shocked to read this, but they probably have babies who waken more often or who may have colic.

Encouraging Good Sleeping Habits

To encourage good sleeping habits for your own sake, and your baby's, try these ideas:

1. Keep the baby in a room that is as quiet as possible. Soft background music or records will tend to block out other noises and keep the room more peaceful.

2.   At first, keeping shades drawn and the lights dim will also encourage restful sleep. When baby is awake, of course, let the sunlight in.

3.   If possible, do not keep baby in the same bedroom with you. Snoring and moving about in your sleep may quickly awaken a baby.

4.   If baby must share a room with a sibling, taking care of the older child's needs and the baby's can challenge you. Sometimes a curtain or screen may allow the older child some privacy and the baby his own area as well.

After the third or fourth month, the amount of sleep needed decreases fairly quickly into a morning and afternoon nap, a fussy evening, and a longer night's sleep. Allow the baby to join the family on a reclining infant seat, or give him some entertainment, such as crib toys tied across the bed, so he can bang on them without hurting himself. Such activities will be good exercise and will prepare him for his next rest time.

Crying It Out. If your baby is not sleeping through the night by at least six months, ask your doctor if it's all right to let him cry it out. If he feels your baby no longer needs a night feeding, you may safely harden your hearts and prepare for a bad night. The first night your baby will cry at least twenty to thirty minutes, perhaps longer. You will be mightily tempted to go and rescue the poor dear. We urge you not to do so. The "poor dear" can quickly turn into a tyrant whom you will learn to resent. Sometimes crying can cause a baby to choke. Watch and listen for this, but if he keeps on crying, you'll know he is fine. After he is asleep, tuck a clean diaper under his head, or move him away from the soiled area. Do not awaken him.

The second night he will cry a little; rarely will he cry on the third night. Give your child lots of daytime attention so he won't be neglected and you won't feel guilty! If you wait too long to break the night-waking cycle, it will become harder by the week. You may similarly leave your baby in his crib in the morning until reasonably close to the time you normally arise (unless, of course, that is noon!).

By one year to eighteen months of age, daytime sleep decreases to one afternoon nap for most babies, and levels off there until four or five years of age, when the nap may no longer be needed.

Sleep Disturbances

Between one and two years, you may count on your baby's having some sleep disturbances that are quite different from those of the six-month-old. At this age, babies may waken screaming and crying in what seems to be fear. My guess is that they have frightening dreams, but they have no vocabulary to describe them. At any rate, such an episode demands some cuddling and kisses. Don't overdo it, but hold and comfort the child before you put him back to bed. Keep a dim night-light on, and perhaps some very soft music. A cuddle toy or blanket may also provide security. This, too, will pass. The calmer and more reassuring you can be, the more quickly it will pass. Don't be tempted to take the child to bed with you. He will promptly learn to love that, and *none* of you will sleep well.

Regular Schedules Best

Children are at their best with a regular schedule. Here is a suggested pattern that you may adapt and find useful.

1. Evening is a restless, fretful time for most babies and continues to be for older infants. So focus on making it a cozy, happy time.
2. Plan the children's evening meal when they are hungry (but not starved) and keep it a happy time.
3. Let them play, hopefully with their father, as hard as they like for an hour. This will consume their restless energy.
4. Help them unwind with a small snack.
5. A warm bath (without water fights) might come next, with its relaxing comfort. After a bath, our children loved to be encased in a big towel and held in hiding for a few minutes.
6. Time now for clean bedclothes, a rocking, singing, and reading time. Bible stories can be a regular part of this ritual, and then the delightful prayertime and tucking in bed.
7. Be in charge. Tell the child a few minutes ahead of time what will be coming next, and then see to it that it does. Do not allow your child to command your attention once he is in bed.

Set these habits early in your child's life, when you *know* you are still in charge. As he grows, modify the routine to fit his needs and yours. Avoid letting bedtime become a power struggle!

The Bedtime Power Struggle

If that has already happened, try something like this:

1. *Tell the child kindly but firmly that bedtime hassles are going to stop.*
2. *You decide what your evening routine will be, and tell the child. (He may or may not believe you.)*
3. *At each step of the evening schedule, forewarn your child about the next phase—then do it!*
4. *Any self-respecting child will test you—he can't give in too easily or you may think he's a sissy. Expect to be tested.*
5. *Do not give in. Do not allow the child out of bed for drinks, potty, and so forth. You may call to him once to remind him of the rules, but not beyond that.*

For an especially strong-willed child, sit outside the room, or by his bed—but do not talk to him or respond except to firmly return him to his bed. He may test you for over an hour.

After the first night, the testing time shortens. After the third or fourth, it will almost always disappear.

Remember—*you are in charge.* Your child cannot feel safe if he is stronger than you. This applies to any area of life. Count on it! Notice his relief when you again are in command.

You will not damage your child by winning such power struggles. He wants and needs you to be strong. If you are uncertain and waver, the child will have to take control!

Giving Up the Nap

You may well wonder how to know when your child is really ready to give up a nap, and when he is manipulating you. Our youngest child is a fine example. At the age of three and a half, we noticed she could not sleep at night. She went to bed by our usual routine, but when we went to check on her an hour or two later she would be wide-awake. She wasn't begging for drinks, the potty, or any attention. When she didn't get a nap one day, she fell asleep promptly at the earlier hour. Seeing this happen for several days convinced us that she just couldn't sleep that much.

Sleepy children rub their eyes, whine, get frustrated quickly, and have droopy eyelids. Do not excuse all misbehaviors as signs of tiredness! But do remember that all of us have a shorter fuse when we are really tired.

As your child matures, continue to help him understand how much sleep he needs in order to feel his best. This varies from child to child. Helping a child understand and be kind to his unique self will set a lifetime pattern of health for him.

The Child's Bedroom

Keep your child's room primarily a bedroom. Isolating family members in their own rooms too much seems to us to be a means of fragmenting the family. We do not believe each child should have his own television, stereo, and radio unless he needs some quiet music.

Equipment your child will need starts with a good crib (baby bed) and a firm mattress. A tiny baby can fit into a full-size baby bed if it is fitted with bumper pads. The bars need to be close enough to prevent the head from getting stuck.

Linens should include a waterproof mattress cover, fitted sheets that stay in place, and a diaper or other clean linen under baby's face. Another pad under the diaper area will save some sheet changes and make laundry a bit lighter.

We believe a portable crib or playpen is nice if you are traveling or visiting. Usually babies don't need them at home unless you have a really cold floor. By the time baby is crawling, he will only be frustrated by a playpen.

Blankets work for nighttime warmth only until your baby starts moving about. Nice zip-in sleep wear is certainly more comfortable on cold nights. If you live in a warm climate, of course, you may not need those.

Colors in baby's room, if you have a choice, may be bright or soft, depending on what you want for your child. Bright colors and lively music may stimulate a placid baby nicely. An energetic infant, however, may need softer colors and more soothing sounds. Be alert to your baby's special needs. Night-lights are usually a necessity for both parents and children, for vision as well as security.

Selecting a Bed. By two or three years, your child will almost certainly be bumping about the ends of his crib. This is the time to choose his bed for the next several years, unless you have one vacated by an older child. A sturdy single (twin-size) bed is best. Bunk beds are preferable, we think, to a double bed, for several reasons: most children sleep better alone; the bunk bed arrangement allows space for another child, or later, for a friend to spend the night, and uses less floor space.

Give the child a chance to shop for the new bed, if possible. If he is to inherit one you already have, introduce the idea of moving to him gradually. It is a big move to a little child. He and that crib have been very close! If possible, keep the crib and the new bed in the same room for a while, and let him choose where he wants to sleep for a few nights. He will soon find himself more comfortable in the big bed, and be willing to put away the baby bed. Such a gradual transfer is helpful for the child who is giving up a bed to a younger child or a baby.

Sharing a room with brother or sister can create many problems, but also some closeness. Keep in mind the "squatter's rights" most of us feel about our own territory. Your understanding and patience will smooth out most of the bumps in the path toward real friendship between your children.

Crib Death

An illness that must be mentioned is *Crib Death*. It has come to be known as S.I.D.S. (Sudden Infant Death Syndrome). Even after years of careful study, we still do not know what causes it. Choking, colds, thymus glands, and many other symptoms have been carefully evaluated, but none of them fits as the cause. We simply do not know.

The typical scene is one in which a parent, thinking a child is sleeping too long, goes to waken him, and finds him dead. The shock and horror of such an event are describable only by those grief-stricken parents who have tragically had to live through such a crisis. Almost all such parents suffer an immense sense of guilt. Rarely, if ever, has there been any negligence or fault, but they naturally assume that. Sometimes there is anger at the medical profession, or parents may blame each other, or another child. Anger is a part of any grief process, but it should not be focused on another person. Each one involved in such a sudden loss needs support and love to make it through.

If you or anyone you know has to endure a sudden infant death, you may want to know about a support group. You may write to the National Foundation for Sudden Infant Death, Inc., 249 W. 34th St., New York, N.Y. 10001.

8
Winning the Eating Game— The Nutrition Factor

A finely tuned engine requires a precise mixture of fuels to run at maximum efficiency. When such an energy source is not supplied, the engine becomes damaged and will not function.

Your child's body is a bit like that engine. It is infinitely more complex and has a great many safeguards and balances built in to protect it against dysfunction. However, the fuel supply, with is essential ingredients, is well understood.

The basic components of your child's fuel and energy supply are these:

BASIC NUTRITION COMPONENTS

Carbohydrates

These are starches and sugars and they are present in fruits (fruit sugar or fructose), milk (milk sugar or lactose), grains, vegetables, and sweeteners such as honey, syrup, and sugar (sucrose). Within the body, these sugars are acted upon to become glucose, or blood sugar.

The digestion of carbohydrates begins right in the mouth. There is an enzyme in the saliva called *ptyalin* that starts to act upon the complex molecules of sucrose and starches, beginning to get them ready for the body to use.

In the stomach, the acids and mechanical action of the stomach's motion break these substances down even more. In the small intestine, more enzymes from the liver and pancreas continue this process. Insulin, an enzyme from the pancreas, is especially needed to complete the digestion of glucose and make it available for the body's metabolism.

Glucose is the energy source of your child's body. When he doesn't use it all, it is converted into fat and stored to be used later.

Fats

These are oily substances, chemically complex, that are found in meats, milk and its products, egg yolks, and many plants and their products. Examples of vegetable oils are corn, olive, coconut, banana, and safflower oils.

Fats begin their digestion in the stomach, where the acids and enzymes begin to break them down. They are acted upon by bile and other substances from the liver, and lipase, an enzyme from the pancreas. Eventually fats become a variety of "fatty acids," and these may form fat to be stored in a child's body or they may be converted by the body's complex fuel system into glucose for energy.

Proteins

These extremely complicated substances are found in all kinds of meats, egg whites, milk and cheese, and some vegetables, especially the bean family.

Proteins need to be broken down by chewing, but their digestion begins in the stomach, where the digestive juices start the long process of making them usable by the body. The digestion of proteins also includes enzymes from the liver and pancreas, and eventually they become amino acids. These are the building blocks of the body's tissues, and your child will need plenty of them during his growing stages. Proteins also may be converted to glucose or blood sugar, and can provide energy for the body.

Minerals

These are found as trace elements in the body. *Phosphorus* and *calcium* make our bones strong. *Sodium* and *potassium* help our circulation to function in supplying nutrients to all the body's tissues by balancing fluids in the tissues and cells with fluids in the blood vessels. *Lithium* is needed by the brain and nervous system. *Iron* and *copper* are essential for our red blood cells. Minerals are normally found in vegetables, meats, and eggs. *Magnesium* also is important in nerve and muscle functions and the building of proteins. It is present in adequate amounts in nuts, whole grains, and beans.

Vitamins

Vitamin A. This is important for good vision and healthy skin and hair. It is found in the yellow fruits and vegetables, egg yolks, milk, cheese, and animal fats, especially fish oil.

Vitamin C. This is important in the capillaries (tiniest branches of the veins and arteries). When it is lacking, these break and bleed easily. It also helps strengthen the mucous membranes. Many authorities believe it helps to prevent colds by its action on the mucosa of the nose and throat. Vitamin C is present in citrus fruits, tomatoes, berries, potatoes, and some yellow vegetables.

Vitamin D. This is very important for healthy bones and skin. It is found in eggs, fish oils, and usually is added to milk and cereals. No matter how much vitamin D is in the body, it is of no use without the action of sunlight on the skin. So be sure your child gets out of doors for a while on sunny days, even if you live in a cold climate.

Vitamin B. This once was thought to be one vitamin, but it is now known to be a complex of a number of vitamins. These are riboflavin, thiamine, pyridoxine, niacin, vitamin B_{12}, pantothenic acid, folacin, choline, and biotin. The B vitamins are found in meats, green, leafy vegetables, nuts, and whole grains. They prevent a variety of diseases of the circulatory and digestive systems, blood, and nervous system.

Vitamin E. This is not well understood but has an effect on the muscles, blood vessels and the formation and strength of blood cells, and the central nervous system. It is found in oils, fruits, vegetables, and whole-grain products.

Vitamin K. This is present in green vegetables, especially alfalfa leaves and in certain fish. It helps the blood to clot normally and prevents hemorrhaging.

Glucose

The metabolism of glucose is important in several regards. First, an even supply of it needs to be maintained if your child is to have the energy to use in daily functioning. When a diet is unbalanced and there is too much glucose, the body may produce extra insulin, which burns it up too fast. This can cause a condition called *hypoglycemia* or low blood sugar. The diagnosis of low blood sugar requires a five-hour-long special series of tests that measure the body's glucose after taking in a large amount of sugar. This is called a *glucose tolerance test.*

Hypoglycemia. When a child's blood sugar bounces from high to low very quickly, he will often act excited or hyperactive, and then become lethargic and irritable. It is as wrong to punish a child for a behavioral problem that is caused by a biochemical imbalance as it is to permit him to be mean due to a behavioral disorder. Your doctor can tell you if hypoglycemia is a problem only by the glucose tolerance test.

You may, however, try an experiment yourself. Remember that proteins and fats metabolize slowly, but evenly, into glucose. Try balancing your child's diet more thoughtfully with less sugars and starches and more proteins. A little fat goes a long way, because it contains over twice as many calories per unit of weight as do proteins and carbohydrates. If you discover that your child's activities and moods level out with this dietary change, you will have real reason to suspect some abnormality of glucose metabolism. We suggest you see your doctor for the glucose tolerance test and keep your child's diet lower in carbohydrates and higher in protein. This should control the problem.

Another very important fact about glucose relates to the disease *diabetes.* In this syndrome, the pancreas simply does not secrete enough insulin. We feel that you need to understand diabetes even if no one in your own family has it, since almost every family has friends or relatives who are diabetic.

DIABETES MELLITUS

Hereditary Disease

Diabetes mellitus is a hereditary disease; therefore a family history of diabetes is important. However, screening tests to find children who might become diabetic are not successful, and often the diagnosis is not made until the child appears at the doctor's office with the symptoms of excessive thirst, excessive urination, and excessive hunger. Sometimes the patient first appears at the doctor's office or at the hospital in diabetic coma. We believe that children with a family history of diabetes should have an occasional blood sugar test taken to determine the possibility of early diabetes.

Diagnosis

The diagnosis of diabetes actually depends upon laboratory data. It is a very simple thing to check urine for glucose, and any diabetic has the equipment to do this. Therefore, quite often within a family where there is an adult with diabetes, occasional spot checks of urine are done by the parent for the child. If there is sugar in the urine, a blood sugar determination should be obtained as soon as possible.

THE CHILD IN DIABETIC COMA IS ONE OF THE EMERGENCIES OF MEDICINE, AND HE SHOULD BE ADMITTED TO THE HOSPITAL IMMEDIATELY. THERE, SPECIFIC PROCEDURES ARE UNDERTAKEN FOR THE RAPID TREATMENT OF THIS SERIOUS COMPLICATION.

Long-term care of the child with diabetes mellitus is aimed at maintaining a healthy state and permitting the child to participate in any activity which he finds to be of interest, or for which he has talent. This is an obtainable goal with insulin therapy. Both parents and children need understanding of the problem and must cooperate with each other in its management.

Understanding the Basics

There are a few basic factors which we try to teach both the parents and child with diabetes mellitus. The first thing we stress is that his childhood can be perfectly normal and that he will mature, with the proper insulin doses, just as other children do. His choice of study, athletic participation, or school activities need not be any different from the nondiabetic child. We try to reassure parents that, even though the disease is hereditary in nature, there is nothing that parents did or did not do that would have precipitated the disease in their child. There is no reason for parents to harbor any guilt about this fact. We also like to reassure both the diabetic child and the parents that, if the diabetes is well controlled, he will not have any more difficulty in recovering from other types of illness than the nondiabetic patient.

It is very important that both the parents and the child realize that the long-term effects of uncontrolled diabetes can be very severe. If the child can realize this early in life, can learn to accept his disease, and can be taught to believe that his life can be relatively free of problems if he exercises some discipline, he may avoid the severe and disabling complications of diabetes in later life. The difficulty often is in teaching the child that his daily discipline is aimed toward the long-term management of good health care.

No attempt will be made in this book to discuss the role of diet, the different types of insulin, or the insulin dosages required. These things will be taught to you by your personal physician or by other personnel who are skilled in diabetic instruction. Other information can be obtained from the American Diabetes Association. (Consult your local phone directory.)

ROLE OF FATS

The subject of fats in the diet becomes most important when you consider its role in weight control and in the problem of *arteriosclerosis* (hardening of the arteries) in later life. We once believed that a child's diet did not need to be concerned about such issues. We now have evidence that raises the possibility that such complications in older people began, very silently, in childhood.

We know that fats which are saturated with hydrogen are especially likely to cause arterial diseases. Saturated fats are those found in animals and their products—milk, butter, and cream. Coconut oil is also rich in that kind of fat.

Use Low-fat Products

Monounsaturated fats seem to do no harm. But polyunsaturated fats are the very safest. Corn oil and safflower oil are excellent, and can be found in liquid form as well as solids like margarine or shortening. *We strongly recommend that you use low-fat milk as soon as your baby is off formula, and always use polyunsaturated fats.* The prevention of diseases of the heart and circulatory system begins in childhood.

Fat Cells

We also have evidence that obesity (overweight) in adults has its origin in childhood. The development of a large number of "fat cells" is the by-product of gaining too much weight early in life. Even if a child loses weight as he grows, these fat cells lie dormant, or empty, ready to fill with fat again when too many calories are taken into the system.

Too high a level of protein, without a balance of some fats and carbohydrates, may create stress for the kidneys. The waste products of the metabolism of proteins are excreted as a chemical called *urea* in the urine.

PLANNING BALANCED MEALS

The proper balance in proteins, carbohydrates, and fats, as well as all the vitamins and minerals, then, is necessary to maintain ideal health and nutrition for your child. In order to be certain that your family actually has the essential elements needed, consider organizing your meals around the following groups of foods:

Milk and Milk Products

Babies start life needing from eighteen to twenty ounces of milk daily. As they grow, this amount increases to about double that quantity. As other foods are added to the diet, however, the milk may safely be decreased to sixteen ounces a day by one year. Usually it should increase slowly to three eight-ounce glasses daily by eight or nine years of age, and stay at that level.

For Milk Dislikers. Many children seem to dislike milk, and it is quite permissible to flavor it with vanilla and a little honey or some artificial fruit flavors. Since chocolate contains caffeine, do not overuse it to flavor a younger child's milk. Milk in the form of puddings or ice cream is also permitted, unless your child tends to be overweight. We know that fat is not healthy, so watch the calories lest they creep up in the form of pushing one or another special food. Better a bit less milk and a less obese child, than exactly enough milk and a fat child!

Despite our enjoyment of real butter, we believe you should

avoid it, since it is high in cholesterol-forming elements. Stick to the polyunsaturated spreads and shortening.

Meats, Poultry, Fish, Eggs, Dried Beans, Peas, and Nuts

Since children need plenty of protein to build their bodies' tissues, they should have a serving of meat daily and an egg from four to seven times a week. The serving size may vary from a teaspoonful at six months to four to eight ounces daily in adolescence. Your child's appetite is almost always a safe guide of quantity. Babies, of course, must get used to the feel and taste of meat and eggs. Once they do, their own hunger will regulate the amount needed. So don't weigh and measure servings. Just offer a variety of meats, tender and tastefully prepared, and your child will take what he needs.

While freshly cooked meats, liver, fish, and poultry are the best providers of vitamins and other nutrients, a finicky eater can get surprisingly good amounts of proteins and minerals from hot dogs (weiners). We urge you to keep offering better types of meat, and to add vitamins until you feel confident that your child's diet is well balanced.

Most children act as though they could live on peanut butter alone. A friend took his grandson of five years to an elegant restaurant for a special lunch and, yes, the child wanted nothing but a peanut-butter sandwich! Fortunately, we know that peanuts are rich in easily digested proteins. With plenty of milk (and we find that is necessary to wash down the sticky stuff!) your child will get enough amino acids to thrive. Soybeans and other dried beans and peas are also rich in proteins as well as starch.

Bread, Cereals, and Flour

Since the outer coating of grains contains most of the vitamins and minerals, whole-wheat grains are certainly the most nutritious. The inner portion of grains is primarily starch, but there is also protein called "gluten" in the germ of the grain. It is the gluten that is responsible for grain allergies.

Cereals, especially rice, which is easily digested and rarely causes allergies, should be one of the first solid foods offered to a baby. Start with a teaspoonful and increase to as much as your child wants. After a year, a child should be offered bread or cereal twice daily.

We strongly suggest that you avoid the sugar-coated cereals. A little honey or fruit with cereal can make it appetizing and avoid the empty calories of too much sugar.

Green, Leafy, and Yellow Vegetables

We find that most babies dislike the green vegetables, except peas, and prefer squash, carrots, and sweet potatoes. As they grow older, however, they will often like green beans as a finger food, and they like many vegetables raw better than cooked. It still amazes us that people transform a crisp, tangy raw turnip into a bitter, unappealing (to us!) mess, and then pay for the energy to cook it. Ditto, carrots, and a few other foods. Fresh foods are the very richest in vitamins, so allow your child to have them as soon as he can chew them well.

Cooking, by the way, is necessary to break down the harder vegetables into a form that can be chewed and swallowed. Some raw vegetables come through the intestinal tract undigested unless they are cooked. One serving daily is enough—adjusted in amount to your child's size.

These foods supply vitamins A and C, the B complex, and minerals. They also supply roughage which helps prevent constipation.

Citrus Fruits, Tomatoes, Raw Cabbage, and Salad Greens

These foods are rich in vitamin C, some vitamin A, calcium, and iron. The list includes berries as well as oranges, lemons, limes, and grapefruit. Your child can get accustomed to eating these with very little or no sugar—to his benefit. One serving daily from this group is enough, but more, if desired, will not hurt.

Potatoes and Other Vegetables and Fruits

This group includes beets and turnips, celery, corn, cucumbers, eggplant, okra, and the less common vegetables. Fruits of all kinds not listed above are included. These provide vitamins and minerals, sugars and starches, as well as roughage.

Most nutritionists recommend a potato daily for children and adults, and at least one other food from the list. Serving sizes should be small and the child should be offered less rather than requiring him to clean up large servings that you think he may need. Do trust your child's appetite.

Fast Food Dangers. Today's fast-food industries have brought real danger to every family's good nutrition. The choice of hamburgers and french fries leaves many of the above food categories untouched. Americans consume increasing amounts of "junk foods" or "empty calories" that satisfy obvious hunger and even make your child gain weight. But they do not meet his basic health and nutritional needs.

We forget the scourges of pellagra, beriberi, scurvy, and rickets that resulted from serious vitamin deficiencies. They will recur, if we do not observe wise eating habits.

Special Diets

Special diets are required for certain physical conditions or during periods of illness. The most common specific diet is one that may be necessary due to allergies. There is such a variety of substances that may cause food allergies that we cannot list them. If your child has evidences of allergies, please consult your doctor for a complete evaluation and follow his recommendations. He may send you to a dietitian who is trained to know all the foods that may contain the items your child needs to avoid.

The Feingold Diet. This diet is especially focused on the elimination of the many additives that food-processing companies use. These additives are dyes and preservatives that make foods look appealing and keep them from spoiling. Many parents and nutrition experts believe strongly in the benefits of this rather complicated diet. Others doubt its positive effect. There is nothing in it that can hurt your child, so if you have a child who is hyperactive, irritable, and hard to live with, you may want to try it. Ask your doctor for information about it, go to your local library, or check in the telephone directory of the nearest city under "Feingold Association."

Gluten-Free Diet. Celiac disease is one of the clinical causes of the "malabsorption syndrome" in which foods, though digested, are not absorbed through the intestinal walls into the bloodstream. In celiac disease, this is due to the reaction of intestinal tissues to the protein fraction of grains called "gluten." The presence of this substance causes irritation and swelling of the tissues that prevents the absorption of foods. Large, foul-smelling, fatty stools are expelled, the child's abdomen becomes enlarged from these and the collection of gas. He cannot gain weight and even growth slows down.

Fortunately, celiac disease can be cured by the elimination of gluten. That, however, is not as easy as it sounds, because gluten is present in all grains and grain products, except rice. The elimination of flour means no cookies, crackers, cakes, or pies. The use of rice flour can be tolerated by most victims of this disease, but people tell us it is not as satisfactory for baking as wheat flour.

Organic Foods. There is a great commotion also about organic foods and natural vitamins by some groups concerned about nutrition. We have good friends who are convinced that foods grown only with natural fertilizers and using no chemical insecticides are superior foods. No studies have yet been devised to prove that, but we respect their opinions. You may decide to grow your own, but if you purchase such specially grown foods, you may pay very high prices. By laboratory tests called *bioassay,* natural vitamins have been shown to be no more effective than synthetic ones, and they are much more expensive.

The nutritional needs of older children are of concern to conscientious mothers. Some children learn to dislike milk. Others will not touch green vegetables, and still others refuse eggs or meat. I used to require our daughter to eat a certain amount of meat at least once a day. One day I cleaned out a corner cupboard near her place at the table. There, in neat little rows, were a large number of dried-out lumps of meat. She had surreptitiously slipped them aside, so *I* felt she was getting proper nutrition, and *she* didn't have to choke on the meat! Her health was just fine, and I had one more lesson that young children (under school age) will survive and be healthy on the foods their own bodies crave.

Counting Calories. If you are a calorie counter (and don't count too exactly!) you may want to know your child needs about one thousand a day by one year of age. You may add one hundred calories per day for each year of age up to adolescence. In the late teens the number goes back down and by middle age, it's back to about one thousand, unless the person works or exercises a great deal.

A non-milk drinker over a year of age can get by very well on sixteen to twenty-four ounces a day, and some of that may be in pudding or ice cream. A non-egg eater may get eggs in the same way. True, he will get a little extra sugar, but if you make your own pudding, you can cut down on sugar and use honey or fruit instead. Children need some sugar for energy, anyway. So don't be too worried about that.

More and more of a young child's calories should come from solid foods. But don't memorize the calorie charts. Offer a nice variety of foods; let your child see you enjoying them, and he will soon be asking for more.

Avoiding Snacks. Avoid too many snacks. We see children who eat bits and pieces all day but never eat a really full meal. We think this creates a habit of snacking that's dreadfully bad after forty! Also, it usually fills a child with starches, unless you offer fruits and vegetables. Eating habits are learned early, and they will be with your child for life. Make sure your family's habits are good ones.

Fluoridation

Every time there is an election, one community or another is voting on the fluoridation of water, and some people actively fight it. Such fighting is based on a lack of complete information. An abundance of studies prove that fluorides create wonderfully strong teeth. Their presence is so controllable that there is no risk of overdosing, even if one drank gallons of water. So be sure your child has this protection. If your community does not provide this, get your doctor's or dentist's recommendation for a good oral preparation and then use it.

Vitamins

There is considerable controversy about vitamins and the need to give them to your child as a supplement. Most baby formulas, as well as mother's milk, are well fortified with necessary vitamins and minerals. However, if you are using a formula that is not so enriched, or if you use regular milk, be sure to give extra vitamins to your child. If you have serious doubts that your child is eating enough of the basic foods, give him supplementary vitamins, and if your adolescent rebelliously lives on junk foods, see to it that he is protected with vitamins.

Babies under six months need only vitamins A, C, and D. They come with a dropper marked with the proper dose for each child's age.

Iron. After six months, babies need iron to form new red blood cells. If your child is not eating meat, egg yolk, or green vegetables, give him the three vitamins above plus iron. Be careful about the dose of iron because too much of it can cause damage. Better ask your doctor about iron administration.

At eighteen months to two years, you may stop vitamins. If your child's appetite lags, if he suffers repeated colds or other infections, or if he suffers much stress, an extra vitamin daily seems a good safeguard.

We suggest that you give water-soluble vitamins that will be readily excreted if they are more than the child needs. Fat-soluble vitamins in excessive amounts can collect in a child's tissues and cause some problems. Frankly, we have seen young people overdose on many things, but never on vitamins.

We hope you will pay attention to your child's eating habits. His body is irreplaceable, and giving it excellent fuel will certainly help keep it running more smoothly, for a longer time, than neglecting its care.

MEALTIMES AND TRADITIONS

We believe mealtimes should be happy family occasions, and we strongly recommend establishing and keeping them just that for your family. With the demands shift jobs and other family activities create, this effort becomes heroic, and many families in our community have given up.

A tiny baby is a great problem at mealtime. It seemed that ours always waited for dinner to start crying. Work around that the best you can, because it's only a few months that such evening yelling goes on. By about four to six months, baby's evening habits change. You may even put her in a high chair or reclining seat and let her join you at the table. Feeding her ahead of time will give you a few minutes to eat your own meal.

By nine or ten months, a child will start eating finger foods and may have any table foods he won't choke on. Observing good family eating habits can be excellent training for a child's eating and table manners. As your child indicates an interest, offer her a bite of various table foods, and then her own spoon for eating. Avoid playing or messing in food by removing it as soon as her eating stops. Do not start feeding battles by pushing for "one more bite." Offer a last bit of each variety of food and then put her down to play.

Remember, children eat when they are hungry, so let your child wait until the next meal for more food. It is tempting to offer snacks and supplements. Don't do that, because it spoils the next meal. Such habits form quickly, and your child may as well learn to eat at mealtime with the family. She may, of course, need some water or milk.

Grace

Keep mealtimes happy. We like to start each meal with a prayer of thanksgiving to God. It is a great practice to mention some special area of gratitude now and then for the farmers who work so hard in heat and cold to produce the food; for the harvesters who pick the vegetables and fruits; for the factory workers who process them; even for the mother who finally prepares it! Gratitude takes cultivating, and this is one nice way to work at that. Also, it's a little more difficult to complain about some food for which one has just expressed gratitude!

Attractive Table

In planning menus and preparing meals, do so lovingly. This will prompt consideration for foods that are especially liked. You will find yourself making a table and its contents more attractive if you think lovingly of those you will see there. Avoid a stereotyped menu, and try a new thing now and then. But don't feel badly if the family doesn't like it. Add a candle to your table, or some flowers from your garden, or wild flowers you have found on a walk. There are remarkably lovely flowers called *dandelions* in nearly every yard or along streets. Arranged in a small bowl, they will grace any table for a few hours.

Conversation

Think about your table conversation. During the day look for cute things a child does, something you've heard, read, felt, or experienced. If it is positive and kind, share it. A bit of music in the background and a special centerpiece of your own making can make any meal special.

Some families use mealtime for discussing the problems or misbehaviors of the day. Such topics almost always end up causing scolding or arguments that destroy the joy of being together. Keep problems and discipline out of mealtimes, and discuss them privately with only the persons involved—not the whole family.

Good Table Manners

Good table manners can be taught to children. It takes time, firmness, and a plan, but it makes the difference between good meals and nausea. When children fight, throw food, or misbehave in any way that you parents see as a problem, excuse them at once and give them no more food until the next meal—no dessert, or snacks, or treats. Add a few firm words of explanation that tell them such behavior will not be tolerated, and then drop it. After the second or third experience, almost all children give up such behavior and learn to eat and behave like people rather than animals.

Seat Assignment. We have seen children fight regularly over who sits by whom. We believe this starts a meal with needless tension. Try assigning each child a regular seat. A small name card or a special garden or wild flower can mark it until each child gets accustomed to that place. A creative approach can turn a habitual fight into a pleasant surprise.

As long as possible, keep yourselves and your children out of all activities that seriously interfere with your evening meal together. This can most readily be made a traditional ceremony of intimacy and communication.

Television?—No!

We believe that television competes with all the good things a family meal should be. It is rare indeed that any television program is worth trying to incorporate into your dinner hour. Move your dinner time rather than compete with television, if you must.

Traditions

Traditions serve a vital function in family strength and meaning. Eating together is one of the most special traditions of families in almost every culture. Fixing special dishes for special occasions makes a child's birthday or a visit home from college more meaningful. It says to a child of any age, "I love you. You are so important to me that I remember what you like, and I've taken the trouble to fix it just for you as a celebration."

Thanksgiving, Christmas, and the Fourth of July all mean traditional foods for our family. We hope you will find and carry on your special customs, too. They will help bind your family together.

Part III

Treating a Sick Child

9

General Medical Information You Need to Know

CHOOSING YOUR DOCTOR

When you are considering having a child, one of the issues you need to think about is the choice of your child's physician. There are many rumors of incompetent doctors, and for someone as priceless as your child, you certainly can't risk inadequate medical care. Most such rumors, by the way, are simply that—a report from someone who simply had a misunderstanding.

Medical schools today have high standards of training. It is very difficult to pass the rigid examinations that are required for graduation, and no one can practice medicine without a license. Furthermore, most states now require extensive postgraduate study every year in order to maintain the license.

Two Choices

You have two basic choices regarding your child's doctor—a *family doctor* or a *pediatrician*. Family doctors now are required to have two years of special training beyond the basic medical-school degree. Most of them pass special examinations admitting them to the American Academy of Family Practice. They are qualified to do minor surgery and to diagnose and treat most illnesses that can attack a family. Many of them are qualified to deliver babies, unless there are serious complications, and they are well qualified to care for the medical needs of children.

Family Doctor. Family doctors have the distinct advantage of knowing you parents, and in many communities they will be acquainted with most of your relatives. This knowledge gives your doctor instant awareness of any hereditary illnesses, as well as familiarity with your unique personalities. If a complication should arise that suggests the need of a specialist, he will know such a doctor and can recommend one who will be competent and in whom you can trust.

Pediatrician. A pediatrician is a physician who specializes in the diseases of children. Rarely, if ever, does he do surgery (unless he is a pediatric surgeon), but he can diagnose and treat most of the childhood illnesses. He will call on a bone specialist, surgeon, or other specialists, if necessary.

Pediatricians have three or more years of training after the completion of medical school. They may take special examinations that qualify them as members of the American Academy of Pediatrics. These are difficult examinations, and you may know a doctor is extremely knowledgeable if he has passed those tests.

Making the Choice

We suggest you talk with friends about their baby's doctor. If they have found one who is satisfactory, the chances are you, too, will like him.

If you are new in a community, you may find that your minister is a source of good information. A very reliable channel for referral to a competent doctor is your local County Medical Society, which will be careful to put you in touch with a qualified person.

Your own unique personality and your personal preferences must enter into your choice, as well as the doctor's qualifications. We know some eminently qualified physicians who are insensitive and brusque. Some patients or parents may be left in tears after encounters with doctors like these, while others respect their more blunt approach. You must decide for yourself which qualities are the most important to you. We hope you will find a person who measures up to all of your specifications, but the chances are you'll have to give up a few.

After the Selection Is Made

Once you have selected a new doctor, call his office and talk with his staff. Explain that you are new in town, or that you are expecting a baby and want to get acquainted. Most doctors appreciate a chance to know a family before an emergency hits. Some doctors are so busy, however, that if they were to add any more families to their case loads, they really could not adequately serve them.

Transfer of Records

It will be helpful, if you have used a doctor elsewhere, to ask him to transfer his records to your new physician. Your child's illnesses and immunizations will be important information for the new office to use. Your doctor will not release those records without your consent. Most of us will give them to parents, but to avoid their loss, we prefer to mail them directly to a new physician.

In talking with the doctor, or perhaps his nurse, you may find out about his office hours, the plan he uses in case of emergencies, the fees he charges, and the pharmacy he uses. Be very frank with him about any and all issues that concern you. Have your questions clearly stated and organized to help save his time and yet give you the information you need.

Nurse Practitioner

Some doctors now avail themselves of the assistance of a *nurse practitioner*. She is a nurse who has special clinical training that enables her to check patients for routine visits such as a well-baby checkup. She will notice even the slightest abnormality and will draw that to the attention of the doctor. We believe in this sort of team. It usually means that you have a little more time for questions and teaching from the nurse and the security of two trained and caring people.

Your relationship with your child's pediatrician or family doctor can be one of extreme loyalty and satisfaction. We are always delighted to see or hear from our patients of a number of years ago and they, in turn, seem pleased and gratified to share memories with us.

We wish for each of you and your children that kind of fond and trusting relationship with your physician.

RESPONDING TO SICKNESS

Most parents of sick children experience some very important reactions to that sickness. First they are worried or afraid—and some illnesses still deserve such feelings. Parents also may feel guilty and tend to blame themselves or each other for the sickness. Perhaps they allowed the child outside without proper clothing, and he caught the cold that led to complications. Or even more needlessly, mother has been too busy with housecleaning and has not spent as much time with her child as usual. Fears are not rational, and we often blame ourselves in illogical ways. Unfortunately, people may try to alleviate their fear or guilt feelings by blaming one another, the child, the doctor, or the hospital.

How to Avoid Damaging Reactions

A beautiful resource is available through our Christian faith to prevent such damaging emotional reactions. Trust in a loving God to understand and forgive your mistakes can remove the guilt. Determine to learn from your mistakes so they will not be in vain. Finally, believe that God loves your child and you, and depend on Him to guide your doctor and activate His healing power of your child's body. Draw on the power of God's Spirit to keep you calm, firm, and supportive. Avoid blaming anyone for the illness. On the other hand, sick children tend to worry about themselves and when you, the parents, are anxious about them, it magnifies their concerns. Believe it or not, children do feel guilty for worrying you and causing extra expenses. Such negative emotions rob a sick child of the energy he needs to get well.

Guilt Feelings

This is a good place to explain the difference between real guilt and guilt feelings. With real guilt, you have done something wrong and you know it. You may not want to admit it, but you know you have been careless, neglectful, or downright mean. Your conscience and your thoughts converge to tell you exactly what was wrong about the situation.

Guilt feelings, on the other hand, are not at all explicit. You suffer a vague sense of anxiety, worry, or remorse, but you really do not know what it's about. In the case of a child's illness, you may feel that some slight mistake you made, perhaps long ago, has been such that God is now punishing you through your child's suffering. Such feelings are dangerous because they are not based on facts. As you understand the real truth, you can be free (even now) from false guilt.

Trusting in Your Heavenly Father

We believe God is compassionate, just, and merciful. While the Bible makes it clear that He does not condone willful sins, it is even more clear that He forgives sins, and that He understands our human imperfections.

Your trust in the heavenly Father is a beautiful resource in a time of stress such as a child's illness. You can count on God to understand and forgive your mistakes and wrongdoings, either real or fancied. You do not need to suffer from guilt, but you do need to learn from any mistakes so you will not repeat them. There are many promises in Scripture about God's strength, comfort, and love. Reach out in faith and believe those.

Jesus Christ said, "Suffer little children, and forbid them not, to come unto me: for of such is the kingdom of heaven" (Matthew 19:14). You can be sure God loves your sick child even more than you do. Trust Him to guide your physician and to make His healing power active in your child's body. Such trust and love are bound to be comforting to your child as well as to yourself.

Avoid blaming anyone and especially avoid blaming yourself. Be warm and supportive with your sick child, but don't be too sympathetic. Even your facial expression can make your child feel sorry for himself or afraid that he is even more ill than he is. Watch your child for any symptoms that should be reported to your doctor, but don't panic.

Gather Your Facts Before Phoning

In contacting your doctor or hospital staff, *collect information* as accurately as possible before calling. Get the child's temperature, his breathing rate (if unusual), the area of pain, the type of pain, and any illness to which the child has been exposed. Describe any injury and the appearance of your child in general. Try to avoid panic or its opposite—unrealistic calm. Tell your doctor your worst fears so he can reassure you or alert you.

Don't Be Afraid to Ask!

Many parents complain that their doctor does not take enough time with them or explain things to them. I know what it is to be a busy pediatrician and to have a husband who is a busy family physician. Yet we doctors will take time if you ask. Don't be afraid of your doctor. He really is a human being, and if you ask him to explain a problem, or even to wait while you formulate your question, he will do that. If you use the time you may have to wait (almost certainly you will wait!) to organize your questions and even write them down, you will help him to meet your needs for information and his needs to save time.

VISITING THE DOCTOR'S OFFICE

The timing of the visits to your doctor's office for routine or well-child checkups will vary with your physician's policies.

Three-Week Checkup

We recommend a checkup at three or four weeks of age to be sure that no birth defects have become evident since the baby's hospital examination. Occasionally, a heart defect or dislocated hip simply can't be detected at birth, but is quite evident by three weeks. Your doctor will want to be sure your baby's eating habits and weight gain are normal, as well as his elimination. Baby's body measurements will be taken and your doctor will probably begin a graph that will show you about where your child's size fits among many others. Your doctor will probe and poke, making certain the navel is normal, the skin is healthy, and a boy's circumcision has healed.

Be sure to find out whatever you need to know about your child's next phase of development, his sleeping patterns, and eating habits.

Six-Week Checkup

The next regular checkup will be at about six to eight weeks of age. At that time baby's immunizations will be started. (*See* Protecting Your Child Through Immunization in this chapter.) Thereafter, routine checkups will coincide with the immunization schedule. After the age of two, your child will need routine examinations only once a year, unless there is some unusual problem that must be followed.

Office Visits for Illnesses

Visiting the doctor's office for illnesses is almost always necessary at some time. Be sure to have ready an accurate account of the development of the symptoms. Your doctor will need such a history.

Waiting Time. The nurse will usually take the child's temperature and prepare him to be examined by the doctor. Unfortunately, there is usually a wait at this point. We doctors try very hard to keep on schedule, but emergencies arise that disrupt schedules. You might be amazed at the parents who make an appointment for one child and decide to bring another one or two along for some little (or bigger) ailment. Each child takes a few extra minutes and before long, the best-planned schedule is done for. So we apologize and ask you to bear with us. Be prepared for the wait with a toy, book, or other entertaining item.

Sometimes your doctor will need X rays or laboratory tests. It may be necessary for you to wait for these reports, or the doctor may telephone the results. Many nurses are well qualified to give you such information. We trust you will learn to love her as well as your doctor, and trust her advice and help.

Phone Calls

Speaking of telephones, we had better discuss those phone calls. We always welcome, *at any time,* phone calls about new babies, high fevers, illnesses, injuries, or any question that is urgent. When such calls can be delayed, without risk to a child, until office hours, your doctor will be most appreciative. You cannot believe the number of calls he gets! And he is human, so he needs to be with his family, sleep a bit, and even eat. It is not uncommon, upon seeing a patient in the grocery store, to hear, "Do you mean to say that doctors have to eat, too?" What can one reply?

The mother of one of our pediatrics patients routinely called during dinner. Her opening statement was classic: "Doctor Grace, I didn't want to bother you at the office, so I just thought I'd give you a call at home." Usually there was a question that could well have been asked days later. Don't let the temptation to avoid the necessary wait at the office allow you to take advantage of your doctor!

Bills

Be sure to check with the receptionist about paying your bill. Doctors are usually not mercenary; they do have to eat, pay *their* bills, and the salaries of their staff. Your friendliness and sensitivity to your medical people will be repaid many times over by their gratitude and affection for you!

HOSPITAL STAYS

Taking your child to a hospital can be very frightening. You will find many people there who seem "all business" and apparently uncaring. Often, however, if you will be simple and honest about your fears, needs, and questions, you will find them warm and helpful.

Preparing Your Child

When there is time, explain to your child as much as you can about his anticipated stay in the hospital. Many times you can prepare a child days in advance for a tonsillectomy or some special tests. There are books in your public library with pictures and stories to help take away the mystery and fear for your child—and you. Never lie to your child. There may be painful injections and frightening laboratory tests. Your child will cope with these best if you have been honest about them. You can assure him that you and the nurses will help him and stay by him so he won't feel abandoned.

Calming Your Child

In certain emergencies and accidents, you will have little, if any, time to talk or prepare your child for a painful, frightening ordeal. It is in such crises that God's strength and love may be felt through you, as you depend on Him. It is also at such times that the efforts you have invested in teaching obedience and trust to your child will be repaid many times over. Usually one parent is calmer during an emergency than the other. The calmer parent needs to stay by the child as much as possible until the crisis is over. Your presence will reassure him, help him relax, and insure his transfer of trust to the doctors and nurses. Your child's emotional control and cooperation can make it much easier to take care of him and return him to health.

Never threaten a child with painful or frightening experiences. Many times we have heard frustrated and weary mothers say, "If you don't behave, I'll have that doctor give you a shot!" Small wonder some children are afraid of us. We understand the fatigue of anxious parents with fretful children. Just be firm with them, as well as patient. This attitude will not tire you any more, and it is far more likely to calm a child. (*See* chapter 13 on discipline.)

Packing for Your Child's Hospital Visit

Taking a child to a hospital demands less packing than you may believe. Hospitals are wonderfully equipped with nightclothes, toothbrushes, combs, and almost all a child could need. Nevertheless, all children feel easier with some of their own belongings near them. So take a favorite toy, blanket, book, or wearing apparel, or bring them later. In rare instances something may be lost, but the child is rarely so vulnerable as he is in the hospital, so replacing a lost item later will be well worth it.

Staying With Your Child

Most hospitals now prefer that a parent stay with a child much of the time. If your child is under three years of age, it is very important that you stay. Under two, it is essential! If you need to leave, explain that to your child and show him, on a clock, what time you will be back. Mark the position of the hour hand with tape so it will show when you can be expected, and then *be sure* to be back at that time. Usually a child's hospital stay is brief, and you can sleep later. If it is more than a few nights, however, you will need to have relief. Relatives and close friends who are calm and cheerful will satisfy a child's need for security very well after the first few days. Do not be afraid to ask.

If you plan to leave for a few hours after your child is asleep, tell him so. Have a nurse who will be on duty talk with your child and you. Tell her in front of your child that she is to call you if he needs something special from you when he awakens. Most sick children can understand your needs and those of other family members, so unless there is a true crisis, you need not feel guilty if you leave for periods of time.

Considering Other Children

Be sure to telephone your other children often to reassure them that they are not forgotten, and that the sick child is being cared for. Involve other children in helping at home, praying for the patient, and visiting when possible. Be sure to let them hear your gratitude and pride for their help and support.

Trusting Your Child's Nurses

Be careful to avoid overprotection of your child or interference with the medical staff in any way. But be sure to let the hospital staff know if there are signs that trouble you. To an anxious parent any variation is magnified as a problem, so do trust the staff. It will help their understanding of you if you will frankly tell them you are very apprehensive, rather than going to them with every tiny change in your child's pulse rate or breathing. Balance your efforts at calmness, however, with honest panic if some real crisis develops. When a parent is with a child, the staff may not feel the need to look in as often as if you were not there. You may find it useful to ask the head nurse what she would like in terms of reports from you, and do tell her plainly what you need from her in order to form a good team to help your sick child get well.

SURGICAL PROCEDURES COMMON IN CHILDREN

Any surgery has a way of striking fear in the hearts of most parents as well as the child. Actually, surgical techniques have become so well perfected that you rarely need to become alarmed. We have discussed birth defects and their treatment, which often is surgical, in chapter 7, "The Next Two Years of Life."

Most Common Procedures

The most common surgical procedures are: 1) the removal of chronically infected tonsils and adenoids; 2) the insertion of tubes into a child's middle ear to clear up long-term infections there; 3) the repair of hernias (either in the navel or the groin); 4) appendectomies; 5) repairs of severe cuts; and 6) setting broken bones.

Preparation. Most of these procedures require only a few days of hospital care or only an overnight stay. You need to understand why your child must go to the hospital the day before surgery. First, he needs to get acquainted with the strange new people and all their equipment. If he is calm and relaxed, he will recover more quickly, with less likelihood of complications. Even more important, he needs to have a bit of laboratory work done. Fairly often, we have admitted a child for a tonsillectomy, and the blood count reveals he is just beginning to have an infection or may be anemic. Such conditions would complicate surgery, so anything except an emergency would need to wait. In such a situation, your child will be sent home and will return later for the elective surgery.

Post Surgery. After surgery, children need to be "babied" for a few days, but usually they may do what they feel up to. Your surgeon will tell you what your child may eat and what he may not do. Be certain that you understand these directions. We find that parents are much more conscientious about following orders if they know why such orders are necessary. If your doctor doesn't think about explaining this in depth, ask him. We know doctors are in a hurry, but let us remind you, if you have your questions ready, he will realize they are important, so don't be intimidated.

SURGICAL CONDITIONS OF CHILDHOOD

Tonsils and Adenoids

The removal of tonsils and adenoids is a relatively simple procedure. In order to keep the child quiet, he will be given a shot about an hour or so before surgery. This will make his mouth dry and he will feel drowsy. Sometimes people say silly things when they are under the influence of a "hypo." Be sensitive about repeating such talk.

Anesthesia. A general anesthetic is used for the surgical procedure itself. There are several gases that are currently being used as anesthetic. They are safe when administered by trained anesthesiologists. *Pentothal* is a liquid that is given in an intravenous solution. The only pain is the original prick of the needle into a vein. It is rapid acting and rarely results in nausea later. Once in a while, a patient may be allergic to it. Your doctor will be very careful to choose the best and safest anesthetic for your child.

After the Operation. After surgery, most children take two to four or even more hours to fully awaken. They may be restless and "out of their heads" for a while, and this need not alarm you. After a few hours they will return to normal.

They will, however, have a very sore throat for a few days. They may vomit some bloody material a time or two after surgery. That is from the bleeding that occurred during the procedure, and it will look dark, a little like coffee grounds.

Bright-red Blood. Sometimes a child will spit out or vomit up some bright-red blood. Be sure the nurse sees this. She can tell whether it means the surgical area is bleeding significantly. Once in a while, such bleeding is difficult to stop, and that is why your doctor will want you to leave your child in the hospital for a night after the tonsillectomy.

If your child is doing well the next day, take him home and follow the rules listed above. Also let him chew Aspergum or use some pain-relieving lozenges or tablets. Most children recover amazingly quickly.

About a week after a tonsillectomy, the scabs that always form over a cut will slough off. Very rarely, some bleeding may occur at that time. If this amounts to more than slightly blood-tinged saliva, call your doctor. It is not likely, but he can best advise you regarding the chance of any serious bleeding. *Don't take a chance.*

Ice cream, sherbet, and cool foods are the best nutrients for the very few days your child's throat will be uncomfortable. Let his own appetite guide you, but do avoid any crusty foods that could scratch that raw tissue.

Appendix

Appendicitis is a serious infection of the appendix which is a small attachment to the intestinal tract at the junction of small and large intestines. An attack of appendicitis starts with a sick feeling, a temperature of 100 degrees F. or more, and sometimes vomiting. In a few hours or less, the pain becomes localized in the right lower area of the abdomen. With gentle pressure midway between the hipbone and the navel, there is marked pain, which is even worse upon sudden release of the pressure. These symptoms may be even more sudden in onset or may develop over a period of twenty-four hours.

DO NOT DELAY IN CALLING YOUR DOCTOR, OR GO AT ONCE TO AN EMERGENCY ROOM! APPENDICITIS IS ALMOST 100 PERCENT CURABLE, BUT IF THE APPENDIX RUPTURES, THE CHILD WILL HAVE A MUCH LONGER COURSE AND SLOWER RECOVERY.

Preparation and Anesthesia. The presurgical procedures and anesthetics in an appendectomy are similar to those in a tonsillectomy. The surgical incision will be remarkably small and usually leaves little scarring. Your child will feel sick for some hours after an appendectomy and will not want to eat. Some intravenous fluids will need to be given until the appetite returns and the intestinal tract functions normally. Usually that is within a day or two.

Ruptured Appendix. Rarely, an appendix may become infected so quickly and severely that it ruptures like an abscess into the abdomen. In this case, a drain may have to be inserted through the incision to be sure all of the infected material comes out and the abdomen can heal. Your child will be sicker for a longer time and will need large doses of antibiotics to cure the infection.

THIS IS THE REASON YOU NEED TO REPORT STOMACH-ACHES TO YOUR DOCTOR WHEN THEY SEEM LOCALIZED, AND ARE ACCOMPANIED BY FEVER OR VOMITING.

Hernia

Hernias are caused by weakness in the abdominal wall. They are most common in the groin, but may occur into the scrotum of a boy or in the area of the navel.

You will find a discussion of hernias in chapter 7, "The Next Two Years of Life."

The presurgical, anesthetic, and postsurgical procedures and reactions are very similar to those for a tonsillectomy or appendectomy. Usually, recovery is very rapid, with a minimum of pain. In fact, you may need to spend some energy in keeping your child quiet enough to allow for good healing. Ask your doctor's advice regarding the sort of activity to allow and avoid.

TREATMENT OF INJURIES

Broken bones and severe cuts may often be treated in a doctor's office. Usually a local anesthetic can be injected into the injured area, and the repair can be done safely without hospitalization. Your doctor certainly will not take a chance with your child's safety.

CARING FOR YOUR SICK CHILD AT HOME

A sick child feels much more secure in his own bed, and whenever possible he should be cared for there. Your doctor will need to decide this issue; when there is any question of your child's safety, a hospital stay must be the better choice.

How to Keep a Child in Bed

Keeping a child in bed, however, may be very hard, even when he feels quite sick. He will prefer to be near the family and will be tempted to get up and down for things he wants. Here are some helpful suggestions:

1. Find out from your doctor just how quiet your child needs to be. Usually he can rest on a sofa or in a big chair, if he stays quiet and warm there. He may even be more calm and relaxed there, where he can observe the family, than if he is feeling lonely and isolated in a distant bedroom.

2. Keep an assortment of special toys, games, books, and entertaining crafts handy, and bring out a new or forgotten item each day. A magnifying glass, kaleidoscope, magnet, and bubbles are suggestions for a collection of special equipment that is great for rainy days, trips, and "boring" days, as well.

3. An arrangement of pillows that can help the child sit up or recline will keep him more comfortable and relaxed.

4. Be sure he is not too hot or too cold. It is easy to overwrap a sick child, so watch him or ask if he is too warm.

5. Keep a chart if the child is on medicine. Be sure to give it as directed and check off each dose. Between concern and extra work, it is easy to forget.

6. Try to plan your work by priorities so you may read to, talk with, or rock the child when possible. It is extremely comforting to a sick child.

7. It is especially neat if Dad can spend time with the child.

8. A cardboard box cut out to fit over the child's body makes a great bed table for eating or working.

9. When possible, a flower on the pillow (from your yard)

or a special little treat (okayed by your doctor) will make the day brighter.

10.   Don't oversympathize or pity. A child learns self-pity very soon! A calm, soothing optimism invites a quick return to health.

11.   Other children will often feel neglected and a bit jealous. Having them help some, and remembering to explain the illness and give progress reports, help. Also tell them you appreciate their understanding and patience. Perhaps they may recall when they were ill, or you may assure them they will get "spoiled," too, if they are ill.

HAVING A MEDICAL EXAMINATION

Whether your child is seeing the doctor for a routine visit or some serious problem, there are certain things you may expect to be done. Knowing these basic tests will help you to work better with your doctor and will enable you to know some things to ask about. It is important that you understand your child—sick or well.

Medical History

Most doctors will first take a good medical history. If he knows your child, that history will merely be an update regarding events since the last visit. If the doctor is new to you, he may prefer to take a complete medical history. We like to get our own histories rather than read another doctor's records, simply because we remember them better. Be sure to tell him all the facts, including special family illnesses that may show up in your child; any important events during your pregnancy, especially any illnesses in the first three months; let him know about your baby's development and when he began walking and talking; be sure to tell him about any allergies or illnesses. He probably will want a dietary history.

Examination

Next, your doctor, or sometimes a nurse assistant, will examine your child. This examination is frightening to many young children. A toy stethoscope or play doctor's kit can familiarize your child with the necessary tools. Take a favorite doll or teddy bear along. We often spend a few minutes "examining" a doll to demonstrate the processes and allay the fears of a child. It saves lots of time and tears in the long run! The doctor will check all the body's openings, but rarely will he probe into them except to examine the ears and throat. He will listen to the heart and lungs, but don't expect him to routinely check the blood pressure. He will feel firmly throughout the child's abdomen to be sure there are no tumors or enlarged organs there. He will check the bones for strength and proper development. A good neurological exam may be done partly through inspecting a child's normal behavior and movements, by the history, and by checking the nerve reflexes. He will feel for any enlarged lymph glands to be sure there is no infection. Under two years of age, the baby's head will be measured, as well as his height and weight, to be sure he is growing properly.

Lab Work and X Rays

Laboratory work is not routinely ordered. If it is your first visit, or if there is any concern about an infection or anemia (low red-blood count or lack of iron), he will want a blood count. This involves a prick of the toe or finger, and withdrawing a few drops of blood. Urine is tested only if there is a history of diabetes in the family or some sign of a kidney or bladder problem. A chest X ray will be done only if your child has a positive tuberculosis skin test, or if there is some sign of a chest problem. Other X rays are limited to the diagnosis of a possibly broken bone or other injury.

We are finding a number of people who evidence concern about taking even an annual chest X ray due to a fear of the effects of radiation. In today's cancer-phobic world, one must understand such concern. Let us assure you, however, that your doctor is aware of such dangers. He will weigh that small risk with the more immediate danger or need. Express your concerns, but listen to his answers. Unless you are a specialist yourself, the articles you read, or the rumors you heard, cannot be as reliable as his years of training and experience.

Ask Questions

Expect your doctor to tell you what tests he has done and their results. Find out whether your child is fine or has any problems. You may need to ask whether you are doing a good job as a parent. *Please ask directly* and then ask if there are new things you need to be doing for an illness, or a new developmental period in your child's life. You are justified in all of your concerns. None of them are trivial or "dumb" if they worry you. We hear many complaints about doctors who do not give enough time for such questions and explanations. In fact recently, Dr. Grace's own sister found out about a diagnosis only from her bill! Sometimes you can prevent that sort of brush-off by being ready with your questions and assertive about asking them. Try not to be angry, however! Doctors are busy and pressured, and they also have feelings. Your courtesy and warmth will get you almost anything from him!

PROTECTING YOUR CHILD THROUGH IMMUNIZATION

Even one generation ago, many children died of illnesses that are now totally preventable. Polio used to take the lives of many children and adults every year. Diphtheria was a dreadful word to even think about, and whooping cough killed little babies.

Through incalculable financial costs, and the hard work of dedicated people, none of these diseases need concern you. Yet by the very removal of that concern can come a carelessness that could bring serious illnesses back to childhood, perhaps even to your own child.

Immunization Schedule

There is a simple way to protect your child from almost every known epidemic disease. Here's the list (with explanation of each to follow):

1. At two months, *he receives his first DPT vaccine; the first trivalent polio shot.*
2. At four months, *he needs the second DPT injection; the second trivalent polio vaccine.*

3. At six months, *he must have his third DPT shot; last dose of polio vaccine.*

4. At one year of age, *he receives his first tuberculosis skin test.*

5. At fifteen months, *your child will need the shot for mumps, measles, and rubella.*

6. By eighteen months, *start over again with booster shots for DPT, as well as polio vaccine.*

7. At two years of age, *it's time for another tuberculosis skin test, unless the last one was positive. (See explanation below.) This should be done annually from now on.*

8. Between four and six years of age, *your child needs another round of DPT and polio immunizations.*

9. For immunization of older children, see *explanation below.*

This is the list of required immunizations for the safety of your child. Be aware of what's to be done and when, remembering the importance of follow-through. An explanation of the various immunizations mentioned follows.

DPT. D stands for *diphtheria,* which once claimed the lives of hundreds of children annually. *P* is for *pertussis,* the medical name for whooping cough. While it was deadly only for tiny babies, it was a major illness of childhood only thirty years ago. *T* is the initial for *tetanus* or *lockjaw,* which still occurs in cases of deep injuries, when people are careless about keeping up their shots. This shot will cause some fever and a bit of tenderness and swelling at the area of the shot for a day or two. Your doctor will suggest Tylenol or baby aspirin to relieve this.

The third injection of DPT vaccine, given at six months of age, may cause some fever and discomfort, but usually less severe than the first. If your baby is uncomfortable, give him some Tylenol or aspirin, and tender care. Don't let yourself feel too sorry about it, because your child would be many times sicker for a long time if he caught one of those illnesses.

The Trivalent Polio Immunization. This is given orally. It tastes good and causes no reaction. It will start at once to protect your child against the once-dreaded disease of polio.

Tuberculosis Skin Test. This is not an immunization, but it tells you and your doctor whether or not your child has been infected with tuberculosis germs. If the reaction is positive, it will look red and swollen around the test for about a third of an inch. This means that tuberculosis germs have invaded your child's body in some area, though it may be impossible to know just where. Do not be alarmed at this, because your doctor will be able to medicate and observe your child closely to be sure this infection never develops into a serious, active case of tuberculosis.

After your child once has a positive skin test, he need not have another one, since it will stay positive. He should, however, have a yearly chest X ray to be sure that tuberculosis of the lungs (the most common type) does not flare up unawares. If it should look as though a child has tuberculosis, it can be safely treated at home.

Most children will have a negative skin test. In fact, it is extremely rare in the United States to find a child, even through adolescence, with a positive one. We have not seen a case of childhood tuberculosis for over twenty-five years, thanks to the excellent and prompt treatment that is made possible by the skin-test screening.

If your child should have a positive test for tuberculosis, the shot for mumps, measles, and rubella at fifteen months will wait until your child has received medicine for the tuberculosis condition. Your doctor will advise you about when to have the MMR shot.

MMR (Measles, Mumps, Rubella). This injection is likely to cause a day or two of fever, discomfort, and maybe a fine, red rash. You may feel angry or worried because your baby has to suffer through this reaction. Just think about his suffering through a week or more of much worse illness and risking dangerous complications, and you will not mind the shot or its reaction at all!

Importance of Shots at Eighteen Months. At this age you have to plan on starting all over again with a booster shot for diphtheria, whooping cough, and tetanus, as well as another dose of the polio vaccine. Babies develop pretty good responses to immunizations, but their systems are all better developed by eighteen months and the shots will boost up their protection considerably. Since they are around many more people by now, they will need more immunity.

Importance of Keeping Track of Immunization. (*See* number 8 in list of immunizations above.) We suggest another round of DPT and polio at age four if the child is exposed to a great many other children, such as in a preschool. Otherwise, waiting until kindergarten is fine. You are likely to remember to have a thorough school physical, and the boosters should be given then.

Immunization in Older Children. After the age of six, you should *not* allow your child to receive whooping-cough vaccine. Older children tend to react severely to it, and the danger of being exposed to whooping cough is much less. After the booster at four to six years, your child should have one more polio booster when he is in the *sixth grade.* And all of us need to have diphtheria-tetanus boosters about every five to ten years for life. If you are outdoors people who are active and could be injured in an area where soil could contaminate a wound, we suggest every five years. Less active city dwellers may safely get by with every ten years.

Most schools now require children to have the proper immunizations before enrolling for the year. We feel this is an excellent practice, and a helpful reminder to busy parents who may forget. Do not, however, get so careless, because your child may be exposed to an active case of one of these infections and you both would suffer for it.

Free Clinics. Medical costs are expensive these days. If you cannot afford the cost of immunizations, do not let that prevent your child from being protected. In almost every county in the U.S.A., there are clinics where you may obtain immunizations for your child free of charge. The United States Public Health Service provides for this, and you need not be hesitant to take advantage of that service.

STOCKING YOUR MEDICINE CABINET

Illness is never convenient. No one ever has time for their children to be ill, or for themselves to be ill. Obviously this stems from the very culture in which we live, where we are on a rapid merry-go-round, and where our lives are so structured that anything which tends to disrupt the routine appears to be almost catastrophic. Because of our impatience with illness, the drug industry has been able to flourish and is one of the large industries of this country. We need only watch TV for a period of time to see how many over-the-counter preparations are recommended to us for a wide variety of ailments and illnesses which, if given time alone, would almost always correct themselves.

Time, the Great Healer

Doctors have learned from long experience that time is one of the great healers of life. We have learned that time is on the side of the physician when it comes to the healing process. This is certainly true in the case of the minor ailments, such as the common cold; gastrointestinal changes, such as constipation or diarrhea; and any one of a number of other, lesser ailments, which are annoying but certainly not life-threatening.

As parents, we are anxious that our children recover as rapidly as possible and therefore, upon their complaints, we often rush to the drugstore to find some helpful relief of the symptoms, or decide that we will see the physician at the earliest possible moment. Because of our concern for our children, and our desire to do the very best thing for them, we tend to believe the advertising of the various media. We soon find that our medicine cabinet at home has a large variety of medicines, which perhaps have hardly been used at all, and which will soon be outdated.

Basic Medications and Supplies

There are a few medications and supplies which we believe should be part of every home medicine cabinet. Fortunately this list is not very long. We will list them below and make a few comments about their use.

Aspirin. This is one of the most commonly used drugs today and, fortunately, one of the safest. However, it, too, is not without danger, and if it is taken in overdoses, can have very serious consequences. Therefore, it must be kept out of the reach of small children. The use of aspirin for temperatures and for pain is known to most all of us, and certainly can be used for both of these symptoms early in the treatment of minor illnesses, as well as those which are more serious. The important thing to remember is that if the temperature or pain persists, it must mean that there is something of a *serious nature* going on and, therefore, medical attention should be sought. One rule of thumb for the dosage of aspirin is to give sixty milligrams or one grain per year of age for children. A three-year-old child would therefore receive three grains of aspirin. (*See* also below.)

Be Aware of Dosage. In giving aspirin to children you need to be aware of the dosage in different tablets. Adult aspirin tablets contain five grains or three hundred milligrams. Until you become very familiar with the metric system, we suggest you stick with the old measurements. Proper dosage is too important to make mistakes with a new system. Children's aspirin have only one grain in each tablet. One grain of aspirin may be given for every ten pounds of body weight. When using one-and-a-quarter-grain aspirin, figure on one grain for every twelve pounds of body weight.

By five years of age, most children can tolerate one adult aspirin. These taste bitter, however, and are large enough that few children can or will take them. We feel that baby aspirins are highly useful until the child can take tablets.

Acetaminophen. This is a very effective medication for lowering temperatures. It also has some effectiveness in the relief of pain. It comes in liquid form, and is often given to children because it has a greater measure of safety than aspirin. There are a number of name brands of this medication as follows: Tylenol, Tempra, Liquiprin, and a few others. The dosage for acetaminophen is the same as that for aspirin. However, the concentration of the different preparations varies somewhat and, therefore, one must be careful to give the correct dose. A careful reading of the label will enable you to ascertain the correct dosage for your child based on his age.

Cough Syrups. Almost every medicine cabinet has some sort of cough syrup in it. We would not necessarily recommend that you have cough syrup on hand at all times, since it is readily obtainable through drugstores, which usually are open late in the evening, and often at some of the all-night grocery stores. Cough syrup comes in two forms. One form is called an *expectorant.* It allegedly helps to liquify some of the secretions in the lungs and therefore reduces some of the irritation that is causing the cough. The effectiveness of this syrup is debatable. The other type of cough syrup actually suppresses the cough itself. This type of cough syrup is certainly useful in the child who is not able to sleep because of the persistent coughing, or who finds that he is disrupting the classroom because of the severity of his cough. Not uncommonly, a child will have a severe cough for sometimes a few days (and sometimes two or three weeks) without any particular findings by laboratory study, chest X ray, or physical examination. Quite often there is no temperature accompanying the cough. In these instances, any of the good over-the-counter cough suppressants are satisfactory.

Antihistamines. There are a number of good antihistamine medications which you can buy over-the-counter in a liquid form. These are particularly good for the child who just has a common cold with a runny nose. If a child has no temperature, there is no reason that he cannot take these medications in the dosage which is appropriate for his age. The pharmacist can assist you in choosing from a wide range of these drugs.

Nose Drops. Nose drops can be used to help reduce the amount of nasal secretion and to open up the nasal passages so that the child can breathe through the nose, rather than the mouth. There are a number of good preparations which you can buy over-the-counter. Probably the one that is most commonly used is Neo-Synephrine, which comes in various strengths. Another commonly used nose drop is Afrin. This particular nose drop can be used less frequently than Neo-Synephrine because of its longer-lasting effect. Nose drops are overused, and we suggest limiting their use to three days.

Antacids. It seems today that every household has some antacid in it. The need for the use of antacids in children is quite infrequent. However, sometimes they will relieve the common stomachache which a child might have.

Kaopectate. This and/or other compounds used for the treatment of diarrhea should be used with some caution. In children, the use of Kaopectate is permissible and may help to give a more formed stool. The use of medications which contain paregoric and which can be bought over-the-counter should be used with a great deal of caution, and for the most part are not recommended for children. Occasionally, under your physician's advice, some such medications may be used in order to control or to at least contain more severe diarrhea in children. However, it is our recommendation that these medications not be used unless they have been prescribed by your physician.

Ipecac. Some authorities recommend keeping ipecac in your medicine chest to make your child vomit if he has taken any potentially or really harmful substances. Frankly, we worry about this, because some poisons should not be vomited since they injure the tissues even more on the way back up! You may also have a false sense of security in causing vomiting, thinking the substance is out of the system. The child may have taken it some time before he vomits, and more may have been absorbed than you realize. If you question the poison, call your doctor before giving ipecac.

Antibiotic Ointments. These are handy to have on hand for minor scrapes, abrasions, and minor burns. They prevent many of the skin infections that may complicate such injuries. Ask your pharmacist for one of these products.

Vitamins. The use of vitamins by children has probably been overemphasized. We believe that infants should have vitamins, but after age three or so, if the child is eating well, the necessity for those vitamins certainly diminishes. A well-balanced diet provides all of the vitamins which the body needs.

Vaporizer. The availability of a vaporizer in the home where there are small children is often a lifesaver, particularly if a child gets into respiratory trouble during the night. We normally recommend the cold-steam vaporizer, only because it is a bit more safe than the hot-steam vaporizer.

Additional Supplies. A few other supplies which you should have on hand for your medicine cabinet include the ever-asked-for Band-Aids, adhesive tape, a roll of bandages for dressing wounds, elastic bandage, and some cleansing, antiseptic agent such as hydrogen peroxide, Phisohex, or Betadine, which is an iodine preparation.

Thermometer. Many times we have had parents call and give a good description of a sick child. When we ask, however, about the child's temperature, they do not know, and that robs us of very needed information. So do get (and master the use of) a thermometer. There are two kinds of thermometers—*oral* and *rectal*. The oral type has a long, thin bulb. It should be placed under the child's tongue and held there, with his mouth closed, for about two minutes. Younger children cannot always cooperate well enough to give you a reliable reading. In that case, you may hold it in the child's armpit, with his arm held firmly against his chest for at least two minutes. To get the child's real temperature (normally the oral reading), you must *add* 1 degree F. to the axillary (or underarm) reading.

A rectal thermometer has a short, round bulb so it cannot be broken in case the child squirms (and he will!) while you are taking his temperature. Use a bit of petroleum jelly on the tip of the thermometer and insert it gently into the child's rectum, holding his legs firmly over his abdomen to keep him still. In a little baby, a by-product of this method is the stimulation of his little rectum to move his bowels. So be prepared for that ahead of time by placing a diaper under him. In reading a rectal thermometer, after leaving it in for about two minutes, you need to *subtract* 1 degree F. since the internal temperature is always higher than that in the mouth.

When it comes to reading it, someone needs to invent a better thermometer. The small column of mercury that registers the temperature is most elusive. You must twist the gadget slowly around, while tipping it end to end, until it is exactly the right position. Then you will clearly see the end of that shiny column resting under a number. Next, you must find out if that number is a full degree or a tenth of a degree. When you have put that together, you will have really accomplished something. We hope this diagram will help.

ORAL THERMOMETER

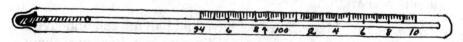

RECTAL THERMOMETER

Some people have worried a great deal when a thermometer is bitten or broken off, lest a child swallow the mercury and suffer from mercury poisoning. Let us reassure you that this does not happen. The mercury is very heavy and it slides right through the intestinal tract and is excreted. So don't be alarmed, but do be very careful. Bits of glass could conceivably scratch the child internally. Even this, however, is unlikely to seriously hurt your child as the slivers become coated with mucus and slide on through.

There are a few other pieces of equipment that are useful, and you may want to keep them in your medicine cabinet.

Rubber Bulb Syringe. You may find this most helpful to use in removing mucus from a baby's nostrils when he has a cold. After he learns to blow his nose, you will find the syringe handy to use once in a while if a child chokes, if he gets a bug in his ear, or for irrigating a cut. Be certain to wash it well inside and out after each use; rinse it with clear water and leave it ready to use.

An Ice Bag. This or one of the new cold packs that "freeze" when you press on them are wonderful for aches and sprains. A jaw that is painful from an extracted tooth, a headache, or a turned ankle, can often be made comfortable by such a cold application.

A Heating Pad. This is another highly comforting item to have handy. After a sprain is twenty-four hours old, in case of many muscular aches and pains, or menstrual cramps, heat feels most soothing. We suggest this precaution, however: Do not use too high a temperature and do not use for too long a time. A medium or low setting will feel almost as good as a higher one. Too much heat for several hours or longer greatly increases the circulation of blood to the area and will raise the body's metabolism in that location. The waste products of the increased metabolism may actually cause more pain.

Emergency Medications. These may need to be kept available in the event your child has an illness that warrants them. An example of this is the use of inhalants in case of an asthma attack; caffeine tablets for a migraine headache; or rectal suppositories for a child who is subject to bouts of vomiting. For all such medications, be sure that the medicine is carefully and clearly labeled. In crises, it is easy to become nervous and you may overlook the medicine or give it incorrectly.

Safety Precautions

Ask your doctor about keeping any emergency medications and how to decide when to use them. Until you feel confident, it is best to call him for advice.

Be very certain, no matter what you keep in your medicine cabinet, to keep it locked and away from the curious reach of young children. Not only should you lock it, but also teach your child that it is always off limits. If your child gets into your medicine cabinet before he is old enough to read well and be trusted to take his own home medications, it is cause for punishment. Whatever disciplinary action you find to be most effective, use it! It may save your child's life.

Child-proof bottles, while helpful, are misleading. Our grandson can pry open child-proof bottles with his teeth while we are still reading the instructions, which are always inverted. *Do not rely on such containers to protect your child.*

Poison-control centers are available in all larger cities and most towns. Have the phone number of a reliable center posted along with the number of your doctor, the police, fire department, and any other emergency numbers. Call it once to see what kind of advice and help the center is prepared to give.

Follow Recommended Dose. It is important to remember that in the giving of medications, one should not give more than the recommended dose. Medicines do not follow the old dictum that if a little is good, more must be better. In fact, quite the opposite might be the result. It is also important to remember that, in the case of minor illnesses, one should be patient and believe that the body has some natural God-given healing ability. It requires only a certain amount of time, and the result will be recovery from the illness.

10
Your Problem Solver for Injuries and Illnesses

INTRODUCTION

In this chapter we will discuss a wide variety of diseases, accidents, and injuries that may afflict a child. They are discussed in this general order: bacterial and viral infections, including those associated with animals. However, the major portion of this chapter will concern diseases and accidents arranged in order according to the part of your child's body that is affected. Some of the general medical information has been discussed briefly earlier, but we feel the repeated material will help you better understand the symptoms and treatment of the various subjects under discussion.

The first body system reviewed is *The Integumentary System* (Skin, Hair, and Nails). Second is *The Musculoskeletal System* (Bones, Tendons, and Muscles). The third system is *The Endocrine System* (Pituitary, Thyroid, Adrenal, Ovaries, and Testes). The fourth is *The Digestive System* (Stomach, Intestinal Tract, and Digestive Organs). The fifth subject under discussion is *The Circulatory System* (Heart and Blood Vessels). The sixth system to be reviewed is *The Respiratory System* (Lungs and Their Branches). *The Nervous System* (Brain, Spinal Cord, and Nerves) is the seventh topic, while the eighth is *The Genital and Urinary Tracts* (Sexual Organs and Kidneys). *The Lymphatic System* (Lymph Nodes and Lymph Vessels) is the ninth to be reviewed, and *The Sensory System* (Ears, Eyes, Nose, and Throat) the tenth. The final system to be discussed is *The Teeth and Gums.*

We conclude the chapter with an important review of Emergency Procedures and A Word About Divine Healing.

THE MORE FAMILIAR CHILDHOOD DISEASES

If you are not sure exactly where a certain symptom fits, don't feel that you are dumb. Sometimes several systems are affected by certain illnesses. Just look in the index, and you will find the topic listed, along with the pages in which it is mentioned.

Allergies are one example of the many parts of the body that can be affected by a problem. Asthma is one manifestation of allergy, and it affects the lungs. Hay fever, also an allergic condition, affects the nose and eyes. Hives, another form of allergy, affect the skin. We hope this arrangement will be convenient and that you will find these descriptions helpful.

When to Call the Doctor

A major question of parents is "When do we call the doctor?" You don't want to be overanxious, but on the other hand, sometimes you are worried. You may feel intimidated by medical people, but we strongly urge you to overcome that feeling. It will damage your relationship with your doctor and prevent the open and trusting communication that both you and he so badly need.

The excellence of your child's medical care depends on these things:

1. *Your doctor's professional skill*
2. *Your skill as parents in noticing symptoms, reporting them, and following through with care*
3. *Your communication and the relationship among yourselves*

To help you in knowing when to call your doctor, we remind you that we have put in boldface, small capital letters the information about symptoms that warrant a phone call and probably a visit to your doctor. Also in this same typeface, we have listed the signs or symptoms that demand you see your doctor at once. It may be that an emergency room in a hospital is nearer. The availability of certain equipment and care there makes an emergency-room visit pay off in a crisis. The hospital, you, and your doctor will communicate and cooperate with each other, so you will get the best of care.

Do have a very convenient place for the following telephone listings:

1. *Your doctor's office and his answering service*
2. *The emergency room of the hospital your doctor uses (hopefully that's the nearest one)*
3. *An ambulance company that you know is reliable*
4. *Your police department (in case you need an escort to a hospital)*
5. *The emergency rescue unit of your fire department*
6. *A poison-control center*

We suggest you call each of these numbers and find out what services they will or will not give in a medical emergency. It has surprised us that some services are extremely poor while others are excellent.

There are a number of illnesses of children that affect the entire body with more or less severe symptoms. These are contagious and often occur in epidemics. Most of them are now rare due to the widespread practice of immunizations. Be sure to read about them, however, because a reminder of their severity will make you very careful to keep up your child's immunizations.

First we will discuss the *bacterial* infections, then the *viral* ones. It is important that you understand these differences, because bacterial infections can usually be cured promptly by the use of the appropriate antibiotics. For the viruses, we have no effective antibiotics as yet. Researchers are busily seeking such medicines, and there are one or two that sound promising. We hope any day to hear of a major breakthrough in such a discovery.

BACTERIAL INFECTIONS

Scarlet Fever

This is a disease that is rarely seen today, thanks to the discovery of penicillin. It is a severe streptococcal germ infection in which toxins or poisons get into the patient's system and cause a bright-scarlet discoloration of the skin.

Symptoms. It almost always begins with severe tonsillitis or a sore throat. When antibiotics, like penicillin, are given, this heals quickly. Without antibiotics, however, the fever stays high, vomiting and headache develop, and the skin turns an angry red color, with a sandpapery feel. Usually there is no redness around the mouth, and this area looks pale. The rash lasts from three to six days and fades slowly. The skin, however, peels off in smaller or larger pieces, and the hair may come out in some unusual amounts. It does grow back, however, so don't be alarmed at this. With proper treatment, scarlet fever is preventable and highly curable.

Scarletina. This is simply a mild form of scarlet fever. It is seen fairly commonly, especially with severe tonsillitis.

Diphtheria

This disease needs to be described, so you will understand why your baby needs the shots to prevent it. It is so rare now that most physicians have never seen a case of it. Only fifty years ago, however, the word struck fear to the hearts of any family.

Symptoms. The bacteria that cause this illness create a severe sore throat and signs of a cold. There is swelling of the tissues and the lymph glands, and thick, tenacious mucus is secreted that sometimes cuts off the airway. The poisons put out by this germ may cause paralysis of certain muscles. The lungs, heart, or other vital organs may also be infected. Death once was an all-too-common result and still occurs rarely in the United States.

Immunization. When I [Dr. Grace] was five years old, I was privileged to be one of the very first children in my community to be immunized against diphtheria. My memory of the fear I knew is vivid. Trying very hard to be brave, I took the first shot I ever had with courage. Our country doctor, a man of great wisdom and congeniality, looked at me with twinkling eyes and said, "Now, Grace, you tell your mother you were the very best one!" I know that doctor is a bit of the reason I myself became a doctor.

It was shots just like that, given by thousands of caring people to millions of children, that have reduced and nearly eliminated these once-dreaded diseases. We want to remind every parent to express your gratitude to God and many dedicated people for the peace of mind you enjoy.

Hospitalization Required. Treatment of diphtheria requires hospitalization so that proper fluids, antibiotics, and antitoxins to counteract the poisons may be carefully administered. Most people who get this rare disease may be cured if treatment is begun in time.

Whooping Cough (Pertussis)

This is another nearly forgotten disease. But if only a few years went by without immunizing children, it would return in severe epidemics.

Symptoms. This serious infection of the bronchial tubes and windpipe causes the secretion of very thick, whitish mucus and irritation of all the respiratory tissues. In order to dislodge this tenacious mucus, the child involuntarily coughs so hard, he turns red or even blue. At the end of such a coughing spell, he draws in his breath with sudden sharpness, creating a crowing or whooping sound—hence the name *whooping cough.*

Children with such a severe cough often vomit from the choking associated with it, adding to the seriousness of the disease by weight loss and lack of fluids. The illness lasts about six weeks, though improvement begins after three weeks. Antibiotics and a special sort of serum containing a substance that will specifically fight the *pertussis bacterium* make this infection less severe than in years past.

Nevertheless, it is a serious illness, especially in tiny babies. So be sure to get your baby immunized as early as possible—

usually at about eight weeks of age. (*See* the section on Immunization in chapter 9.)

Tetanus (Lockjaw)

This is a disease that is caused by bacteria that enters the body through a puncture wound or deep cut. These germs grow only in deeper tissues because they do not like oxygen, as do most of the other germs we deal with.

Symptoms. When such germs begin to multiply deep inside the tissues, they cause redness, heat, pain, and swelling of that area. But the main problem is caused by the poisons (toxins) these bacteria secrete. These toxins affect the nerves and muscles, causing involuntary muscular contractions or spasms. These begin with some aching and stiffness and progress to almost boardlike rigidity. Without treatment, death is very likely due to inability to breathe.

Treatment. Fortunately, medical science has discovered treatment that makes survival the rule, not the exception. A substance called *tetanus antitoxin* is given at once along with tetanus toxoid. The antitoxin, as its name implies, acts against the toxin or poison in the system. The toxoid causes the body to quickly add its own substances to fight against the toxins.

The germs that cause tetanus are harbored in the intestinal tracts of animals, though they are present in nearly all soil. Care in wearing proper shoes in outdoor areas and avoiding wounds by watchfulness for nails or other objects sharp enough to penetrate shoes and skin will help prevent tetanus. Obviously, however, accidents beyond the control of anyone may occur.

Immunization. For this reason, you need to protect *yourselves and your children* against tetanus by having immunization shots. These have proven extremely successful in preventing tetanus. The shots create some local pain and swelling but this lasts only a day or two, and the shots could save your life. (*See* the section on Immunization in chapter 9.)

Allergic Reactions. Some people develop an allergic reaction to tetanus antitoxin when they have had injections more than once. Also, tetanus toxoid may eventually cause an allergic reaction. This is often severe and may cause lowering of the blood pressure, rapid pulse rate, and fainting, as well as an acute, severe asthmatic attack and hives. Any medical person should be aware of this possibility and warn you. However, you also need to be alert to any unusual symptoms on the part of an older child and report these to your doctor.

Tuberculosis

TB is now a rare disease. It is an infection caused by a special bacterium. Usually it affects the lymph glands in the chest and some part of the lung itself. It may affect bones, some part of the nervous system or, rarely, other parts of the body. There are antibiotics that now will control and cure this once very dangerous disease. It is important, however, to diagnose it early and treat it thoroughly. Your doctor should do a skin test on your child when she is one year old and once a year after that. This test will tell you if your child has been infected even a little bit by the tuberculosis germ. If so, your doctor will X-ray her chest and will recommend a special medication for a year, because this germ is very stubborn. He will then re-X-ray the child. If she is well, you may rest assured that she will be fine. Proper follow-up demands one X ray a year. The skin test will stay positive, so don't worry about that.

VIRAL INFECTIONS

Measles (Rubeola)

This disease rarely occurs due to routine immunization. (*See* chapter 9.)

Symptoms. The symptoms begin three to five days after exposure to an active case with cough, fever, headache, and mild vomiting. After a day or two, red spots with white centers (called Koplik's Spots) appear first inside the mouth on the cheeks and throat. The rash spreads from the head and neck over the entire body. The rash is red and feels rough. The eyes are red and burn, the throat is sore, cough is dry and severe, and the fever rides at 103 degrees F., give or take a bit, for several days. After the fifth or sixth day, the child improves fairly rapidly.

The only prescription for measles is rest in bed, lots of fluids, and aspirin to help control the fever and relieve some of the discomfort. A good cough syrup prescribed by your doctor will help the cough some.

There are a few complications that may occur after measles such as ear infections, bronchitis, or pneumonia. Your children need never go through this if they have one relatively painless shot!

Three-Day Measles (Rubella)

Sometimes called German measles, this is a miniversion of regular measles. It lasts a total of three days, is mild, and rarely if ever has a complication, unless it happens to a pregnant woman in the first three months of her pregnancy. Then, about 25 percent of the time, the baby will be born with blindness, deafness, or other serious birth defects. Be certain that your child is immunized against rubella!

Mumps

This is a viral infection of the glands that secrete saliva. They are called *parotid glands* and they are located in front of each ear in the cheeks. You can feel with your tongue the openings of the parotid glands on each side.

Symptoms. When they are infected, these glands swell to several times their normal size, and the opening is red and puffy. Usually the jaws ache, and the glands hurt when anything is eaten that stimulates the flow of saliva, such as pickles or sour foods. There usually is some headache, a moderate fever— about 101 degrees F.—and loss of appetite. The whole process from onset to health is from five to seven days. There is no treatment. Rarely the infection has been reported to occur more than once.

Danger to Boys. The danger of mumps is with boys. For some reason, especially if it occurs near the time of puberty or later, mumps may spread to the testes. If an infection occurs there, it causes swelling, severe pain, and fever. It may damage the testicle enough to cause sterility. For this reason, every boy ought to be immunized against mumps. It is advisable for girls also to be vaccinated to be sure they do not contract such an infection when they are older, and could be much sicker from it.

Chicken Pox

This viral infection is almost universal in childhood. Many times the first evidence of chicken pox is a small blister on the upper back or lower neck. The blister looks like a tiny teardrop on a red base, and is tender and itchy. There is usually a fever of about 100 to 101 degrees F., a mild headache, and symptoms resembling a mild cold. The sores spread over the entire body, and even into the mouth. Rarely, they extend into the throat and may cause a severe cough. Some children get by with only a few lesions, while others are covered with them. No one can explain this.

Stop Scratching! It is important to keep a child from scratching in order to prevent secondary infections and scarring. Little children may need mittens to protect them, and older children must be encouraged to refrain from scratching. Your doctor may recommend calamine lotion or other soothing applications to relieve the itching. Certain prescription-type antihistamines may also help to relieve the itching. The worst of this illness will be past by the fifth day. The blisters dry and form crusts. Though the itching is not as bad, it is tempting for children to pick off these crusts. Help them not to do so. If they are left to fall off when they are ready, there is much less danger of unsightly scars.

Roseola

This is another viral infection of young children. With this disease the child is extremely irritable and has a high fever—about 103 to 104 degrees F. He may even have a febrile convulsion (*see* later in this section). Upon a thorough physical exam, your doctor will find nothing extraordinary, and probably will tell you to administer aspirin, watch, and wait. About the time you are convinced that you can't take one more hour of such fussing and worry, the fever will drop almost instantly, and the child will feel dramatically better. It is then that a red, flat rash will break out all over the body. It will last two to three days, disappear, and your child will be well. There truly is no treatment, and there are no known complications. It usually occurs in children under eighteen months of age. The appearance of the rash after the fever breaks distinguishes this disease from measles.

Fifth Disease

This is a nondescript rash with variable symptoms. It is called by this name because there are four other childhood diseases with comparable rashes—measles, rubella, scarlet fever, and roseola. It probably is caused by one of many known viruses. The symptoms are very mild and the rash is usually the only sign of any illness. The real name is *Erythema contagiosum,* and it is usually epidemic in nature.

PET OR ANIMAL-ASSOCIATED INFECTIONS

There are a few diseases of people that are shared with and caught from pets or animals. You need to understand these because they may be extremely serious.

Rabies

This is one disease that still frightens both parents and medical people. It is a viral disease that is common among animals. It apparently is carried by some animals, that is, bats and skunks, without any symptoms. If they bite other animals or people, however, it will cause severe infection that is almost always fatal if not treated preventively.

Symptoms. An animal or person with rabies is affected in the nervous system. The nerves become inflamed and stimulate the muscles to become sore and stiff. The muscles in the neck and throat are affected first, and eating or swallowing becomes extremely painful. The patient allows saliva to collect in the mouth rather than to swallow it. Eventually the muscles which control breathing become affected, and death occurs.

Catch the Animal. Rabies occurs only after a bite by a rabid animal. Sometimes the animal evidences the signs of being infected by staggering and drooling of saliva. At other times such signs may not be present. If an animal bites you or your child, try to get someone to catch it alive safely. Never do this barehanded, and always avoid bites—especially on the trunk of the body. The virus spreads slowly along the nerve tracts, and a bite on the hand will give time for preventive treatment, while a bite close to the central nervous system and brain will not allow enough time. If the animal can be caged, send it to a veterinarian's laboratory. He can see whether or not it is infected. If the animal dies, its body should be taken to such a laboratory for testing. Even a dog in the neighborhood must be observed for several days to find out if it is in the early stages of rabies.

Prevention—Not Treatment. There is no treatment for rabies, but it can be prevented. All household pets should be immunized against rabies with booster shots every two years. No safe preventive shots are yet available for people. However, if someone is bitten by an animal suspected of being infected, a series of twenty-one rabies shots can be given that will prevent it, unless the bite is too close to the brain. These shots must be given once daily. They are given in the abdominal muscles, because there is a danger of paralysis of the muscles in the area around the injection. The abdominal muscles, should they be so affected, cause less problems, and handicap normal functioning less than any other muscles in the body.

A very few people with intensive care of a life-support type have now survived rabies. But do be careful to protect your pets and beware of wild animals. *Do not teach your child to be afraid of animals, but do teach him caution.*

Cat-Scratch Disease

This is a viral infection that is associated with a bite or scratch by a cat.

Symptoms. It is characterized by swelling, redness, and pain in the lymph nodes of one area of the body. While this illness is usually mild, sometimes there is fever, and the child feels quite sick. Actually, any small injury, not necessarily a cat bite or scratch, may result in this disease if it becomes infected. Though the original injury heals, there is a secondary problem with infected lymph nodes.

Treatment. Cat-scratch disease lasts from two to eight weeks and rarely has any complications. There are no antibiotics that will cure it because it is a virus. But the child's own body almost always will fight off the infection. If your child has a scratch or bite by a cat or other pet, of course, you will watch it carefully. Even if the animal is well itself, it can cause a localized infection in your child.

If soreness and swelling occur in areas near such an injury, see your doctor. He will need to verify the diagnosis and help you be sure that healing is complete. Sometimes viral infections may be complicated by (or mixed with) bacteria, and this might require antibiotic treatment.

Parrot Fever (Pittacosis)

This is rare in a severe form, but mild cases are not uncommon. In fact, the symptoms resemble viral pneumonia. (*See* Pneumonia later in this chapter.) But sometimes it is more serious and needs special antibiotic treatment. It actually is caught from birds, but not necessarily parrots. It may be caught from chickens, turkeys, pigeons, and other birds or fowl.

Q Fever

This is a disease carried by sheep, cattle, and goats. It is spread by ticks, which bite an infected animal and then people, or it may be spread directly from animals to people.

Symptoms. It is rarely serious and is characterized by fever, headache, general muscular aching, and a cough. In fact, there may be findings in the lungs resembling mild pneumonia. The disease is treated with antibiotics and almost always is cured promptly.

IF YOUR CHILDREN ARE AROUND CATTLE, SHEEP, OR GOATS AND DEVELOP THE SYMPTOMS DESCRIBED ABOVE, BE SURE TO SEE YOUR DOCTOR.

Encephalitis

Here is another disease that is carried by animals and spreads to people. In this case, the animal is most likely to be a horse and the tiny creature that carries it is the mosquito. (*See* Neurological Illnesses later in this chapter.)

Rocky Mountain Spotted Fever

This is a disease usually affecting both people and small, wild animals. If a hard tick bites one of these small, infected animals, then bites a human, it is likely to inoculate the causative agent into that person. It occurs throughout North America, not just in the Rocky Mountains as the name implies.

Symptoms. The symptoms of this severe illness begin within two to fourteen days of the tick bite. They begin with fever, severe aching, and a rash that actually produces bleeding into the skin that looks like bruises. That is the source of the name *spotted fever*. When this is not treated, pneumonia or heart problems may develop.

Prevention. This disease can be prevented by vaccination. If you plan a camping trip, or live in an area where this disease is likely to occur, you should have your children (and yourselves) immunized. It also can be prevented by avoiding or quickly removing any ticks. The best method of removal is to grasp the insect by the head and chest by a fine forceps and gently pull until it comes off. In case you have not dealt with ticks, they are tiny insects that latch onto human skin for dear life by their mouth parts. It is hard to remove them. Some time-honored methods are: to apply kerosene; heat, as in a match flame; or fingernail polish, which causes them to suffocate. Be certain that the head is not left embedded in the skin, even if you must pry it out with a needle. The use of tick repellent in the clothing if you must be in tick "country" can also prevent their bites.

IF, HOWEVER, ANY OF THE ABOVE SYMPTOMS BEGIN WITHIN A FEW DAYS OF A TICK BITE, SEE YOUR DOCTOR AT ONCE, AND TELL HIM OF THE BITE AND THE SYMPTOMS. THERE ARE NOW EXCELLENT ANTIBIOTICS THAT WILL CURE THE DISEASE IN A FEW DAYS. BUT IT IS IMPORTANT TO TREAT IT EARLY!

Tularemia

This disease is carried by all kinds of wild animals and may be caught from them by hunters. If your children go hunting with their dad or anyone, warn them about this disease. It may be caught by insect bites or from eating inadequately cooked wild meat, as well as by contamination of a scratch or break in the skin while cleaning the animal.

Symptoms. It begins with one of three general symptoms:

1. There may be a red, swollen infection at a spot where an infected animal may have touched an open scratch, or perhaps a bone may have pricked the skin in cleaning the animal that had been hunted and killed. The lymph nodes then swell and become tender all over the body; there is fever; and the patient will feel very sick.

2. Stomach upsets after eating wild meat or drinking contaminated water may be followed by infected lymph glands through the throat and entire abdomen. It is important to think about the possibility of this if you or your family have been hunting or have eaten such food.

3. Lung involvement occurs in all forms of tularemia. It is manifested by a dry cough, and sometimes there is blood-tinged sputum coughed up.

THE TREATMENT FOR ALL TYPES OF TULAREMIA IS THE PROMPT USE OF ANTIBIOTICS. WHEN THEY ARE NOT GIVEN, HOWEVER, IT MAY BE FATAL, SO BE SURE TO GET THE VICTIM OF SUSPECTED TULAREMIA TO A PHYSICIAN AT ONCE!

THE INTEGUMENTARY SYSTEM
(Skin, Hair, and Nails)

The skin is a complicated tissue composed of two layers: the *epidermis* or outer layer, and the *mesodermal* connective tissue (or dermis), which helps attach the skin to the body.

In the epidermis there are cells that become dead and dry, continually sloughing off—unnoticed as in dandruff or simply dry scales. Under this surface layer of cells are hair follicles and hair, nails, the outer layer of the teeth (the enamel), and sweat and oil glands. In the female breasts, the mammary or milk glands are a special part of the skin. The wax glands in the ears, and some special glands in the eyelids, complete the structures that are all a part of this important system of the body. Actually

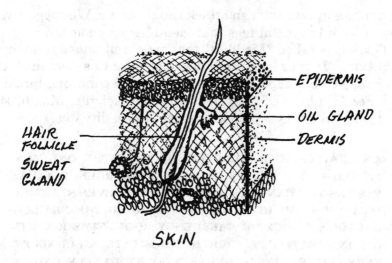

SKIN

the nails and outer layer of the teeth (enamel) are formed from the epidermis.

The diseases of the skin are classified here as *allergic, bacterial, viral, fungus, insect* and *weed irritations,* and *injuries* or *accidents.*

Allergic Diseases of the Skin

Hives. These are one of the manifestations of allergies. Asthma is an allergic reaction in the lung tissue; hay fever similarly affects the lining of the nose; and hives show up in the skin. They range in severity from a fine, mildly itchy rash to "wheals" or extensive swelling of the skin. The eyelids may become puffy or even swell until they are almost shut. The lips may also swell, as well as the hands and feet.

Severe Symptoms. Very rarely, the body may react with all of its tissues affected by an allergy. In such cases, the nose will itch and run, and an asthma attack may develop. This severe, generalized reaction is called *anaphylactic shock,* and it is quite frightening. When such a situation develops, rare as it is, it is most commonly due to an insect sting. Bees and hornets are the usual offenders. Less frequently such an extreme reaction is due to a variety of other substances. If you or your child has ever had such a response to a stinging insect, you need to be very careful to avoid them, and you may want to carry some medication to use in case such an attack should occur. We suggest you wear one of the metal tags that identifies your allergy.

These tags called "Medilert" tags may be obtained from most drugstores. If your local store does not have this item in stock, they may be obtained by writing Speidel Distributors, Inc., 897 Fee Fee Road, P.O. Box 1779, Maryland Heights, Mo., 63043. Our local druggists say their product is a quality one.

AN ANAPHYLACTIC REACTION SUCH AS THE ONE MEN-TIONED ABOVE IS A TRUE MEDICAL EMERGENCY. GO AS FAST AS YOU CAN WITH A CHILD (WHO IS EVEN STARTING TO MOVE FROM HIVES TO WHEEZING) TO THE NEAREST DOCTOR'S OFFICE OR EMERGENCY ROOM. TIME IS CRITI-CAL IN TREATING IT, SO DO NOT HESITATE. AN UNNECES-SARY TRIP, IN CASE HE GETS BETTER BY HIMSELF, CAUSES ONLY A LITTLE INCONVENIENCE. GETTING THERE TOO LATE MAY CAUSE A FATALITY.

Treatment. For ordinary hives this is quite simple and there is no great urgency except for the discomfort and itching. These, however, may be intense.

We believe you should always consult your doctor when your child has hives. If he knows your child, a phone call may take care of the problem. But if the reaction is severe, he may need to see the child to determine the need for stronger medication than you have at home. Usually your doctor will telephone a prescription that relieves the itching and counteracts the allergic substance. Almost always, hives disappear as quickly as they come. While you are waiting for the prescription to be ready, put your child in a warm baking-soda bath. It will relieve the itching a bit. Alcohol sponging or a lotion such as calamine may also help the itching. Your child will be grateful, at least, for your efforts.

Causes. More often than not, we cannot ascertain exactly what substance causes hives. We do find, however, that hives occur when a child is excited or especially worried about something such as a school examination. When they occur frequently, a dietary history and careful evaluation of the environment can help identify the offending material.

Insect Stings. See Insect Bites this chapter.

Eczema. This is a skin condition that usually begins in infancy. Probably it is an allergic condition that affects the skin in a specific way. Various foods, such as eggs, corn, and milk, have been blamed. So have a variety of other factors such as soap, woolen or other rough fabrics, pets, and emotional problems.

Symptoms. The symptoms of eczema are itching and scratching. The signs are a raw, reddened, weepy rash, especially common in the folds of the arms and legs. In infants the rash is common on the face as well.

Treatment. Treatment is aimed at relieving the symptoms. Avoid soap over the affected areas. Avoid any foods known to cause a flare-up of the rash. Encourage the child to avoid scratching. Mittens on a small child may help. The use of any drying agent such as alcohol (its sting often feels better than the horrible itching!) or calamine lotion will relieve the itching somewhat.

Hydrocortisone ointment in 0.5 percent strength is remarkably effective in treating eczema. You may now buy this without a prescription under a number of different brand names. Ask your druggist for the most economical one. Dry the affected area and rub in the ointment very well.

In using any ointment, you need to rub it into the affected area as thoroughly as possible. There are sweat and oil glands in the skin into which the ointment needs to penetrate if it is to be effective. Smearing it on top is not enough. This is an example of the importance of parental courage and firmness. Pressure on a tender area causes some discomfort and your child will want you to stop the treatment. Now, do not be mean or unnecessarily rough. But explain the reasons for what you do, and then do it, firmly and gently. Comfort the child afterward without undue pity. As he improves, help him know that the pain of the treatment made possible the comfort of the healing. This is a lesson for all of life—not just an isolated situation!

Bacterial Infections of the Skin

Impetigo. This infection of the skin is caused by *strep* (streptococcal) germs. *Staph* germs may also be found in such infections. These bacteria are commonly found in the nostrils, skin, or mouth without serious symptoms. Through a mosquito bite and subsequent scratching, as well as any injury or irritation of the skin, these germs may invade the protective outer layer of skin and get into the layer of skin that is warm and moist enough to allow the germs to grow and multiply. They do not, however, spread deeply or widely enough to cause *cellulitis* or blood poisoning. They just cause a slightly uncomfortable, pinkish spot that oozes a bit, and then forms a yellowish or greenish crust over itself. It spreads slowly and may occur on other areas of the body.

Treatment. Gently soaking off the crusts and removing them to expose the pink area beneath will enable you to apply an antibiotic ointment. Rub this in well, and it will quite quickly cure the local infection.

In order to prevent the very serious complications that rarely follow strep infections, however, most doctors give several days of antibiotics by mouth as well. We strongly recommend such treatment.

Boils, Carbuncles, Sties. They are skin infections usually caused by staph germs. These are common in warm weather and may keep spreading or recurring. A boil usually starts as a red, firm swelling in the skin. It may have initially been a tiny pustule, or there may be only the red, painful bump. This lump will slowly enlarge and gradually will become soft and perhaps yellow in the center. Sometimes this will burst, and blood-tinged pus will flow out.

Treatment. In the treatment of a boil, it is necessary to remove with gentle pressure or sterile tweezer a firm center plug or "core." If this is not removed, the infection is likely to recur.

Be very careful to avoid severe pressure in squeezing a boil lest it spread germs in bruised tissue and cause cellulitis to occur. (*See* Cellulitis under Heart and Blood Vessels later in this chapter.) We have found it helpful to gently massage an antibiotic ointment into the skin around a boil to help prevent the spreading of bacteria.

We also found the following procedure to be helpful in people or families who have frequent, recurrent boils, sties, or other staph infections. We know that many people harbor staph bacteria in their nostrils without any problem there. Picking the nose, however, is one of the most universal habits of American people, and this habit allows staph bacteria to get under the nails and on the fingers. By rubbing the eyes or scratching another area of the body, these bacteria may easily be introduced into tender tissues, where they may set up a serious infection. Using an antibiotic ointment in the nostrils every morning and evening for one week will very often get rid of those troublesome intruders and stop their spread. Ask your druggist for a good antibiotic ointment.

Viral Infections of the Skin

Herpetic Paronychia (*Viral Infection of Fingernails*). A child who has a fever sore or herpetic mouth infection may easily spread this infection to the nail bed and cuticle by chewing on his nails or sucking his fingers.

Symptoms. In such an infection, the skin about the nail becomes an angry red; it may be "weepy" or moist, and is tender. If it gets under the nail, it may cause a loosening of the nail from the nail bed, and the nail may even come off. In order to cure this infection, in fact, the nails may have to be removed since the virus "hides" under them and will continue to grow there.

Treatment. Quite by accident, we discovered that soaking such infected areas in ordinary rubbing alcohol dried the area, and many times completely cured the infection. Alcohol stings and causes considerable discomfort at the first touch, but most children felt that this sting was a welcome relief from the constant low-level pain they felt anyway. New nails that grow out will usually be healthy, if they are not reinfected.

Since this is not life threatening, many parents allow this infection to run a long, painful course untreated. Do not do this. If home remedies do not help, call your doctor or visit him and let him help you.

Shingles (*Herpes Zoster*). This is a viral infection that affects the sensory part of one particular nerve tract. Some authorities believe it may be due to the chicken pox virus that stays "asleep" in parts of a certain nerve, and later becomes active again. At any rate, the rash (though localized) looks very much like chicken pox. While this disease is rare in children, it does occur.

Symptoms. The symptoms are usually mild—a slight fever and general discomfort, followed by pain along the course of one single nerve. It may be on the face, neck, arm, or chest. The pain along this nerve may be severe or only mildly itching in nature. The rash that breaks out is watery, but the blisters break and crusts form.

Treatment. There is no treatment, except calamine or other lotions to relieve the itching, and some pain-relieving medication. Usually aspirin or Tylenol are adequate.

It is possible for this infection to reoccur, though eventually the body does seem to develop an immunity. Be careful that your child does not scratch the blisters and then rub his eyes. Such an infection in the eyes can be serious.

Fever Blisters and Cold Sores. These are also caused by a herpes virus. They usually occur in the mouth but many spread to the lips and around the mouth on the skin. (For further discussion, *see* Mouth and Throat, later in this chapter.)

Warts. They are a scourge of childhood! There are many superstitions about their cause and cure. For all the annoyance they cause, we really know very little about them. We believe they are caused by a virus and not by playing with toads! We have found them curable—with time or by cauterizing them with a tiny electric needle (under a local anesthetic) or with special chemicals. We do not believe that burying a dishrag in a cemetery at midnight will do it!

Plantar Warts. The only painful warts are those occurring on the sole of the feet. These are called *plantar warts* and by their pressure into the foot, they become most uncomfortable. Plantar warts are less likely to disappear by themselves than are the ones on the hands. By the way, warts may grow anywhere on the body, but the hands are by far the most favored location. Plantar warts may be removed surgically or by treatment with an electric needle. This is, of course, done relatively painlessly under a local anesthetic. The healing takes about two weeks. X-ray treatment, once used to cure plantar warts, is no longer recommended.

Fungus Infections

Ringworm. This is a round, small, reddened area on the skin that is itchy, a bit scaly, and tends to heal in the center as it extends from the border. It is caused by a microscopic organism that gets into the skin, grows, and causes irritation there. This is very contagious among children and is commonly caught from pets, such as cats or dogs. When it gets into the scalp, it will cause the hair to fall out in infected areas.

Diagnosis. If you suspect this infection, call your doctor and ask him to see your child. He can quickly diagnose it and needs to know it is not impetigo, allergy, or some other problem. He will give you a prescription that must be taken long enough for healthy new hair to grow out and the fungus to be destroyed. This is distressing to most mothers, but it is not at all an emergency and can be cared for at your convenience.

Athlete's Foot. It is a common ailment of older children who frequent the wet showers of gymnasiums—hence the term *athlete's foot.* It is caused by a fungus different from ringworm and causes peeling and cracking of the skin, especially between the toes and on other areas of the feet. It lives in warm, moist areas, such as shower stalls, and is *highly contagious.*

Treatment. Most families do not even consult a physician for this, but treat it with home remedies. These include the following: 1) Keep the feet as dry as possible by removing shoes and wearing sandals, or cutting out the toes of old tennis shoes. 2) Use an antifungal powder, such as Desenex. This does not require a prescription and can be found in all drugstores. The feet (and socks, when they must be worn) should be dusted well with this. 3) Clean cotton socks should be worn daily if closed shoes are necessary. They should be soaked in a strong bleach solution to prevent reinfection. 4) Bathtubs and showers need to be disinfected with any good household chemical after bathing. 5) Use of personal sandals or thongs in school showers and regularly disinfecting them can prevent recurrences.

When such measures do not produce a cure, do call your doctor for further advice.

Jock Itch (Tinea Cruris). This is a fungus infection of the groin, common in adolescent males. It shows up as a reddish, scaly, itchy rash scattered in patches, and is usually limited to the groin. It is readily curable, using the same sort of powder or ointment as in athlete's foot. Cortisone creams are effective in treatment.

Tinea Versicolor. This is a fungus infection that may occur over the upper part of the chest. It is scattered in irregular patches that are scaly, itchy, and yellowish-brown in color. Tinea versicolor is relatively uncommon. For treatment and a definite diagnosis, see your doctor.

Insect Bites

Mosquitoes. These are the most common biting insects, and their itch can be highly annoying. There is no treatment for bites, but several things may relieve the itch—rubbing alcohol may sting but this often feels better than the itching. A bit of pressure over the bite with the edge of a clean fingernail helps. Again, it is the mild pain of this pressure that temporarily relieves the itch. Avoid deep scratching, since this may inoculate germs into the bite and cause infection. Usually these last only a few days.

Occasionally a mosquito will bite soft tissues, and the swelling, without the firm skin to stop it, may become great. We have seen eyelids swell shut and a boy's whole penis enlarged from a single bite. This rarely if ever means that this is a serious reaction, and does not imply a developing anaphylactic reaction. Applying cool, moist packs may reduce the swelling and discomfort, but bites will heal in such areas just as they do anywhere.

Chiggers. These are tiny insects that live in the grass. They love to burrow under tight socks or shorts and get into the skin, where they cause intense itching. Soaking chiggers with alcohol will usually kill them, but the itching will last several days anyway.

Ticks. These are also insects that bite and cause trouble. Ticks lock their heads into the skin and can readily be seen hanging on. It is tempting to pull them off, but they will sacrifice their lives for the sake of "hanging in there." So use any powerful toxic substance that will not hurt the skin—gasoline, kerosene, turpentine, alcohol. Soak the insect with this. He will finally relax his jaws and fall off. Covering him with nail polish is said to work, as does greasing him with any ointment. They work by suffocating him and getting him to relax and drop off. Use a good antiseptic to cleanse the bite and a Band-Aid to help soothe the sting. Watch for any sign of infection over the next several days. If you are in an area where Rocky Mountain spotted fever is endemic, call a doctor. Some authorities recommend using tweezers to pull ticks out. If you suspect this disease is found in the area, use tweezers, but be sure to get the head out, as well as the body. The theory behind this is the possibility of the inoculation of the infectious material into the victim's skin by the death of an insect. Plucking it off alive will hopefully prevent this.

If you are in tick country, to protect your child as well as yourself, use a good insect repellent. Spray it over the body, where it may be exposed to the ticks, and the clothes, as well, because ticks may stay in clothes for hours and bite later! As always, prevention is better than a cure!

Bees, Wasps, Hornets, Yellow Jackets. These large stinging insects usually sting only when attacked. Never step on one, swat at him, or annoy him. Believe me, it will pay to give him wide berth! No matter how careful you are, however, you may inadvertently challenge one of these creatures and he will let you have it. The pain of this sting is immense! It will send cold chills over the body and cause goose bumps for hours.

Treatment. Try to remove a bee's stinger by flicking it out, if possible. The pain is nothing compared with the pain of the sting! If you can't remove it, don't worry. Your body will swell up around it and eventually push it out. Covering the sting with mud, moist soda, an ointment, or whatever you may find, will relieve the pain slightly. And take heart, you *will* recover!

Allergic Response. Rarely, people may have an *allergic response* to the sting of such an insect. They swell rapidly at the site of the sting and also get hives or general swelling of the body. When this affects their lungs, they may go into *anaphylactic shock.*

THIS IS AN EXTREME EMERGENCY. GET THIS PATIENT TO A HOSPITAL AS QUICKLY AS YOU CAN. TAKE SOMEONE ALONG TO PERFORM ARTIFICIAL RESPIRATION, IF NEEDED. WHEN A PERSON HAS SUCH A REACTION EVEN ONCE, HE NEEDS TO WEAR A "MEDILERT" TAG, AND HIS DOCTOR MAY GIVE HIM AN EMERGENCY KIT TO CARRY, AT LEAST WHEN HE IS IN AREAS INHABITED BY STINGERS.

Spider Bites. Spiders are everywhere. Rarely do they bite people. Just as with other insects, when people ignore them, they mind their own business. Curious children will poke at insects, however, and sometimes they inadvertently touch them in some way. Most bites are from brown spiders, and though they cause painful, swollen areas, the bite is not a threat to your child's life. The black widow spider may cause more serious illness.

Black Widow. A black widow spider is named that because the female eats her mate after mating. She is a glossy black color, and on the underside, she has bright-red markings in the shape of an hourglass.

IF YOU KILL SUCH A SPIDER AFTER SHE HAS BITTEN YOUR CHILD, TAKE IT AND YOUR CHILD TO THE EMERGENCY ROOM OF THE NEAREST HOSPITAL AT ONCE.

Symptoms. The spider's bite may go unnoticed at first, or there may be two tiny red spots where the bite occurred. Within fifteen minutes to as long as a few hours, there is swelling, heat, and pain in the area of the bite. This is followed by severe cramping of the muscles in the area, and then over the body. Rarely, the victim may go into shock, the respiration or heart may fail, and death may result.

Giving special medication in the veins can be lifesaving. There are some antivenin medications available in areas where these spiders are numerous. *Do not wait; get to your doctor or hospital at once if you feel there is a serious possibility of a black widow spider bite.*

Ants. These insects occasionally bite children and can cause some pain and redness at the site of that bite. Red ants especially are notorious for this. A bite from a fire ant can cause anaphylactic shock. In the U.S.A. there are few known poisonous ants. In South America and Africa, in the tropics, there are some ants that are known to be seriously toxic to human beings.

Blister Beetles. These are not uncommon in North America. Beetles are fascinating to children since many of them have an iridescent color, and they feel hard. Some beetles secrete a mild toxin that may cause blisters where they walk across the skin or are touched. This is not serious and requires no treatment except perhaps a mild disinfectant.

Snake Bites. These are rare in most parts of the U.S.A. and require emergency-room treatment. Rarely, however, on a camping trip such a luxury may not be within reach. If you suspect a poisonous snake bite, at once make a tiny cross cut through the skin, squeeze and suck on the area, carefully spitting out the venom you thus may remove. Put a tourniquet above the bite to slow down the absorption of the venom into the bloodstream. *Get medical attention as soon as possible.* Remember to release the tourniquet every few minutes for a few seconds to avoid serious circulatory damage or blood clots.

There are small snakebite kits available in most drugstores. Take one along if you expect to be around snakes. And be sure to wear heavy walking boots. Snakes can't bite through them.

Scabies. This is a contagious infection of the skin caused by a tiny insect that burrows into the skin and tunnels through it. The itching is intense, and children will scratch until the area may bleed. The distinguishing feature of this is the formation of "tracks" with little bumps or raised areas along these tracks. They are highly contagious through touching, and need to be diagnosed and treated by your doctor. A complete cure is to be expected and the itching improves in a few hours. *Be sure to use a disinfectant* in laundering the child's clothing and linens, and watch for several days for any possible reinfection.

Head Lice. They are actually tiny insects that find their way into a child's hair, where they like to live. The insects themselves move about, causing itching and scratching. The eggs, however, stick like glue to the hairs, where they may be seen by anyone. They are about twice the size of a pinpoint, yellowish in color, and shiny. They spread rapidly through a group of children, such as a classroom, due to the scratching and later touching of other children or their belongings.

Many parents feel disgraced over the fact that their child may have head lice. Lice are associated with carelessness and filth, so to keep lice may indicate some fault. But catching them is easy, and the condition often epidemic in a school or a classroom. You certainly need not feel embarrassed about an infestation of head lice.

Treatment. You will need to call your doctor, and if he questions your diagnosis, he will want to see your child. He will need to prescribe medication, in the form of a shampoo or lotion, which is highly effective. You will need to disinfect the linens and clothing of the infected child. Usually everyone in the family should use the medicine to prevent the spread of the lice. Be sure to watch for a week to see if there is a reinfection.

Swallow Your Pride! With all forms of such pests as well as intestinal parasites, you need to swallow your pride and report them to the parents of your child's playmates. Their children may have caught them, too, and they may not have symptoms that are as noticeable or parents who are as watchful as you. Not only will you do them a favor in catching an infection early, but you may prevent your child from being reinfected by his friends!

Contact Dermatitis

Chemicals. These may be responsible for certain skin rashes. In children, the most common one is soap. This may be the soap used in bath or bubblebath solutions, or it may be laundry detergents or bleaches. If your child itches, shows redness, or develops a rash after a bath, or after sleeping on freshly laundered linens, try eliminating soap. Use the very mildest soap you can find and only in areas of the body that perspire the most. You may need to resort to the Ivory Snow for laundry (without bleach) that you used when your child was a tiny baby. If the rash clears in a few days, you may be sure of the cause. Keeping only the milder soap on hand will probably cure this. A common offender is various bubble-bath products which children enjoy.

Woolen fabrics. These may cause skin rashes and itching in children with tender skin. Even over an undershirt, a woolen shirt may cause irritation. Other fabrics may cause a similar reaction, but no other kind is as common as wool. Sometimes knitted sweaters made of exceptionally soft wool yarn can be tolerated. Try them and see, but be grateful for synthetic yarns if your child is truly sensitive to woolens.

Weeds. They are potentially producers of severe contact dermatitis. While almost any plant may cause a reaction on someone, the most universally toxic weeds are poison ivy, poison oak, and poison sumac. They are wild plants and vines that grow throughout the United States and Southern Canada. They are most common in wooded areas.

Recognize Them. Poison ivy grows as a vine. The leaves always grow in clusters of three; they are dark green with indentations on the edge. The trunk is tough and "hairy." Poison oak looks like ivy except that it grows in clumps or low bushes instead of vines. Sumac has more leaves in each cluster.

These weeds are covered with an oily substance that is irritating to almost everyone. Within a few hours to a day or two, the exposed area becomes red, extremely itchy, and little fluid-filled blisters form. Wherever this fluid spreads (or even the oil itself on the exposed skin), it will cause more such areas. It is extremely uncomfortable and often requires medical care.

The treatment of weed dermatitis includes:

1. *Immediate application of strong soap and water to remove the oils. Rubbing alcohol may also be useful in removing them.*
2. *After the itching develops, a drying, soothing lotion such as calamine or caladryl or more rubbing alcohol will help to relieve it.*
3. *Usually any oil or grease-based preparations will only serve to spread the rash. One exception is the cortisone or hydrocortisone preparations. You may now purchase these directly from your druggist. They provide much relief from the inflammation and itching of ivy dermatitis.*
4. *In a severe reaction, you may need to see your doctor. He can prescribe a cortisone medication to take by mouth that will fairly quickly control the problem. It is not unusual, however, to have a flare-up of the condition when the medication is stopped. Sooner or later your body may simply have to recover by itself.*

Prevention. Poison ivy dermatitis may be prevented in most people, if they become immunized against it. This may be done through shots, or by taking repeated small doses of a preparation by mouth. It takes three to four months to build up your immunity, so plan ahead if you are a camper or hiker. Wear heavy boots and socks when you walk in wooded areas, and *always be on the lookout.* Prevention is so much easier than a cure!

Skin Diseases of Unknown Cause

Alopecia areata. This is a fairly rare disease of the scalp that involves the loss of hair in a small area. Loss of all of the hair may result from high fevers, such as once occurred in untreated scarlet fever. It may also be the result of lead or other chemical poisoning, and it often follows the use of chemotherapy for cancer. The localized loss of hair, however, is not well understood. We do not know what causes it, and the only treatment we have is the local use of steroid creams. These are limited in their effectiveness. Sometimes the hair grows back as unexplainedly as it fell out.

> BE SURE TO SEE YOUR DOCTOR IF YOUR CHILD DEVELOPS THIS PROBLEM. IF IT BECOMES MORE WIDESPREAD OR DOES NOT IMPROVE, HE PROBABLY WILL WANT YOU TO SEE A DERMATOLOGIST.

Cheloid. This is the formation of excessive scar tissue in the area of a cut. This tissue is red in color for some months, but it fades with time. The tissue appears as a raised, rough, "gristly" feeling enlargement of the healing scar from a surgical incision or an accidental cut. It is not serious and the only harm is the disfiguring effect it creates.

Treatment. In some cases, this can be surgically removed, and with steroid treatment, the incision may heal without cheloid. No one can guarantee that, but if your child has a severe scar of this type where it can be readily seen, he will certainly be grateful for any attempt to remove it.

Pityriasis rosea (Rubra). This is a common skin irritation that resembles ringworm. It is a rash composed of round areas about one-half inch in diameter. They are most numerous on the upper front of the chest, but may break out anywhere on the body. The outer edge of the circle is slightly raised and reddish in color, while the inner area is pale and scaly. There is mild itching. No treatment is necessary and it will heal within three to four months.

Psoriasis. This is a disfiguring ailment of the skin that sometimes affects children. It is more common in adolescents. Again, we must report that no one knows the cause of psoriasis, though most authorities believe it involves some stress factors, since many patients evidence a high level of anxiety, fear, or other emotional problems. Neither psychotherapy nor cortisone (steroid) treatments help appreciably.

Symptoms. Psoriasis is evidenced by reddish, slightly moist areas that become covered with heavy, grayish crusts. The crusts are firmly attached, and if they are removed, the raw area underneath tends to create more of them. They affect the elbows and knees, but may occur on the scalp and over the body as well.

Treatment. The best treatment available is the vigorous use of cortisone-type ointments or creams. These are limited in their effectiveness, but they do help considerably.

Vitiligo. This is a condition that is the opposite of freckles. For no known reason, scattered areas of skin turn pale, or even whitish, and lose their normal pigmentation. There is no pain, and no scaling or itching are reported. Sometimes the color returns when the child is in sunlight, but in some cases the condition remains unchanged no matter what is tried. Fortunately, some cosmetics can cover up the difference in color, and it need not be a serious problem.

Acne

This is a major skin problem of teenagers, and it causes them untold embarrassment. Apparently it has some connection with the hormone secretion associated with puberty, because it is rarely present before puberty and often is worse in girls just prior to each monthly menstrual period. Acne may occur later in life and generally lasts over a ten-year period.

Acne also occurs in young people who have oily skin, and it tends to run in families who have this skin condition. Various foods may aggravate the problem, and rich or greasy foods, those containing chocolate, and various milk products, are often blamed. Other authorities, however, believe that foods have no effect on acne. Poor skin care is certain to aggravate acne, though that alone does not cause it and many acne victims are exceptionally careful in their hygiene.

Besides the psychological reasons for treating acne, it needs to be treated to prevent its becoming disfiguring.

Bacteria invade the oil and sweat glands of the skin where they cause an infection. This starts as sore, red bumps which progress to yellow pimples. These may be large and ulcerate when they drain, leaving deep scars as they heal. Such scars may be treated by dermatologists or plastic surgeons, but they cannot be completely removed.

While acne rarely can be completely cured, it certainly can be effectively treated and greatly improved. The following are suggestions for treating acne:

1. *Consult your doctor. He can prescribe antibiotics to be taken orally and in a lotion form in a roll-on applicator. An antibiotic ointment may be useful but is obviously greasy. Remember to thoroughly massage the surface medications into the skin.*

2. *Despite the disagreements about foods, we believe in eliminating rich and oily foods: chocolate, in any form, cola drinks, nuts, milk products, except skim milk and cottage cheese, and foods or medicines containing iodine (though some authorities believe that iodine does not affect acne).*
    Do eat plenty of the basic foods described in the chapter on nutrition in the book. Drink plenty of water.

3. *Keep the skin clean by careful washing and brisk rubbing to remove the dry epidermal scales and to help press out the oil secretions. Keep the skin soft but use an astringent such as denatured (rubbing) alcohol or cold water to constrict the openings of the pores—after careful cleansing, of course.*

4. *The ultraviolet rays of sunshine are good for the skin, but avoid excessive amounts in order to prevent searing the epidermis, locking in the oil and bacteria that result in acne.*

5. *Getting plenty of rest and moderate exercise are excellent health habits, though they will not cure acne.*

6. *Cosmetics may be used if they are not made of heavy oil bases, are used sparingly, and cleansed carefully before retiring.*

Be aware of the essence of true inner beauty, and develop those qualities while you patiently await the improvement of the external blemishes that are so annoying.

Accidents and Injuries

Abrasions or Severe Scratches of the Skin. These are common with little children. Usually these need only gentle, thorough washing and the application of a kiss and a Band-Aid. Sometimes there may be ground-in particles of gravel or dirt that must be picked out with a tweezers, or lifted out with a sterile needle. If you are squeamish about cleansing a very dirty abrasion, see your doctor. We have seen some very serious infections result from scrapes that have been improperly cleansed. Permanent scars may result from such neglect.

Treatment. Hydrogen peroxide is a good cleanser and rarely causes much, if any, pain. After drying, we recommend covering the area with an antibiotic ointment. You should keep such a medication in your medicine chest. It soothes the skin by keeping out air, prevents contamination with bacteria, and usually keeps bandages from sticking and pulling off crusts when changed.

Blisters. Unusual rubbing and pressure against the skin in a localized area may cause a blister. The skin, irritated by the pressure, accumulates a little pocket of serum. This protects the tenderness, but also causes pressure and pain.

Warning! It is tempting to prick the blister and drain it. Do not do so! This allows infections to get started that may become serious.

Treatment. The application of a Band-Aid relieves some pain and protects the blister from dirt. By bedtime, you can usually remove any bandage, and let the area dry to form its own protective crust. The next day, if it looks fairly dry, leave it open. If, however, there are moist areas, or if the spot is located where it may be irritated further by clothing or motion, reapply a dressing until healing is complete.

Treat by stopping the pressure. Use a bandage; wear different shoes. Change position in the use of tools, and so forth. Allow the blister to heal. If it breaks by itself, apply an antibiotic cream, a bandage, and watch for any sign of serious infection. (*See* Cellulitis later in this chapter.)

Lacerations or Cuts. Most cuts should be seen and repaired by your physician. Often they are deeper and more extensive than seemed apparent at first. An ugly scar may result from the best of home remedies.

Unless the cut is bleeding profusely, however, you need not panic. Put pressure on the area to stop bleeding. Wrap gauze about the area, or a clean towel, if it is a larger cut, and head for your doctor's office.

RARELY A CUT MAY BE DEEP AND EXTENSIVE ENOUGH TO CAUSE DANGEROUS BLEEDING. IF YOU SEE A SPURTING TYPE OF BRIGHT-RED BLOOD, AN ARTERY HAS ALMOST CERTAINLY BEEN SEVERED. PUT TIGHT PRESSURE ABOVE SUCH AN INJURY BY TIGHTLY TYING A STRONG CORD, A HANDKERCHIEF, OR ANY STRIP OF FABRIC ABOVE THE AREA. RELEASE THE PRESSURE FOR A FEW SECONDS EVERY THREE OR FOUR MINUTES TO RESTORE THE CIRCULATION, AND REAPPLY PRESSURE. GO AT ONCE TO THE NEAREST HOSPITAL OR DOCTOR'S OFFICE.

If the patient becomes faint, have him lie down with the head lower than the body.

Tetanus shots. These were once recommended after any injury. Newer studies, however, show that if a patient has had a booster shot for tetanus within five years, he does not need one.

Bruises (*Hematomas*). Severe bruising may cause great pain. These may occur from a fall, bumping into an object—especially one with sharp edges or corners—or a blow. There is swelling and discoloration of the area either at once, or more commonly, within a few hours, depending on the depth of the injury. The discoloration is due to the breaking of small blood vessels inside the skin. If this is fairly extensive, the blood that leaks into the tissues will spread over a fairly large area. A blow about the eye will usually cause extensive swelling of the eyelid and blackening of the skin—hence the term *black eye*.

No Real Treatment. Given time and patience, bruises will disappear. Usually in the process, the discoloration becomes ugly greenish, bluish, and yellow, as the blood cells break down and are finally reabsorbed and excreted. There is no treatment for bruises. Cold packs immediately after a blow or bump or pressure over the area may reduce the bleeding into the tissues and cut down somewhat on swelling. After twenty-four (24) hours, warm packs may relieve pain and help reduce the swelling and discoloration a little bit faster.

Possible Complications. The only complications of any concern are related to infections that rarely occur at the site of the blow. *When a child bruises very easily and extensively from relatively minor bumps, you should let your doctor know.* He will probably order studies to rule out any possible disease of the blood cells and circulatory system.

Burns. Burns may be caused by heat, chemicals, or sun. They are classified in three groups—*first-, second-,* and *third-degree* burns.

Symptoms. A *first-degree burn* has redness of the skin and pain. The pain usually subsides in a few minutes to a few hours. The redness lasts from three to five days.

Second-degree burns are red and become blistered. This means the burn has damaged the outer layer of the skin and serum or fluid collects under it, pushing it out into the blisters. Pain is quite severe, and lasts longer than in first-degree burns.

Third-degree burns extend through the layers of the skin, damaging or destroying the oil and sweat glands as well as the nerve endings. The skin is seared and feels hard or crusted. After the first shock of extreme pain, there may be numbness, until the dead skin sloughs off. This will expose countless nerve ends in raw and tender flesh beneath the skin, and again there is excruciating pain.

First-degree burns from heat require no treatment except tenderness and a warning to prevent further burns by possible carelessness. Any soothing ointment will help the pain subside faster, we believe.

Second-degree burns, if they are smaller than a few square inches, may also be safely cared for without a doctor's attention. Be careful to gently apply a soothing, pain-relieving ointment.

Do *not* rub it in. A fairly loose dressing of gauze (to keep away air currents that add to the pain by moving the hairs in the tender skin, and to shut out germs) is wise. *Do not open the blisters.* The fluid in them is ideal food for bacteria, which can enter through even the smallest needle prick. If they should burst of their own accord, gently press out the fluid and apply an antibiotic ointment.

> **IF A SECOND-DEGREE BURN IS VERY LARGE AND SEVERELY PAINFUL, TAKE THE CHILD TO SEE YOUR PHYSICIAN. HE MAY NEED TO RECOMMEND SPECIAL CARE, OR EVEN A FEW DAYS IN A HOSPITAL. IF THE BURN HAS STARTED TO HEAL AND THEN TURNS RED, HOT, AND PAINFUL, YOU WILL NEED TO SEE YOUR DOCTOR TO DETERMINE IF THERE IS A SECONDARY INFECTION.**

> **THIRD-DEGREE BURNS, UNLESS THEY ARE VERY SMALL, SHOULD BE SEEN BY YOUR DOCTOR. VERY EXTENSIVE BURNS OF THIS TYPE OFTEN REQUIRE HOSPITAL CARE AND EVEN SKIN GRAFTING BY A PLASTIC SURGEON.**

Chemical burns. These should be treated as heat burns except for this action: *They should at once be flooded with cool water for as long as there is any chance of the chemical itself remaining on the skin.* If you know the chemical is an acid, dust the area of a first- or second-degree burn with baking soda. If the substance is known to be an alkali, vinegar may be poured over it. *When in doubt, use only water.*

Sunburn. First-degree sunburns are common and rarely cause trouble or serious pain. A good lotion to soothe and soften the outer layer of skin is enough treatment.

A second-degree sunburn, however, is much more painful. Marked redness, pain, and blistering, which is slow to develop, occurring over fairly large areas of skin, can produce an illness of some severity. Bed rest with moist packs or baking-soda baths may provide some relief.

The various "caine" medicines such as Surfacaine, Solarcaine, and so forth, may relieve pain, but an allergy to them is common. Hydrocortisone ointments, now available directly from your druggist, along with aspirin, are the best home treatment.

**IF THE CHILD REACTS WITH CHILLS, FEVER, AND VOMIT-
ING, CALL YOUR DOCTOR. HE MAY NEED TO GIVE ORAL
CORTISONE IN SOME FORM, AND STRONGER PAIN-RELIEV-
ING MEDICATIONS.**

**THIRD-DEGREE SUNBURNS ARE POSSIBLE BUT UNLIKELY.
IF IN DOUBT, SEE YOUR DOCTOR!**

Sun Poisoning. An interesting by-product of exposure to too
much sun is a condition sometimes called *sun poisoning.* The
sun, especially in an early exposure to a large amount of rays,
will stimulate secretion of oil and sweat in the skin glands. At
the same time, it may sear or dry the outer layer of skin (the
epidermis). This locks in those secretions, producing irritation
with severe itching. The skin feels bumpy and is dry. The best
treatment is a warm bath followed by a firm rub to remove dry
outer skin. Rub into the skin a good cream or cortisone-type
ointment to soften the epidermis and open the pores. This may
take several days to completely return to normal.

Prevention. Sunburns are best treated by prevention! Allow
children in direct sun only thirty minutes at a time (or even
less) until they have begun to tan. Use a good sunscreen lotion
or cream, that lets through the less harmful rays, until your
child has adjusted to the sun. Suntanning creams and lotions
contain a chemical that quite effectively screens out the more
harmful, burning rays. Our local pharmacist assures us that on
the label of such a preparation, there will be noted a percentage
figure citing the strength of that substance and its effectiveness
in preventing sunburn. If in doubt, ask your pharmacist.
Usually blond and red-haired children are fair-skinned and will
burn much more quickly than darker-complexioned children.
Be alert to your child's special needs and to risks and dangers of
all sorts, and you will save yourself, as well as your child, much
needless pain.

Finger and Toenail Injuries. You are most fortunate if you
have never had to deal with a child who has had a finger caught
in a car door, or in some way crushed a nail! These are severely
painful (though not dangerous) injuries. Teach your children to
check carefully for anyone's hands on a door frame before closing the door. And avoid being in such a hurry that you forget
that rule yourself!

When it happens, however, apply ice or cold water at once. If none is available, allow the child to put the finger in his mouth. The gentle pressure of his own tongue will be soothing. Usually nail-bed injuries cause blood to be released from the capillaries and collect under the nail, separating it from the flesh. After the first few minutes of intense, throbbing pain caused by the pressure under the nail, the pain eases somewhat and will disappear. If the bleeding is more severe, however, the pain will last for hours.

GO TO YOUR DOCTOR WITH SUCH A HURTING CHILD. HE WILL BE ABLE TO RELEASE THE PRESSURE WITH A SIMPLE PROCEDURE, AND DRAIN OUT THE BLOOD THAT HAS COLLECTED THERE. HE WILL BANDAGE IT TO PREVENT INFECTION, AND YOU WILL NEED ONLY TO WAIT FOR THE NEW NAIL TO GROW.

As the injured nail grows out, keep it trimmed, and watch for the separated part to approach the end of the nail bed. It will be loose and may catch on clothing, tearing the still-attached part a bit. To avoid that pain, trim the injured end with a nail scissors. The new nail will be ready to protect the fingertip very soon. A few days with a little Band-Aid will be helpful.

THE MUSCULOSKELETAL SYSTEM
(Bones, Tendons, and Muscles)

Introduction

The bones make up the skeleton or framework that supports and gives strength to the body. They are composed of a *protein matrix,* in which minerals (notably calcium and phosphorus) are deposited. At the ends of the long bones there is a special area called the *epiphysis,* which allows for your child to grow. At the latter stage of adolescence, these close or harden so growth stops. In girls, the growth usually slows down or stops a few years earlier than in boys.

In the center of the bones, the *marrow* exists. It is softer than the rest of the bone and contains many blood vessels. Some of the circulating blood cells are formed in the bone marrow.

Cartilage is essentially soft bone that has not been hardened by the deposit of minerals. The lower ribs, the nose, and some parts of the bones in the hands and feet are cartilage early in a child's life, though they "calcify" and harden later on. The nice thing about this little miracle of divine planning is that children suffer less fractures or damage due to these softer tissues. Almost every child, for example, gets a finger caught in a door at sometime. Yet very rarely, if ever, have we seen such a finger's bones broken before early adolescence.

The *muscles* are made up of protein and a great number of blood vessels. They are attached to each other and to bones by ligaments and tendons, which are smooth, very tough tissues. The tendons and ligaments help hold the bones together, as well as attaching the muscles to the bones.

Infections in the Bones and Muscles

Infections in the bones were once the dread of every physician. If patients recovered at all, they were often left with severe deformities. With the advent of antibiotics, however, bone infections are almost unheard of and are almost always cured completely.

Osteomyelitis. This is an infection of a bone. It may follow an injury, even a fairly minor one, such as a bruise; or it may occur without any known cause. The most common culprit in causing it is a staphylococcus germ commonly called *staph.* This bacterium apparently can get into the bloodstream through the nose, where it often lives quite harmlessly, or throat, and then becomes lodged in a bone.

Symptoms. The symptoms of osteomyelitis are these: 1) fever that comes and goes, usually spiking up to high levels of 103 degrees F. or more; 2) a general sense of fatigue, weakness, and feeling sick; 3) pain over the infected bone—though this is not always true. Laboratory tests give very special information and X rays usually reveal the infected area of a bone.

Treatment. This illness used to be severely crippling, but in today's world, a cure is highly likely!

THE CHILD WITH OSTEOMYELITIS NEEDS TO BE IN A HOSPITAL. COMPLETE REST, SPECIFIC ANTIBIOTICS, AND CAREFUL WATCHING ARE POSSIBLE ONLY IN SUCH A SPECIAL SETTING.

Treatment specifically includes: 1) making the affected bone absolutely immobile, as well as keeping the body at rest in bed; 2) giving an antibiotic that is specifically tested to prove its effectiveness against this particular germ. This may need to be given, in a solution of fluids, directly into a vein, in order to ensure that it reaches the infected area in a degree of strength that will really be curative; 3) good diet containing nourishing foods, vitamins, and minerals to encourage healing of the bone; 4) careful reevaluation of the infected bone to be sure it is completely well. If healing is not complete, the infection may flare up, and the germ may then be able to resist the antibiotic, making healing much more difficult.

As in all serious illnesses, you need to trust your doctor and follow his recommendations. If this is impossible with one, do ask for a consultant, or even change doctors.

Bone Cancer. This is rare in children, but it deserves mentioning. Sometimes such a disease is first discovered through a fracture that is the result of a very minor injury, or even without an injury. It may show up as an area of constant pain, and at times it is evidenced through swelling in the bone.

Tumors of the bone almost always require extensive surgery, but this may cure the disease and save a young person's life. *If your child shows any of the above symptoms, be certain that he sees a qualified specialist for treatment without delay. Your family doctor is the best source of such a referral.*

Myositis. This is an inflammation or infection of a muscle. Perhaps because of the extremely good blood supply to carry away infection-causing substances, muscular infections are extremely rare.

Symptoms. Occasionally, however, viruses attack one or more muscles, causing severe pain. The most common site for this is in the neck. Nearly every child will awaken some morning with boardlike stiffness and severe pain when he tries even to move the neck. This is called *wryneck* or *torticollis.* It is probably caused by a virus, and often has tender lymph nodes associated with it.

Treatment. The treatment usually includes tender, loving care. A heating pad, gentle massage, and pain-relieving medication are helpful in tiding the child through this truly uncomfortable problem. It rarely lasts more than two days with any severity. We have never seen any serious complications.

Injuries to the Bones and Muscles

Sprains. A sudden twist or turn of a joint may cause a jerk of a ligament (which attaches two bones together), or a tendon (which attaches a muscle to a bone). This snap stretches that tissue suddenly, causing intense pain. Furthermore, such an accident ruptures small blood vessels, allowing blood to escape into the tissues. This causes swelling and discoloration, like a bruise.

Treatment. Cold or ice-water packs to the injured area at once will help stop the swelling and relieve the pain. Most doctors still recommend applying an elastic wrap or taping the sprained joint (usually an ankle) to partially immobilize it and give it support. The pain will automatically limit its motion for some time. After the first twenty-four (24) hours, warm packs or a heating pad may be applied. Such heat probably cannot penetrate deeply enough to increase healing, but it feels better.

Possible Broken Bone. If there is any question about the extent of the injury, *take your child to your doctor.* He may be able to verify that it is, indeed, a sprain. There is a possibility, however, that a bone may be broken, and an X ray will tell you that. Signs that will guide you are these: 1) localized pain or tenderness over a bone and inability to bear weight or move the injured part (a sprain may have pain, but it is more generalized and not so severe); 2) deformity of the injured part; 3) the swelling lasts longer and may be more extensive than a sprain. A small crack in a bone, however, may show none of the above signs, except a deeper and more lasting pain. Yet that small crack could become a major fracture with any additional stress. *So do not hesitate to get your doctor's opinion and an X ray.*

Baseball Finger. A common injury to the fingers is caused by a blow against the end of a finger. Since this often occurs in attempting to catch a baseball, it is called a *baseball finger*. The blow pushes the bones of the finger against each other causing some bruising, swelling, and severe pain in the joints or knuckles. A small splint will relieve the pain and help such an injury to heal. You may devise your own splint from a popsicle stick, a cotton ball to pad it, and some tape to hold it in place. The pain will subside in a few days. If it does not, or if there is any doubt at all, please see your physician. At times a bone may be chipped, and will require X rays and special treatment.

Dislocations. A severe jerk or pull on a bone may cause it to be separated from another and pulled out of position at a joint. A common place for this to happen is at the shoulder, or sometimes the elbow. There is severe pain and inability to move the extremity at that joint. *This always needs to be seen by a doctor.*

Treatment. After a dislocation, some degree of immobilization is necesary for a week or two. A sling or elastic bandage usually is adequate. Just as in a sprain, the ligaments and tendons are stretched. Immobilizing them allows them to heal so the stretching does not become permanent, allowing further dislocations to happen more easily.

Fractures. Simple fractures or breaks in a bone are common in active children. The most usual areas are the wrist and forearm, the collarbone, and the ankle. Usually there is some deformity, always severe pain, and some degree of swelling around the injured area.

> WHEN THE ABOVE SYMPTOMS ARE PRESENT, TAKE YOUR CHILD TO YOUR DOCTOR. IT IS WISE TO MAKE A SPLINT OUT OF A SMALL BOARD OR STICK, PADDED WITH A TOWEL. TIE THIS WITH STRIPS OF CLOTH, ABOVE AND BELOW THE INJURED AREA OF THE CHILD'S INJURED EXTREMITY.

Most fractures of this simple type can be treated in a doctor's office and put in a special brace or a plaster cast. In children, you may expect healing of a small fracture in three to four weeks. A larger one may be kept in a cast from six weeks to three months.

Compound fractures are more severe than the simple ones. In these, the bone is dislocated and the jagged ends have cut through the skin. The dangers here include the likelihood of infection and injury to large blood vessels or nerves. For such a fracture, cover the area with sterile gauze, or even a clean cloth, if the accident takes place in an area where dust could blow into the wound. Do not, however, lay a dirty cloth over the wound.

CALL FOR EXPERT HELP IF THIS SORT OF FRACTURE OCCURS IN A LARGE BONE, THE SKULL, OR THE SPINE. IN THE FOREARM OR LOWER LEG, IF SUCH HELP IS NOT READILY AVAILABLE, MAKE A SPLINT OUT OF STICKS, PADDED WITH ARTICLES OF CLOTHING, TOWELS, OR WHATEVER YOU HAVE. TIE THE LIMB ABOVE AND BELOW THE INJURY TO THE SPLINT, AND CAREFULLY PLACE THE CHILD IN THE BACKSEAT OF A CAR, WITH THE LIMB ELEVATED, AND GET TO THE NEAREST HOSPITAL. IF THERE IS EXTENSIVE BLEEDING, APPLY PRESSURE ABOVE THE AREA, BUT DO NOT TOUCH THE BROKEN SKIN, UNLESS YOU HAVE TO. IN MORE SEVERE INJURIES, ESPECIALLY NEAR THE SPINAL CORD OR BRAIN, IT IS SAFER TO WAIT FOR HELP THAN TO RISK AGGRAVATING SUCH AN INJURY. COMPOUND FRACTURES, AND MANY THAT ARE DISLOCATED, REQUIRE HOSPITAL CARE. YOUR DOCTOR WILL NEED TO DETERMINE IF SUCH CARE IS NECESSARY AND FOR HOW LONG.

Injuries to Muscles. Any sprain, dislocation, or fracture will also involve pulling or bruising of muscles. Sometimes, however, through overuse or a blow to the area, a muscle may be damaged independently of other injuries. Injury to a muscle is evidenced through pain and weakness. While there may be swelling, it is hard to diagnose unless it is extreme.

Another problem with pain in the muscles is what we call the *overuse syndrome.* A dramatic example is the young person who has been relatively inactive and then starts training for track or football. After the first day, the youth may suffer such intense muscular pain that he is incapacitated. Such reactions may be milder and more localized from less obvious overuse. But the cause is similar. It is not dangerous.

Treatment. The only treatment is aspirin, warm baths or showers, and rest. Young people should be encouraged to work out slowly in training for a sport. They need to exercise every day in order to keep their bodies healthy and their muscles in shape.

Charley horse is a common sports term for localized spasm of parts of a muscle. No one knows why only an area is involved, but any coach or physical-education instructor is familiar with the problem. The usual treatment involves rest, massage, and sometimes splinting with an elastic wrap.

Tennis elbow is rare in children, but may occur in adolescents. It is an irritation of the tendons of the elbow or, occasionally, the wrist. From overuse or repeated sprains, that tendon becomes inflamed and painful. The pain radiates down the arm and into the little and ring fingers. Usually rest is sufficient treatment. It is important to teach your child to relax the muscles of the affected arm completely, as often as possible, in order to gain the needed rest. A snug elastic wrap may relieve the stress about the affected area. Rarely special medication may be given by your physician.

Ganglion cyst is commonly found on the inside of the wrist. This cyst is only mildly painful. For reasons no one knows, a tendon in the wrist may become slightly swollen and tender. It is probably due to overuse or a minor injury that causes swelling in the sheath or covering of a tendon. The fluid that produces the swelling stays localized in the cystic area. With time and rest, some of these cysts sometimes disappear. A sudden sharp blow, as with the edge of a heavy book, may break the cyst though it might reform.

Rarely, such a cyst may become large enough to cause pressure and pain that are so severe it warrants surgical correction. This is surprisingly technical surgery, and a poor result can cause limited movement of a child's wrist. So we suggest postponing surgery as long as possible. If it must be done, seek a surgeon who is skilled in this type of work. Your family doctor or pediatrician can safely recommend someone to you.

Severe Muscle Cramps. Part of a muscle may suddenly go into a cramp. It becomes excruciatingly painful and cannot be made to stop at will, as can most muscular motions. The treatment of a sports trainer is to massage the area, and with the side of the hand, strike a firm blow to it. Often this breaks the spasm and relaxes the muscles. Sometimes a splint or firm taping of the area prevents a recurrence of this painful condition.

Deep Cuts. Injury to muscles may include *deep cuts*. When this happens extensively to the substance of the muscle itself, it may need to be repaired surgically. A tough layer called a *muscle sheath* encases each muscle. If it is torn or cut, it may need repairing to keep the muscle in functioning condition.

A cut to the hands or feet or any joint may involve the severing of a tendon. Tendons may, of course, be cut elsewhere, but hands and feet are most commonly injured in this way. This will stop normal functioning of that muscle.

**IF ANY CUT RESULTS IN LOSS OF A SPECIFIC AREA OF MO-
TION, BE SURE TO SEE YOUR DOCTOR AT ONCE. WAITING
MAKES REPAIR MUCH HARDER.**

Growing Pains. Growing pains are an age-old diagnosis made
by parents as well as doctors. During growth spurts of early
grade-school years and at adolescence, aches and pains of intense proportions may occur. These are severe enough to
awaken a child at night. Nothing can be seen on X ray or physical examination, and it is tempting to accuse a child of making
up the pain to get attention.

We both believe, however, that this pain is real. It may be related to the rapid growth and stretching of the bones themselves or the ligaments that attach the muscles to the bones.
Perhaps it is something we haven't yet thought of. At any rate,
you need to treat it as you would any other pain—with empathy
and encouragement, but not pity or overreaction.

Rubbing the aches gently, giving aspirin, a heating pad, and
your tender, loving care will usually restore some comfort and
sleep. It is always useful to teach a child to be a bit stoic with
this sort of pain. (*See* the section on Grief in chapter 16.)

Growing pains are not to be confused with rheumatic fever. In
the latter, there is redness, pain, and swelling in various joints;
there is a low-grade fever, and laboratory tests are abnormal.
None of these are true in the growing-pains syndrome. Please
do not take a chance, however, by diagnosing this by yourself.
Ask your doctor!

THE ENDOCRINE SYSTEM (Pituitary, Thyroid, Adrenal, Ovaries, Testes)

The hormonal system has the extremely important function
of regulating the growth and development of your child's body.
There is an amazingly intricate interaction of the brain, the pituitary gland, the thyroid gland, the adrenal glands, ovaries,
and testes. We do not know much about the thymus and pineal
glands but they, too, have their input into this complex system.

Pituitary Gland

This affects the growth of your child. Too little causes dwarf-
ism, which may be mild or severe. Too much of the growth hormone causes giantism and, eventually, deformities associated

with that. Along with nearby parts of the brain, it has an effect on salt and water metabolism.

Diabetes Insipidus. This problem, due to malfunction of the pituitary gland, can affect young children though it is rare. In this disease there is a lack of certain hormones that help the body preserve water. Far too much water is poured out through the kidneys, resulting in extreme thirst and the drinking of a great quantity of water. The resulting loss of salt and potassium may create a biochemical problem, so this illness requires expert care. It can be treated with drops of *pituitrin* (a hormone from the pituitary gland). Evaluating this complex illness will probably require the consultation of a specialist, called an endocrinologist.

Thyroid Gland

Thyroid hormones keep your child's body functioning appropriately at its own metabolic rate. It helps burn the body's fuel in a regular fashion, supplying energy and helping maintain the healthy functioning of the body. The thyroid gland may become infected with various bacteria. Such an infection will cause swelling and pain over the gland, fever, and abnormal laboratory findings. Antibiotic treatment will cure this in a few days.

Viral Infections of the Thyroid. These, on the other hand, may last for weeks or months and tend to reappear. The use of cortisone (or similar substances) will often cause improvement, but when it is stopped, the infection may return. Viral thyroiditis may occur after mumps but several viruses have been cultured from such infections. Eventually thyroid infections do go away and rarely, if ever, is there a serious complication.

> THE SYMPTOMS ARE PAIN AND SWELLING OVER THE FRONT, CENTER AREA OF THE NECK. THERE MAY BE FEVER AND SORE THROAT, PAIN WITH SWALLOWING, AND ENLARGED, TENDER LYMPH NODES. IF YOUR CHILD HAS SUCH SYMPTOMS, BE SURE TO SEE YOUR DOCTOR.

Goiter. This is an enlarged thyroid. The thyroid enlarges in an attempt to supply enough hormones. Mild enlargement is present in most adolescent girls and some boys. In parts of the country where there is a lack of iodine in the food, such swelling can become huge, disfiguring, and uncomfortable. The use of iodized salt has nearly eliminated this once-common problem. Large goiters may have to be removed surgically once they occur.

Symptoms. Too much thyroid output can cause rapid heart rate, weight loss, and trembling. A sense of nervousness and apprehension are common.

If your child has any of these symptoms, be sure to see your doctor. The imbalance in thyroid hormones can seriously affect your child's health. Yet this can be easily diagnosed and treated by your physician.

Adrenal Glands

The *adrenal glands* have a great deal to do with the way your child's body handles stress. When he is afraid, special secretions from these glands make his heart beat fast, his breathing speed up, and his muscles become tense. This prepares him to fight or run for his life. Other secretions help fight off or control various illnesses. Still another helps regulate the blood pressure.

Any infection or tumor of the adrenal glands is so rare in children or adolescents that we feel you needn't consider them. If such a condition arises, your doctor will recognize it.

Ovaries and Testes

The ovaries and testes produce estrogen and testosterone at the time of puberty. These sex hormones produce the various characteristics of femaleness and maleness. (*See* chapter 15 on Adolescence.)

Birth defects involving these glands are discussed in chapter 7, "The Next Two Years of Life." In the case of mumps, boys may have an infection of the testicles that can seriously damage or destroy these glands. (*See* Viral Infections earlier in this chapter.)

THE DIGESTIVE SYSTEM (Stomach, Intestinal Tract, and Digestive Organs)

How It Works

This part of the body is extremely complex, but we will outline it for you simply. The digestion of food begins with the mouth, tongue, teeth, and salivary glands. The teeth and tongue begin to mechanically break up the food, and an enzyme in the saliva, called *ptyalin,* helps to digest the starches and sugars in the food. It continues with the swallowing reflex, which goes into effect when the food reaches the back of the tongue and throat. This automatic reaction pushes the food down a tube that extends from the throat, through the chest into the upper end of the stomach in the abdomen. This tube is called the *esophagus,* and its muscular walls contract in waves that get the food into the upper stomach. A valve opens to admit the food, and closes to keep it in the stomach. The only time that valve reverses its action is in case of a vomiting episode.

Once in the stomach, food is mechanically squeezed to break it up still more than the mouth and teeth already have. It also is acted upon by the secretions from the stomach, acid and enzymes, to make it ready to pass on into the intestinal tract.

Food passes out of the stomach through another valve that shuts to prevent the contents of the intestines from getting back into the stomach. The presence of partly digested food in the intestines prompts the emptying of bile and other chemicals from the liver, and insulin (along with other substances) from the pancreas into the small intestines. These chemicals finish the digestive process by making the changes that enable the food to be absorbed into the tissues to supply energy and the building blocks of tissues for the growing child.

Parts of food that are eaten are not digestible, and these pass on into the large intestine, where they eventually are eliminated in the bowel movement.

Here are some of the common illnesses that affect the digestive system.

Infections of Mouth

Herpangina. This infection is in the back part of the mouth and throat, caused by one of several herpes viruses.

Symptoms. There are many small, bright-red spots that become ulcerated, scattered over the soft palate, tonsils, and entire back of throat. There is severe pain, so that eating and drinking are difficult. There may be one or two degrees of fever, but rarely is it high unless the body's fluid level gets low, due to difficulty in

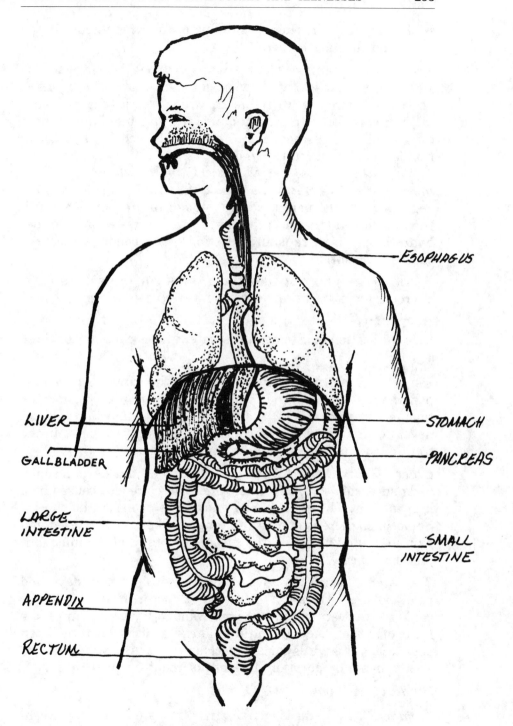

DIGESTIVE SYSTEM

swallowing. Usually there is swelling of the lymph nodes in the neck, and they are tender.

Treatment. Treatment of herpangina includes mouthwash, gargles, and pain-relieving chewing gums or swabs. Since this is caused by a virus, there are no known antibiotics that will cure it. Therefore, keep your child quiet, and give him liquids and a bland diet until his body can (and it will!) recover. This infection lasts about seven to ten days.

While there is no specific prescription available, a visit to the doctor's office may be advisable if: 1) the fever goes over 101 degrees F.; 2) the pain is severe enough to prevent sleep; 3) if the mouth gets dry and urination slows down—warning of dehydration; 4) if there is any question of a secondary infection, such as tonsillitis.

> **THE POSSIBILITY OF DEHYDRATION IS THE ONLY REASON TO HIT THE PANIC BUTTON AND GO TO THE EMERGENCY ROOM.**

(*See* the section on Stomach Flu, later in this chapter, for these signs.)

Herpetic Stomatitis. This is caused by the same virus as herpangina but it affects the front of the mouth, the lips, and the tongue. No one knows why these two similar infections almost never occur at the same time, or why one child is infected in the front of the mouth and another in the throat.

Other Herpes-Caused Infections. Everyone has an occasional fever sore, cold sore, or canker sore. These are also caused by a herpes virus. They are usually on the lips or inside the cheeks. Sometimes there is one on the tongue. They are scattered and painful, but do not cause the severe symptoms of the infections just described.

Treatment. Usually these sores heal within a few days and rarely, if ever, warrant a visit to your doctor. If your child has canker sores very often, you may want to try giving him some form of a lactobacillus culture. These healthy bacteria often counteract this virus and help clear it up. Ask your druggist about such a preparation. It does not require a prescription.

Stomach Ailments

Stomach "Flu." This is characterized by pain in the upper center of the stomach, usually with loss of appetite, nausea, and vomiting. It is usually limited to a few hours up to twenty-four hours. Pain that is sharp or dull may come and go. Similar symptoms may affect other family members to one degree or another.

Other Symptoms. There is often lower abdominal pain—griping or cramping in nature. It is not localized and comes and goes over several hours or days. It is common for diarrhea to accompany the pain. It may be severe for a few hours or even for a day or two.

Treatment of Stomach Flu

1. Withhold food for either vomiting or diarrhea as they are described above.

2. For vomiting, give Coca Cola syrup (obtainable from most drugstores), one teaspoon every fifteen minutes for four doses, and one teaspoon every three to four hours if nausea and vomiting continue. For one- to two-year olds, give one-half teaspoon. Under one year, give one-quarter teaspoon.

3. For lower intestinal cramping and diarrhea, give Kaopectate or a similar preparation—one tablespoon after each bowel movement up to six doses per day. Under one year, one teaspoon is enough. Preparations with paregoric should be given with caution and *only* on the advice of your doctor.

4. Start clear liquids (such as weak tea), carbonated beverages (such as ginger ale, 7-Up, and so forth), fruit-flavored gelatin or bouillon—in small sips. More than an ounce at a time may result in more vomiting. Gradually increase the amount as it is tolerated.

If improvement does not occur in twelve to twenty-four hours, call your physician's office. He may add a prescription in the form of a rectal suppository or medication to stop stubborn vomiting and to slow the diarrhea, or he may need to see the child.

IF THE CHILD HAS FEVER OF 100 DEGREES F. OR OVER, STOPS URINATING, APPEARS VERY LISTLESS; IF THE MOUTH AND TONGUE BECOME DRY OR THE EYES LOOK A BIT "SUNKEN," INSIST THAT HE BE SEEN BY YOUR DOCTOR OR IN AN EMERGENCY ROOM.

This indicates possible dehydration and may necessitate hospital care. Your doctor will need to know how many times the child has vomited, how many bowel movements he has had, and about how much fluid your child has kept down within the past eight or twelve hours. *Try to keep an estimate of this information,* if your child has very severe vomiting or diarrhea.

Food Poisoning. Stomach flu is not related to eating a certain food. *Food poisoning,* however, which causes symptoms like the flu, attacks most of the people who have eaten a contaminated food at one time or within a few hours of each other. Food poisoning usually begins within eight to fourteen hours after eating and lasts thirty-six to seventy-two hours.

Food poisoning resembles stomach flu in its symptoms of severe vomiting and diarrhea. Rather than a virus, however, the cause is bacteria which have contaminated foods. The symptoms usually affect all of the people who have eaten the spoiled food, and such symptoms begin within a few hours after the food is consumed. The symptoms are often severe for a few hours but may last a day or two. It is not uncommon for food poisoning to require hospitalization for the dehydration that ensues.

Treatment for Food Poisoning. In milder cases the treatment is essentially like that for stomach flu. It is wise, however, to allow the stomach and intestinal tract to be emptied before giving medication or liquids, in order to rid the body of the bacteria and their toxic substances.

Stomachaches of Questionable or Undetermined Origin. Gas in the intestinal tract may cause pain, if a large enough bubble collects to cause ballooning or stretching of a small section of the intestine. This is short-lived, and gentle pressure or massage removes it. While the child does feel pain she does not feel or act sick, and no treatment is needed.

Overeating is a possibility in considering stomachaches. Occasionally children will go on an eating binge. A fruit tree in the neighborhood can invite a "gorging" bout; or sometimes a bag of cookies or candy can become a temptation too big to resist. Overindulging in a delectable food can cause such stretching of the walls of the stomach that severe pain results. This is better prevented than treated, but usually patience and gently rubbing the upper abdomen will relieve the pain. Occasionally, a child may vomit which, of course, rapidly relieves the distension and the pain.

Some emotional problems are accompanied by habits of overeating. If your child is sneaking food, nibbling incessantly, and gaining weight too fast, you need to investigate the cause. In our experience, children who overeat are lonely, worried, and need more affection and fun. If you cannot discover the underlying needs and troubled feelings, do consult a child psychologist. An evaluation early on, *before* the eating habits become entrenched, can prevent this compounded problem from getting out of hand.

Tension stomachaches are characterized by their association with anxiety-producing situations. In a tense, anxious child, just facing a day of school may cause this discomfort. These pains are usually vague, but the child may localize them in the upper-center of the abdomen. The feeling may be similar to the tight, knotlike feeling adults experience in the pit of the stomach under stress. This pain is not necessarily imaginary or "made up"—there often is real pain. A child may, however, be using it as an excuse. Try to differentiate real pain (even that produced by anxiety) from manipulative techniques that are clearly contrived. Do not allow a child's dishonesty to gain him a day off!

Intestinal Parasites. These usually produce no symptoms, but at times they may cause vague stomach distress. Tapeworms and pinworms are the most common parasites and are caught from other children, or possibly pets. While most parents are horrified at them, they are common, curable, and need cause no worry.

Pinworms are tiny (about one-quarter inch long) threadlike worms that are white, movable, and reproduce in the large bowel (or colon). They are spread from child to child by the "anal-oral route." A child who has these complains of itching about the rectum, and inevitably scratches—especially at night, when these tiny creatures move to the rectum and lay their eggs. The eggs become embedded under the nails, and later rub off on toys, other children's skin, and any item touched. From here they readily get into the mouth, the intestines, and set up a new infection—in the same child or other children.

Parents are always horrified by finding worms in a child's stool. There is certainly no shame in a child's having pinworms, but it is a shame to neglect the necessary treatment and cure.

Symptoms. If you see these creatures moving about in a freshly voided bowel movement, or see them in the rectal area at night when your child awakens itching, you will know that you need to call your doctor. *Now this does not demand a night call, since he cannot treat your child until the pharmacy opens. It is not an emergency. Your doctor gets many night calls that are emergencies, so let him sleep, and call his office the next day.*

Treatment. Meanwhile, sit your child in warm water to soothe the skin, apply petroleum jelly to protect him, and go back to sleep. Your doctor will probably call in a prescription that usually involves one dose at once and a repeat dose in one week to get rid of any reinfections. The entire family and any closely involved friends need to be treated at the same time to prevent reinfecting each other. Disinfect the underwear, linens, and toys. Cut the child's nails to decrease harboring of the eggs. Check the stool periodically for three to four weeks, and then forget it.

If you suspect pinworms but can't find them, call your doctor. He can do special tests that will enable him to reassure you one way or another.

Roundworms are large, long worms that fortunately are not common, because they produce surprise and horror when seen by a child or his parents. These are caught, like pinworms, from other people or, rarely, from animals. *They are unmistakable, and a phone call to your doctor will usually be all that is required to get a cure on the way through a prescription.*

While worms are not an emergency, they do need curing since they rob their victim of necessary food elements and result in anemias and weight losses.

Tapeworms are flat, segmented, intestinal parasites that are excreted through the intestinal tract in sections about one-half inch long and slightly wider. The worms that remain inside consume a large amount of food and may cause weight loss in the child. If your child eats a great deal, does not grow and gain weight in proportion, and is pale and listless, you need to suspect some form of intestinal parasites. If your own inspection does not reveal these creatures in the child's bowel movement, call your doctor. He will ask for a stool specimen and have it examined in a laboratory.

Stomach Ulcers. While common in adults, stomach ulcers are rare in children. When present, these are characterized by burning pain in the pit of the stomach that is relieved by milk and other bland foods, and made worse by spicy, fried, fatty, or greasy foods.

If you suspect such a problem, do call your doctor. He may prescribe medication and a diet to help decide whether or not the child needs X-ray studies.

IF, HOWEVER, THE PAIN IS *NOT* RELIEVED, OR IF THE CHILD VOMITS BLOOD OR PASSES STOOLS THAT ARE STICKY LOOKING AND BLACK, THE CHILD MUST BE SEEN EVEN IF IT MEANS EMERGENCY-ROOM CARE.

Other Digestive Problems

Acute Viral Hepatitis (*Infectious Hepatitis*). This is an infection that for no known reason "settles" in or attacks the patient's liver. It is caused by a virus and comes on slowly and quietly.

Symptoms. The symptoms that first warn us of this illness are 1) some nonspecific gastrointestinal symptoms, such as loss of appetite, nausea and vomiting, or some constitutional symptoms, such as fatigue and weakness. 2) Dark-brown urine is often an early sign and usually occurs before any sign of jaundice of the skin. Yellow tinge to the whites of the eyes may be the first sign of an impending jaundice. However, many patients with hepatitis may not develop jaundice. 3) The bowel movements may become very light in color, described as a "clay-colored stool." 4) Itching skin may accompany the jaundice. 5) Joint aching and pain sometimes occur. 6) The liver (in the upper right area of the abdomen) usually enlarges somewhat and becomes tender.

Bile. These symptoms come from the fact that the infection keeps the liver from accomplishing its usual duties, one of which is the putting out of a dark-green fluid called *bile*. This collects in a sac outside the liver through a system of bile ducts, and is emptied into the small intestine as it is needed to help digest foods—especially fats. The bile, therefore, backs up into the bloodstream and collects in the tissues, or is put out through the urinary system.

Diagnosis. This is made by the above symptoms plus very accurate laboratory tests. We have very sensitive blood tests to determine the type of hepatitis. There are three types of this disease. The *first* is caused by *Type A Virus* and occurs most commonly by the fecal-oral route. *Type B Virus* and *Type Non-*

A, Non-B Virus are spread by needle stick or mucosal injury. Your doctor will determine the type and will advise you about it.

Treatment. Be sure to see your doctor at the very first hint of jaundice (the yellowish color of skin, or the other symptoms listed above). This is not an emergency, but the earlier it is diagnosed, the more probable it will be curable. Your doctor will tell you: *Keep the child very quiet*—rest reduces the stress and enables the body's energy to focus on healing. *Avoid all fats in the diet*—the body cannot digest them, and they make demands on the sick liver that it cannot perform anyway. Protein and carbohydrates are okay. Usually extra vitamins are given to help the liver to be nourished and offer it every chance to recover.

Laboratory tests will be taken as often as your doctor believes necessary to be sure recovery is complete.

You will know that your child is recovering by improved skin color, and the return to normal color of urine and bowel movements. As the child improves, it becomes increasingly difficult to keep him quiet, yet this is really important in complete recovery.

Contagion. This disease is contagious through the fecal (bowel) material. To prevent its spread, those who attend to bowel disposal, wiping the rectum, and so forth, need to wash hands very carefully, and sterilize a bedpan or clothing that may be soiled. It is possible that several members of a family will be sick with this in succession.

Prevention. There is now a highly successful means of preventing the spread of this illness. If your family has been exposed, your doctor may want to give them injections of gamma globulin. The danger of this illness is in leaving a damaged liver that may impair a person's health permanently.

Constipation. This is a condition of the bowels in which the stools become firmer, larger, and harder to move than normal. Rarely is this serious in a child, but many parents worry about it excessively. We tell parents not to worry unless the child goes beyond four days without a movement. It is extremely rare to have a parent call back. You need to understand that bowel habits vary from one person to another. Some people have a movement after every meal. Others have one only every second or third day. Get to know your child and his natural functions.

Constipation can usually be prevented by balancing a child's diet. Breast-fed infants absorb so much milk that very little needs to be excreted. Be sure, however, that breast-fed infants are given some water. Formula-fed babies can easily have their bowel movements made softer or firmer by increasing or decreasing the richness of the formula with water.

Solid Foods and Constipation. As your baby starts on solid foods, you may not realize that he is getting too little fluid. He may become constipated from this, so be sure to offer him water as well as milk from time to time.

When your baby starts on strained or solid foods, balance the proteins with some roughage foods, such as green vegetables and fruits. Applesauce and bananas are excellent "normalizers," helping the stools to be formed but not hard. Use good common sense and avoid worry. Constipation need rarely if ever be a problem.

On those rare occasions when your child does have a problem, your doctor, or even your druggist, will tell you about a laxative that is mild enough for your child. Use it only rarely, so your child will not become dependent on it.

Hirschsprung's Disease. In a very rare situation, a child, from birth, goes a number of days without moving his bowels. He then passes a very large stool or requires an enema to have one at all. If this is true of your child, you need to consult your doctor. Such a child may have Hirschsprung's disease. In this very rare case, the nerves that supply the lower colon and rectum are not normal, and the usual reflex to empty the bowels does not take place. Surgical procedures can correct this in most cases. This needs to be done as early as possible to prevent extreme stretching of the walls of the large bowel.

Gastrointestinal Bleeding. Bleeding from the gastrointestinal tract in children is not a very common problem. Occasionally, if a child has had a lot of vomiting, there can be some blood-tinged material in the vomitus itself. However, this is the result only of the severe irritation of the gastric mucosa, and should not cause any undue alarm. *If a child has gastrointestinal bleeding, causing black, tarry stools, then the cause of that bleeding must certainly be investigated.* This obviously would have to be done by your physician, and X-ray studies would probably be necessary.

Occasionally a child will have some bright-red blood in the stool from bleeding in the lower portion of the colon. This can be the result of a little ruptured hemorrhoid inside the rectum, or less commonly, from a polyp which exists in the lower intestinal tract. *Any type of bleeding, even though it is bright-red, should certainly be checked with your physician if it reoccurs.*

Gallbladder Disease. Gallbladder disease is a very uncommon illness in children. We have seen gallstones in children at age twelve requiring surgery, and cases have been reported as early as age nine, but this is unusual. The history of gallbladder disease in children is not unlike that of adults. There is pain in the right upper quadrant of the abdomen, just below the rib cage. There may be, prior to such problems, a history of indigestion and some intolerance for certain foods, such as those which are highly seasoned, fried, fatty, or greasy. Family history of gallbladder disease is also important. The diagnosis of gallbladder disease and gallstones can only be established with certainty by X-ray study.

Poisons. Injuries to abdominal organs are discussed in the section on Heart and Blood Vessels, later in this chapter. Of primary concern in the stomach and intestinal tract is the possibility of swallowing poisons. We will discuss this under three headings: *medicines, caustic chemicals,* and *aromatic chemicals.*

First, medicines. Children are extremely curious and will put anything into their mouths to see how it tastes. When medications are left in places accessible to children, be sure they will find them and try them out! Even the new so-called child-proof bottles that defeat us adults, are quite easily opened by the strong jaws of a child. Keep them out of reach, and teach every child in your house they are *off limits.*

Treatment. If, despite your best precautions, a child gets into your medicines, *make him vomit at once.* Some authorities recommend syrup of ipecac for every medicine cabinet. It is a powerful emetic, and in one or two tablespoon doses will make the most stubborn child vomit. We do not personally feel comfortable with ipecac. Sometimes, a length of time may have gone by since the child took the forbidden medicine, and too much of it may have been absorbed. By giving an emetic, you may have a false sense of security. If you do use it, be sure, at least, to call your doctor and get his advice on further treatment or observations that are needed.

Further Measures for Removing Poisons. Other time-honored measures that may induce vomiting include sticking a finger or smooth, blunt object down the throat to initiate reflex gagging. A slightly beaten raw egg or a teaspoon of powdered mustard from your spice shelf in a little warm water may cause vomiting. It has been our experience, however, that such methods often fail, and valuable time is wasted in the efforts to employ them.

If you cannot get the child to vomit enough to thoroughly empty the stomach within ten or fifteen minutes, take him at once to the nearest doctor or hospital. Take along the bottle from which he took medicine, and some estimate of how much he swallowed. The doctor will usually insert a rubber tube through the child's nose, draw out the contents of the stomach, and wash it out with a sterile solution. He will tell you what to look for in the next few hours, and probably will lecture you about keeping medicines away from children! Do listen to him.

Second, caustic chemicals. These include all or most of the materials in your laundry room, kitchen sink, and workshop.

Household ammonia, drain and oven cleaners, bleaches, acids of any kind, and detergents all contain poisons that could kill your child. These chemicals burn the tender tissues of a child's throat, and hence you will only aggravate the irritation if you try to get the child to vomit them.

FOR SUCH POISON INGESTION, RUSH THE CHILD AT ONCE TO YOUR DOCTOR'S OFFICE OR THE NEAREST EMERGENCY ROOM. TRAINED MEDICAL STAFF WILL WASH OUT THE CHEMICAL AND INSTRUCT YOU REGARDING OBSERVING AND CARING FOR YOUR CHILD. FOR SOME SUBSTANCES SUCH AS LYE, THEY MAY NEED TO OBSERVE YOUR CHILD IN THE HOSPITAL FOR A FEW DAYS.

Third, aromatic chemicals. These usually are made from petroleum or similar *hydrocarbons*. The common items in this group are gasoline, lamp oil, turpentine, furniture polish, car waxes (liquid), paint thinner, insect sprays, and any oily, strong-smelling substance.

These chemicals cause trouble through the inhaling of their fumes into the lungs, or absorbing the poisons through the blood vessels, from which they enter in the lungs, causing a chemical pneumonia. There is no special treatment for this, though most children in our experience do recover completely.

IF YOUR CHILD TAKES ONE OF THESE FLUIDS, GET HIM TO A HOSPITAL OR DOCTOR'S OFFICE AT ONCE. EXPERTS WILL EMPTY THE STOMACH THROUGH A STOMACH TUBE AND WASH IT WITH A HARMLESS OIL THAT WILL ABSORB AND REMOVE MOST OF THE CHEMICALS. YOUR CHILD WILL ALMOST CERTAINLY BE ADMITTED TO THE HOSPITAL FOR OBSERVATION. AT THE VERY LEAST, THEY WILL GIVE YOU WRITTEN INSTRUCTIONS AND YOU WILL NEED TO KEEP IN CLOSE TOUCH WITH YOUR DOCTOR FOR SEVERAL DAYS.

General observations on poison ingestion:

1. Do not be deceived because a child does not appear to be ill after taking something. The effects of aspirin or turpentine poisoning will not show up for some hours. Some poisons affect the liver or kidneys and may not show their toxic effects for several days.

2. Do not rely on a friend or relative. They may be ever so helpful, but unless they are experts on poisons, they may advise you wrongly. Activated charcoal, for example, is commonly recommended and useful in neutralizing certain poisons, but is useless in others.

3. Even when you think a substance is harmless, for example, certain kinds of ink, it may not be entirely harmless. So never hesitate to call your doctor. Many communities have poison-control centers or an emergency room may specialize in this problem. *Post the phone number,* so you can call quickly in case of an emergency.

4. Get as much information as possible about the amount and kind of substance swallowed and when it was taken. This can help your doctor immeasurably.

THE CIRCULATORY SYSTEM (Heart and Blood Vessels)

The heart and blood vessels are described in chapter 7, "The Next Two Years of Life." Problems such as anemia and leukemia may occur at any age, but the symptoms are similar to those in younger children.

Diseases of the Circulatory System

Diseases of the heart and blood vessels are very rare in childhood. Once in a great while, a viral infection (such as in severe influenza) may attack the heart muscles. The heart cannot beat effectively in this case, causing symptoms of fatigue, shortness of breath, and pain over the heart. The pulse is fast and often irregular at times.

IF YOUR CHILD SHOULD DEVELOP THESE SIGNS, THEY WILL BE QUITE APPARENT. DO NOT HESITATE TO CALL YOUR DOCTOR AND REQUEST THAT YOUR CHILD BE SEEN THAT DAY. HE SHOULD DO AN ELECTROCARDIOGRAM OR SEND YOU TO A CARDIOLOGIST (A DOCTOR WHO SPECIALIZES IN THE HEART).

Treatment. Treatment of a viral infection of the heart needs to be started, at least, in the hospital. *The need to observe and promptly treat any signs of heart failure requires trained medical people.* Your doctor will be careful to explain to you all the aftercare and precautions. These depend on each patient, and how extensive the infection is.

Blood Poisoning (*Septicemia*). This is a serious illness that usually follows a relatively small injury or infected spot such as a pimple. Even a bruise can result in blood poisoning. It is caused by the entry of bacteria into the blood vessels, in which they may be carried to various parts of the body, setting up infections.

Symptoms. 1) Around a scratch, cut, bruise, or pimple there develops an area of increasing redness, pain, heat, and swelling. 2) The redness extends out in streaks, usually outlining veins beneath. 3) If this stage is not treated, severe chills and fever are likely to develop. 4) The person feels very sick and, in the days before antibiotics, the patient would often die within a few days.

You need to see your doctor at the stage of the appearance of red streaks. He may then take tests to determine exactly the cause and extent of the infection and which antibiotic is likely to destroy these bacteria. The child can be very safely treated at home under medical supervision. Probably your doctor will have you apply warm soaks to increase comfort, keep the infection from spreading, and to keep you so busy you won't worry so much.

IF YOUR CHILD SNEAKS OR SPEEDS PAST THE STAGE OF LOCAL REDNESS, HEAT, AND PAIN, AND SUDDENLY GOES INTO FEVER AND CHILLS, DO NOT HESITATE. TAKE YOUR CHILD AT ONCE TO YOUR DOCTOR, AFTER PHONING, OR TO AN EMERGENCY ROOM.

Cellulitis. This is an extensive infection of tissues surrounding a relatively small, innocent-looking infection such as a pimple, insect bite, or scratch. Everyone has bacteria on the skin at all times. In warmth and high humidity, when the skin is usually soft or tender, or when the body's defenses against infection are down, these bacteria may attack and invade the deeper tissues more extensively. The body may not be able to fight off these bacterial invaders and so the infection gains a foothold and spreads.

Prevention. When your child scratches or picks at a sore, he helps those bacteria gain entrance to the deeper tissues and worsen the condition. So prevent a serious skin infection by the use of an over-the-counter antibiotic or antiseptic ointment. (Ask your druggist for a good one.) Apply it with firm massage into the skin around the sore and apply a Band-Aid to prevent picking.

Treatment. If it is too late for prevention, and you see the spot getting red and sore (usually this takes a few days), call your doctor's office for advice. His nurse will probably advise hot, moist packs, dressings, and a callback in twenty-four hours.

If the sore is not better by the next day, or is even worse, your doctor will want to see the child. He may need to give an injection to be certain the antibiotic gets into the circulation and reaches the tissues. (Sometimes antibiotics by mouth may be vomited or are poorly absorbed from the intestinal tract.) He will probably prescribe more antibiotics to be sure that healing is complete and there is no relapse.

IF THE CHILD IS NOT BETTER AFTER THE SHOT OR ORAL ANTIBIOTICS AND SHOULD GO INTO THE SEVERE FEVER AND CHILLS DESCRIBED IN BLOOD POISONING, BE SURE TO RETURN TO YOUR DOCTOR OR EMERGENCY ROOM.

Raynaud's Disease. This is a rare disease of the circulatory system. It affects the minute muscle fibers in the capillaries and the connective tissues of the blood vessels. This results in the clamping down of the blood-vessel walls, essentially closing off the circulation. The hands and feet become cold and ache from the poor blood flow. Cortisone and its related medications are the only known medical treatment.

Biofeedback. A new field of study called *biofeedback* offers, however, some hope for this and a few other illnesses. It is based on the belief that people can willfully control the parts of their bodies that were once thought to be under the regulation of the nervous system alone. By careful training, people can learn to relax those "involuntary" muscles and improve their circulation, their heart rate, the function of their stomach, intestines, colon, and other bodily functions.

Rheumatic Fever. This is a complication of streptococcal disease. In this case, it appears a few days to several weeks after an untreated strep infection, such as a strep throat, or even impetigo. The joints all over the body become red, hot, and painful. The child feels unable to move and is truly very sick. Along with the inflammation of the joints, there usually is a similar tissue reaction in the heart—often affecting the valves that open and close to allow proper separation and pumping of the blood from veins and arteries into the body. Many adults today still suffer the effects of the scarring of the heart valves from rheumatic fever, though surgical procedures can now correct many of these problems.

PLEASE BE CERTAIN THAT YOUR CHILD IS SEEN PROMPTLY AND PROPERLY TREATED FOR ANY POSSIBLE STREP

INFECTION. IF YOU NOTICE ANY OF THE ABOVE SYMP-
TOMS, CALL FOR AN APPOINTMENT WITH YOUR DOCTOR.
BE ALERT, AS WELL, TO THE PRESENCE OF UNUSUAL FA-
TIGUE, LOSS OF APPETITE, AND COMPLAINTS OF JUST
NOT FEELING WELL. THESE ARE SIGNALS FOR MEDICAL
ATTENTION!

Some parents mistake these serious symptoms for "growing pains" and ignore them. Eventually, the pain and fever will disappear, but when untreated, rheumatic fever may leave permanent, serious heart damage. Growing pains have no physical signs that can be demonstrated, such as fever or swollen, aching joints. There are no abnormal laboratory findings with growing pains. Do not risk a diagnosis yourself. If there is any doubt, let your doctor decide!

Injuries to Heart and Blood Vessels

Heart. Accidents or injuries to the heart are extremely rare and when they occur they are, unfortunately, likely to be fatal instantly.

Blood vessels. These however, are commonly cut or crushed in even minor accidents. Bruises have been discussed earlier in this chapter, as have cuts or lacerations. This additional information, we believe, will be helpful:

1. Distinguishing venous from arterial bleeding may help you to evaluate an emergency as compared with a less dangerous incident. *Blood from a vein is dark in color.* It flows or oozes out steadily and can be stopped fairly easily with pressure. This is because venous blood is flowing more lazily back to the heart from the tissues.

2. *Arterial blood,* on the other hand, is being forcefully pumped by the heart to the tissues of the body with its fresh supply of oxygen. *It is bright-red in color and comes out in spurts that coincide with the beat of the heart. Any serious bleeding needs medical attention, but arterial bleeding should be taken care of promptly, while venous bleeding can wait for you to make a call, change clothes, or whatever you may need to do.*

3. *Internal bleeding* is very rare, but it is important that

you recognize its signs. Abdominal bleeding is very rare in any organs other than the spleen and kidneys. A serious blow to the liver or other abdominal organs could, of course, injure them, but such injuries would be beyond the help of most parents.

After any apparently serious injury, watch your child for several hours for these signs:

1. *Tenderness or pain in the abdomen with muscle "guarding" or stiffening when you press on the stomach*
2. *A feeling of light-headedness or actual fainting*
3. *Cool, pale, and clammy skin with sweating*
4. *A fast, weak heart rate—over 120 at rest*

IF THESE SIGNS DEVELOP, DO NOT HESITATE. TAKE YOUR CHILD AT ONCE TO THE NEAREST HOSPITAL. EMERGENCY SURGERY MAY BE REQUIRED THOUGH X RAYS AND VARIOUS TESTS WILL NEED TO BE DONE TO BE SURE.

THE RESPIRATORY SYSTEM (Lungs and Their Branches)

How It Works

The lungs are protected within the chest wall, which is ingeniously devised to allow flexibility for expansion and contraction. The expansion of the lungs takes in fresh air with its oxygen, and the contraction phase pushes out the carbon dioxide from the body's metabolism. This function is very much like a bellows blowing air out and taking it in.

Throat. The respiratory tract is structured like an upside-down tree. The throat divides into two passageways. One leads to the stomach, and the other, leading to the lungs, is like a hollow trunk of a tree. There is a trapdoor that guards the tube (*trachea*) into the lungs, so no food or other material gets into the breathing passageways. The trapdoor is the voice box or Adam's apple and is protected above by the *epiglottis,* a projecting structure that protects the vocal cords. These open and close to let air in and out, and they vibrate as we talk or sing to make the various tones we use to modulate or vary our talking. The vocal cords and the epiglottis help keep out foreign bodies that could create a bout of choking.

Chest. In the chest, the trachea or windpipe branches three times on the right and two on the left. Each branch leads to one section of the lung called a *lobe.* There are three lobes on the right side of the chest, and only two on the left. Each main bronchial tube branches into many short tubes, and each of these immediately rebranches into countless tiny and ever-tinier branches, until they reach the minute air sacs called *alveoli.* There the actual "work" of breathing takes place. The expansion and contraction of the muscles between the ribs, the diaphragm and, at times, the abdomen and neck certainly are at work, too, but their purpose is like a bellows—to take in and push out the air. The actual exchange of gases, as mentioned above, takes place through extremely fine tissues in those alveoli. The alveoli, in a sense, are like the leaves on a tree.

In fact, leaves take in the carbon dioxide people breathe out and turn it into their green coloring matter, called *chlorophyll,* and thus put out oxygen. This exchange between plants and animals is an example of the fine balance in nature that keeps our world the sort of place it is. It is difficult to envision such perfection without the hand of the Perfector!

Nose. The nose is part of several systems, and it is hard to know just where to discuss it. It is a sensory organ, since it contains the cells by which we smell. But it also leads into the throat and is the usual passageway for air. So we will discuss it in several places.

In the passageway of the nostrils, there is a constant flow of mucus that washes out dust, pollen, and germs that are in the air we breathe. Furthermore, there are fine hairs, called *cilia,* that beat outward in a waving motion. They help the mucus trap the foreign bodies and move them back outside. A sneeze is the body's way to help push out larger particles, such as pepper or dust, that could irritate the tender tissues in the lungs.

Sinuses. There are seven areas called sinuses that are cavities in the bones around the eyes and nose. Normally these sinuses

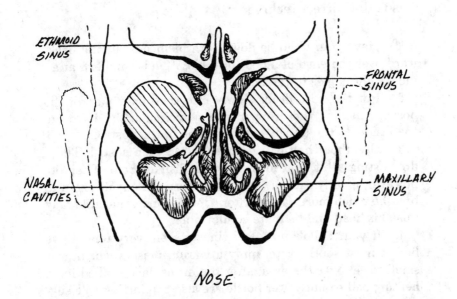

ETHMOID
SINUS

FRONTAL
SINUS

NASAL
CAVITIES

MAXILLARY
SINUS

NOSE

help give resonance to our voices and also help manufacture the mucus that cleans out the nostrils and upper throat. Occasionally these become infected from a cold or sore throat.

Such an infection is called *sinusitis,* and it causes swelling of the passageways that normally carry out the secretions into the nose. If the swelling is severe enough, those passageways become blocked. The secretions then build up in those bony cavities and cause severe pain.

Infections of the Respiratory Tract

Sinus. A true sinus infection is rare in young children, since the bones in and around the nose are quite soft and the sinus passageways are quite broad. In children past nine or ten, however, such infections are possible. If there is no fever, we suggest a good nasal spray or drops and a decongestant such as an antihistamine. (*See* Stocking Your Medicine Cabinet in chapter 9.)

Using Nose Drops. Here is a handy tip on the successful use of nose drops. Many people find them useless, and this is why. They carefully drop them into the bottom of the nostrils, where they quickly run into the throat and are swallowed.

This is the correct technique:

1. Have your child lie down with his head hanging backward over the edge of a bed (or table, if he is smaller), at almost right angles to the body.
2. Put the nose drops slowly into the upper part of the nostrils, moving the dropper in a semicircular fashion from the inside, to the upper, to the outside of the nostril.
3. Use about half of a dropper full in each nostril. These drops sting a bit, and most children dislike them. They do, however, greatly relieve their discomfort and enable them to breathe much more easily. After a few seconds, the child may raise his head and be more comfortable.
4. If your child's nose and sinuses seem very tender, we find it most soothing to apply a warm, moist washcloth or small towel over the area, after the drops have soaked in. A heating pad or hot-water bottle are also comforting. We suggest using heat for only ten or twenty minutes at a time.

Do not use nose drops *more than four times a day* and *not more than three days in succession.* After a few days' rest, they may be used again.

Common Cold. The symptoms of this widespread nuisance are well known! The nose is stuffy, red, and sore from sneezing and wiping. There is a profuse watery discharge, which later becomes heavy and yellowish or green-tinged as the cold progresses. The eyes are watery and usually there is a headache.

Treatment. Almost always the drainage from the nose irritates the throat and causes a nagging cough and sore throat. Rarely is there any significant fever. No matter how you treat (or even if you ignore) a cold it seems to last about a week. Home treatments are adequate for the average, run-of-the-mill cold: pain relievers, nose drops, cough syrup, hot tea, fruit juices, and tender, loving care.

Vitamin C. Many people now are convinced of the usefulness of Vitamin C in preventing colds. We know this vitamin strengthens the mucous membranes of the body, so it seems logical that their resistance to the viruses that cause colds would be improved. Try it if you are susceptible to colds. Use a water-soluble brand, and give four times the minimum daily amount recommended for your child. (Any cereal box has this figure on its side panel!)

Call the Doctor? These are signs to help you decide whether a cold is severe enough to warrant a call to your doctor.

1. *A fever that goes over 100 degrees F.*
2. *A cough that is not relieved by the usual cough syrup in your medicine cabinet (See Stocking Your Medicine Cabinet in chapter 9.)*
3. *The development of an earache*
4. *The occurrence of severe respiratory distress, pain or tightness in the chest, or labored breathing*

Croup. Sometimes a common cold begins or goes into an irritation of the larynx (voice box), windpipe (trachea), and bronchial tubes. In its milder form it is characterized by hoarseness, a dry, barking cough, and some discomfort with breathing.

In its more severe form, croup can attack suddenly while the child is sleeping—and often does. The child labors for every breath, and it is indeed a frightening experience.

CALL YOUR DOCTOR AT ONCE, AND HE WILL TELL YOU WHETHER THE CHILD NEEDS TO BE SEEN.

Meanwhile, do this:

1. Turn on a shower full force, with hot water, and hold the child in the bathroom (*not* under the shower), as comfortably as you can. Do your best to be calm, and try to relieve the child's panic. Fear tightens up every muscle, and just soothing him may ease the distress a little.

2. If relief is prompt, the child's color is good, and his breathing is easy enough to allow him to sleep comfortably, cancel the call to the doctor. Watch the child a bit and go to sleep nearby.

IF THE CHILD'S BREATHING DOES NOT EASE, HOWEVER, OR IF HIS COLOR IS DUSKY AROUND THE MOUTH, OR IF YOU ARE SEVERELY FRIGHTENED, HEAD FOR THE EMERGENCY ROOM OR YOUR DOCTOR'S OFFICE.

Occasionally a child with croup has to be admitted to the hospital. Treatment there almost always involves putting the child in a clear plastic "tent" with cool mist and oxygen. If you can stay calm and supportive, remain with your child until he is really better. If you tend to hover and feel anxious, however, step outside of your child's room and get calm. Children quickly copy parents' fears and this can aggravate their illness.

Other medications usually will include decongestants, cough preparations, and probably antibiotics. Cortisonelike medications are very useful in controlling the inflamed and swollen condition of the tissues.

Bronchitis. This is an infection of the larger branches (called bronchial tubes) of the lower respiratory tract. It usually spreads from an infection or cold in the nose and throat. Often there is a low-grade fever, a severe cough, and a feeling of tightness in the chest. The cough, dry and racking at first, usually becomes looser and produces thick mucus. The child feels and acts moderately sick, but usually is much better within a few days.

If the fever is over 100 degrees F., call your doctor. He will probably see your child to make sure this is not pneumonia, and give him some prescription-type cough preparation and antibiotics. Rarely is this serious enough to panic.

Bronchiolitis. This is an infection of the finest branches of the respiratory tree. It is characterized by very shallow and rapid breathing with a wheezing sound. It usually starts as a cold but worsens fairly rapidly and severely. It sounds like asthma but it is caused, not by an allergy, but by an infection.

Treatment. Many times bronchiolitis can be treated at home with decongestants, cough medicine, and antibiotics, if there is fever or other indication of a bacterial, rather than a viral, infection. The child needs a good humidifier, and the best kind puts out cool mist, rather than hot steam. The coolness helps reduce the swelling in the irritated tissues.

If your child is not improving, or if his respirations (breathing) become more labored, you need to see your doctor. He probably will give you stronger medication and can tell you what to watch for in case your child needs to go to the hospital.

If your child skips over this intermediate stage, he may show these danger signs:

1.   *The muscles of the neck and abdomen contract to assist in the labored breathing*
2.   *The rate of breathing jumps from the usual fourteen or so per minute to thirty-five or forty times per minute*
3.   *His color loses its usual rosiness and turns pale or bluish around his mouth*

IF THESE SYMPTOMS DEVELOP, TAKE YOUR CHILD TO THE EMERGENCY ROOM AND THEN CALL YOUR DOCTOR.

Pneumonia. This is an infection of the lung tissue itself. The illness has gone beyond even the tiniest branches of the bronchial tubes and has invaded the air sacs themselves. This hinders the exchange of the waste gas (carbon dioxide) for fresh oxygen. It creates a serious biochemical condition of the whole body. Fortunately, pneumonia is almost always limited to one area of the lung, so there is enough healthy tissue to keep the sick child safe.

Viral. When pneumonia is caused by a virus, there is little fever, or none. The cough may be severe, but the general sense of well-being is not lost to the degree it is in bacterial pneumonia. Breathing is fairly comfortable. Viral pneumonia is commonly called *walking pneumonia.*

Bacterial. Pneumonia that is caused by bacteria is more severe in its manifestations. It causes chills and a high fever, rapid, labored breathing, and a sense of being very sick. There may be no cough at first, or there may be a dry, racking cough. The child has no appetite and simply wants to lie still. The labored breathing seems to consume all of the child's strength.

When these symptoms exist, see your doctor at once:

1.   *A fairly sudden onset of high fever, over 103 degrees F.*
2.   *A sense of heaviness or pain in the chest*
3.   *Rapid labored breathing*
4.   *A feeling of being weak and sick*

IF YOU CANNOT REACH YOUR DOCTOR, AND IF THESE SYMPTOMS ARE ALARMING IN THEIR SEVERITY, DO NOT

HESITATE TO GO TO THE NEAREST EMERGENCY ROOM. A CHEST X RAY AND BLOOD COUNT WILL QUICKLY DIAGNOSE PNEUMONIA.

While pneumonia is almost never cause for panic or crisis, it does need to be treated promptly. The treatment for bacterial pneumonia includes: 1) strong doses of an antibiotic, usually by injection, so it will work faster and more effectively; 2) cough medicines to relieve the fatiguing, dry cough and loosen the mucus; 3) aspirin to control the fever; 4) large amounts of fluids to help keep the temperature down; 5) keeping the child as comfortable as possible with or without covers, according to the way he feels. (He will go from chills to sweating fairly quickly.)

Asthma. This looks and sounds much like bronchiolitis. The muscle fibers that open and close the bronchial tubes become irritated by certain substances, and that irritation causes those muscles to tighten up, so the bronchial tubes close, causing obstruction to the air flow. The lungs collect some fluid as well, and breathing becomes noisy, rattly, wheezy, squeaky, or tinkly in sound. So much energy is invested in breathing during a severe attack, that the child may be able to do very little else but breathe.

Diagnosis. Asthma can be very accurately diagnosed by a history of the attacks and a good physical examination. The exact substance that triggers the allergic response, however, is not so easy to track down. Various foods, pollens, dust, animal danders, molds, and a variety of other substances have been found to cause it.

It is important to find out what the culprit is and try to eliminate it from the diet or environment. An *allergist* is a doctor who specializes in the exact diagnosis and treatment of allergies, and if your child's problem is severe, we suggest you consult such a specialist and follow his advice.

While we know that asthma attacks are precipitated by allergies, we know that emotions also influence its occurrence. Fears, anxiety, and worry all are found to be common elements in the asthmatic child's personality. These certainly are a result of a severe attack, but we also believe they are a factor in causing asthma as well.

Treatment. If a substance such as pollens in the air cannot be avoided, your allergist may recommend desensitizing your child. This involves tiny injections of very dilute, sterile preparations of the offending material. The strength of the solution gradually increases to a maximum that is the most the child can take—without an asthma attack. After some months or years, some children seem to recover from or outgrow their allergies, and these shots can be stopped.

There are several medications and treatments that will relieve the asthma attacks while the child is being desensitized.

1.   Aminophylline, theophylline, antihistamines, adrenalin, ephedrine, and cortisone (or its related substances) are all useful. Your doctor may need to try various ones to find the best one for your special child. Their effect tends to decrease over a period of time, so he may need to change medications. You and your doctor must work well together to adjust doses and relieve this distressing problem.

2.   Sprays and inhalants are of several kinds. They may be prescribed or purchased from your druggist. They work rapidly, but relief doesn't last too long. Usually they need to be used along with the medications listed above.

3.   *Reassurance and calmness* are extremely important in allaying an asthmatic child's fears. His anxiety will make the symptoms worse, and many children go into even worse attacks when they are upset. A gentle, firm manner is comforting. Remind your child that previous attacks have gone away, and tell him he will be better shortly.

4.   When the usual medicines fail to control an attack, the child may go into a severe bout. These signs need to be noted:

1.   *A marked increase in the breathing rate, which is normally about fourteen per minute*
2.   *Extreme wheezing and pushing to get the air out of the chest*
3.   *Pale or dusky color about the mouth*
4.   *Retraction of the neck and abdomen, as the muscles there strain to help breathe*

IF THESE SIGNS ARE PRESENT, GO TO YOUR DOCTOR'S OFFICE OR AN EMERGENCY ROOM. HOSPITAL STAFFERS

CAN GIVE INJECTIONS THAT WILL RELIEVE SUCH ATTACKS PROMPTLY.

With any asthmatic child, be calm, clear, and definite about every aspect of life. Do not overprotect or pamper him, but avoid threats or extreme anger that could seriously frighten him. In turn, teach an asthmatic child to be honest and open about his feelings. Fear and anger can be appropriately expressed, and a child needs to be taught how to do this. Help him understand the problems that create such emotions, and then help him find solutions so he will not be left helpless in such fear or frustration. Many asthma attacks can be prevented or made less severe by teaching this way of life to a child.

Accidents and Injuries of the Respiratory Tract

Foreign Bodies. As described previously, a substance sometimes slips through the trapdoor of the larynx into the respiratory "tree." It finally lodges in a branch too tiny to let it pass, where it may cause the lung tissue beyond to collapse for lack of air. This causes coughing, some pain, and more or less difficulty breathing, depending on the size of the area blocked off.

Treatment. If any such symptoms remain or occur after a choking episode, see your doctor. A chest X ray will reveal such a problem. He will need to send your child to a specialist to remove the object, restore the lung's functioning, and prevent serious complications. Even if the symptoms seem minor, be sure to cooperate. Later complications can be serious indeed.

Accidents. These mishaps may break ribs fairly easily in older children. In younger ones, the ribs are softer and more flexible, so they "give" instead of breaking so easily. Observe carefully any child who has suffered a chest injury.

Ribs. A broken rib is painful and will not be difficult to discover. It may, however, puncture a lung, allowing air to escape into the chest cavity, and finally cause a lung to collapse. If this is happening, you will know it because:

1. *There is severe pain over the entire chest*
2. *The child's breathing becomes labored and his color will turn pale or dusky*

3. *He may feel faint and seem in shock, with rapid pulse rate and cold, clammy skin*

THESE SIGNS SIGNIFY AN EMERGENCY. GO AT ONCE WITH THE CHILD TO THE NEAREST HOSPITAL. THE DOCTORS WILL X-RAY THE CHILD AND GIVE HIM SPECIAL TREATMENTS TO REMOVE THE TRAPPED AIR, PREVENT INFECTION, AND PROMOTE HEALING OF THE LUNG.

Other Causes of Lung Rupture. Rupture of the lungs may occur from other injuries, and it may happen spontaneously for no known reason. It occurs in babies with hyaline membrane disease and in children suffering from cystic fibrosis.

In almost every case, a *pneumothorax,* as this is called, is entirely curable. But it does require expert medical care in a hospital. Know your doctor and rely on his judgment.

THE NERVOUS SYSTEM (Brain, Spinal Cord, and Nerves)

The anatomy and function of the nervous system are described in chapter 7, "The Next Two Years of Life." The severely disabling birth defects are discussed there as well.

Viral Infections of the Nervous System

There are several viral infections of the nervous system that we need to discuss. These diseases are especially serious and may be fatal.

Reye's Syndrome. This is a combination of damage to the liver and the brain following a seemingly minor viral infection. There is severe swelling of the brain, usually sudden in its onset. The liver becomes infiltrated with fat and fails to function well, and the blood-sugar level falls. It is most likely to affect children from six months to fifteen years of age.

Symptoms. After a cold or mild stomach flu, a child may seem perfectly well for a few hours or even several days. If he develops Reye's Syndrome, he will begin to vomit repeatedly, fairly quickly become delirious, and then go into a coma. He may suffer convulsive episodes. The fatality rate is 25 percent or more.

Treatment. Treatment of this disease requires hospitalization. Extremely careful management of fluids and the body's delicate balance of systems may mean the difference between life and death, or recovery and permanent nerve damage. Since there is no specific cure, however, no matter how expert the medical attention, some children simply may not survive.

Of those who do survive, most recover fairly completely. A few, however, may suffer mild to severe brain or nerve damage. This disease is certainly one that merits all of your faith in God's will and provision for you as well as your child.

Encephalitis. See Convulsive Disorders, later in this chapter.

Bell's Palsy. This is a weakness or paralysis of the muscles of one side of the face. It is rare in children. It may follow a cold or other viral infection. The signs are a loss of taste on the front and one side of the tongue, a weakness of the muscles around one side of the mouth, cheek, the eyelids, and the forehead. There is rarely any pain, but the muscular weakness is disfiguring and frightening. Most patients recover completely.

Treatment. It is important to see your doctor if your child evidences the above signs. He will probably give him cortisone in some form and will recommend extra rest. Bed rest, however, is not necessary.

Shingles. This subject is discussed in the section on Skin, Hair, and Nails earlier in this chapter. While it is an infection of a nerve, the first evidence is that of pain and blisters on the skin.

Headaches

An aching head may be a symptom of a number of illnesses. The most common illnesses that cause headaches are: *tonsillitis, earaches, flu of all kinds,* the *common childhood illnesses,* and almost any *bacterial* or *viral infection.* Such infectious agents send poisons into the system that cause fever, aching, and often an upset stomach, as well as a headache. The treatment of such a headache is involved with treating the underlying infection. This may be simply rest in bed or antibiotics and pain relievers.

In *sinus infections* or a *severely congested nose from a cold* or *hay fever,* there may be a localized headache. It usually is present over and under the eyes, around the temples, or over the bridge of the nose. Sinus infections are rare in children. *Sometimes an antibiotic is necessary to clear up such an infection, but usually nose drops and decongestants, along with a pain reliever, will take care of it.*

> **A FEELING OF PRESSURE IN THE HEAD, ASSOCIATED WITH SEVERE VOMITING (FORTUNATELY RARE), MAY BE A SIGN OF A SERIOUS DISORDER. THE MOST LIKELY IS MENINGITIS OR ENCEPHALITIS, OR EVEN MORE RARELY, A BRAIN TUMOR, OR BLOCKAGE OF FLUID DRAINAGE AROUND THE BRAIN. THESE WILL BE DISCUSSED IN THIS CHAPTER.**

Eyestrain. This may cause headaches. Usually this pain is due to muscle strain from the child's squinting in order to see better.

Other Causes of Headaches. If you wear a tight hat or a scarf tied about your head, you may experience a severe headache and not realize it is from the pressure of the hat or scarf.

Such a headache may occur from the tension of the scalp caused by tight muscles. The scalp is actually a long, flat tendon that connects muscles in the forehead, over the ears, and in the neck. As these muscles contract during prolonged times of anxiety or worry, they may act exactly like a constrictive hatband, causing headaches. Just feel those muscles, and if they are hard and ache, *make them relax.* They will obey you, and in a short time this sort of headache will disappear.

Migraine headaches are "mavericks" in their origin. We believe there are physical causes, but we have seen people recover from them through psychotherapy, too.

Migraine headaches are extremely rare in young children, though we do see them in adolescents. They usually occur on only one side of the head. They are often preceded by peculiar disturbances of the vision, such as blind spots, flickering, or spots before the eyes. There may be vomiting with them, but this does not mean there is a brain tumor. The physical basis for these is unknown, but some authorities believe it may involve a tightening or spasm of blood vessels.

If your child has one of these headaches, notify your doctor. You should, of course, try aspirin or Tylenol and rest. But if it is a true migraine, your doctor can give you a special medication that will give relief.

Convulsive Disorders

There are three main types of convulsive illnesses in children—*febrile convulsions, idiopathic epilepsy,* and *Jacksonian epilepsy.*

Febrile Convulsions. These occur in young children under three. The fever usually is high, and it may be related to a variety of underlying infections or illnesses. Rarely, even a low-grade fever of 100 to 101 degrees F. may cause a convulsion.

Symptoms. In a convulsion, the child's eyes roll up, and there are uncontrollable contractions or spasms of the muscles all over the body. While it seems to last an eternity, such a convulsion usually lasts only a few minutes at most. The child may be drowsy afterward.

Treatment. Obviously treatment is to get the temperature down quickly. While one person is calling the doctor, another should place the child flat on his back with the clothes removed. Using ice water, or a mixture of alcohol and water, sponge the neck, arms, groin, and ankles, where the large blood vessels are closest to the skin. The cool water will absorb the body's heat, and the temperature will go down. *Do not put a convulsing child in a tub* since he could jerk out of your control and get water in the lungs.

YOUR DOCTOR WILL WANT TO SEE YOUR CHILD OR HAVE HIM SEEN AT A HOSPITAL AS SOON AS YOU CAN GET HIM THERE. DO TAKE HIM IN FOR A DIAGNOSIS AND FOR TREATMENT OF THE ILLNESS SO THE CONVULSION WILL NOT RECUR. THE DOCTOR WILL USUALLY WANT AN ELECTROENCEPHALOGRAM TO RULE OUT A MORE SERIOUS FORM OF EPILEPSY.

Idiopathic Epilepsy. This is a big word that simply says we don't know what causes this kind of seizure. We do know it runs in families, and that it is accompanied by an abnormal discharge of electrical impulses from part of the brain.

There are three forms of idiopathic epilepsy: *grand mal, petit mal,* and *psychomotor.*

Grand mal epilepsy occurs after a sort of warning called an *aura.* It begins with loss of consciousness, then builds to major jerking spasms of all the muscles of the body; usually there is loss of urinary control, and sometimes bowel control. It will rarely last more than a few minutes, and is followed by a period of drowsiness or sleeping for an hour or so.

Treatment for Grand Mal. Treatment involves protecting the patient. Lay him on the floor with a rug or blanket under him if possible. Hold the head on one side to keep the tongue from falling back in the throat. If possible, put a padded wooden object in the mouth to prevent biting the tongue.

If there are other people about, ask them to leave to protect the patient's privacy and dignity. When appropriate, as in a classroom, explain a bit about this illness to take away any fear or rejection of the child.

Petit mal is characterized by a brief loss of awareness of the surroundings. The child does not fall, and there are no muscle contractions. After a few seconds, the child resumes normal activities and may not realize he has had a seizure. These seizures may occur in clusters, rarely, or regularly. We do not know what makes them occur at one time and not another.

Psychomotor seizures are mysterious and may be dangerous. The patient slips from one state of being into quite a different one. He may start for one destination and end up in another, not recalling how he got there or what he did in the interim. A classic example of this is the Dr. Jekyll and Mr. Hyde story, through few cases are so complex or dramatic.

Diagnosis of Epilepsy. Besides the symptoms and signs listed, this disease is diagnosed by a special test called an electroencephalogram (E.E.G.). This test is much like an electrocardiogram that tests heart function. Tiny electrodes are placed over the head with fine wires that lead to special paper. The electrical impulses that are put out by the brain are recorded by a fine pen on this moving roll of paper. Doctors and technicians who have studied thousands of such tracings can see if and where there are abnormal electrical impulses.

Treatment of Convulsions. We know that certain anticonvul-

sant medicines can control most of these convulsions and seizures. Special dietary controls may also help. Be sure to keep
your child, if he is afflicted with this problem, under excellent
medical care. Teach him to recognize the onset of a seizure, and
where to lie down to protect himself. Help him tell a teacher or
other adult that he will need help during such a seizure. And
teach him how to live as normal a life as possible.

The final general kind of epilepsy is called *Jacksonian,* after
the person who first described it. This almost always follows
some type of brain injury. It is limited to one part of the body as
a rule. It may spread to include the rest of the body in a grand
mal seizure, but it always starts with one area. The treatment is
the same as for idiopathic epilepsy.

Encephalitis. This is a viral infection of the brain tissue. It may
complicate a viral infection elsewhere in the body, such as measles or influenza. Epidemic encephalitis, however, is spread from
animals (most commonly horses) by an insect vector—the mosquito. If such an insect stings an infected horse, and then stings
a person, it is very likely to inoculate that infection into the
person.

Symptoms. The disease starts with a headache, stiffness of the
neck, fever, and vomiting. It progresses to a deep sleep or even a
coma, depending on the severity of the infection and the resistance of the body of the victim. There may be a recovery in a
week or ten days, or the patient may worsen or even die.

Treatment. This is limited to supportive measures, such as intravenous feedings and control of the body's chemistry. There
are no antibiotics that affect this virus.

Meningitis. This disease affects the tissues that surround the
brain. The medical name for the layers of that tissue is *men-
inges.* Due to the infection, there is a swelling, and excess fluid
collects around the brain and spinal cord, producing pressure
that causes severe headache and boardlike stiffness of the neck.
Usually there is a high fever, and there may be vomiting and
convulsions.

Cause. In children, the most common bacterium to cause meningitis is *hemophilus influenzae,* type B. This has a slower

onset, is generally less severe, and recovery is more rapid than an infection by a bacterium called the *meningococcus*. The latter occurs rapidly, is severe, and is somewhat more likely to be fatal or to leave some complication.

Treatment

IF YOUR CHILD EVIDENCES THE SYMPTOMS LISTED FOR EITHER ENCEPHALITIS OR MENINGITIS (FEVER, SEVERE HEADACHE, SEVERE STIFFNESS OF THE NECK, UNUSUAL DROWSINESS, WITH VOMITING OR CONVULSIONS) SEE YOUR DOCTOR OR GO TO YOUR HOSPITAL EMERGENCY ROOM AT ONCE. DO NOT WAIT UNTIL MORNING AND DO NOT BE CONSIDERATE OF YOUR DOCTOR. EVERY HOUR COUNTS AND YOU WILL DO HIM AND YOUR CHILD A FAVOR BY CALLING. HOSPITAL CARE IS ABSOLUTELY NECESSARY FOR SURVIVAL.

Brain Tumors

Brain tumors fortunately are rare in children. There are many different kinds, and they become more complicated to discuss than are helpful. *These, however, are the signs of any type of brain tumor you may need to recognize:*

1.   *Headache* is usually present when a brain tumor is developing. Sometimes it develops suddenly and lasts. In other cases it may come and go, and sometimes there is no headache, even with a large tumor.

2.   *Mental changes* may take place, depending on the location of the tumor. A tumor in the front part of the brain may cause personality changes that are so subtle, you may feel your child has an emotional problem. In other parts of the brain, no changes in mood or behavior are noted at all.

3.   *Speech disturbances* are not uncommon, but they also occur only if the tumor is in or near the area of the brain that controls speech.

4.   *Visual disturbances,* such as blurred vision or double vision, may make parents suspect eye problems. Be certain that such visual symptoms are evaluated by a medical doctor who can be certain about the possibility of a tumor.

5. *Disturbances in balance and motion* are especially common in the *cerebellum* or center-of-balance area of the brain. Other locations, however, may also cause such symptoms.

6. *Disturbances in sensation* may involve pain, numbness, or loss of taste, touch, smell, or hearing.

7. *Convulsions* may occur as a sign of a brain tumor, just as they do in epilepsy. Special diagnostic tests can tell what the cause is.

8. *Nausea and vomiting* are common signs of many illnesses. They also may be symptomatic of a brain tumor, but this symptom is always accompanied by other signs as well.

The tests your doctor may recommend will include one or more of these: special kinds of X rays; an electroencephalogram (brain-wave tracing or E.E.G.); an examination of the spinal fluid; and a CAT-scan. (This is a special kind of X ray that reveals any change in the density or type of tissue at any depth in a given area of the body. It is a highly reliable diagnostic tool and will clearly locate for a skilled physician the site of a tumor, if one is there.)

Treatment. Surgical procedures can successfully cure many brain tumors. Malignant or cancerous tumors, of course, are less curable, but they are very rare in children.

Injuries to the Brain and Spinal Cord

Bumps and Bruises. These are as common to the head as any part of the body. If your baby has a fall (all three of ours did) that involves a possible head injury, don't panic. Pick him up and check him for any marks or disfigurement. Comfort him and lay him down—*but watch him.* If he goes back to normal playing or some fussing at the indignity of it all, he will probably be just fine.

Check the baby's skin color and the pupils (dark centers) of the eyes. If the skin stays pink and the pupils constrict to light and dilate (or enlarge) in shadows, you may be even more sure the child is fine.

Concussion. If the fall was a bit harder, or the child landed on the wrong place, however, he may have a concussion. This is a jolt that causes a slight bruising or swelling of a child's brain. The signs are these:

   1.   The child becomes pale and listless. He will not want to eat and may vomit. He will have a severe headache. The pupils may react more slowly, and one more than the other.

   2.   *If your child shows these signs, do call your doctor.* He will probably want to see the child, but he may ask you to watch him a few more hours. You may let the child sleep, but check his eyes and general condition every hour or so. If the child improves, the doctor may do nothing more than check the reflexes and general condition. Most concussions from children's falls are mild and leave no effects.

SHOULD THESE SIGNS WORSEN, OR THE CHILD CONVULSES OR LOSES CONSCIOUSNESS, DO NOT WAIT. CALL YOUR DOCTOR AND TAKE YOUR CHILD TO THE NEAREST HOSPITAL.

Subdural Hematoma. This is bleeding below the heavy tissue that covers the brain. From a few days to as long as three weeks after a blow to the head, there is slight danger of this complication. Rarely, a tiny blood vessel is torn by a child's fall or the swelling resulting from it. This may allow blood to slowly ooze into a pocket below the tough tissue that encases and protects the brain. The blood acts as a foreign substance and may draw more body fluid into the sac. When or if the fluids create enough pressure, the following symptoms may be expected:

1. Nausea and vomiting
2. Inequality of pupil size and reaction to light
3. Blurring of vision, though you cannot evaluate this in infants
4. Disturbances of speech
5. Weakness or paralysis of some muscles
6. Convulsions or fainting spells
7. If the soft spot is open, it may *be fuller than usual (depending on the size and location of the hematoma)*

IF ANY OF THESE SIGNS DEVELOP, CALL YOUR DOCTOR
AND GO TO HIS OFFICE OR HOSPITAL AT ONCE.

Surgery can correct this problem, but it needs to be performed before the child becomes seriously ill.

Spinal-Cord Injuries. These are rare, but leave tragic crippling
in their wake. Any injury that causes a snapping of the backbone, with stretching or tearing of the spinal cord in that area,
will produce spinal-cord damage. Sports and diving injuries are
especially dangerous to the neck area, where injuries may cause
complete paralysis of the body.

ANY INJURY, ACTUAL OR SUSPECTED, OF THE BACK AND
SPINAL CORD NEEDS EXPERT CARE FROM THE FIRST MO-
MENT. ANY WRONG MOVES CAN WORSEN THE INJURY.
CALL AN AMBULANCE, POLICE, OR ANYONE EXPERIENCED
IN FIRST AID. IF NO ONE IS AVAILABLE, FIND A STRETCHER
OR MAKE ONE OUT OF LONG POLES AND A BLANKET. THE
PERSON SHOULD BE HELD RIGID WHILE TURNING ONTO
HIS STOMACH, AND SHOULD BE TAKEN AT ONCE TO THE
NEAREST EMERGENCY ROOM.

Special equipment and techniques for care can make improvement possible in some victims. Spinal-cord injuries, however, have a poor prognosis for much actual recovery. Many
heroic victims, however, have made wonderful contributions to
our world. Even tragedy may have its compensations!

THE GENITAL AND URINARY TRACTS
(Sexual Organs and Kidneys)

The kidneys, ureters, bladder, and urethra are described in
chapter 7, "The Next Two Years of Life," as are the ovaries and
testes.

These parts of your child's body are essential to his life and
obviously to his or her ability to bear children. Being aware of
possible illnesses, then, can help you to prevent these diseases,
or at least their serious complications.

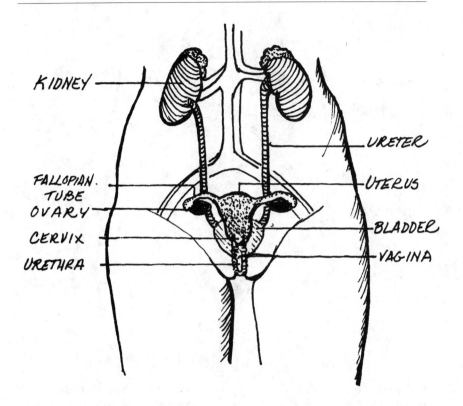

KIDNEY

URETER

FALLOPIAN
TUBE

UTERUS

OVARY

CERVIX

BLADDER

URETHRA

VAGINA

FEMALE GENITOURINARY SYSTEM

Infections of the Genitourinary Tract

Mumps orchitis. This is an infection of the testicles, caused by mumps. A boy's testicles may become swollen, hot, and extremely painful. Complete bed rest is necessary, but there is no other effective treatment, except that in severe cases, making an incision in the tough, fibrous covering of the testicle will relieve pressure and possibly prevent subsequent sterility. Not uncommonly, one or both testes may become sterile, and such a boy will not be able to conceive a child.

Immunization. Mumps vaccine, now available everywhere in America, will prevent mumps, along with this tragic complication. Be sure your children are protected.

The ovaries are rarely infected except in case of venereal diseases. (*See* chapter 15, "The Seesaw World of the Adolescent.")

Epididymitis. This is an infection of the excretory ducts or tu-

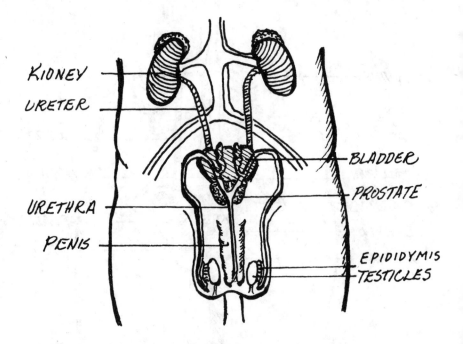

MALE GENITOURINARY SYSTEM

bules leading from the testes to the vas deferens. In case of an infection, either viral or bacterial, the entire scrotum may become swollen, hot, and tender. The testes are not involved, but areas attached to them or near them will show signs of infection.

Treatment. Be sure to take your son to the doctor as soon as possible. You do not want to take a chance on such an infection spreading to the testes themselves. Usually with rest and antibiotic treatment, this infection is cured in only a few days. There are rarely, if ever, any complications when this is treated promptly.

Cystitis—Bladder Infection. This is quite common in girls, because the channel (the urethra) from the bladder to the outside of the body is quite short and the opening fairly big. This allows bacteria to enter and cause an infection. While there is lower abdominal pain with this, the major symptom is that of frequent, painful urination. Often there is a little blood in the urine, and the urine looks cloudy. The abdominal pain that is present is in the area just above and even directly under the pubic bone in the very lowest, central area of the abdomen.

There may or may not be pain when pressure is applied, and usually there is no fever.

If you suspect a bladder infection, call your physician. He will probably want to see your child, and he will need a specimen of the urine in a clean container, marked with the name and date.

Meanwhile, encourage the child to drink clear liquids—as much as possible—to help prevent the infection from getting into the kidneys, where an infection is much more serious. While waiting for medical care, sit the child in warm water. It will help relieve the pain, which may be severe.

Treatment. The doctor will almost always give your child a special antibiotic to cure the infection. He may need to culture the urine to identify the germ that is causing the infection, and to find out what medications will be effective against the causative organism. To do the culture, your doctor may need a catheterized specimen of urine. He, or his nurse, will carefully cleanse the tissues around the opening of the bladder and gently insert a soft, small tube that will drain out a specimen of urine into a sterile bottle. This is needed to eliminate bacteria that normally are on the skin and would contaminate the urine. Children may act and feel upset over such a test, but your calmness and firmness can help them to cooperate. It is not as painful as it is frightening.

Repeated Infections. If your child has repeated infections of the bladder, your doctor will probably recommend doing some special studies to see if there are any abnormalities of the urinary tract that may need to be remedied.

Nephritis. This is an inflammation or infection of the kidneys. We will discuss two types: *glomerulonephritis* and *pyelonephritis.* These are technical terms to describe some very understandable diseases.

Glomerulonephritis is caused by a reaction to the toxins or poisons that are put into the body by a serious streptococcal infection, usually in the tonsils. This poison causes the tiny collecting tubules that pick up and drain off urine to swell, preventing the normal excretion of urine. As the body collects these fluids, the tissues become puffy, and the eyelids look swollen. These damaged kidney tubes allow red blood cells to slip through the usual fine screen, and many of them pass out of the circulation and are discharged in the urine that is excreted, so the body becomes anemic and weak. One of the normal body proteins also slips through, and is lost in the urine. The diagnosis is based on these physical signs, the history of strep infections, and the examination of the urine in a laboratory.

The child who has such symptoms needs to be seen as soon as possible by a doctor, though this is not a real emergency. It develops slowly and takes some days before anyone could really recognize it, so do not panic.

Treatment. Your doctor will almost surely want your child to have bed rest at home. He will probably prescribe an antibiotic to be sure the strep infection is completely cured. But the kidney will have to heal itself. Your child will need to limit salt and decrease his protein intake, since the digestive waste products of protein are excreted through the kidneys. He should drink a moderately large amount of water to keep the poisons diluted somewhat. If there are complications, such as increased blood pressure, or some permanent damage to the kidneys, there are good medications to control the symptoms. In the very rare event that more serious damage could result, there is even the possibility of a later kidney transplant. So do not despair, if your child should develop nephritis.

Pyelonephritis is a bacterial infection of the kidney. Usually it follows or occurs along with a bladder infection, but it may occur suddenly with a high fever, chills, and severe back pain.

> THIS INFECTION NEEDS TO BE TREATED VERY PROMPTLY AND MAY EVEN WARRANT A TRIP TO THE EMERGENCY ROOM. AN INFECTION MAY SPREAD RAPIDLY AND COULD LEAVE SCARRING THAT WOULD RESULT IN PERMANENT KIDNEY DAMAGE.

Rarely, a patient with pyelonephritis needs to be in the hospital for special laboratory tests and treatments that monitor and promote healing more effectively.

Follow-up. You do need, however, to be certain that your doctor follows your child's progress with you. He will need to check urine specimens, blood studies, and your child's blood pressure to be sure healing is complete.

If such infections occur several times, your doctor will probably want you to take your child to a *urologist*. He is a specialist in diseases of the urinary tract and can find out if there is some injury or birth defect that makes such infections a special risk. Many such defects can be corrected, making your child's health more secure.

Nephrosis. This is a rare disease of the kidney in which the tissues that make normal functioning of the kidneys possible simply do not work. The kidneys allow proteins to slip through the screening devices, causing excess proteins in the urine and decreased proteins in the blood. Due to lack of protein in the bloodstream, fluids escape into the tissues and abdominal cavity, causing swelling. Nephrosis usually occurs between two and four years of age, and often used to be fatal. Now, however, treatment with cortisonelike medicines and other drugs can control it for many years. Antibiotics for even minor infections are important to prevent further stress in the kidneys.

Injuries of the Urinary Tract

Kidneys. In children's games, wrestling, and fighting, a blow to the back is common. If such a blow lands in the right area in the small of the back, it may cause a bruised kidney. The symptoms are:

1. *Pain in the injured area that may be mild or severe depending on the severity of the swelling that may occur*
2. *Blood-tinged urine that will be noted within a very few minutes or hours*

Such symptoms need to be reported to your doctor as soon as you are aware of them. He will need to see your child and a specimen of the urine. He will decide if the child can be watched at home or may need hospital care and diagnostic procedures.

Urinary Bladder. Accidents to the bladder are rare, since it is well protected by the pubic bone. With a sharp blow, however, over a full bladder, it could rupture. The signs of a ruptured bladder are:

1. *Disappearance of the sensation of the full bladder with
    its need to urinate*
2. *Voided urine is bloody*
3. *Gradual development of abdominal pain and swelling*

SHOULD YOU NOTE THESE SYMPTOMS AFTER AN INJURY
OR BLOW OVER THE BLADDER AREA, GO AT ONCE TO THE
NEAREST HOSPITAL, WHERE IT CAN QUICKLY BE DETER-
MINED WHETHER THERE IS CAUSE FOR ALARM. IF SO,
SURGERY WILL BE NEEDED TO CORRECT SUCH AN INJURY.

Genital Injuries

Female. The common injuries to a girl's genital area are these:

*The insertion of foreign bodies into the vagina in an attempt
to masturbate or explore the body.* We have never seen such a
condition, except in emotionally troubled girls. They have
sometimes been previously attacked sexually, thereby arousing
intense guilt or fear that are shown through hurting themselves.

*The appearance of blood or scratch marks in the vaginal
area need to alert the parents, so they may help such a child
get proper medical attention. If there is reason to suspect sexual abuse of the girl, you may need to seek counsel to help her
overcome any fears or guilt and regain a healthy attitude
about her genital area and sexuality.*

"Straddle" injuries: A fall onto something sharp or the
pressure from a bicycle accident against a girl's vaginal area
could tear her hymen (the tissue that covers the vagina) or
bruise the labia (lips that protect the vaginal area).

We find some parents who fear that such accidents are a
child's excuse or a cover-up for premature sexual activities.
Other parents claim a daughter has suffered an accident when,
in fact, there may have been serious sexual abuse perpetrated
on her.

Child-Abuse Laws. Under present child-abuse laws, everyone is
required to report to child-welfare authorities any suspicion of
child abuse. Some parents themselves are involved in sexual
abuse of their children (*see* section on Child Abuse in chapter
16) and fear discovery. Do not blame your doctor if he reports
suspicious injuries; laws require him to do so. If you are inno-

cent, that will be shown. *If not, this may be your opportunity to get help for a very destructive and powerful habit.* At any rate, take a girl with any vaginal injury or bleeding to your doctor. He will see if the injury has penetrated deeply enough to do serious physical harm. And if so, he will get the help she needs to become a perfectly normal young woman.

Male Genital Injuries. Injuries to the *penis* are very rare in our experience. Bruising, insect bites and, rarely, the inserting of a foreign body by a boy into the penis are seen. These are easily treated, but you need to find out why a little boy might put an object into such a tender area.

As in little girls, boys are not uncommonly molested by older children, arousing strong sexual feelings and curiosity. Ask your child about such events, and do not hesitate to ask for an evaluation by a specialist in children's emotional problems if you suspect such a problem. A clean bill of health will comfort you, but taking care of an early problem could prevent more serious problems later.

A bruise is possible to a boy's *testicles* and *scrotum,* but it is rare. It is likely to occur only by a sudden bouncing fall onto a bike seat or similar straddle-type injury. This injury will be apparent through swelling, pain, and discoloration of the scrotum and testes.

Apply ice packs at once, and call your doctor. Rarely would such an injury require surgery, but the doctor's following the child's recovery with you will enable him to pick up any possible signs of a complication early enough to prevent its development.

THE LYMPHATIC SYSTEM (Lymph Nodes and Lymph Vessels)

The lymphatic system serves two main purposes. One is to protect the body's tissues from infections, and the other is to supply fluid and nutrients to the tissues of the body.

Protective Function

Lymph Nodes. The protective function is performed by an intricate network of *lymph nodes* that are scattered, a bit like beads, along a vast network of lymph channels. When bacteria, viruses, or any dangerous materials come along, these nodes act like a screen or sieve and collect them. Many times these nodes themselves become infected in performing this protective function.

Infectious Mononucleosis. This is usually a mild illness, though it may be severe! It usually involves tenderness and swelling of the lymph nodes of the head and neck—especially notable is the enlargement of those nodes in the upper back of the neck, and back of the head, and those beneath the jaw. There is a sore throat, which may be mild or severe. There usually are generalized weakness, fatigue, discomfort, and aching occasionally so severe as to require bed rest.

So far as we know, this is caused by a virus. There is no specific cure.

Diagnosis. This is made by symptoms plus very specific laboratory tests. If the symptoms your child describes are severe, a visit to your doctor is necessary. While this disease goes away and complications are very rare, the course is prolonged, and general fatigue and weakness are such as to need medical attention.

Treatment. Expect your doctor to examine your child, take blood tests, and instruct you in his care. Such care will include: 1) bed rest until the temperature is normal; 2) extended rest times when activities are begun again; 3) vitamins to replace those missed by a poor appetite; 4) sometimes cortisone (or one of its related medications); 5) again, let us explain that antibiotics are not useful in curing this illness, though they may be given to prevent or to treat a secondary bacterial infection in the raw and painful throat.

This disease is rare under five years of age in our experience, but is not uncommon in older children. It is spread by coughs, sneezes, or droplets spread in ordinary conversations. It has been called the "kissing disease" for decades, because of its frequency among dating teenagers.

Lymphadenitis. This is an impressive word for an infection of the lymph nodes. While this may occur as a secondary symptom of some other primary infection, it may occur without any known cause elsewhere in the body.

A cold or flu may manifest itself only by swollen tender lymph nodes in the neck. These can be felt as firm, tender knots in the neck. They last seven to ten days, and gradually return to normal. They may stay slightly enlarged and firm for many weeks or months.

Such an infection in the abdomen is called *mesenteric adenitis*. It resembles appendicitis in some cases, so closely, in fact, that an appendectomy must be considered. It is, however, an infection of the lymph nodes through the abdomen, much like that affecting the neck.

Lymph glands behind the knees, in the groin, in the armpit, and in the chest are more unlikely to show infection unless there is an infection nearby.

Hodgkin's Disease. This is, fortunately, very rare in children. It is a form of cancer, but its progress is very slow, and treatments are remarkably effective. Patients sometimes go into remission for long periods of time, and they may believe they are cured. The outlook for such patients is much better than it was even a few years ago.

Symptoms. This disease is first noted by the presence of an enlarged, exceptionally hard lymph node. Usually, it is first discovered in the neck. To be definitely diagnosed, such a node needs to be removed and studied under the microscope. Doctors who are specialists in diagnosis can tell very accurately whether or not this is Hodgkin's disease, and the appropriate treatment can begin at once.

Be certain that your child, if he ever should have Hodgkin's disease, is under the care of a reliable cancer specialist. A *hematologist* or *oncologist* is a doctor who knows the best treatments for such a disease. Do not settle for anyone—no matter what he claims—who has less training than such a specialist. He may be able to work with your family doctor or pediatrician, especially if you live a long distance from a large medical center. Such specialists often see people from a great distance, and recommend treatments that can be given nearer your home.

Lymphedema. Sometimes the ducts or channels that carry the lymph or fluid that helps nourish the body's tissues become damaged. Occasionally they may be partially blocked from a birth defect; or the damage may be the result of a serious infection or injury. In any event, the lymph tends to collect in the tissues, causing swelling that becomes somewhat firm. It may even cause tightness of the skin and stiffness of the muscles in the areas affected.

Lymphedema may be severe and even crippling in its effect, though this is, fortunately, very rare. More often, the system reestablishes enough of the lymphatic flow to keep the child's body functioning. Once it reaches a balance, it may not become any worse. The most common areas involved are the thighs, and this is due to injuries in the groin. Very rarely, surgical drainage may relieve this condition, at least temporarily.

THE SENSORY SYSTEM (Ears, Eyes, Nose, and Throat)

The ears, eyes, and nose are sensory organs, along with the tongue and skin. These functions are described in "The Next Two Years of Life," chapter 7.

In this chapter we are concerned with the illnesses, infections, and injuries that may affect these priceless parts of the body.

The *nose* is the organ of smell as well as the upper part of the air passageway to the lungs. It also is the receiver of drainage from the sinuses. (*See* Respiratory System earlier in this chapter.)

The *eyes* are organs of sight. They are connected by nerve tracts to the visual center of the brain, as well as the cortex or outer covering of the brain. It is here that the sights our eyes see are interpreted, recognized, and remembered.

Ear Infections

Sense of Balance. Our *ears* are organs of hearing. In addition to hearing, the inner ear is involved, along with part of the brain, in our sense of balance. When a child twirls, as on a merry-go-round, or just for fun, the structure of the inner ear twirls, too. When the child's motion stops, however, the fluid in that structure will go on turning, creating a sense of dizziness.

Motion sickness is due to sensitivity of the inner-ear mechanism. Some children, as you know, have much more of a tendency to motion sickness than others. They can't ride in a car comfortably, let alone a merry-go-round or Ferris wheel. They

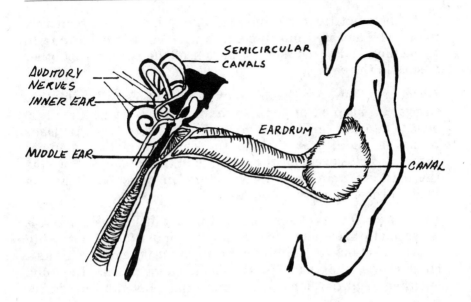

EAR

may even vomit from such dizziness. Usually, motion sickness lasts only a short time after the movement stops.

Allergy-Caused. Sometimes such dizziness (or vertigo) is caused by allergies, or a cold, that causes irritation or swelling in that inner ear. This creates serious loss of balance, nausea, and general misery, sometimes for several days. The treatment of this is the use of decongestants, such as antihistamines. Dramamine and Marezine are available without a prescription and help motion sickness, as well as the vertigo just described. These medications, however, make a child very sleepy. For auto trips or plane flights with children, that may be an added advantage. If you want to take your child to an amusement park, however, his fun will be greatly impaired by the drowsiness.

Deafness. This may be a condition with which a child is born. (*See* "The Next Two Years of Life.") Or it may be the result of a serious illness that could damage the auditory nerve. It may occur from serious injuries affecting the eardrum or tiny bones that conduct sound waves to the nerve endings.

Causes. One of the causes of deafness that can be prevented in most cases is that of repeated infections that are neglected. An eardrum that swells can easily rupture.

If this is not treated properly, hearing may be permanently impaired. Repeated infections also may cause trouble due to thickening and scar-tissue formation of the eardrum or other tissues in the ear.

Earaches. These are the dread of parents of a small child. Few things can keep all of you awake all night like a genuine earache. There is a tiny tube called the *eustachian tube* that leads from the middle ear (behind the eardrum) into the upper throat. It helps even out the pressure in that area and prevents the eardrum from breaking with sudden pressure, such as a blow to the ear or even a big yawn.

Eustachian Tube. The problem with that little tube is this—it is especially short and wide in children under four. So it easily allows infections to get into the ear from the nose or throat. As a child grows, the shape of the head changes, and the tube lengthens and develops an *S*-shape that prevents such infections.

Dangers in Ear Infections. More than being painful, ear infections involve some danger, as well. The pressure of the fluid that builds up in that little chamber blocks off the very tube that allowed the infection to get started. If it is not treated promptly, it will cause the eardrum to break. If this happens, you will know it because there will be blood-tinged, pussy discharge from the ear canal. Once the drainage occurs, the excruciating pain stops, and finally the ear will heal. The danger, however, is that the eardrum may not heal well or there may, after several bouts of this, be enough scar tissue to impair the hearing.

Symptoms. These symptoms will help you know if you need to call your doctor:

1. *Severe pain that is not relieved by aspirin, ear drops, or the use of nose drops to try to open that offending little tube*
2. *Fever over 100 degrees F. that accompanies an earache, indicating a bacterial infection*
3. *Drainage of material from the ear canal*
4. *A loss of hearing in an ear that has been aching or that has drained*

You do not need to rush to an emergency room with an earache. Just go to your doctor's office on the day it occurs, or even call him if you know your child is susceptible to earaches. He will decide if he needs to see the child (he usually will) or can telephone for a prescription.

Treatment. The treatment of earaches involves the relief of pain as soon as possible. Your doctor will probably give you a prescription for pain-relieving drops to use at once. *If you see any sign of drainage, however, do not use drops.* We do not want to get oil into that middle-ear area.

Next, an antibiotic should be started to cure the infection. Most doctors start with an injection that will work quickly, but will follow that with oral antibiotics. Be sure to give this to your child for as long as the doctor says. Many times the pain is quickly relieved, and the child feels better, but the infection will flare up in a few days if it is not really cured. It will take five to seven days for this to happen.

Oral decongestants help cure an earache by reducing the swelling in the nose, throat, and eustachian tube. Nose drops add to this part of the healing process. Use them several times a day for two or three days.

Tonsillectomy. When a child suffers frequent earaches, your doctor and you may feel concerned about serious damage to that ear. He may recommend the removal of the tonsils and adenoids. These are lymph glands located in the throat and behind the nose, which help localize colds and infections. They may help block off that opening into the middle ear, however, and their removal helps keep it open and prevents middle-ear infections.

Tube Insertion. Another very useful treatment is the insertion of tiny plastic tubes through the eardrum to keep fluid from building up in that middle ear. These tubes may safely be left in place for many months, and then removed. They do not lessen a child's hearing, and will prevent infections. You need to be careful, however, to keep water out of that ear until the tubes are out, and the eardrum is healed.

External Otitis. This is an infection of the canal of the ear. It is commonly called *swimmer's ear,* and is caused by bacteria that easily grow in a moist, warm area such as an ear. A swimmer's ear begins by itching in the canal. It progresses with a watery or thick discharge that may be white, yellowish, or green-tinged. The drainage becomes chronic, and the itching and minor discomfort are annoying. Rarely, however, are they likely to make a child feel really sick. He may not hear very well, but usually even the hearing is not seriously lessened at first.

Treatment. Over a period of time, however, an external otitis can damage the eardrum, cause a more serious infection, and even some hearing loss. Call your doctor about such an infection. He should see your child, clean out the ear, and show you how to treat it. It is wise to have him recheck the ear until it is completely well.

Precautions. If your child is highly susceptible to ear infections, you may need to have him use earplugs when swimming, or keep his head out of the water, or both. Ask your doctor's advice.

Ear Injuries

Injuries to the ears are due to two causes: a) sticking a foreign body into the ear canal; b) a blow to the ear with sudden, strong pressure against the eardrum. A hard slap over the ear or some diving accidents are examples of such a blow.

Prevent such injuries by teaching your child to avoid ever inserting anything into his ear. Never slap or allow anyone else to slap a child on the ear.

However, no matter how careful you are, such injuries happen. If your child complains of pain and you see blood coming from the canal, call your doctor for advice.

IF THERE IS BLOOD COMING FROM THE EAR, IF YOUR CHILD CANNOT HEAR A WHISPER OR WATCH TICK IN THAT EAR, AND IF YOU CAN FIND OUT THAT THE ITEM STUCK INTO THE EAR WOULD BE SHARP ENOUGH TO RUPTURE THE EARDRUM, GO TO YOUR DOCTOR AT ONCE.

An eardrum ruptured by pressure will have jagged, rough edges. Unless these are repaired properly, your child's hearing may be permanently damaged.

An annoying accident is the entry of the canal by an insect. The child who can talk will tell you it is there. Holding a flashlight to the ear almost always attracts the insect and he will crawl out. Holding the child still is the hard part because the tickling is intense! Should this not work, you may drop in some sweet oil, ear drops, or even lukewarm water and the bug will float out. At least this will kill it and stop the buzzing and tickling.

The Nose

The following problems affect the nose and its functions:

Hay fever. This is an allergy that affects the nose, rather than the lungs. It resembles a cold, but it lasts a very long time. The symptoms of hay fever are:

1. *There are frequent "clusters" of sneezes.*
2. *Almost constantly the nose feels stuffy or is runny. The secretion is watery.*
3. *The eyes are red, watery, and uncomfortable. Both the whites of the eye and the eyelids are affected.*
4. *Inside the nose, the tissues are pale-gray and glistening, as contrasted to a cold, in which they are red and angry looking.*
5. *There may be a dull headache from the pressure of the stuffy nose, but it is not as severe as in a cold.*
6. *Almost always, there is a history of other family members having asthma or hay fever.*

Treatment. The treatment requires a visit to your doctor to diagnose and determine the cause of this allergic phenomenon. The diagnostic procedures are like those for asthma, and desensitization shots may be necessary when symptoms are severe. Other treatments are:

1. *Antihistamines* which will counteract the swelling and nasal discharge. Unfortunately, they make most people drowsy, and you may be able to give them only at night.
2. *Decongestants,* such as ephedrine, will help reduce the swelling and dry up the discharge, but it may speed up the heartbeat and act as a stimulant, keeping a child awake at night. Your doctor will need to help you adjust dosages and balance these side effects.

3. *Nose sprays* will give prompt relief, but it doesn't last long. When you use them too long or too frequently, they may become irritating and actually can make the swelling worse. Do not use nose drops more often than four times a day, and not more than three days in a row. After a few days, you may use them again.

4. *Cortisone* or its related substances may be needed in severe cases. We like, however, to save it for the most severe attacks, because it, too, has some side effects.

5. Rarely, you may need to see your doctor or an allergist regularly for hay fever. We have never known it, however, to be an emergency.

Bacteria commonly invade the nasal passages and seem to stay there with little evidence of pain or infection. Children with *bacterial rhinitis,* as this is called, will have a yellow or green-colored thick nasal discharge. They tend to have crusts that form on the middle of the nostril, which they pick. Such picking may result in nosebleeds and more crusting.

Antibiotics, in an ointment or spray, as well as taken orally, will cure a nasal infection. Your doctor will need to prescribe the oral medication.

Nose Injuries

Foreign Bodies. Young children universally love to poke their fingers into small openings. This includes their own ears and noses as well as light sockets. Often, as they suck their thumbs or fingers, they tickle their noses with a fuzzy blanket. Once a family brought in a child with only a complaint about the child's foul-smelling breath. It was true! And the cause was a plug of blanket fuzz the child had stuffed up his nose. Removal was easy in the office, but we do not recommend that parents try too hard to remove foreign bodies from their child's nose or ears. It is easy to do more damage than you help, especially if the object is hard, like a bead. If the child is old enough to cooperate, have him blow the nose fairly hard. A tickle to the nostril may cause a sneeze that will dislodge and remove the item.

If these measures do not work, however, take the child at your convenience to the doctor's office for the removal of the foreign object.

Nosebleeds. These are caused by injury, by picking the nose, or sometimes they occur spontaneously.

Nose picking is a common habit. Sometimes it is due to nervousness, but often it is caused by annoying or painful crusts of dried mucus in the nostrils. As a child picks these, bleeding will often result from the raw tissue beneath. Almost all of children's nosebleeds come from the sides of the septum or cartilage that divides the nostrils. About one-quarter to one-half inch up the nose on this structure, there is an area with so many capillaries that it even has a special name, *Hesselbach's triangle.* It is here that most nosebleeds originate.

Treatment. Knowing that makes treatment of a nosebleed simple. You do *not* need to put ice on the neck, a pack under the upper lip, or have the child lie down. Simply do this:

1. Have the child blow his nose to clean out any blood clots.

2. Have the child sit quietly and practice breathing through his mouth, while you firmly pinch his nostrils together, creating pressure against the septal area described. Your thumb and forefinger will generously cover it. If the pressure causes pain, release it slightly.

3. Keep an eye on your watch, hold this pressure for five minutes. The child will get restless, but *do not let up sooner* or you will have to start all over. An older, reliable child, can hold his own nose.

4. After five minutes, release the pressure gradually, and tell the child to hold his nose still for five more minutes. He will feel like wiggling or rubbing it. Do not allow him to do so, unless you want to repeat this process.

5. After several hours, apply, very carefully, a small bit of petroleum jelly or other ointment. This will soften the crusted area and help keep the child from picking it.

Broken Nose. A break of a young child's nose is very rare, due to the softness of the cartilage tissues until three or older. A fall or blow with a moving swing, and so forth, can strike the bridge of the nose, crushing the fine bones, and causing severe bleeding and pain.

Treatment. Pinch the sides of the nose together to create gentle pressure and stop the bleeding. *We recommend taking the child at once to your doctor or hospital.* No serious harm is done by waiting a few hours, or even a day or so, but a broken nose needs setting to prevent its growing crooked, and to prevent blockage of the air passages.

Eye Infections

Infections of the eyes are of two types: *bacterial* and *viral.*

Sties. Bacterial infections commonly occur in the tiny oil and sweat glands in the eyelids or in the hair follicles of the eyelashes. We commonly call these *sties.* They are painful, red, swollen areas. Usually they point or come to a head, drain, and heal. They do, however, tend to spread, since the drainage is loaded with bacteria. In the warm, moist climate of the eyes, these bacteria readily set up new sties.

Occasionally they penetrate deeper and cause infections that may require a doctor's care. Do not take a chance on your irreplaceable eyes. If a sty does not heal promptly, see your doctor.

Pinkeye (Conjunctivitis). Viral infections cause redness, itching, and pain of the lining of the eyelids and of the eyeballs themselves. Very often there is a mixed infection of bacteria and a virus called *pinkeye.* Actually there are several kinds of infectious agents. This condition, common in childhood, is highly contagious but rarely serious.

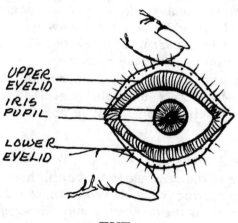

UPPER EYELID
IRIS
PUPIL
LOWER EYELID

EYE
(front view)

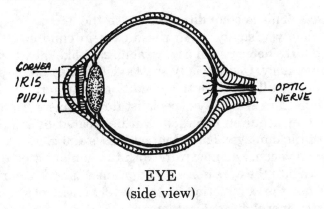

CORNEA
IRIS
PUPIL

OPTIC
NERVE

EYE
(side view)

Symptoms. The usual course of pinkeye is this: A child goes to bed at night feeling well, but having some itching in the eye. He may only feel that he is more sleepy than usual. In the morning, however, he awakens, but finds he cannot open his eye. Usually it affects one eye at a time. The secretions from the infection dry on the eyelids at night, literally crusting the lids together. Soaking the eye with warm water will open it, but the eye is red and very painful. Your child should be allowed to miss school to keep the infection from spreading, but also to let him rest the eye, treat it with medication, and promote complete healing.

Calling the Doctor. Call your doctor if your child has any infection in the eye. He can determine by telephone whether he needs to see your child, or can simply telephone a prescription. For an infection, the patented medicines are not adequate. *Do not waste time with them.* This is one time price is not a major issue. If the eyelids and skin around the eyes are swollen, red, hot, and tender, *call your doctor at once.* These are rare but important signs of a more serious infection that needs treatment at once.

Other Eye Problems

Color Blindness. This occurs in about 5 percent of males and is extremely rare in girls. The usual problem is one of distinguishing between red and green colors but occasionally other colors, too.

Doctors have special charts that will diagnose the condition. While there is no treatment, it is useful for your son to understand this visual problem. He will need to learn traffic lights, for instance, and will require help in matching colors in wearing apparel.

Cataracts. This is a condition in which the lens of the eye becomes cloudy. Usually when these exist in children, they are due to a birth defect, such as a viral disease like measles during early pregnancy. Occasionally such a defect may be hereditary. Your doctor will diagnose this condition fairly early in life, but you will need to see an eye specialist for treatment. Congenital cataracts or acquired cataracts can be treated by surgical removal of the damaged lens. Contact lenses and glasses can give fairly good vision, and new work with the implantation of artificial lenses into the eyes holds great promise. Surgical correction must await the completion of the development of the eye, in order to properly fit artificial lenses.

Glaucoma. This is an eye disease that is rare in children, but needs early detection and treatment. In fact, it is usually a birth defect, if it does occur. It is evidenced by swelling in the front part of the eye. The pupil and iris (dark center and colored area) are enlarged, and the eye feels firmer than normal. Surgical as well as medical treatment can help this, but it needs to be treated by an eye specialist.

Eye Injuries

Foreign Bodies. The most common injuries to the eyes are caused by the presence of foreign bodies in the eye or a blow or bruise causing a so-called black eye. (*See* the section on bruises.)

Anything not normally in the eye will cause severe discomfort. Even an eyelash or a speck of dust will cause the eye to weep for attention. Many such specks may be removed by pulling the upper lid out over the lower one and having the child blow his nose. Often a facial tissue or soft handkerchief may be touched gently to the speck, and it will stick to it and come out. Do not be too forceful in trying to take care of this yourself.

When to Go to the Doctor. When a foreign body is hard, such as a grain of sand, or if it is sharp, such as a piece of glass from broken spectacles, or when you cannot remove it with the above procedures, go to your doctor's office. He can remove it without the risk of further injury. A scratch to your child's eye with his own fingernail, or someone else's, or a sharp object, also demands a visit to your doctor. Put a patch of gauze or folded handkerchief over the eye. Tape it with transparent tape. The doctor will probably determine the extent of the injury, give you some medicated drops, and bandage the eye shut for a period of time. Such a scratch often injures the cornea, the eye's protective outer covering. If it is not treated, an infection could result in scarring and possibly impairment of your child's eyesight.

IF THE EYEBALL HAS BEEN HIT WITH A SHARP OBJECT OR BY A SEVERE BLOW, GO AT ONCE TO YOUR DOCTOR OR TO THE NEAREST HOSPITAL. SUCH AN INJURY NEEDS IMMEDIATE ATTENTION. BLEEDING FROM OR INTO THE EYEBALL OR EVEN SEVERE DISCOLORATION OR SWELLING ARE SIGNS REQUIRING URGENT MEDICAL CARE.

Black Eye. This usually involves the eyelids and bony area about the eye itself. Many times the eyeball is red due to broken capillaries in the whites of the eye. This looks dreadful, but it is not serious and will disappear before the bruise is gone.

Treatment. Cool or ice packs to an injured eye bring some relief from pain and may decrease the swelling. Mild pressure also helps prevent swelling. Blows about the eye often involve a laceration, as well. Usually this will be over the bone above the eye, or occasionally over the cheekbone below. Such cuts need to be seen and repaired by your doctor to prevent dangerous infections or ugly scars.

Red Eye. Other insults may also result in a red eye. Usually the red, watery eye is due to pollen, dust, allergies, or infections. During a coughing bout or vomiting episode of unusual severity, tiny capillaries may break or open up enough to allow red blood cells to escape into the tissues. Other less-common causes are seizures or convulsions, or severe straining such as with a hard bowel movement.

It is important for you to understand this symptom so you and your child will not worry about it. You need not do anything about it at all.

Injuries to Throat and Larynx (*Voice Box*)

Most injuries in this area are due to foreign bodies. Children love to put objects in their mouths as much as they love to

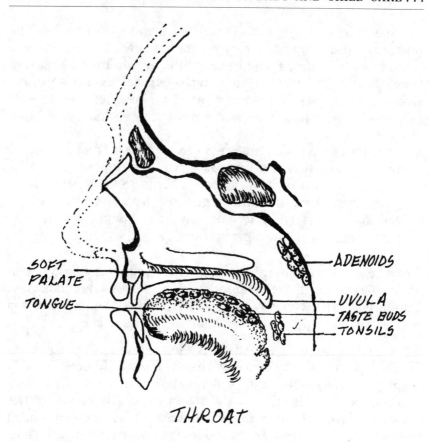

SOFT PALATE

TONGUE

ADENOIDS

UVULA

TASTE BUDS

TONSILS

THROAT

put their fingers in their noses. And all too often those objects get caught in the throat. Fortunately, most objects are too large to go through the opening in the voice box. You can often take them out, or the child will swallow them. We have seen a child who had secretly swallowed twenty-five (25) pins pass all of them without any complication. We do not however, recommend giving children access to such items.

Removing Objects. Do be extremely careful, however, in taking objects out of a child's throat. Probably no mother can afford the luxury of long or ragged fingernails, and this is one example to explain why. In reaching in the child's throat, hold his head firmly with one hand, insert your finger into the side of the mouth and throat downward, until it is under the object, and lift it carefully out. The child's reflex to choke or gag will help you bring it out.

Any object that is in the larynx or windpipe is quite another problem! Usually the presence of any object in these areas will cause severe coughing and choking. Often this will dislodge and expel the material, which may be food.

Heimlich Maneuver. Occasionally, however, the reflex of coughing is not enough, and the material may get stuck. It may partially or entirely block the air flow. If the child begins to turn pale or dusky in color, turn him upside down and give him two or three sharp slaps between the shoulder blades. If this does not remove the obstruction, place the child in a sitting position, and put your arms around him with your one hand grasping your other in front of him. With your fists, or the heel of your hand, in the pit of his stomach, give him two or three bear hugs in quick succession. This creates pressure against the child's diaphragm, and very often will dislodge the material by such pressure from below. This method was devised by Dr. Henry Heimlich of Cincinnati, Ohio. It is called the *Heimlich Maneuver* and has saved many people from choking.

IF NONE OF THESE MEASURES IS SUCCESSFUL (AND THEY TAKE LESS TIME TO DO THAN THEY DO TO TELL!), WAIT NO LONGER, BUT GET THE CHILD TO THE NEAREST EMERGENCY ROOM. TAKE SOMEONE ALONG TO USE MOUTH-TO-MOUTH RESUSCITATION TO HELP THE CHILD TO BREATHE.

The doctors may have to do a tracheotomy to save the child's life. This is an incision below the voice box through the windpipe to allow placing an airway into the tracheal area. Removing objects may take some time, and once your child is breathing, that can be done.

For little babies, and even older children, keep a rubber-bulb syringe handy. It can be most useful in withdrawing food, mucus, and so forth, that may cause choking. Keep any small items out of reach of your child, and you will avoid most choking emergencies.

The Tongue

Infection of the Taste Buds. There are countless rough spots over the surface of the tongue called *taste buds.* These sensory organs distinguish sweet, sour, salt, and bitter tastes. Most of our taste experiences, however, come from the sense of smell. Occasionally one or more of these taste buds become swollen and tender. Commonly such an infection is due to a herpes virus and accompanies fever sores in or around the mouth. This infection will last a few days and disappear by itself. No treatment is necessary.

Ranula. This is a swelling of a mucous gland or cyst under the tongue on one side only. Usually it is painless but may cause speech disturbances. It can be drained by your doctor, though rarely it may need to be treated surgically.

Geographic Tongue. This is one with round, smooth, red patches with slightly raised gray margins. These areas spread from the back of the tongue forward and on both sides. It means absolutely nothing, so do not be alarmed. Such patches come and go, and eventually disappear.

THE TEETH AND GUMS

Once your child's teeth are in his mouth, you have several concerns related to their care.

Influencing Factors

There are several factors that influence the strength and health of your child's teeth.

Genetics. Some families simply have the genes and chromosomes that make for weaker bones and less-healthy teeth. Nothing can be done about that except to take the best care you can of the teeth your child has inherited. Early detection and treatment of such defective teeth can make the best of the ones a child does have.

Illness During Pregnancy. There is some evidence that serious illnesses during pregnancy may have a damaging effect on baby's tooth buds.

Proper Nutrition During Pregnancy. This is also important to your baby's teeth. You need plenty of vitamins, minerals, and proteins for the formation of strong teeth in your developing baby.

Illness in a Baby's Early Life. It is likely that high fever and the toxic effects of serious illnesses in infancy may damage the developing tooth buds. Such effects are usually present only in the temporary teeth, so you may hope for better health in the permanent ones. An exception to this is the six-year molar. It starts to calcify at birth and may be affected in serious illnesses, thus causing early loss of this key tooth.

Diet. Children who eat a diet rich in sugar, invite tooth decay. Those who lack calcium and other minerals and vitamins, because of a poor diet, also may form poor teeth that decay easily. Sugars and starches dissolved in the saliva stay in the mouth for long periods of time. They create a climate that encourages the growth of bacteria, and these bacteria promote tooth decay.

Dental Hygiene. Removing food particles and getting rid of that sugar-rich condition can be readily accomplished by regular brushing of the teeth. As soon as the first tooth erupts, it should be brushed! *You* will need to do this for your child until she is about four years of age. Use a soft brush, and begin teaching your child to brush her own teeth after each meal. Let her watch you brush, and you will find that she will want to brush, also. Let her do it her own way at first, and finish doing it for her. Our dentist's rule of thumb is this: When a child can tie her own shoes, she can brush the teeth effectively—not before.

Fluoride. Be sure your child gets enough fluoride in the water or in special vitamins, to allow strong teeth to develop. This is especially important as the permanent teeth are forming at birth.

Care of the Teeth

Obviously, this begins during pregnancy and continues in providing good nutrition for your baby. Keeping him healthy will give him added protection against poorly formed teeth.

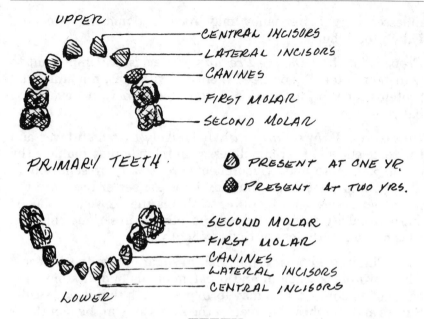

UPPER

— CENTRAL INCISORS
— LATERAL INCISORS
— CANINES
— FIRST MOLAR
— SECOND MOLAR

PRIMARY TEETH

🦷 PRESENT AT ONE YR.
🦷 PRESENT AT TWO YRS.

— SECOND MOLAR
— FIRST MOLAR
— CANINES
— LATERAL INCISORS
— CENTRAL INCISORS

LOWER

TEETH

Once those teeth are there, however, you need to help your child to care for them conscientiously.

Watch his diet and avoid sweets, soft drinks, and sugar- or starch-containing foods between meals. Milk in the digestive tract has minerals that help build strong teeth. In the mouth, however, it, too, may linger to encourage bacterial growth and tooth decay.

Have him brush those teeth after meals. Even a drink of water, or washing out the mouth with water, will get rid of much of the food or milk residue that encourages bacteria to grow around the teeth and gums. (A dentist friend once demonstrated to me [Dr. Grace] the value of eating an apple. He asked me to eat one and then to run my tongue over the surface of my teeth. They felt amazingly clean and smooth. He said there is an enzyme in apples that has this cleansing effect on the teeth, and strongly recommends eating that fruit regularly. Perhaps the old adage, "An apple a day keeps the doctor away" is still true, and applies to the dentist as well!)

When your child is between two and three, begin regular dental visits. The first visit or so may be useful just to acquaint your child with this important person and the complicated equipment in his office. He needs to like and trust his dentist if he is to be able to cooperate in future care of his teeth. Choose your child's dentist partly because of his ability to work successfully with children.

Decayed (carious) teeth may seem unimportant in a child of four or five, but do not be deceived. *It is entirely possible for a badly decayed baby tooth to spread its damage to the forming permanent tooth below.* Dentists usually repair or pull temporary teeth to prevent such damage, as well as to keep your child's mouth in good order. X rays are often necessary to accurately diagnose the extent of a cavity. Your dentist will not use X rays needlessly. Most dentists like to see a child twice a year, but if your child has "problem" teeth of any kind, he may need to see him more often.

Flossing teeth is now recommended by dentists and dental hygienists, as soon as a child is able to do this. Dental floss is a strong thread that is either coated with wax or especially made so it will not injure the gums. It should be cut into a length that is easy to handle, pulled between the teeth to the gum line, and gently passed back and forth for a few strokes. This cleans out the food particles that collect there, and helps prevent the formation of *plaque* or mineral deposits on the teeth. The friction also is good for the gums and makes them tougher.

Fear of dentists is a universal feeling. It is a wonder that any small child can tolerate a dentist's office at all. But if you can get over your own nervousness, it will certainly help your child to be more relaxed. We strongly recommend that parents stay in the waiting room while the dentist and the assistants take over for you. They are trained to handle a child's fears as well as his teeth.

When we took our youngest child to the dentist for the first time, we'll admit, we were worried about her response to the new environment. She was not quite three, and with a sober face, she trudged down that hall away from us. In a short time, she was back with a tiny toy prize and a smile. The dentist said that she had simply closed her eyes and sat absolutely quiet. Every child has more ability to cope with strange situations than we usually believe. Each does it in a special way, and we need to trust them to find that.

Dental Problems

The common problems of a child's mouth are discussed under Infections of Mouth earlier in this chapter. In addition to those, there are some dental conditions that need your attention.

Carious or Decayed Teeth. This is the most common dental problem. The causes of this have been listed above. We know good dental care will catch such problems early and correct them promptly. The new dental equipment, such as the drill with water cooling, makes a visit to the dentist much more comfortable. The less your child dreads those visits to the dentist, the more likely it is that he will go willingly and keep up the good care of his teeth.

Abscessed Teeth. When a cavity is not filled promptly, it enlarges slowly but surely. It may finally get into the center part of the tooth or the root canal. This part of the tooth contains nerves and blood vessels that go down into the bone that holds the teeth. Bacteria thus have access to tissues in which they multiply and set up an infection. Such an infection causes pain that becomes intense, swelling, and (sometimes) infection in nearby lymph glands.

Formerly, abscessed teeth were inevitably pulled. Now, fortunately, dentists can treat such an infection with antibiotics, drain the abscess, and clean out the decayed part, filling it with a special substance to prevent further decay. This is called *root-canal work.* It is expensive and extensive, but very often can save a tooth.

Broken Teeth. In the falls and fights of childhood, it is common to break off a piece of a tooth. Sometimes the rough edges can be filed, and the tooth will survive very well. In other cases, when the broken piece is large or has broken off close to the nerve, a cap will have to be made to cover the edges of that tooth. Such caps used to be made of gold and were expensive and, to some, unsightly. Now they may be made of material very much like the tooth and are hardly noticed.

Dislodged Teeth. This is a tooth that is completely knocked out. Usually such injuries involve the upper front incisors, and they affect the appearance as well as the pleasure of eating. A missing tooth may be replaced with an artificial one. This can often be done in a way that fastens the new tooth into the old socket, so it looks natural and functions almost like the original tooth. Amazingly, dentists can sometimes replant the dislodged tooth, and it will actually stabilize, at least for some time, and function as well as ever. All teeth that are loosened, even so-called baby teeth, should be splinted, just like a broken bone, since the teeth *are* bones in bones.

Plaque or Tartar. This is a deposit of minerals on the teeth, especially at the gum level. It is very hard and must be chipped and polished away with special tools. Unless it is removed, cavities will tend to form, and the gums may be damaged. Later in life such problems may be severe and require painful and extensive repair. Using floss will help prevent this condition.

Bleeding Gums. When a child's toothbrush shows evidence of blood streaks on it, you'd better look at his mouth. It may mean that the gums have become soft from poor care, due to the toothbrush being too hard, failure to brush the gums at all, or perhaps that there is some abnormality of the tissues. Some dentists recommend the use of a Water Pik.

Importance of Brushing. Have your dentist or hygienist show your child how to brush his teeth. He needs a brush that is soft, according to our dentist. A harder brush may be painful, so the child does not brush thoroughly, or it may actually scratch or injure the gums. Good brushing uses an up-and-down stroke, following the ridges on the teeth, then a gentle, thorough job on the gums, as well as on the grinding surfaces of the teeth. The stimulation of gums makes them firmer, increases the circulation, and promotes a healthy mouth.

Trench Mouth. Bleeding gums may indicate an infection. One such infection of the gums is called *Vincent's angina,* also called *trench mouth.* It is caused by a germ that spreads quickly and creates swelling, tenderness, and bleeding throughout the mouth. Antibiotics, such as penicillin, will cure this quickly, and it needs to be treated to prevent serious damage to the gums. Trench mouth is no longer considered contagious.

Lack of Vitamin C. This may also cause bleeding of the gums as well as in other parts of the body. One of the effects of vitamin C is to strengthen the tissues that compose the tiniest blood vessels (capillaries) throughout the body. When that vitamin is not present in adequate amounts, the capillaries allow blood to seep through, causing easy bruising and bleeding gums.

Some very rare blood diseases also cause bleeding and bruising to occur throughout the body. Your dentist or doctor will be aware of that fact and will recommend tests to rule that out.

Crooked Teeth. These are a common problem among children. It has become almost a necessity for every child to have beautifully straight movie-star teeth, even though the cost now runs into thousands of dollars. Certainly it is helpful to a child's sense of personal loveliness to have even teeth, but there are also good health reasons for having orthodontic work done. By straightening the teeth, there are fewer deep crevices in which food particles and bacteria may hide. There should, then, be less decay and better dental health.

Malocclusion. Furthermore, severe *malocclusion* (or the failure of upper and lower teeth to fit together properly) may cause trouble of other sorts later in life. When the jaws do not fit together symmetrically, a condition like arthritis may develop in the joint of the lower jaw and the skull. This is painful and incapacitating. It should be prevented rather than cured.

Good health depends on good nutrition, and good nutrition depends a good deal on good teeth. So take care of your child's teeth and cooperate with your dentist. It's one thing that pays, even though it costs!

EMERGENCY PROCEDURES YOU MAY NEED TO KNOW

There are several lifesaving measures that you need to master. Most of these must be taught through demonstrations, but try to become familiar with them. Watch your newspapers and television, or listen to the radio for available classes (that usually are free) where you may learn these techniques.

Cardiopulmonary Resuscitation

C.P.R. means *cardiopulmonary resuscitation.* It is a method of creating pressure on the heart and lungs to stimulate breathing, and even to revive the functioning of a heart that has stopped beating. This procedure has saved many lives, and you need to be trained in using it. It could save the life of your child.

Mouth-to-Mouth Resuscitation

Mouth-to-mouth resuscitation is a method of artificial respiration for a person who has stopped breathing, but whose heart is still beating. In a small child, the mouth of the rescuer is placed over both nose and mouth of the baby, and regular, slow breathing is used. Be careful to avoid strong pressure on breathing out (which is the patient's breathing in), to avoid overexpanding the lungs.

On an older child, hold the nose shut, and simply breathe into and out of the mouth. The rescuer's mouth must be held firmly over the patient's in order to create the vacuum effect that is needed to start his own breathing.

Prevention of Drowning

The victim needs to be helped to drain out and vomit out the water from both his lungs and stomach. To do this, put the patient on his stomach and lift him up firmly by putting your hands, clasped, over the pit of his stomach.

Firm but guarded pressure on the lower ribs will squeeze more fluid out of the chest. It is necessary to have the head lower than the chest, so the fluid can drain out completely.

After removing the water (or other fluid), mouth-to-mouth resuscitation may be used to initiate breathing.

Time is short in reviving a person who has serious respiratory or heart failure. While you may never need to deal with such an emergency, every parent should know how to use these techniques, in case of a crisis. Attend classes, practice the procedures, and when your children are old enough to do so, require them to learn. Possibly, your child will save your life!

A WORD ON DIVINE HEALING

In the midst of today's spiritual renewal, there has been a great resurgence of faith in miraculous healing. My own [Dr. Grace's] mother strongly believed in God's healing, and many of my friends join me in that belief as well.

Biblical accounts of healing are numerous and go back to the days of the Old Testament. A Syrian king, Naaman, was cured of leprosy upon the advice of Elisha, the prophet, who told him to dip into the Jordan River seven times. Jesus' healings were too numerous to list, and included the ultimate physical miracle of restoring the dead to life. We have no problem believing the truth of any of those miraculous healings. Down through the centuries, further validated accounts testify to the miraculous intervention of God to heal and save people in times of need.

Such healings occur today, although due to a lack of faith, perhaps not with great frequency. And, unfortunately, some people have been guilty of the presumption of healings that God has not seen fit to perform. We have seen diabetics, in all good faith, taken off their lifesaving insulin long enough to die because of its absence. Children with epilepsy have been claimed to be healed and have been taken off their anticonvulsant medications, only to return to horrible seizures.

Many parents suffer agonies of guilt over their lack of faith and blame themselves for a child's illness or death. We hope you will not do this. We must allow God's sovereignty and forgiveness to rule in our lives and follow the guidance He gives us in difficult circumstances.

There are important miracles that do take place every day. Three days ago I cut my fingers deeply on a broken glass, and already they are healing. Three years ago I broke my ankle. A doctor sacrificially went through years of costly training, so he could put those broken bones together in straight alignment. Those bones are perfectly healed and strong again.

Often we forget that *natural healing* is a miracle. Our bodies are "fearfully and wonderfully made" and their tendency is to get well, no matter what. Aging, neglect, and carelessness may interfere with healing and health, but God's creative processes are truly marvelous.

The discoveries and dedication of the entire medical and pharmaceutical fields are easy to take for granted. Because there is no longer a single case of smallpox in the world, we may forget the genius and courage of Dr. Edward Jenner, who saw the similarity between pox in cows and in humans, and developed a vaccine that today has wiped that scourge from our earth. This, too, is a miracle! You may want to thank God for Doctors Charles H. Best and Frederick G. Banting, who discovered that insulin could be taken from animals and given to people to save their lives and health.

Our God is not limited. What *is* limited is our ability to understand the mystery of His laws, the whys, whens, and wheres of His touch in our lives.

Occasionally God does some supernatural healing through a miracle of timing in natural events. A brother of mine suffered a hernia while lifting a new cook stove in our parents' kitchen. He was not especially dismayed, but went to a surgeon to arrange for its repair. Our mother believed profoundly in God's power and asked Him to heal her son, so he wouldn't have to go through the pain and inconvenience of surgery. When he returned to the doctor for the presurgical physical examination, the man discovered that my brother had an abscess in that groin. Surgery, of course, was postponed. When the abscess healed, the doctor found that the scarring it produced had sealed off the weak tissues causing the hernia. It would be easy to see this as a series of coincidences. We choose to see it as God's loving response to the prayers of our mother.

God's control over the atoms and molecules is easy. He gave to people, however, the control over their own decisions, feelings, and attitudes. When people choose to submit to God, to have courage, to see something beautiful in the worst of circumstances, that, to me, is a huge miracle.

Two young women are equally miracles. One, Kathy Miller, was critically injured in a car accident. By all medical criteria, she should have died; yet she lived. By the most rigorous tests that were done, she certainly should never have walked or talked again, but she was restored to an exuberant life. Kathy is a winner.

Joni Eareckson also was in an accident. Severely injured, she lived but did not recover. She is markedly handicapped physically. Yet her spirit was healed. She evidenced no self-pity, and by the transcendence over her handicap, she, too, witnesses to the miraculous power of God. He gives her courage to live with the incredible limits of her physical condition. Perhaps we get too dictatorial as to how God should perform His miracles!

Now we know God still does miracle healings. He does them through men and women of special faith, and He does them directly to people of less spectacular but equally profound faith. Do not be afraid to ask for your miracle. But in a world much more committed to skepticism than faith, do trust God, the Father, to do the sort of miracle He knows is made to order for you or your child!

Part IV

Rearing a Confident Child

11
The Components of Personality Development

Surely one of the greatest concerns of most parents is "What sort of person will my child become?" Whatever his looks, abilities, and interests are, it is the kind of human being he is that will bring you joy and pride—or heartache.

Webster's New World Dictionary defines the personality as "Habitual patterns and qualities of behavior of any individual as expressed by physical and mental activities and attitudes."

CLASSIFICATIONS OF PERSONALITY

There are three major qualities useful in classifying and describing such habit patterns and qualities.

Extrovertive or Introvertive

Extroverts are people who are trusting, open, and readily become involved with people and situations outside themselves and their own homes. They are talkative and tend to be "joiners."

Introverts, on the other hand, tend to live within themselves. They are quiet and choose their own private pursuits over joining groups. They prefer to have few friends, but those are usually deep and meaningful relationships.

Optimistic or Pessimistic

By nature, perhaps, but certainly by life's experiences, some people expect the best. They describe the sky as "partly sunny," if they see even a patch of brightness.

The pessimist, on the other hand, plans to join a Pessimists' Club, but restrains himself for fear he will be struck by lightning while on the way. He routinely finds and expects the very worst!

Energetic or Placid

While the first two categories probably are learned, we know that a child's energy level is evident at—and even before— birth. In examining newborn babies, we find some who are alert and respond to any stimulation with great energy. Others sleep through an entire examination and barely react to the noise and jolts that are necessary to test their reflexes. You mothers of more than one child may have noticed that one was active before birth, and another worried you by his inactivity.

Dr. Stella Chess, a child psychiatrist and professor at Bellevue Hospital Center, affiliated with New York University School of Medicine, has studied such babies. She has discovered that many parent-child conflicts relate to differences in energy levels of parent and child. This is especially true of mothers who usually spend the most time with a child. A placid mother who is blessed with a child of high energy may be drained and frustrated by trying to keep up with the child's needs. It is not difficult to see how each would contribute to a vicious cycle.

You can easily see that in any one person there will be some balance in all three of these personality qualities. You may be a placid, pessimistic extrovert, an energetic, extrovertive optimist, or any other combination.

WHAT HELPS FORM THE PERSONALITY

Heredity

We have just seen that a part of the personality is present at birth—the high- or low-energy aspect—but even this may change somewhat as a child develops. The intelligence and physical appearance and bodily functioning are partially hereditary. We know intelligence is also influenced by a baby's early environment, and that a child born with a big nose can be transformed through plastic surgery. Many of us believe that heredity, while it plays a part, is not as important as it was once thought to be. And that's good, because we can do more about problems if we are not bound by the limits of heredity.

Home Environment

Significant influences in a child's home environment are not those of equipment and space. Instead, they focus on the people who compose the family—what they are like, and how they feel and react toward each other.

Security of the Marriage. It has been aptly said, "The best gift you can ever give your child is a set of parents who truly love each other." We hope you settled that before you had a child. If not, do so now. Love is a decision, a commitment, and a discipline. Choose to accept each other as you are; love the good; overlook the problems you can't change, and work together at changing those you can! Chances are, another spouse wouldn't be better, only different!

Unconditional Love of Each Child. Perhaps you dreamed of having a gentle blue-eyed girl with blond, curly hair and had a brown-eyed, bald-headed, active boy instead. Forget your dream, and learn to love every bit of that boy. Think of your baby as a surprise package from God. You may explore it only a layer at a time. See what God has put there to enjoy and·prepare for a special purpose someday! Lay aside your expectations, and as he grows, explore with him what his gifts and interests are. Guide those, but don't try to remake him into your "clone" or puppet.

Start Early With Fairness and Reasonableness. Learn to "read" your child, and sense his natural likes, dislikes, and readiness for the next stage in developing. Keep *exploring* more than *expecting!*

Provide Security Through Your Consistency. Get together, Mom and Dad, on your rules and how to train and manage your child. It helps form a climate in which he can safely explore and develop his true personality. Always follow through on threats or any disciplinary measures, as well as on promises.

Work for Balance. One of the advantages of having two-parent families is that of the natural check-and-balance system you can be to each other. If you parents use your differences in this way, instead of fighting over them, your home will be much happier and your children, better adjusted!

Such balances include protection versus letting a child risk and explore; freedom versus structure, leniency, and strictness—and so many more. Look for the extremes, and you will know much more about the balanced centers of life.

Practice Clear Communication. Children are so fresh and simple in their communication. Relearn from them how to be more precise and understandable. So many painful feelings come from poor communication.

Strive for Peacefulness. Your home will really reflect your inner being. If you are restless and disorganized, the chances are your home will be noisy and cluttered. If you are energetic and organized, your house will reflect that even by the colors and arrangements you choose. If you are calm and "together," the atmosphere of your home will be that. God's Word says, "Thou wilt keep him in perfect peace, whose mind is stayed [fastened] on thee..." (Isaiah 26:3). Be whoever you are, but make that pleasant for everyone about you.

A child's personality is fairly well bent by eighteen months of age, and really set by three years. That does not mean he cannot change. Habits and attitudes can always change, but the basic tendency to be intro- or extrovertive, optimistic or pessimistic, and energetic or calm, will be likely to stay as they developed early on.

Accentuate the Positive. If you have cultivated habits of finding the best in yourself, your spouse, and your child, as well as in life in general, you will cultivate optimism. If you have encouraged your child to talk by listening to him with respect, the chances are he will be more outgoing. And if you allow him to grow and explore with protection but also with freedom, he will find his own best energy level and use it creatively.

Environment Outside the Home

This aspect of your child's life is largely beyond your control. It is fortunate, therefore, that your home is the most significant force in his early personality formation.

His Expectations. Each child takes with him into the world the degree of trust and the attitudes that he has acquired at home. By the habits of behavior he has learned, he will set up other people to fit into his expectations. So, if you have been reasonable, gentle, and firm, the chances are your child will respond to his kindergarten teacher as if she were similar. By the respect and obedience he shows to her, he is likely to merit her appreciation and respect. When significant adults outside the home are very different from you, however, your child will be confused and perhaps afraid.

Your Interpretations. This is your cue to interpret to him something about other kinds of people. Your child may incorporate the quality of understanding into his personality. Be careful lest you teach your child that there is something bad about everybody. There are many extremely critical people who seem to build their own ego strength from the debris of those they tear down.

You do need to teach your child reality if his personality is to fit into this world. A child with too much trust and optimism can be duped and destroyed by dishonest and dangerous people. Teach your child *not to talk to strangers* when he is away from you, and instruct him *never to go with a stranger anywhere.* This is teaching him good judgment.

Growth Means Expansion. As your child grows, he needs to have his personal and geographic boundaries expanded. His curiosity will push for this and if you are observant, you will know it's time for him to move out. Help your child's personality to develop by giving him choices, opportunities to become creative, and requirements for responsibilities. Balance the activities that promote such growth at home with those at school and in church.

The Teenager. As your child approaches the teens, continue to enlarge his room to grow. Help him learn to think clearly and to develop a philosophy of life. Continue to teach him of God's plan for his life, and how He has guided you in decisions and your growth in wisdom. Steel yourself against the pain of losing your child. Only by losing him, the child, can you finally gain him as a friend for life.

Since personality development takes place so early in life, let's focus in more detail on certain aspects of your child's early life.

EARLY PERSONALITY DEVELOPMENT

A Swiss psychologist named Jean Piaget studied in depth a number of children. Dr. Piaget is co-director of the Institute of Educational Science in Geneva, Switzerland, and a professor at the University of Geneva. For more than forty years he has been an authority in scientific investigation into the origin and development of intellectual faculties in early childhood. He came to believe that the earlier and the more actively a baby was stimulated, the more intelligent he might become. While we still believe in heredity and its limits on the intellect, there is much truth in Piaget's ideas. As a baby's senses of touch, sight, taste, hearing, and motion are excited, they send messages to his brain that make it function in some way to interpret, recognize, and later remember these experiences. The more it works, then, the more efficient a brain ought to be. And so, it seems, it is.

Colicky Babies

Babies who have colic get lots of attention because their family can't bear the crying. Studies show that babies who had colic grow up to have significantly higher intelligence than comparable babies without colic. Now don't wish for a colicky baby! But do practice spending a lot of time playing with and enjoying your baby. It will benefit you and probably will help him.

Keeping a Balance

Remember the importance of balances in life, however, and be sensitive to your individual child. If he is already extrasensitive, be more soothing in your manner of playing with him. If he is too placid and calm, be more energetic, but don't try to make him become something he isn't.

A friend of ours described a visit to his new granddaughter. His daughter had taken great pride in having a "good" baby. She would lie in her crib for hours without crying, and demanded little attention. This friend realized, however, that good babies can unknowingly be neglected. He and his wife spent much of their time enjoying and playing with this responsive baby. After they left, their daughter was stranded with a baby who cried for attention and was not so "good"—but much healthier emotionally.

Enjoy Your Baby

Try to see your new baby, not as a burden, but as an exciting new person to cultivate and enjoy. The more you treat him this way, the more likely he is to develop just that sort of personality.

If you hope to avoid training your child to be pessimistic, catch him being good and give him your pleasure and approval. Too many parents attend to a child mostly when he has needs or is crying. Be happy and excited about him and reflect the joy he can feel in himself, as he grows.

On the other hand, a baby needs to cry and make some demands if he is to understand his strength. Appropriate energy and aggressiveness develop when a child's actions call forth the parent's reactions. You won't find the perfect balance in attending and responding, but your search will help you get there.

As your child grows, your skills will grow. And eventually you will find you have a beautiful child on your hands—one who is loving and trusting, exploring and curious, and willing to be finally independent.

FAMILY POSITION

There are certain components of a child's personality that we believe are related to his position in the family.

The Oldest or Only Child

This child, of course, gets the undivided time and attention of both parents. He does not need to compete for that and can feel quite secure. Oldest children frequently show a tendency to want to please the parents. They are generally loving, verbal, and responsive. They show a remarkable degree of responsibility. In fact, it is sometimes necessary to slow them down in that respect, or they become trained worriers.

Parents tend to overreact to their first child. They worry,

overprotect, and often overdiscipline. They call doctors and grandparents frequently, write everything down in the Baby Book, and take lots of pictures.

The Second Child

Now the *second child* is quite different. He is usually more independent but not so responsible. He is, in fact, somewhat lackadaisical. While he may be bright and verbal (since he learns more readily from the older sibling), he also may be less motivated to achieve.

It is easier to understand the second child if you consider the parents' opposite practices. Having realized that they overdid it with the first one, they certainly aren't going to repeat those mistakes! So they make a few of the opposite ones. They let him cry longer for attention, worry a lot less, and maybe ignore him some. He learns his independent ways from that, but may not feel as close to you.

If the second child becomes the youngest, he may get enough extra attention to make up for the earlier bit of neglect. If he becomes a middle child, however, he may become quite lost and feel relatively insignificant. This position risks some real harm to a child's self-esteem and his overall personality.

Middle Child

If you have a *middle child* (or several), be especially aware of the possibility that he may feel relatively unimportant. That may be due to his own inferences that the oldest and youngest children get an undue share of your attention. To counteract such fears, find the energy to share your interests with him, and in every way show and tell him that he is just as loved and special as the others. Watch grandparents and other relatives, so they do not unknowingly leave out the middle child.

Third Child

Third children often have a very decided advantage over the first two. Parents have explored both extremes and have a feel for better, middle-of-the-road practices of parenting. By their calmer, more confident approach, the third child often is more secure and develops more self-confidence. He is loving, fairly ready to please, and conscientious without as much worry as the oldest.

Often the third child talks late, because he learns how to get the older siblings to talk for him, or to understand his sign language. He may become a charmer, and it is quite possible to really spoil him. It is such a child who can get his parents to believe his mischief is "cute," and he can get by with so much that he becomes a con artist. Avoid that by thinking ahead ten years. If your charmer of four or five acts as he does now, at sixteen or eighteen years of age, will it be funny or dangerous? Discipline him accordingly, and you will prevent such problems.

Later Children

Later children may repeat any of the above patterns or form their own unique pigeonholes in the family. This is influenced by their temperament, the spacing of time between them and their brothers or sisters, and events that may take place.

The Youngest Child

The youngest child may be especially enjoyable, or he may become a problem. Sometimes parents just wear out and let him get by with less training and discipline. Sometimes older children resent the greater freedom he has and tend to "pick" on him. He may be overprotected or kept dependent by a parent who needs to be needed. This is a formidable list of dangers. But being aware of them is usually enough to help you overcome them, and raise that youngest child to be a fine adult.

INFLUENCES OF RELATIVES

Grandparents and other relatives can add to or detract from a child's personality health. My [Grace's] grandmother was totally deaf and materially dependent on my parents. But she was my main comfort in childish sadness and a steadfast example of courage and faith. Her acceptance of her handicap still inspires me! I remember a special cousin's notice of me as a secret assurance that I was special—worth her attention. Negative influences can be just as profound—but damaging. Here are some of the problems related to relatives and some suggestions for dealing with them.

Physical Resemblances

If the relative your child resembles is handsome, there may be no problem. If he is less attractive, you or your child may see some of his undesirable traits mirrored in this relative.

When a family resemblance is a problem, you may solve that by discussing it openly. Point out the positive features of that person, or help the child compensate for his apparent defects by developing qualities of character that transcend appearance. *Forbid teasing or name calling about any physical trait or habit.* Be careful that you, as parents, do not unconsciously feel that your child is inferior due to any physical defect.

Behavior Resemblances

Dr. Grace once worked with a family whose son resembled a relative. While the relative was quite handsome, he unfortunately went to prison for some major crimes. The parents were afraid their son could become like that relative, because he looked like him. By their tension and fears, they were pushing him in the very direction they dreaded.

Resemblance to a Deceased or Divorced Spouse

It is not uncommon for a child to be so much like a lost loved one, that he is a constant reminder of the pain or frustration associated with such a loss.

In the above instances, the cure is the same. 1) Get the facts straight. Resemblance does not mean this is the same person. See your child for himself and let go of the identity of the other person. 2) Finish your grief about the lost person or his failures. 3) Consciously release your child to be himself. Rather than concentrating on similarities, focus on his unique individuality.

Mirroring One's Own Faults

There are times when a child closely resembles you—his parent. It is your own qualities that either endear or estrange him.

If you see traits you dislike in yourself (sometimes because your own parents disliked them) in your child, reread the solutions above. They will work in freeing your child. Try them on yourself—you may also become free to be lovely!

Similarity to Your Parent

Again, if this is a favorable trait, it rarely causes a problem (unless you become partial to the child). Sometimes, however, such a resemblance brings out all of the struggles you once had with your own parent. When those old memories and feelings stack up on a current situation, they may become overwhelming. In such a situation, sit down, and in prayer and meditation try to really understand that problem parent. Name all of your resentments, and as you understand why they exist, let go of them. You will then be able to honestly forgive that parent. Review the section above, and we believe you will have solved this problem.

FURTHER ROLE OF PARENTS IN DEVELOPING PERSONALITY

Misinterpretation of Child's Behavior

Traditionally, parents see behaviors as having certain meanings. These do not always hold true. At times parent-child problems date back to birth, and the fact, for example, that the child never wanted to be held. Mothers describe such babies as "stiff," and unable to be cuddled. Almost always, as we talk, they discover, seemingly for the first time, that they had felt as if the baby rejected or disliked them. They unwittingly fell into a bit of rejection in return. Stiff babies are not *un*loving! They just have active, strong muscles.

Sometimes curious or mischievous children are felt to be mean or rebellious. Rarely is this true. They simply are more energetic and extrovertive. It is their unique personality. So train this child and help him to be considerate, but don't punish or try to change him.

Parents' Values and the Child's Personality

By the time people become parents, they have consciously or unknowingly formulated their value systems. This will include or exclude sports, music, reading, school achievement, personal appearance of one type or another, certain jobs or careers, spiritual qualities, and so on.

When a child's personality and aptitudes happen to coincide with the parents' value system, all is well and good. The child's need for approval will be met, and he and the parents will probably get along well.

Conflicts. Unfortunately, this is not always the case, and many a child's natural tendencies are at crosscurrents with the parents' values. They may love him just as much as the other child, but their approval will not be as genuine. Children have such keen sensitivities to their parents; you simply cannot fool them. They will feel your lack of enthusiasm, and be hurt by it.

We are talking now about a child's native abilities, not his behaviors. The latter need to be trained and controlled. His abilities and his basic personality, however, are his. You may help him balance those facets of it that we have discussed. But accept him and love him wholeheartedly *as he is!*

Please remember that God the heavenly Father created and planned for your child as He did you. Trust Him. He will help you and your child to find fulfillment and usefulness that will bring you peace and joy throughout your lives!

12
The Necessity of Spiritual Training

In our day, it is tempting to look for the easy ways in life. Perhaps the search for ease has unknowingly invaded even the spiritual areas of life. You need to teach your child the qualities of living that reflect the spirit of Christ. Perhaps He could wave a magic wand and give those to us. But knowing the physical, mental, and emotional complexities with which He created mankind, God carefully told us in Proverbs to train up our children in the way they should go. When they are old, they will stay in those paths. As you look at yourselves now and recall how you were as children, you will no doubt understand that statement from Proverbs 22:6. Let's consider how you may train your children in some beautiful habits.

SELF-CONTROL

Meaning of Self-control

Temperance is the quality of self-control in conduct, expression, or the indulgence of various desires. In the New Testament we are advised to "add to knowledge, self-control, and to self-control—patience" (*see* 2 Peter 1:6). Theologians originally felt this to be so important they called it one of the four cardinal virtues.

Control is a badly misunderstood term. When our family was learning to snow ski, we often saw warning signs that said, "Don't ski out of control!" and nearly every day, someone who ignored such signs ended up with parts of his body in a plaster cast. *Control* did not mean *stop skiing*, it only meant "Go only

337

with the speed and over only those areas that you can handle without hurting yourself."

Self-control is exactly like that. Allow only those emotions, behaviors, and attitudes in your life that are positive and loving. Paradoxically, sadness, fear, and anger can also be positive and loving. Stay in control of them and do not let them wreck you.

The word *temperance* as it is used in the King James Bible comes from a Latin term meaning "to mix in due proportions." Mixing all the many components of life in good proportion is temperance or self-control, and is a quality bringing resilience and strength—like tempered steel—to life.

Teaching Self-control

Here are some suggestions for teaching self-control or self-discipline to your child.

Start in Infancy. Start in infancy by understanding your child's feelings and needs. He is born with fear and anger. The fear may save his life, if you teach him to develop it into *caution.* It may restrict him, on the other hand, if you overprotect him and keep him from exploring because of *your* fear. Anger can tell someone a child is in pain and can bring out the correction of the injustice of a sticking pin—or the pain of the social ills in our world. By contrast, anger that is out of control can murder and destroy.

Control Yourself. Be in control of your own fear and anger, and you will provide the sort of example and care for your little baby that will lay the foundation for self-control.

Guide Him. As your child grows, he will need your warning and your external controls through protecting and guiding his exploring body. Keep his boundaries tight enough to protect him, and expand them enough to keep him growing. *Require your child to do something every day that he'd really rather not do.*

Letting Go. As soon as he evidences the ability to manage his own temper, behavior, and responsibilities, let go of helping him. Show your pride in his toilet control, consideration of friends (when he'd rather be selfish), and helping you (when he'd rather play). Your pride will mirror his own beauty and keep him steadfast.

Importance of Understanding Himself

A major element in teaching self-control is helping the child identify and understand his feelings. When he knows what can anger him, he may deal with it before it becomes explosive, while he can control and use the anger in a healthy way. The same principle applies to fear, and even excitement. It's as normal to be afraid as to be angry. Use that fear to teach caution, not to hide in panic.

1. *Teach your child the vocabulary of his emotions.*
2. *Interpret the needs that accompany these feelings.*
3. *Help your child to ask for these things clearly.*
4. *Avoid giving a child the reward of special attention for explosions. Help him gain control, and then talk out the needs and their solutions.*

With older children, you may only need to strengthen the habits begun earlier. If you missed it then, start now. Explain to your child what you are doing and seek his cooperation. It can be done.

Adolescent Loss of Control

Adolescents often go through a period of losing control. Their bodies change so rapidly, they may not have the physical energy to call upon to help them. They feel so confused at times about wanting to grow up or stay young, that they act like children.

One of the best ways to deal with this is to explain to your teenager that it is normal, and nearly everyone feels this way. Reassure him that this time will pass, and he'll find out who he really is. Meanwhile, show him he can count on your support and backup control. Then practice that. It makes no sense to scream and yell at a confused adolescent to control himself!

Most teens need comfort and reassurance when they lose control—more than they need lectures or punishment. Consequences may be necessary, too, but they should be administered with empathy and kindness, along with firmness.

OBEDIENCE

Obedience is a quality that is sadly lacking in many children. In 1 Samuel 15:22, God reminded Saul that "to obey is better than sacrifice." It certainly is more difficult because it demands giving up some of one's will and rights. Obedience is compliance with a request or command.

Importance of Obedience

In the life of a child obedience can be lifesaving. Crisis situations that require his cooperation are not uncommon, and a child's safety may depend on it. Obedience in the best sense is for one's good and *not* to establish a system of tyranny.

In recent decades, the mental-health field has advocated the establishment of children's rights and power. Child abuse is tragic testimony to the need for such considerations. As always, however, the pendulum of life swings from one extreme to the other, and currently we are seeing the consequences of too little obedience. In the Christian home this should not be, and disobedience is directly contrary to God's values as told in Samuel's writing.

We believe that no one can become a good leader without learning to be a follower—one who can obey orders before giving them.

Teaching Obedience

Here are some ideas in the teaching of obedience:

1. *Select one issue at a time that involves obedience,* such as leaving a special item in its place, and not playing with it (for a young child).

2. *Decide on the consequences for disobeying the command,* and then settle down with the child. Tell him that vase, for example, is off limits. He may not touch it.

3. *Whenever the child reaches for that vase, repeat a firm "No!" and reinforce that, if necessary, with a firm swat.* Simply restraining the child may be adequate discipline. But under no circumstances is the child allowed to have it. Stick

with both the child and the object until you are reasonably sure of his obedience.

4. *Then step out of the child's sight, and see if he has learned the lesson well.* It is one thing to obey under a parent's threatening stare, and quite another to do so by a child's own control.

If he was just waiting for his chance to disobey, you will need to repeat the routine. Doing this when a child is one or two years of age is a difficult task. When he is four or five, it is heroic. But be encouraged! Each succeeding lesson becomes easier. And remember that his submission to your protective, guiding, authority will make it easier to obey the authority of the heavenly Father.

Teaching the Older Child. An older child will not learn as easily as a younger one, but do not despair. He, too, can learn. With a child who can understand, discuss the importance of obedience. There are many examples, good and bad, to illustrate that point. Once your child can see the value of obedience, ask him to help you with a plan for mastering that. Again, start with one issue, such as turning off the television to do homework. Prepare both the child and yourself for the hardship that will be, but go ahead and put the plan into effect. Praise him when he complies, and do feel good about your own efforts! When he struggles against the new plan (and be sure he will!), just remind him of his agreement, and help him follow through. Don't expect him to be happy. That feeling will come when you thank him later for letting you help him learn to obey!

MEEKNESS

Meaning of Meekness

Meekness is a misunderstood quality of the Christian. Its true definition means "not inclined to anger or resentment." The present common inference of meekness is "spineless or spiritless," but the earlier biblical meaning was "pleasant, gentle, not seeking revenge." Being pliable and teachable are wonderful qualities that, in balance, would make all of life's relationships pleasant and worthwhile.

Everyone has had some encounter with a know-it-all person who is anything but teachable. It is often the opposites of certain words that help us understand their true implications. This is true of *meekness*. You do need to balance being teachable with being discriminating about truth and falseness.

How to Teach Meekness

If you are to teach this quality to your child, you need to understand and value it yourself.

1. *Your best way of teaching meekness is by modeling it.* You can learn as much from your child (almost), as you teach him. Let him know that, and he will reciprocate by being willing to learn from you.

2. *In making decisions and coming to agreements, stay open to facts.* Avoid arguments that prove your personal point of view and stick with ideas that make the issue logical and fair.

My [Dr. Grace's] mother was likely to be stern about things we might and might not do. Usually there was no discussion. I resented that attitude but was helpless to do much about it. One day mother caught me pecking away at my brother's typewriter. Looking up in fear and dread, I awaited the lecture she usually gave. I still recall my surprise when she calmly said, "Gracie, that is fun, isn't it? But you'd feel badly if something broke. Better leave it alone." Even as a child, I felt comforted by her effort to understand my feelings and to learn from me. That experience meant more than all of her lectures.

3. *In early childhood, your spirit of making sense out of your child's life (and yours) can instill into him this appropriate sort of pliableness.* My parents' discipline and examples helped me see the reasonableness and sense in life. It began in me a lifelong search for meaning in the happenings of life.

Explaining the need for proper rest, play, nutrition, and all sorts of ideas, can help your child to become teachable and open-minded.

In grade school, countless experiences may be used in several ways. A child may rebel against people or practices he dislikes, or you may help him gently fit into the situation and learn from it.

Coping With Difficult People. One of our children had an elementary-school teacher who seemed impulsive and unfair. Several parents became irate and wanted to get her fired. We felt she was not really bad enough to warrant that, and we chose to help our child understand and cooperate with her. Throughout life, there are difficult people. The earlier a child can learn to get along with, and even help them, the better off that child is. By such efforts to interpret others to your child, you are making him gentle and pliable enough to be tolerant.

Meekness in the Adolescent. Here the fruits of teaching meekness begin to ripen. A child is now able to reason on an abstract level, and can think through many of life's trying and puzzling times and people. He is likely to be loved by others who yearn for an understanding and flexible friend—one who will learn with them and from them, as well as share with them.

A man named James once wrote, "Who is a wise man and endued with knowledge among you? let him shew out of a good conversation his works with meekness of wisdom" (James 3:13).

GENTLENESS

"The servant of the Lord must be gentle unto all" (*see* 2 Timothy 2:24).

Meaning of Gentleness

Gentleness means *refined, polite, moderate, not rough or harsh.* Like meekness, it is rejected as a desirable quality by aggressive people in today's world. I have a favorite poster, however, that says succinctly: ONLY IN REAL GENTLENESS IS THERE STRENGTH. ONLY IN TRUE STRENGTH CAN THERE BE GENTLENESS.

Years ago a popular magazine advertisement for a motor oil declared: TOUGH! BUT, OH, SO GENTLE! That is the Christian concept of gentleness. Strong and tough, but sensitive and responsive. When I [Grace] was a child, I was often sick with strep throat infections. My mother was very gentle to me then, but the strength of my farmer father's very being was the most comforting and reassuring in his gentle care of me.

Teaching Gentleness

Teaching gentleness to an infant is a joy. Handle him with strength, but practice moving slowly and deliberately with your baby. Cultivate a soft tone of voice. Even in the house, the softness of the sound level, the degree of light, and the texture and color of fabrics can be soothing and soft.

As your child grows, you can learn to discipline him with the gentleness of genuine strength. As each child varies in his energy level, you will need to balance your strength and gentleness in different ways. Dr. Grace loved the hospital X-ray technician where she trained in pediatrics. The technician could quiet the wildest of frantic children, as if by magic. One day Grace asked her for her secret. She demonstrated it to her. While holding a crying child firmly, the technician whispered in his ear. He simply had to hear what she was saying, and in order to hear, the crying stopped. Once she had the child's attention, she could explain away the fears and gain his cooperation. A gentle touch!

Defending Himself. When a child has to contend with rough, bullying playmates, he may need special instruction in the tough side of love. Being able to defend one's self is necessary in many neighborhoods. In fact, a child may earn respect only when he can stand up to the toughies. You can instruct him in how to do this without unnecessarily hurting the other child, yet stopping his attacks. Help your child to understand, forgive, and restore reasonably kind feelings to the other child.

In adolescence, the temptation is strong to become sophisticated, macho, and calloused. Your encouragement and modeling are extremely important during these years to help your child stay gentle and kind.

Close relatives had taught their son to avoid fights. Obediently he had done that, but a classmate persisted in hurting and even bruising his arm in a sly fashion with a single knuckle of his hand. James took this without retaliation for an entire semester, but after discussing the situation, he and his dad decided it was enough. Waiting and ready, the next time the boy jabbed his arm, James coolly and calmly—but very firmly— gave one back. The boy was so amazed he barely stifled a yelp. Once more he attacked, and James returned the blow in silence.

Neither boy discussed the event but the attacks stopped. There was a new respect of James for himself as well as by his classmate.

In older children who have not learned to be gentle, you will need to do some teaching about its value and true meaning. As your child understands that and sees it in your life, he will be more likely to work at developing that special quality.

FAITH

"Now faith is the substance of things hoped for, the evidence of things not seen" (Hebrews 11:1).

Meaning of Faith

Faith is unquestioning belief in God. It implies complete trust, reliance, and confidence in Him. Faith is closely related to trust, but the latter is usually understood to be a basis for positive regard toward someone we know. Faith is a belief in someone whom we do not see or know with our physical senses.

How to Teach Faith

Infants. Teaching faith has its foundations in trust, and that needs to be developed from birth on. As you respond consistently to your tiny baby's hunger, wetness, boredom, or pain with the satisfying of those physical needs, you are helping him to learn faith. He calls, and you respond again and again. The more you can keep your mood tender and kind, the more secure your child can become in his trust. The greater the degree of structure and relative consistency you can offer, the more solidly will the trust be built. And that trust is the foundation on which faith will one day be built.

Preschoolers. In preschoolers, with all their exploring nature, you have still more opportunities to teach faith. Explain the life cycle of a caterpillar and a butterfly, and you have taught your child a marvelous pattern of birth, life, death, and life. It will help you comfort him when he must experience a loss through death.

Encourage the curiosity and wondering of your child. Faith will grow through questioning and honest doubts. Never discourage true searching on the part of a child.

Be a Model. Model for the child your own life of faith. Even now, I [Grace] am convinced that our shoes wore longer in the era of the depression because of Mother's prayers. She knew we could not often afford new ones, and prayed over every shoe we ever purchased!

Pray with your child, and ask God to show Himself to your little child in His own unique way.

My own faith in God is sometimes portrayed in my memory of my father. After a ride on a tractor or wagon, he would always reach the ground first, and he would say, "Jump to me, Gracie!" No matter how far it looked, I jumped without hesitation, for I knew he would never let me fall.

Spoiling a Trust. A little girl with whom I [Grace] worked had serious emotional problems. She was nervous and had nightmares. It was almost impossible for her to concentrate in school. She related this story from her childhood. Her strong daddy would sit on the floor and say, "Run to me, Janie!" The little girl would run as fast as her chubby legs could take her, and he would enfold her in his arms in a big bear hug. Every so often, however, instead of catching her with a hug, he adroitly slipped aside, and Janie would crash headlong into the rough wall behind him. She showed me the scars on her nose and cheeks from her crashes. This man taught her to mistrust. All too many parents aren't "there" for a child who needs them, and they spoil his sense of trust.

School-Age Children. As they study science and world geography, they can grow in their faith. Share in your child's growing knowledge, and add to it the wisdom of your understanding of God's creation. We have no way of knowing how God created matter and the universe, but many brilliant scientists believe that He did so. You certainly can be confident about God's power and intelligence in the creation.

Teach your child about storms, earthquakes, and tornadoes. As he understands them, he will be less fearful and can learn some things about protecting himself. Teach him about the incredible individuality of fingerprints and the uniqueness of snowflakes. If you live where there is snow, give your child a good magnifying glass and help him examine fingerprints and snowflakes. He will see that no two are ever alike!

Adolescence. In adolescence, your child is usually ready to be confronted with the need to confirm the faith you have taught him. His own spiritual birth is an event at which God must preside, so avoid pushing a child to a premature new birth. On the other hand, do not take for granted that he will take this important step of faith on his own. Watch him for signs of interest and readiness, pray for guidance, and lead him into that leap of faith into the heavenly Father's arms.

Adolescents are natural doubters, and we believe this is healthy more than alarming. Faith is the unquestioning belief in God, but doubt is the questioning and exploring that often leads to belief in God. We see God as being so wise and powerful that He welcomes honest searchers and doubters. Encourage your child's questions and doubts, and help him find the answers. In the end, his faith will be even stronger.

God's love for your children is much stronger than your own. He had Luke tell us that wonderful story of the son who left home and wasted his inheritance on wild living. That son, however, returned, and his father, who watched for that return constantly, saw him when he was still far away. What a celebration it is when a child returns. That's when your faith pays off!

PATIENCE

"... knowing that tribulation worketh patience; And patience, experience; and experience, hope" (Romans 5:3, 4).

Meaning of Patience

Patience is the will or ability to wait or endure a hard time without complaint. It is a grim reality that patience comes only out of some degree of pain. That makes a problem for the "Now" generation who have been taught to seek pleasure and avoid pain!

Teaching Patience

Nevertheless, as Christians, patience is a quality that must be developed, and here are some ways you may teach patience to your children.

In Infancy. Avoid immediate response to a baby's normal demands. It won't hurt him a bit to wait a few minutes for his attention, and it will begin to train him, through small discomforts, to be patient.

Now do avoid the other extreme of making a baby wait so long that he becomes angry at the real injustice of it all, or gives up in despair. It's another of those hard-to-find balances in life, and just when you've figured it out for one child, you may have another who is so different in temperament, that you have to start learning all over again. Of course, that process is teaching *you* patience!

There is a great piece of advice that the apostle Paul left for us to think about. It applies to the avoidance of practices that destroy a child's patience. ". . . Don't keep on scolding and nagging your children, making them angry and resentful. Rather, bring them up with the loving discipline the Lord himself approves, with suggestions and godly advice" (Ephesians 6:4 TLB).

Toddler and Preschooler. He can tolerate a fairly long postponement of his wishes, and he needs to learn to accept some definite commands and *nos.* You must distinguish between wishes and needs at this age. Needs for food, rest, and affection should be met regularly. Wishes for new toys, sweets, and delayed bedtime may require a negative response. It is the way you say *no* that makes the difference. An irritated or angry reply will prompt fear or resentment. A quiet, "I understand. I used to like to stay up, too. But you need your rest, and I see your eyes looking sleepy, so off you go," can help a child accept the limits of life with patience.

On shopping trips, make it a practice to get a special "thing" only on rare occasions. Our grandson, from the late twos, has accepted such negative responses to his frequent requests with a philosophical, "Perhaps tomorrow!" His mother told us that she has always tried to keep her promises to him. When she says he may have the item later, she really gets it for him. So he is developing trust as well as patience.

Grade-School Children. These youngsters get a heavy dose of the trials that work patience. They must give up some playtime for homework. They need to have household responsibilities, so there is a loss of more freedom. Parents and teachers are often reminding them to finish book reports and projects.

Be sure to give your schoolchild plenty of encouragement, little irritability or nagging, and all the honest praise you can. This positive approach can help him make it through some rough years!

The Adolescent. He needs patience as he hits the really frightening prospect of approaching adulthood. He has a variety of teachers to please, as well as parents (and possibly a boss and co-workers if he has a job). Being almost within reach of adult freedoms, he is still bound by the restrictions of childhood.

Be very sensitive to the deep and confused feelings of your teenager. Help him to grow slowly toward the freedom that carries more responsibilities than he can see. And do avoid the imprisonment of keeping him for too long under your orders. Use your authority sparingly, and depend more on his own self-control. Remind him of the need for endurance. His athletic experiences and observations are a fine model for helping him see the need for patience.

As with almost all adolescent issues, help your child understand facts well enough to choose well. Use your position primarily to nudge gently if he veers to one extreme or the other.

GOODNESS

"The fruit of the Spirit is . . . goodness . . ." (Galatians 5:22).

Meaning of Goodness

Honest goodness means striving for excellence in living. It is virtue, the essence of right living. Unfortunately, as language changes, many words lose their original dignity and value, and come to have a slang meaning. *Goodness* is such a word. It now is seen as "goody-good" or implies a "holier than thou" attitude. Be clear in your understanding of goodness.

Teaching goodness to your child demands some sort of measuring stick. However *you* understand morality and excellence will determine how good you or your child may be.

Jesus said, "There is only one who is good and that is God" (*see* Luke 18:19). In this respect, therefore, it is as God imparts His goodness to us that anyone can be good. Goodness is His gift.

How to Teach Goodness

Humanly, however, there are disciplines by which parents can begin to direct a child toward goodness.

1. *Teach and model excellent standards of ethics in your home, work, and neighborhood.* (We have such a neighbor. He does good deeds for everyone in a quiet, natural way that may go unnoticed—a good man.)

2. *Train your child to do good things for you or for others in his own way.* Our youngest child gave a New Testament to a neighbor one day, when she was only six. The next week, that neighbor was killed in an accident. That was a good deed, done in simple obedience to God's prompting. Being honest, considerate, and helpful are all evidences of God's goodness in a life.

3. *Watch the newspapers and TV for examples of people who evidence goodness or evil.* Teach your child the contrasts in life, so he will have a basis for good choices.

KINDNESS

"Be ye kind one to another, tenderhearted, forgiving one another . . ." (Ephesians 4:32).

Meaning of Kindness

Kindness is a way of doing or being benevolent. It includes sympathy, friendliness, gentleness, and generosity. Even in disciplining your child, you may do so kindly. My [Grace's] mother's kind manner of dealing with me about playing with my brother's typewriter was more effective and memorable than all of her lectures or punishments. Kindness is not passive. It is a positive manner of life.

Teaching Kindness

Teaching kindness cannot be done without modeling it. You may teach forever, but if you do not live kindly, your words will be largely wasted.

Infants. From the first day of your *baby's* life, parents, begin the habit of kindness to each other, as well as to him. This habit will be well formed by the time your child is old enough to try your patience.

As your child grows and begins to play with friends, observe his manner of interacting with others. Tell and show him how to practice kindness with them. You can firmly require this behavior of your child without behaving unkindly yourself.

Schoolchildren. Abstract concepts are easier to explain to this age group, and they can understand the real meaning of kindness. Being kind at this age, when others are not, is very hard. You can teach your child, however, to understand the inner fears that prompt rudeness and aggression on the part of other children. Their very negative behavior can motivate your child to even greater efforts to be kind. We have seen very young children learn to think compassionately—to be gentle and kind. Your child and you may learn that, too.

Adolescence. The insecurity and identity search may make your child temporarily short in kindness. Being kind, we believe, demands a core of real self-worth. So don't descend to your teenager's level of rudeness and anger. Be firm and strong, but gentle and kind. With your consistency, he will return even more readily to his own belief in kindness as a way of life. A group of parents with whom we meet regularly are supporting one another in this sort of discipline with their teenagers. It has been both reassuring and exciting to hear how well such an approach works!

PEACE

"Let the peace of God rule in your hearts ..." (Colossians 3:15).

The Search

Probably few qualities of being are as sought after as peace. Ironically, the more we search for it, the more it eludes us. Peace comes at the cessation of war or strife. It is quite right that John said, "Let the peace of God rule. . . ." As we get our lives in balance, stop fretting, and learn to trust, the peace of God comes to us.

The most important sense of peace is that which comes within each one who stops his inner struggles and learns to rest in Jesus Christ. This usually happens individually, but it spreads, and makes it possible for us to live in peace with others.

While peace is certainly desirable, there is a time for conflict. We have seen parents seek peace "at all costs." They have given up their responsibility and rightful authority in favor of peace. We call this laziness or passivity and do not condone it. When you need to be firm and battle out certain issues with a stubborn child, do so. The peace will return when you have successfully waged such necessary battles! You do not need to stay in battle array forever!

Teaching the Concepts of Peace

Teaching appropriate concepts of peace to children who live in a conflicting world is a real challenge. Begin with yourselves, parents, and each other. When you have some disagreements, settle them and return to peace and love. Beware, lest you seek the false peace of denial or pretense. We see many Christians, who believe they should always be peaceful and victorious, covering up their honest feelings of frustration or anxiety. You will only find them cropping up in disguised ways, so go ahead and admit these negative emotions. You can think about the problems that produce them, and resolve the issues once and for all. Pretending them away only robs you of inner peace, instead of restoring it.

Peace is one pole of a dynamic process. Only by upheaval or warfare can we, by contrast, even define peace, let alone value it. In teaching peace to children, please remember this polarity. Children do fight and disagree. Infants are born with anger. So be certain, in your children's battles, that the issues are clear. Help them finish their disagreements according to your family rules for such "fights." Then close those issues and return to peace again. You may, over time, help your child discover that true peace is the life-style he enjoys the most. The good feelings of peacefulness usually are preferable. However, when families value peace *too* much, they paradoxically live in the constant unrest of unresolved struggles.

Peace of God. It is extremely important to teach your child how to return to the inner peace of God. The loss of that sense comes about when one's conscience comes into serious conflict with his wishes or feelings. An example of this is the wish to play ball when the conscience says, "You need to be doing some homework." Many adults keep themselves in constant turmoil by thinking of something they should be doing instead of whatever they are doing. How useless!

Resolving Conflicts. Teach your child (and yourself, if you need it) to resolve conflicts of such damaging sorts by choosing carefully what to do and when to do it. Help him to gather the facts, talk or think about them, and then make a decision. He may find that by planning, he can play ball and still have time to study if he doesn't dawdle. By studying carefully this evening, he can feel free to play ball the next evening. Teach him how to find time to take care of his needs for fun and play, as well as for responsibilities in school and at home.

In gathering facts, sometimes one's own needs are all that must be considered. Often, however, the needs and feelings of others must be thought of. This complicates matters considerably, since one does not always know what the other person really is needing. Help your child find a courteous way to ask and to balance his own and the other's feelings and needs. Through negotiation and taking turns, remarkably fine solutions are possible.

The Element of Trust

In peace, there is an important element of trust or faith. A child will be at peace if he can trust his parents' wisdom and love. Through this, he will finally learn to trust his own judgment and decisions, and will stop worrying over mistakes, real or imagined. Ultimately, it is trust in the energy, wisdom, and protection of the heavenly Father that restores peace.

Submission

Peace usually also involves submission. When I cannot have my way, I can stay angry, or graciously yield this point, and choose to give in on this issue. Such submission is not slavish. It is courageous and mature, willing to take turns at having one's own way.

In every conflict of life, the ultimate power we each retain is that of choosing. We may only be able to choose how we will react or feel, but it is at that point that we can choose real peace, by leaving the final decision to the heavenly Father.

LOVE

"... God is love" (1 John 4:8).

"Let your older women teach the younger women to live quietly, to love their husbands and children" (*see* Titus 2:4).

Role Definitions

Anger and fear are born with each child. They are easily recognized. Love, however, must be taught. Historically, it is the mother who is the gentle, soft influence in the family. Her breasts nurture and comfort the baby; her voice may be softer; and her instinct usually is to protect and nurture her young.

The mother's soft love may well be balanced by father's physical strength, energy, and protectiveness. These role definitions are commonly rejected these days, but we still believe in them. This is biologically sound, since God put such instincts into animals. If you prefer to mix the male and female roles, certainly you have the right, but do find some way to help your child learn to identify himself. It is difficult to love one's self without a sense of who one is!

Meaning of Love

Love is much more than a feeling. Perhaps everyone has a slightly different sense of what love is. Certainly it is a choice. (I must choose to act in a loving way, whether I feel it or not, if I am to be consistent in parenting.)

Once you make the choice to be loving, the next step is to practice self-control and discipline yourself to carry out the loving way of life. Love is expressed in our actions as well as our words, and either without the other leaves an emptiness.

Love expects the best from others and will settle for nothing less. It is willing to be tough as well as tender. It is willing to enter into another's hurts and share the pain—whether it is a bruised knee or the loss of a friend. It is willing to take certain risks, such as letting go of a child when he is ready for more independence.

To be real, love must begin with God. He is love. It is in the personal awareness of His love for you that you can then love yourself. Jesus told us to love our neighbor *as* ourselves. He knew that we cannot really love anyone else until we do love ourselves. Now He was speaking, we believe, about a healthy respect for one's self as His created child—not an egotistical, self-centered, me-first sort of love.

Family Love

Parents. In a family, love needs to be solidly established between spouses before bringing a child into a home. Significant studies show that parents who are at ease and are satisfied with each other have children with much greater self-esteem than those who lack these qualities. Parents who fail to show such love for each other often put down one another, and end up losing the love and respect of their children.

Be careful to resolve the conflicts between the two of you before you talk too much with your child about love.

Young Children. Finally, the love of both parents ideally envelopes the children. This love is from birth to death with varying expressions. The infant needs gentle, tender, cuddling love. A toddler enjoys playful tossing and tickling as expressions of affection, as well as more cuddling.

Middle-School Years. In the middle grade-school years, most children need to receive affection in private, and need some space away from parents in front of their friends.

The Adolescent. Unless he is quite secure, the teenager needs still more privacy. But he also craves some expression of your love in physical ways. Try this in playful ways and in the privacy of bedtime. Don't worry; he will come back to loving you more expressively when he matures.

Teaching to Be Loving

Teach your children to be loving by these policies:

1. *Demonstrate esteem for each other and them.*
2. *Never insult a person you love.* Guide and criticize constructively by such comments as, "You can do better than that!"
3. *Listen with respect to your loved one's ideas.* You may disagree and challenge, but do not insult the person by name-calling or belittling him or his ideas.
4. *Stay in tune with the other's needs and feelings.* If you don't know what he needs, ask.
5. *Practice courtesy with your loved ones.* "Excuse me," or "I'm sorry," or "Thank you," are still in style.
6. *Be aware of your facial expression, gestures, and tone of voice.* Try to make them match, and if you must register anger or disapproval, return them to loving regard, as soon as possible.
7. *Be honest.* Don't act gruff when you're really sad or worried. Don't act hurt when you're angry.

Love is, by choice, vulnerable. A popular philosophy of today says, "You have only as much power to hurt me as I will give you."

By contrast, the Christian says, "If I love you, I will choose to be transparent with you. I will give you the power to hurt me, but not to destroy me."

T.L.C. has come to mean tender, loving care. We believe it may also mean *tough,* loving care. Love may need to be tough at times to provide the discipline and protection your children need. Tough love sets limits, enforces them firmly and consistently, with fairness and kindness.

JOY

"The fruit of the Spirit is love, joy, peace ..." (Galatians 5:22).

Meaning of Joy

Joy is a very glad feeling of happiness, delight, and great pleasure. There seems to be something absolutely essential about the presence of joy in human beings. When joy is missing, or in short supply, people go in search of a substitute. What they find that *seems* like it are excitement, thrills, and even danger.

Religious teachings, unfortunately, have been accused of being mournful more than joyful, and all of us have known Christians who seemed to demonstrate that. As we see the troubled lives about us and contrast them with the wonderful life God really wants us to have, we can allow ourselves to feel "down." It is truly comforting, therefore, to know that the Bible lists *joy* as one of the fruits of the Spirit!

Teaching Joy

Infants. In an infant, you may teach joy by the way you interact with him. Your exuberance in his very existence will be felt by him every time you touch him. Be sure that the sounds around him are joyful at times, as well as soothing. The tinkle of a music box sounds so happy; so can the sound of your voice, as you talk or sing to him. The delight of every one of a child's senses can be an expression of delight at God's superb job of creating that baby.

Motion of an object, or his own body, can be fun, and baby's grasping of your nose or hair, that brings a response from you, can make baby chortle with delight. He needs activity to feel joy.

The Growing Child. As your child grows, build upon these early experiences of his own physical senses. Help him to explore a variety of sights, sounds, touches, tastes, and motion. Swinging, climbing, and jumping are experiences children can share with great joy among themselves. Just watching healthy children at play is a joy.

Add to the experiences he already has enjoyed, new ones involving groups of friends, teachers, and pets. Our youngest child, Wendy, had a teacher whom all of us will remember. She stimulated the students' learning in every good way. But best of all—she loved them. Our daughter frequently told about the children gathering around this wonderful lady's desk: "We cuddled around Miss Smith today, and she told us the neatest story!" The joy of "cuddling" made the entire second-grade year a memorable one.

Even the losses and grief of life are made bearable by the memory and certainty of the restoration of joy.

The Adolescent. In adolescence, there is joy, as well as concern, over new freedoms and growth toward independence. Dating is another whole area of joy—as well as some anxiety. Help your teenager to have such wholesome sexual attitudes and controls that dating will stay joyful.

Finding a job and earning their own money is usually a joy for teenagers, even though there is some worry mixed in. One hot summer evening, our son, age thirteen, came up to me [Dr. Grace] showing his well-developed biceps. He remembered the year before and said, "Mom, last summer I was so bored, I didn't have anything to do but watch television. But this summer is *great.* I'm busy doing yard work, I have a great tan, and look at these muscles. And I even get paid for it!" He was full of the joy of achievement and its rewards.

The Fruits of the Spirit

Those of you who are Bible students will recognize in all of these qualities the fruits of the Spirit, which are listed for us in Galatians 5:22 and 23: "But the fruit of the Spirit is love, joy, peace, longsuffering [patience], gentleness, goodness, faith, Meekness, temperance [self-control]. . . ."

When parents plant the seeds of these basic traits, they await maturity and the cultivation of the Holy Spirit to grow and produce these lovely fruits. Wouldn't it be exciting to live in a family where each member lived out these qualities constantly? You can know this if you practice them, teach them, and submit to God's work within you and your family.

13
The Importance of Loving Correction

In child-rearing practices, we have seen a great many changes in the last four decades. In feeding, doctors have swung from rigid schedules to child-demand feeding, and from lots of strained foods early in life, back to milk-only for the first six months. We've gone from rustic to "prissy" in dress, and back to very casual wear.

Probably in no area of a child's life, however, have we shifted so far—and sometimes so unreasonably—as in the area of discipline. Many young parents (and older ones, too!) have been very confused by these contrasting philosophies. Let's see if we can think through this mass of conflicting ideas and arrive at some basic common sense.

How do you want your child to turn out?

CHARACTERISTICS OF EMOTIONAL HEALTH

These are some characteristics of an emotionally healthy person. Perhaps they can guide you as you set your sights on some goals that will help your own child. We would like every child to become:

1. A loving adult who is capable of understanding and caring about himself and others
2. A careful adult who has learned how to achieve bal-

ances in his life—who values and appropriately expresses both his aggressiveness or anger and his vulnerability or fear—one who controls these without hiding or exploding them

3.   A responsible adult who lives up to his own best, has an appropriate sense of duty, and is trustworthy

4.   A cautious adult who shows good judgment by finding and considering most of the facts involved in making life's decisions (not just his own selfish viewpoint or wishes)

5.   A wise adult who knows how to learn from his own and others' experiences, and applies such learning to new situations

6.   A creative adult who values his God-given talents and uses them for his own joy and the betterment of others

7.   A courageous adult who will take appropriate risks but not those that needlessly may hurt anyone

8.   An adult who knows how to lose as well as how to win

9.   An adventurous adult who explores more than he expects, but who expects the best of himself and others

10.   A reverent adult who values life as a gift from God and who protects that life through proper care and knowledge

11.   A flexible adult who can adapt to necessary changes when they are not damaging, but who holds to principles that dare not change

12.   An achieving adult who is motivated to reach goals, but who will not sacrifice his integrity by taking avantage of others

Wouldn't the world be a wonderful place if we all lived in such a fashion? We believe that children can be trained to become adults with some of these qualities.

BECOMING A GOOD DISCIPLINARIAN

Understand Yourself

In order to be a good disciplinarian, you need to *understand yourselves,* as parents. There are many ways to define one's own self, and we have chosen a vocabulary that is part of Dr. Eric Berne's *transactional analysis theory.* Dr. Berne was a well-known psychiatrist from Carmel, California. In working with a patient who was a highly intelligent professional man, Dr.

Berne saw him demonstrate several different aspects of his personality. One attitude was clearly childlike; another, quite mature and intellectual; and the third, either protective or critical, like a parent. From these observations and countless more, Dr. Berne and others developed a school of psychological thought called "Transactional Analysis." (*See* Bibliography.)

The Child in Us. Each of us has a part of our lives that is remarkably like the *Child* we once were. We adults express feelings, wishes, and imagination very much as we did when we were children. Most of us adapt or modify such expressions to suit various adult situations, but the basic Child is always there. He varies from loving to frightened to angry feelings, depending on what happens.

The Adult. We also have a compartment of our being that is logical, thoughtful, and *Adult*. Given reliable facts, the Adult computes and comes up with good answers and decisions. Many times these facts, however, are clouded by the wishes and feelings of the Child part of us. If in childhood, we were spoiled and became tyrannical, as adults, it could influence our logic negatively.

The Parent. The third major division of our personalities is the *Parent* who sits within, making judgments, or taking care of our wishes and needs. The critical, judgmental Parent is needed to bring into a balanced submission the willful Child, and the caring or nurturing Parent is important in comforting us when we are in need.

As you identify these parts of you, we hope you will determine which ones are out of balance, because they will dangerously influence some destructive methods of discipline.

For example, if you live too much through your wishes and feelings, you will find yourself frustrated and powerless. You will tend to fight with your children as if you, yourself, were a child. If you are too coldly intellectual, you will tend to stifle your children's natural feelings. And when you are too critical or too caring, you may discourage your children or make them overly dependent.

You can see, then, how very important it is that you understand all the facets of your own life. By knowing them, you may use the strengths and protect the weaknesses. Use your intellect to size up the situation that needs attending to. Use your criticalness to discipline, your nurturing, caring capacity to administer that discipline in a kindly way, and your feelings to understand those of your child. Use your childlike sense of need to remind you to lean on the wisdom and power of God. That's being a whole person and using all of your personal resources!

Definition of Terms

DISCIPLINE is a word that comes from the Latin. In its most meaningful definition, it is the process of teaching and results in learning. By such a mechanism, the results that are listed above can be achieved.

TRAINING is a word that originated also in a Latin word meaning "to pull or drag." In rearing children, then, we pull them along in the ways they should go. (And sometimes that is literally what good parents do!)

Common Mistakes by Parents

There are at least seven common mistakes that parents make which defeat their otherwise good training and discipline.

1. *Inconsistency.* When a child is required to do a job or behave in a certain way one day, but not the next, he becomes confused. In such a situation, he will test out his parents to see if they mean business. This testing out looks like rebellion, and so it prompts some anger in the parents. The anger will make most parents even more harsh on bad days, and probably will feed into their sense of guilt and a tendency to "rescue" the child the next day.

2. *It's naughty, but "cute"!* Some children are born-and-bred charmers. They can do dreadful things with a masterful look of mischievous innocence. It takes a truly wise and far-sighted parent to resist such charm. Many times we have seen parents scold such a child with grins on their faces. The child can't be blamed entirely for his choice of believing the grin. Resist such a charmer when he is in serious error and be *congruent*—that means make your face, words, and feelings all say the same thing.

3. *Rigidity.* Situations sometimes do warrant your being flexible. Now this is a tough balance to find. Being unbending

will eventually cause real rebellion, but being too flexible results in the confusion of inconsistency. The best picture to help you is that of enlarging the enclosure of a young colt. As he grows, his fences must be pushed back, or he will break them down. So know how your child is growing and decrease the limits as he evidences his ability to be responsible.

4. *Permissiveness.* In a well-intended attempt to show respect to children and to allow them to grow up uninhibited, there is now a generation of very easygoing parents. They have ended up with the tail of a monster. In a scholarly series of studies, Dr. Stanley Coopersmith, of the University of California at Davis, has shown that children of strict, consistent parents evidenced significantly greater self-esteem and general success than children of permissive parents. Children have neither the experience nor abstract reasoning ability with which to make many decisions until their teens. They need limited and guided choices early in life—a few decisions to make independently by seven or eight, with gradually increasing freedom until the early teens. By adolescence, most young people make many of their own choices.

5. *Lack of clarity about rules.* Mothers may allow privileges that fathers refuse, or vice versa. Sometimes rules are too detailed, creating constant hassles, or they may be too vague. Good discipline demands clear-cut principles that cover lots of details. For example, "You are not to hurt your brother or sister, physically or with words!" That means no biting, hitting, scratching, name-calling, and so on. You do not need to list those and then find you forgot "no kicking!"

6. *Excessive gentleness and patience.* That may surprise some of you. But children do not understand or respond well to infinite patience. There needs to come a point at which you, the parents, take no more! The child needs to believe you mean what you say, and you may practice firmness without guilt. The Bible clearly says of a father, "Whom he loves, he chastens" (*see* Hebrews 12:6). You are not likely to chasten if you don't lose patience. "Be ye angry, and sin not: let not the sun go down upon your wrath" (Ephesians 4:26).

7. *Failure to follow through.* You may be ever so clear, congruent, and balanced in your strictness and leniency, but if you fail to follow through, the game may be lost. After you tell your child to do something and he doesn't do it, you need to punish

him according to your plans and policies. That will let him know you mean what you say. But don't forget, the punishment becomes discipline only when the child does what he was supposed to do, and begins to do so regularly.

Good Training Concepts

The best time to begin training your child is at birth, though you will really be training yourselves then. The attitudes and habits you form early will be easier to achieve in a way that will serve you well later. Let's list some concepts that you may practice from birth:

1. *Be consistent.* The way you structure your baby's feedings, bath time, playtime, walks, and general care is important. Baby needs roughly the same pattern in his life, day after day. Now I'm not speaking of bells and alarms! But once your child establishes his hunger, sleep, and waking habits, you need to keep yourself and him settled into a regular pattern in your day's activities. Taking charge of that will begin to establish your authority. Considering special needs of your baby will give him significance and security.

2. *Be reasonable.* Babies certainly are not judges of reason. And you are not responsible to please them with two reasons for everything you do. You should, however, have reasons. You will grow in self-confidence and healthy authority when you know why certain events happen as they do. Later on, your child can be influenced and will have a greater sense of fairness if you do explain your ways.

3. *Be understanding.* That does not mean "Be permissive." It does mean that you need to be aware of the fact that babies' feelings and needs are closely entwined. Understanding implies that you see what their behavior means. For example, very early in life, children cover their anxiety and fear with anger and aggressiveness, but you should always respond to the deepest feeling and need. It is the target. At two, Andy was cross and impudent to his grandmother, who was baby-sitting. Understanding that he missed his mother—and was covering that sadness with anger—enabled him to discard the anger, cry out his real tears, and be comforted.

4. *Be aware.* Most of us have certain dreams for our children. As they grow up, however, they rarely fit into those

dreams. We may not be as accepting and aware of each child's reality as we need to be and often try to mold them to our original wish. Tune in to your individual child. Learn his limitations and capabilities. Help him to accept those limits and realize to the fullest those capabilities he has. Let your dreams fit within the framework of these.

5. *Be realistic.* Parenting is not easy and it certainly is not convenient. The sooner you discover and accept those facts, the sooner you can get on with it. One set of parents wanted children, but they believed they could have them and still retain the life-style they had enjoyed before the children came. Their oldest child became pregnant at fifteen. The second child had a problem with stealing, and the youngest ran away from home. There are sacrifices in being an adequate parent. Refusing to make those, with poise and grace, may cause a far worse sacrifice—emotional health.

6. *Be a team.* Being one of a pair of parents is hard work. Going it alone is nearly impossible, and we salute you wonderful and courageous single parents who manage and do it so well! If you are part of a pair of parents, however, be sure to talk out your differences and come to a basic agreement about your expectations, policies, and means of enforcement. When you disagree about a child, either keep it cool or disagree beyond his hearing. Children feel guilty and afraid when they know they have caused a problem between you, even though they may go ahead and take advantage to get their way.

If you're a single parent, seek out a friend or relative to serve as a "sounding board" and be a backup for you when you need that.

Dealing With Varying Emotions

There are several important emotions that you, the disciplinarian, are likely to encounter in yourself. Dealing with them appropriately can be grueling!

Anger. Without some anger, most parents would not discipline their children at all. Please be honest about your anger; but do control it. Some severely troubled children with whom I [Dr. Grace], have worked are terrified of their parents' anger. My mother had a policy that worked well. She took us through that big farmhouse to the farthest room. I believed she did that to allow our anxiety to increase, and it did! Years later, however, I overheard her telling a friend that she did that to allow her own temper to cool. It worked both ways. Do find your own method and use it.

Guilt. When parents become too angry, they may give in to remorse and guilt. Out of such emotions, they may apologize, rescue, or undo the good part of a special disciplinary action. Now when you do wrong in some way, you need to admit it and apologize. But don't do that when the basic lesson needs to stand. One evening I [Dr. Grace] had been exceptionally hard on our son about his irresponsibility, and sent him to his room to think it over. Then I began to picture how little he was, and felt I may have taken out the frustrations of my difficult day on him. The more I thought, the worse I felt. Finally I cut a slice of chocolate cake and took it, with a glass of milk, to his room. He looked up as I entered with my peace offering and said, "Mom! You just spoiled the whole thing!" How right he was!

Do not discipline your child, by the way, by creating a sense of guilt in him regarding the way he "makes" you feel. If a child does wrong, point it out. He needs to realize what was harmful about that. A healthy child will feel some remorse and guilt, and these emotions may prompt his reforming. For those, a child needs forgiveness from you, God, and himself. Do not, however, blame your child for upsetting you, giving you a headache, and so forth. Your reaction is your responsibility.

Helplessness or Despair. A child will eventually lose respect for a parent who gives in to self-doubts and helplessness. At the time, such feelings in a parent may make a child feel shame and guilt, and he will give in. Later, however, he may become disgusted and turn away. No child should feel stronger than his parents.

Resentfulness. A friend of ours described her punishments as a child. Her mother would lecture her regarding her evil ways, spank her, and then treat her coldly for several days. That mother clung to her resentments about the girl's misbehaviors to the point of rejection. Hanging on to resentment spoils good discipline. After an experience of that sort, a child needs to be forgiven and held in the embrace of the parent to demonstrate being restored to love again.

Good discipline should bring about obedience and respect without fear; a balance between giving in and yet preserving the child's dignity and individuality; behavior that includes personal safety and consideration of others, and eventually self-control.

DEALING WITH DISCIPLINE BY AGE GROUP

Good discipline demands knowledge of what each child is capable of doing and understanding at a certain stage in his life. Children vary a great deal in their abilities, but perhaps these rough guidelines will help.

Discipline in Infancy

At this early stage of life, a baby cries out in pain or from fear. In times of hunger or discomfort, he will sound angry, but is not capable of anger as adults know it.

One father we know reportedly spanked his babies from birth on when they cried. This would seem totally uncalled for and even dangerous. A baby's cry can warn the parents of illness, and is his only way of communicating.

The foundation of good discipline is trust, so give your baby consistent, loving care, security, and enjoy him. Play with him and talk to him. He'll respond in the same way as he grows.

In the infant, try to anticipate enough of his needs to avoid excessive crying. But allow enough crying so the child feels his importance. Your loving, consistent response to his yells develops trust.

From Nine to Fifteen Months

During these months, children are exploring and learning to walk. They want to touch everything, bang it, and taste it. Most breakable or harmful things need to be placed out of reach. Every child, however, must learn the meaning of *no*. To teach that all-important lesson of limits is essential and relatively easy now. Choose your time and the issue. Ceremoniously work it out with your child. He will help you to choose the issue by his special fascination for something.

With our son, the issue was an expensive book titled *Gray's Anatomy*, a classic of textbooks. The bright pictures fascinated our toddler, and he repeatedly grabbed it, nearly tearing the pages. One Saturday afternoon, I [Dr. Grace] sat on the floor with him beside the bookshelf. When he reached for the book, I sternly said, "No, Lyndon!" Avoiding my gaze, he reached again, and I firmly held back his little hand. As soon as I released my grip, he grabbed again. This time I firmly rapped his hand. He stamped his feet and cried, and I sat and cried. Being a strong-willed child, he repeated this painful ceremony at length, but I held out and finally that battle was won—for both of us. *Gray's Anatomy* was safe; Lyndon had learned to accept limits; and I had established parental authority. Other issues needed to be settled later, but each became a bit easier.

From Eighteen Months to Two Years

From birth through the second year of life, a child needs to be within sight or hearing of an adult at all times. That is confining and inconvenient—and *necessary*. It can also be fun, if you keep priorities in order and learn to enjoy and play with your child.

Rather than coping with the disasters of an unattended child, you take charge. Place him near you as you do other things. Think of new items he can safely enjoy. A wooden spoon and cooking pan can become a fine drum without injuring your eardrums. Various lids and utensils from your kitchen will intrigue him because they are new. Avoid items that could hurt him or the house.

Reach out to your child for a hug now and then. Stop whatever you are doing to play with him a few minutes, just for fun, and don't wait for his cry to command your attention. He can learn to be good for your interest rather than bad.

Those "Terrible Twos"

By the age of two, children understand a great deal, but they usually do not possess the vocabulary with which to communicate. We believe that much of the frustration of two-year-olds has something to do with that. They are also curious explorers, and have little experience with reality. Up to now they've had everyone's attention. They've been cooed at, changed, fed, picked-up-after, and their slightest wish has been Mom's command. About two, they begin to get a picture that shows that's about over. Now they have to feed themselves, use the toilet, and get scolded for climbing up the bookshelves.

Here's what a two-year-old needs in the area of discipline (teaching):

1. *He needs "live language."* That means Mom and Dad need to talk directly to him, taking time to look at him and wait for a response.

2. *He needs to understand the rules.* Those rules should be limited to two areas: a) those that are lifesaving, like staying out of laundry supplies and the medicine chest; and b) those that have long-range importance, like respecting the rights and feelings of other people.

3. *You parents need to understand and believe his limitations.* This can be especially difficult if you have a child who is large, physically. You may forget he is just two. Twos can't help spilling, dropping, exploring, and feeling frustrated. Practice patience and firmness. It's a good idea to get your "spiller" to help clean it up a bit. It may help him try harder to hold on. Be sure his spoon, cup, and plate are as spill-proof as possible.

4. *As nearly as possible, get all the caretaking adults to have similar rules and consequences.* Inconsistency is confusing and will slow down your child's learning.

5. *Don't forget to follow through.* That's even more important with kids than it is in a golf game! Be sure you remember praise! A report to Daddy about a special achievement of the day or a "thank you for eating so neatly" will give your child an excuse for feeling good. It also may train him to thank you for your efforts.

6. *Remember with twos as well as younger children to avoid crisis-to-crisis living by planning fun for every day.* Peanut butter sandwiches and milk are a picnic in the yard—and spills don't count on the ground. A walk around the block or the yard can open up a magic world to a child, if you are creative. Children love to walk on a wall—holding your hand if it's high. Rolling in leaves or grass is another form of ecstasy to a child. Be sure he has old clothes that can be stained. Play together, keep up cuddling, rocking and singing, or reading.

The need to set limits, be consistent, loving, and firm can be taxing. But the more you put into it now, the easier it will be later.

Temper tantrums are the dread of most parents. They can be frightening if your child is a breath-holder. *But you can handle them if you believe you can.* See the section Problem Behaviors in chapter 17 for more information on tantrums.

The Thrilling Threes

This time will inevitably arrive if you can just hang on through the twos. Almost as if by a miracle, a three-year-old becomes less resistant, more manageable, and fun again. They are ready to play actively with other children and can take turns—something a two simply is not ready to do. Here are some characteristics of most threes.

Characteristics of Threes. In *socializing* with children, each three-year-old needs to be given time to do it his own way. Andy waits in the doorway at Sunday school for a minute, eyeing the whole scene. Slowly and quietly he moves to the toys, starts to throw a ball to another boy, and then expects it back. He is learning to share, and loves the contact. Adults who understand will not push. Giving a child plenty of time and space, yet being there when he panics, will help him make it in this important job of developing socially.

This is the time for a child's *imagination* to reach full bloom. He needs toys that can be used creatively to make planes, bridges, or animals. You will need skill to know what he made without insulting him. When he asks you if you know what he has drawn with his crayons, and you really can't see anything but scrawls, you might say, "Oh, I'll bet you can't wait to tell me!" Usually, that's true. If he persists, use your imagination and tell him it looks like an inchworm or a leaf, and then, of course, expect him to say, "It's a dog!" He wins, and he needs to win. Don't argue, and don't try to make him draw a better dog. There's time for that later. Now he needs to just create.

In *pretend playing,* be sure both you and the child keep pretense and reality clear. Both are fine, but occasionally, a child may confuse them and that is a problem. Also, keep reality as much fun, at least part of the time, as pretending is.

Children need heroes. At three, they can adopt story or television heroes readily as their very own. It is your responsibility to be sure their heroes are good ones. Screen the television programs very carefully, even cartoons. And learn to tell stories. Daniel and Esther from the Bible are still special heroes to Grace, and she learned about them from stories her mother told her as a child.

If you are a single parent, or if your family has special stress during this year, when your child is three, use special precautions. Your child can imagine frightening things as well as happy ones. Take time to explain issues to him, in simple terms. Reassure him of your love and his safety. Don't overprotect or mollycoddle, but just be aware of his worry and respond to it.

Even though a three-year-old doesn't need as much supervision as a younger child does, he still should be observed by frequent spot checks. You may guide him into healthier play and social interactions, and he will be reassured by your interest in him.

By three years of age, your child should be able to control his aggressiveness and selfishness. He ought to stop biting, kicking, hitting others, and be able to share toys and take turns. Require him to do that. He should be able to eat his meals with the family with some degree of neatness, though he may be excused from the table earlier than others. He usually can play creatively for twenty to thirty minutes without direct adult attention. Most three-year-olds can use the toilet with very little adult help, and they can dress themselves, except for buttons and shoe fastenings.

Spankings. The older a child is, the less we believe they need spankings. Discipline (teaching) can often be accomplished verbally by clear, firm statements and patient follow-through. There may be times, however, for you to spank a preschooler. Do so ceremoniously. Take the child to a private area and explain to him what he did that was wrong, and why it was wrong. No long lectures, please! Tell him that a painful result to such a hurtful action will help *him* to know how others feel. Spank him with something that will not hurt too much, and let him cry it out. Then hold him, let him feel your forgiveness and love, and once more clearly tell him what you expect him to do from this time on. *Then forget it.*

Alternatives to Spanking. Some children are so sensitive and others so stubborn, that spankings may actually make them worse! Be sensitive to your child and use the least severe method you can that will teach the lesson he needs to learn. Some suggestions for a three-year-old are:

1.   Send him to his room to think about how to change his misbehavior. After five or ten mintues, go to him, talk it over, love him, and let him go.

2.   Time-out. This is a time-honored custom involving standing in a corner (or sitting on a chair) where you can watch him. It works best for a child who might tear up his room if he were sent there alone, or one who is too sensitive and could feel unduly rejected.

3.   The loss of a privilege. Not allowing a child to play with a special toy or friend for a day may teach him to value and respect them more. This method should be used when a child is too rough or inconsiderate. We do not believe in allowing children to break toys or hurt people out of anger.

4.   Do teach your child what he may do to express his anger. Help him verbalize it, understand it, and decide what to do about it.

Frustrating Four-Year-Olds

This is the era of "Whys?" and "Hows?" Four-year-olds are entering more into real things, though they certainly have not given up their pretend world. They want to know how birds fly and why the ants live underground. Their curiosity is endless and their questions remarkably profound. At times the world can be frighteningly big, and fours need plenty of attention. Keep an encyclopedia handy and look up some of the things your child brings up. That helps you to avoid glib replies, encourages your child's interests, and teaches him the wonderful habit of reading to find out about his world. Also, it helps when you really don't know! Above all else, do not ignore your child's priceless will to explore. His future success in life will have much to do with what he learns now. Be sure he learns that learning is fun!

Attention-Grabber. We're not forgetting that you are human! It's perfectly all right to postpone questions for a while, but children can't remember the point too long, so you need to remember what they asked. You may also be alert to the possibility that your four-year-old is demanding your attention through questioning or incessant talking. Avoid such indirectness by stopping whatever you are doing (when you can), and really listen and respond to him. As the quality of your attention improves, the quantity will become less. Children grow so fast. After five, your child will be in school, and he will never again be as truly yours as he is in the preschool years.

Explorer. Your four's exploring demands that he dismantle things to see what makes them move or tick. You will be tempted to think this is destructive. It isn't at all, since he wants to learn, not destroy. Keep old appliances that he can't get hurt with, and show him how to take them apart. Be certain, however, that he knows all useful articles are off limits. Toys should be those that can be built and taken apart often. Magnets and a magnifying glass can occupy some fours for a long time. Fours like babies of any kind, but they need help in handling them.

Preschool? Preschool may be a great idea for your three- or four-year-old. We believe in them for children who enjoy or need social times with other children, or for those who need help in developing learning skills. Do avoid early frustration, however, due to too many expectations. The fad for teaching preschoolers to read has hopefully faded. While it seemed so precocious, and gave parents much to brag about it became apparent that by the third or fourth grade, the early readers were no more advanced than others.

Expectations of Your Four. Here are some expectations you may rightly have of your four-year-old:
If your previous training has been good, he will usually be obedient. If he does not mind you, work out a plan for being more clear, firm, and effective in your discipline. Tell him what you want, help him do that—or wait for him to do it; then let him know that you respect and appreciate him and his efforts.
Most of the time he will play well with friends, and may begin to show the qualities of either leadership or following. Please accept both with equal pride. Even good leaders usually start out as fine followers. While this world certainly has few great leaders, it is certain there are few good followers. Continue to encourage consideration of others.
There will be plenty of spills, breaks, and falls. Teach your

four to clean up and mend these and to take proper precautions. Rarely, if ever, does a child need to be punished for such things. One of my [Dr. Grace's] major regrets is the anger I expressed to our son over torn trousers and jeans. It seemed that every Sunday his good pants were torn someplace in the course of playing with friends after church. Now I would quietly mend them with gratitude that such happy times would give him a sense of joy in the church and his friends there.

Many fours still take afternoon naps, but some are ready to stop them. A quiet time in the afternoon seems advisable. Lying down and looking at books, or listening to stories or records will balance his activities with rest, and keep you close to each other if you share that time with him.

Many sensitive and imaginative children will have bad dreams at times. Now, as when he was younger, go to the child or welcome him to your bedroom. We believe children deserve comforting and reassurance that dreams are not real.

Be sure to take him back to his own bed. He can learn quickly to enjoy spending the night with his parents, and will devise excuses for doing that. Most authorities agree that sleeping with parents is not a good practice, psychologically or practically.

Eating habits are usually set by four, so you need only be watchful to keep them good. Avoid too many snacks and make those fruits and vegetables more than sweets. Offer each child small servings of the family's meal, and give seconds when some of everything is eaten. Many children prefer vegetables raw, and most of them are more enjoyable and their vitamin content is more active when they are uncooked. We recommend raw vegetables and fruits whenever possible.

General Informaton About Disciplining Fours. Since they are curious, give them reasons for rules and discipline. Many times children will give up some of their power in the interest of fairness and logic. Do not, however, get sidetracked into arguments. Listen to the child's feelings and wishes, and honestly consider them. Make your decision, help your child understand it, and then firmly follow through.

A friend described her son, who was grouchy at times. One morning he asked for milk. When his mother fixed his glass, he refused it and demanded orange juice. She prepared that, and he immediately requested grape juice. Such a child usually needs to be given two choices, and then be required to stick with one. If he refuses it, put the drink in the refrigerator until he stops fussing.

Contrary to popular opinion, children do not have to be happy all the time. Life has many frustrating and sad experiences, and children can learn to handle these. Eventually happiness comes from within us. You may say to a grouchy child, "Sally, I can see you're upset right now. I feel that way, too, at times. Why not just sit down for a minute and think it over. Then come and we'll talk about it together." You do *not* need to make her happy. But do expect her to get over her grouch, and meanwhile, keep yourself at peace.

What Works Best. Disciplinary methods for fours that usually work best are:

1. *Tell them a few minutes ahead of time when they are going to need to change activities.* Follow through with that change, but don't expect them to like it—liking is not so important as doing.

2. *Tell them you appreciate their cooperation.* Using big words with fours sometimes helps them feel more grown up. It tells them you expect them to be mature people.

3. *Spanking is still appropriate for some children.* If it works, use it, but try other means of discipline, too. Remember, punishment is a means to an end.

4. *Time-out, going to his room, and losing privileges become increasingly useful if you add to them the logic and the requirement that the actions you deem necessary be done.*

It takes extreme courage and patience, but do wait it out with a stubborn or irresponsible child. I [Dr. Grace] used to nag our daydreamer child and ended up making both of us miserable. Making the expectations clear and the consequences meaningful is enough—if you don't spoil it by rescue tactics. If Johnnie doesn't stop playing when the final call goes out for bedtime, you cut short his story period by the time he dawdled. That gets him to bed on time, and protects his rest. The next day he is likely to remember the price he paid, and that will help him choose to respond. If stories do not interest Johnnie, of course you choose another type of consequence that is important to him.

School Discipline

After starting school, children receive a good deal of their discipline at school. It is extremely important that you and the school staff cooperate. If your child misbehaves at school, you need to firmly express your displeasure. But you also need to help him know how to handle the kinds of problems he will meet there. The complexities of large numbers of classmates from widely varying backgrounds creates confusion. Take time to get enough information to help your child understand his peers, and know how to get along with them. He needs to know how and when to stand up to another child's bullying, and how to reach out to a child who is shy. He needs to show respect for authority, but needs to let you know if that authority is out of line. Be careful to get accurate information about school situations before assessing discipline.

Homework

Schoolchildren need to do their assignments to their best ability. Find out if that requires *homework*. For most children, we believe it should. Homework emphasizes the profound importance of learning; and it helps you parents to know what is being taught your child. Sometimes you may disagree with a certain philosophy, and you need to help your child understand your point of view. Homework can also teach resonsibility. And finally, by having a set time for it (during which nothing else takes place), your child is not so likely to "forget" it or leave important projects until the last minute.

The Forgetful Child

If your child forgets books, supplies, or lunch money, don't be too quick to take them for him. A trip home or a late assignment may be a small price for the acquisition of a mature sense of responsibility. If it is truly unusual for your child to forget, or some unusual circumstance arises (such as a rare family crisis), you may find it fair to relent. Use good judgment and not pity, and you'll usually do the right thing.

Nonphysical Discipline

Methods of discipline for school-agers rarely need to be physical. Clearly think through with the child what is wrong, why it's wrong, and what needs to change. Discuss this *with* him and not *at* him. Find out what will most effectively help him learn this, and see to it that such a course of action is taken. If your grade-schooler does not begin to discipline himself, adolescence will be much more difficult.

It is harder and more time-consuming to *teach* than to *punish*. It is usually infinitely more worthwhile!

TEACHING RESPONSIBILITY TO CHILDREN

Meaning of Responsibility

Responsibility depends on the ability to distinguish between right and wrong. It involves thinking and acting rationally, and learning to be accountable for one's own behavior and decisions. It results in becoming trustworthy and reliable. Responsibility and good discipline are as interwoven as feelings and needs. They always go together.

We used to believe that children learned responsibility by parents' making them do their jobs. And it is important to follow through, as you know if you've read any of the section on Discipline. But it takes more than follow-through! That may only superimpose the parent's conscience on the child. Pinocchio, in that wonderful story, was lost when Jiminy Cricket (his external conscience) disappeared.

Responsibility by Degrees

A better plan is to give your child choices of increasing degrees of importance. Ideally, you started at two years of age, and by now your child is a veteran at making wise decisions. If you missed that, however, don't worry. Start now! But do it now with a little pomp and ceremony. Tell your child you've just learned that he is in need of some experience at decision making. Tell him how you arrive at your decisions. (Think this part out ahead of time!) Then work out with him a plan for taking into account the necessary information, discussing it with some reliable person, and coming up with good conclusions. Then let him have at it. Stand by without an "I told you so!" and help him correct mistakes and learn from them. Congratulate him on good choices, and *let him know what was good about them.*

During all of my [Dr. Grace's] grade-school years, my mother did a wonderfully wise thing. She always took me to choose the fabric for my new school dresses. During the process of sewing and fitting those clothes, she consistently had me show them to friends who dropped by. I can still hear her say, "Didn't Gracie make a fine choice? She always likes the dainty little prints!" I recall feeling so pleased with myself.

AREAS OF RESPONSIBILITY

There are three areas of responsibility we will discuss: 1) actions; 2) relationships; 3) materials and money.

Responsibility in Actions (Jobs)

1.   At home

As early as *one year of age,* a child will learn to accept limits and obey certain orders. He can, for example, help pick up toys before bedtime, or learn to stay out of areas that are dangerous.

By *two years,* a child can pick up his toys with only a little help. He can obey requests for helping by doing simple tasks, and becomes more reliable about staying within limits. He still needs much supervision and protection.

At *three,* most children are well on the way to being responsible for using the toilet, dressing themselves, playing safely and considerately with other children, and can help parents. They can follow two- or three-step requests such as, "Please get the flashlight, turn it on, and bring it to me."

By *four or five,* children can button and zipper clothes and a few may be able to tie shoes. They often get through a meal without spills, and are better coordinated in general. They can give up their own wishes at times in the interests of others, and are capable of cooperating with a group, such as a class. They can transfer respect for and trust in authority people from parents to teachers and other adults. They need guidance in whom to trust and whom to avoid.

2. At school

Elementary-school children have a great many responsibilities thrust upon them suddenly. They must learn to mind a new adult who changes at least every year. They have to adjust to some twenty-five other children in competitive situations for seven hours a day. They are confronted daily with parents' disapproval if they do not achieve successfully.

Begin Now. This is a heavy burden, but it can easily be managed if you have been teaching responsibility at home. If you have not done that, please begin now. Discuss with your child the idea that he deserves to succeed and be proud of himself. Let him know that in allowing him too much freedom, you have unknowingly let him down. Tell him that you will be changing the old ways, and convince him that you must have his help. Together, set up a plan that will assign some fair and manageable duties to each child. Work out a system to remind him daily to do them, and then make that system work. Such a plan should include school behavior and studies, as well as homework.

Problem Children. For several years, Grace has worked with problem children in school. Generally, they are underachievers and have behavioral problems. In many of these cases, the children have few responsibilities at home. When even a small job is asked of them, it is rarely enforced consistently.

Give your child a share in keeping your home livable. Teach him how to assist you in a variety of tasks, and then assign a fair amount of responsibility to do them on his own.

Keep a Chart. Keeping assignment charts for younger children will help them develop habits of responsibility. Such charts, however, are useful only if you parents keep using them consistently. Stars for successfully finishing jobs can be a reward to your child. But your praise and respect are the best reward, and will teach him the ultimate prize of self-respect.

Responsibilities in Interpersonal Relationships

1. Honesty

One of the major problems in relationships is that of dishonesty. It may be blatant or subtle, but it is destructive. People are dishonest with each other when they pretend to feel one way but actually feel another. Pretending to be hurt when you are angry, or acting angry when you are truly afraid or worried, is not honest. It is confusing and brings about responses that add to such confusion.

Emotions are God-given, and in their refined state, are uniquely human. Animals know love, anger, and fear, but not the many branches and shadings of these that people experience. So do not deny or disguise your feelings, but understand and express them appropriately.

Accepting One's Feelings. Please help your child to accept all of his feelings by accepting them yourself. Show him how to communicate those emotions by your own example. Teach him how to express them without hurting anyone, and in a manner that has respect and dignity. And guide him in identifying the needs that match his feelings. He can then get the need met and the painful emotions may be healed.

Vocabulary of Feelings. It is extremely important that you teach your children the vocabulary of feelings. There are three ways to do this:

1. *Put your feelings into words.* Be sure that your words, your real feelings, and your facial expression all match. That is what we call being "real," and it is believable. Do this with each other as parents, as well as directly with your child.

2. When you see your child looking sad, angry, excited, afraid, and so forth, *tell him the word.* Then ask him what has made him feel that way, and help him find a solution to the problem.

3. *Read to him.* Several books for children are now available that help them understand and express feelings.

2. Thoughtfulness

Very young children of even two or three can learn to be sensitive to the feelings and needs of others. You need to teach your child how to respond to them. This involves the quality of *empathy* or feeling with another.

How to Teach Thoughtfulness. You can teach this beautiful quality by your reaction to your child, your spouse, and others. Discipline yourself to enter into joy, sorrow, or any other emotion with sincerity and simplicity. Then guide your children to do this with you and others. Teach them the words to say, and tell them what to do. Grace has often said to our children, "I'm really tired this evening, will you rub my back?" or "I feel sad after hearing people's problems today. I need a hug." They seem to be pleased to be needed by their mother, and she avoids taking advantage of that.

Finally, when your child hurts, physically or emotionally, comfort him. And then use his pain to teach him how others feel. Children are naturally self-centered. They do not stop to consider how others feel unless someone teaches them.

3. Friendliness

How to Teach Friendliness. The Bible says, "A man that hath friends must shew himself friendly . . ." (Proverbs 18:24). That is just as true today as it was thousands of years ago. Children need to be encouraged to be interested in the lives and activities of others. Being congenial, willing to give and take, caring, and exploring ideas and concerns of one another are the qualities of friendships.

In his perceptive book *Four Loves,* C. S. Lewis described friendships as the "Oh! You too?" experience. A child who likes to play dolls will recognize that experience when she finds another child who also enjoys dolls. Help your child to discover and develop individual interests and skills, so he will be able to find others with whom to share such activities.

4. Generosity

Today's philosophy is generally a self-centered one. It takes special effort and awareness to teach generosity to children who, by nature, are selfish. Being generous is a bit easier if the child has the quality of empathy.

How to Teach Generosity. During the years of the depression, most people were poor, and our [Dr. Grace's] family certainly was. Very rarely, however, my father would buy a small bag of candy, and that was a great treat. I would ask for a piece the minute we were out of the store. Even now I recall Dad's exact words: "Let's wait till we get to the car. Other children on the street can't have candy, and they will feel bad to see you eating it." I knew how that felt, and I was willing to wait to save another child pain. Had my father not explained that fact, I probably would have grown up less aware of others' feelings.

It is easier for some children to share than others. And it is easier to be generous with certain things than others. Help your child in the difficult task of being generous with things he really values, if you want him to master the quality. Your respect and praise will make it worth the effort, until your child grows up enough to realize it for himself.

It is good to remember in teaching generosity, that each of us needs some of our own private "turf" and belongings. We believe this is not selfish and, in fact, provides the core of security that makes generosity possible. There are some items no child should be required to share.

5. *Respect*

How Not to Teach Respect. To a person, the teachers with whom we have worked professionally (several hundreds of them) say that children are losing the quality of respect. Our society has tended to take away our heroes. We are told all the bad qualities of the people we admired. While honesty is necessary, perhaps we have gone beyond that and have lost respect. Not only do children evidence lack of respect for heroes of the past, but for most (or all) authority figures of the present.

When we as adults criticize and put down others, we unwittingly may be teaching our children disrespect. A familiar bumper sticker reads: QUESTION AUTHORITY. And there is some value in questioning leaders who may have lost their integrity.

The other extreme, however, is to mistrust and derogate so many people that we respect no one.

The Meaning of Respect. Respect means consideration for others and courteous regard for them as individuals. It is evidenced by:

1. *Learning to disagree in an agreeable manner.* Holding an opinion different from mine does not make you (or me) a bad person.

2. *Giving others privacy in their space and feelings.* Teaching children to enter someone else's room only after knocking, or to share thoughts and feelings, is respectful, but probing and demanding usually are not.

3. *Noticing another's mood and responding sensitively to that shows respect; telling others a bit of how we feel or what we need is also an expression of respect.*

4. *Being responsive to others is respectful.* We have been with people who are so preoccupied with their own ideas that they never give us a chance to talk—or even respond to them.

6. *Courtesy*

Teaching Good Manners. We rarely teach manners in today's culture in America. Perhaps that is part of the reason for our being disliked as tourists in the rest of the world. True enough, good manners can cover an uncaring or even cruel heart. But that need not be true. Try to give your child the advantage of a loving heart by loving him and teaching him God's love. Then good manners will simply be the natural communication of that loving regard.

Meanwhile, teach your child—*and require him*—to say, "Please," "Thank you," "Excuse me," and the many other expressions of sincere regard for the comfort of others.

Responsibility in Material Things

Very young children have yearnings for things that do not belong to them. They also feel possessive of the things that do belong to them. As Christian people, we have serious responsibilities about possessions, and we need to teach these to our children early in their lives.

1. Teaching appropriate acquisition

First, let's discuss teaching children acceptable ways of getting things it is appropriate for them to have.

Purchasing. When your one-and-a-half or two-year-old child begs for a toy or other item in the store, decide whether it is permissible for him to have it. Explain to him the process of selecting and then *purchasing* the item. Give him the money to hand to the salesperson in exchange for the item, and briefly explain the process again. After a few such experiences, the average child will understand the idea of purchasing. This should avoid a young child's natural tendency to pick up whatever he likes and keep it.

Borrowing vs. Stealing. We had a rule, as our children grew up, that they never brought home toys or any item from friends' homes. That prevented the temptation to steal or even to borrow from them. There are times, however, when children may *borrow* something from each other. Be sure your child takes proper care of it and returns it promptly. Any breaking of that rule should mean the loss of the privilege for a while, until he can be more responsible.

Borrower's Responsibility. Material responsibility means that you do not borrow what you cannot repay. And it means that you always return what you borrowed. My [Dr. Grace's] mother taught us to return borrowed items a little better than they were. If she borrowed a cup of sugar, she repaid it heaped up. A borrowed pair of gloves had to be clean and pressed before they were returned, even to a sister.

Earning an Item. This is a wonderful way to get it, and it can teach your child to really appreciate any possession for which he works. You will need to provide special jobs and arrive at a fair pay scale. Usually children need help to save their money, until they accumulate enough for the article they want. The pride of ownership in such children is a joy to behold. Please give your child this extremely beneficial experience, rather than giving him too much too easily.

Postponement. Teach your child to postpone wish-fulfillment. We adults are largely responsible for raising a "Now" generation by giving children too much too soon. When a child asks for items in a store, it is wise to refuse those requests most of the time. If he throws a fit, remove him from the store. Far from inhibiting or depriving a child, this practice will teach him the value of postponing pleasures, and even of finding he cannot always have what he wants.

Sometimes Never. There are times when a child's wish may be fulfilled "later," and there are times when it may never be fulfilled. The use of candy cigarettes may be ever so appealing to a child. We thought they were a step in permitting children to smoke, so we decided against them. Our son wanted a motorbike, but we had seen too many mangled bodies from accidents on them. So we said *no.* He may have survived anyway, but we used our best judgment to provide protection and avoid needless risks.

2. Proper allocation of allowances

Now, let's discuss the idea of allowances. Many parents routinely give money to their children to spend as they like. There are pros and cons to this issue, and each parent must weigh them and decide.

Advantages that we see to routine allowances are these:

1.   A child has his own money to buy the little things he wants and has less temptation to steal.
2.   As his wants increase, a child has the opportunity to learn to choose what is most important—unless his parents supplement the allowance.
3.   Allowances make possible teaching a child to budget. We do not believe in giving a child free rein with his allowance. Teach him to tithe it for his Sunday-school or church offering. Show him how to save a portion, how to spend some for useful items, such as pencils or paper, and how to spend a little for enjoyment. Someday that child's spouse will be deeply grateful to you!

You may start with ten pennies a week for a four- or five-year-old, and increase the amount according to his needs and responsibility. Many junior-high young people can be trusted with an allowance that covers school and most personal expenses.

Disadvantages:

1.   Children may feel parents *owe* them the allowance, and may be ungrateful or demanding.

2.   Parents may be inconsistent in giving the allowance, causing frustration and nagging.

3.   Children may believe they owe nothing to the family as a unit. We believe every member of a family should carry responsibilities and share in these without being paid.

4.   Parents may be conned into giving a child doles through the week, even though he has squandered his allowance on the first day.

As parents, weigh the advantages and disadvantages and do your best to overcome the latter. Decide together what your policy will be, and explain it to your children. *Review your decision* now and then to see if it still is in the best interest of your child. Situations change and you need to keep up with those changes.

3. Teach sharing

Finally, let us think about teaching material responsibility for others. In a hungry and poverty-stricken world, teach your family to give and share with those who are less advantaged. Most churches have special projects that give to world hunger or local families in need. If you are even a little bit aware, you may find people who are needing something your family could provide. Take the time to do that. And do it with dignity and respect, avoiding condescension and pity. During those depression years of the 1930s, visitors rarely left our [Dr. Grace's] home without some small gift from our garden or chicken house. Even as a child I felt good about that sharing.

It really is possible to raise children with a true sense of responsibility. We hope this will help you to do it!

MOTIVATION

Healthy discipline and a sense of responsibility are part of the formation of healthy motivation. We speak with many groups of parents, and it is common for some of them to ask about non-motivated children.

Reasons for Lack of Motivation

There are four basic reasons for this. We have formulated them from our experiences:

1. *Failure to give children responsibility early in life prevents the development of achieving.*
2. *Overprotecting children, and doing too much for them, often gives them the feeling that they can't accomplish much, and even worse, that they don't have to. Natural laziness goes into effect, as well as a lack of self-confidence.*
3. *Expecting too much and being hypercritical may discourage a child so that he gives up rather than risk failure.*
4. *Taking a child's efforts for granted often becomes discouraging. Your child craves your approval and pride. Remember to show him you feel it!*

To prevent or remedy these problems, review the sections on Discipline and Responsibility earlier in this chapter. The results of success in these respects is the growth of self-motivation. And that's what it finally takes to get young people to succeed in school, in a job, and in relationships.

Guidelines for Motivating

Here are some specific guidelines that will almost always result in a motivated person.
Praise.

1. *This can't start too early.*
2. *Develop the habit of finding something good in every situation.*

3. *Praise must be specific to be credible: "That table just shines from your polishing it!"*
4. *Never follow praise with* but! *Help a child do the best job he can and then give unqualified praise.*
5. *Be honest about your praise. It's okay to disapprove of a child's performance and make him repeat it until it's right. Then you can be honest in your approval.*
6. *Tell someone else about the child's good job, so he can hear it. You may tell his other parent, telephone a grandparent, or tell a friend. Your child will feel the true significance of his effort by its being important enough to share.*
7. *Use care to avoid your child's belief that his good deeds are to your credit. They need to be his.*

Even in older children who lack motivation, we have seen these policies work slowly but surely to bring about improvement.

Gratitude.

Honest appreciation for your child's help or concern is highly motivating for further similar performances. Take time later to reflect back on the situation and how it met a need for you. A smile and hug may pin that down in your child's memory. Be specific, simple, and sincere, but don't run it into the ground!

Success.

It has been our personal experience that success breeds more success. Success is the result of doing a project, finishing it, and finding it worthwhile. It comes in many forms—sports, academic learning, creative projects, games, personal controls of all kinds, and in jobs and careers. For a young child, success must be defined by you parents. Later he will know and enjoy it himself.

Tangible Rewards.

Be careful in this department. Too many children grow up expecting "M&M's"—or money—for everything they do! A glass of lemonade after a long, hot job can be a surprise reward that helps make the effort worth repeating.

Fair and Deserved Punishment.

The avoidance of one of my [Dr. Grace's] mother's scoldings or my father's disappointment in me was a strong motivator in my childhood. Use punishment wisely, but do use it when you feel it is deserved and will promote healthy changes.

Where Credit Is Due

Balance your child's developing sense of pride with healthy humility. By this, we mean help him feel even more excited about his achievements by the awareness of others who have assisted him. To know God has given him certain abilities need not take away from them. In fact, it should help him to value those gifts even more, and take seriously the duty to use them well. The training and input from teachers and yourselves, as parents, the help and support of family and friends, are all part of anyone's success. Teach your child to appreciate those factors and to express that.

MORAL DEVELOPMENT

Defining Right and Wrong

A sense of right and wrong are part and parcel of discipline and responsibility. But it may help you with your children's training to think about what makes an issue right or wrong. For many years, I [Dr. Grace] have defined sin as any act that hurts or diminishes my value in some way; or that hurts or takes away worth from someone else. It was gratifying to read Dr. Karl Menninger's book *Whatever Became of Sin?* and find that very definition in it.

The idea of situational ethics of the last two decades has just enough truth in it to make it spread like weeds. But it has a destructive component, in our opinion. We believe it is partially responsible for the disconnectedness that seems so prevalent in the lives of young people and children. By that we refer to the inability to learn basic life lessons and principles from specific experiences. A child, for example, who cheats in a game and gets caught, does not learn to stop cheating. He also cheats on tests at school and may cheat in sports.

Teaching Morality

Teaching morality to children must become a universalizing influence. Morality becomes the umbrella that protects a child from many drops of misbehavior or deliberate wrongdoing. This includes obedience to God's laws, love and empathy for others, and respect for one's self among other factors.

Part of morality includes the communication of family values and traditions. Many years ago Grace was greatly moved by a book she can no longer locate, called *When Legends Die*. It describes three young people, Christian, Jewish, and Indian. Each has rebelled against the family beliefs and customs, finding himself adrift without meaning in life. By returning to their original moorings, each one is restored to a sense of significance and peace.

Guilt Feelings and Real Guilt

In an attempt to alleviate the painful consequences of guilt feelings, too many counseling professionals have thrown out *real* guilt as well. Guilt feelings are born of a vague sense of wrongdoing without knowing what that wrong is. They keep people miserable and usually are relieved only by professional therapy. *Real guilt* is a painful sense of knowing one has truly broken a law. It involves some remorse and sadness along with shame or embarrassment. True guilt is mankind's good friend, because it motivates growth and change in positive directions. Never foster guilt on children for inconveniencing you, the parent. But when your child breaks one of God's laws and behaves in an unloving way, he is guilty.

Dealing With Guilt

Here are some suggestions for dealing with guilt:

1. *Clarify with your child what he has done that is wrong, and why it is wrong.* Help him put himself in the other person's place, and how he would feel there.
2. *Avoid condemning him.* Jesus said to the woman taken in the very act of adultery (a blatant breaking of one of the Ten Commandments), "Neither do I condemn you!" Let your child know that you, too, have failed and have sinned.
3. *Help your child understand why he did the wrong.* Perhaps he wanted too much to make a perfect test score, so he cheated. It becomes easier to help him avoid cheating

again, if he understands that perfect scores or top grades are less important than honesty.

4. *Think through with your child how he can make right the wrong he did.* This will be painful! Apologizing, confessing, taking one's consequences, all hurt deeply. And that pain is healthy, because it was deserved, and will almost always deter one from future misdeeds.

5. *Help your child remember God's promises of forgiveness.* Lead him in a private prayer of confession. Let him know that you forgive him, and that he must also forgive himself.

6. *Drop the incident and rarely, if ever, remind him of it again.*

Sort through your own moral values. Be sure that your beliefs and your life-style coincide. Then remember to talk about those values at opportune moments. Look for daily-life happenings that will illustrate those values, and casually and simply talk about those events. Many of our best values came from dinner-table conversations during our childhood.

God told His special people, Israel, that they should love Him completely and teach His words "diligently unto thy children, and shalt talk of them when thou sittest in thine house, and when thou walkest by the way, and when thou liest down, and when thou risest up" (Deuteronomy 6:7). By practicing this, your own life will grow in its resources and your children will learn morality in its truest sense.

14

The Fun Side of Family Living

"The family that plays together stays together," said many mental-health posters a few years ago. That philosophy still holds true. Yet many families do not know *how* to play—at least they rarely do so.

At various ages, children are capable of playing with different toys and in different ways.

PLAYTIME THROUGH CHILDHOOD

The New Baby

A baby at birth experiences pleasure when held, when nursing, and probably when being touched and talked to. By three months of age (and often sooner), a baby enjoys looking at and banging on a mobile or a sturdy toy that he may grasp (only reflexly at first) in his own hand. His greatest pleasure continues to be the close attention of loving family members. Get close to a baby's face (if you don't have a cold!), blow in his neck, or tummy, and tickle his feet. Pull on his hands and feet to exercise those muscles, and enjoy his happy laughter as he responds to you.

At Six Months

By six months, a child is highly responsive, laughs and coos readily, and will make you think you'd like another baby just like him any day. Don't listen to that thought, because in a few months he will be teething and crawling and wearing you out! The six-monther will hold onto toys for a while, but he will learn to love dropping them to see you bend over and retrieve them. Be inventive! Fasten toys that are bright, that make noises, and that move a lot, onto his bed or high chair, so he can't throw them away. Continue to play with him physically as much as *you* both enjoy.

At Eight Months

Around eight or nine months your baby will be crawling. Help motivate him to do that by putting toys around his play area. As he crawls to them, he will be developing those important arm and leg movements that help decide his right- or left-handedness. (*See* chapter 7, "The Next Two Years of Life.") He will play happily near you for longer times without your direct attention, but he still needs and wants plenty of that, too. Singing or talking to your child while you are busy will keep the baby happily aware of your presence and more content. This is the time to reorganize your schedule so you can begin to catch up with a lot of household chores you dropped a while ago.

At One Year

At a year, many children are walking and can get into things at higher levels than a crawler, so re-childproof your house! At this age, babies love to poke their fingers into holes, and they enjoy putting items into and out of a container. Be certain that all electrical outlets are covered so the baby won't get hurt. Large beads or small blocks and a box or pail will intrigue him for many minutes. Think constructively now! If you interrupt that in and out process on the "in" cycle, you can actually teach your year-old child to begin putting away his toys! It's so much easier to develop that habit now, than to battle a child of two about it. Learn by watching your child's interests and readiness and think about using that information to your advantage—and his good training.

Twixt One and Two

Between one and two years of age, babies begin to build. They stack two or three blocks—but mostly they knock down the ones you stack! That's not because you did a bad job, or because baby is a destructive monster. It's because she likes to see things move and bounce, and because maybe you will build another one. The play process is important now—not the height of that block tower! Pull or push toys are great at this age. Babies love to cuddle stuffed toys and still like holding, tickling, and romping.

Now Comes Two

As you approach that second birthday, you will become aware of behaviors in your child that seem aggressive and stubborn. They are! That's how your child learns to be a real person, and finds out what he can do or can't do. He wants to explore, and when he is stopped for any reason, he is frustrated.

We believe a two-year-old should be taken out-of-doors a lot. Help him find a safe place to climb, and supervise him so he won't fall! Help him swing, run, and walk on a wall—holding your hand. He will love wild flowers and will tear them up. Caterpillars are a thrill, as are wild animals and birds. As you guide this time of exploration, you will find fewer areas to fight about and can direct his energies into wonderful, constructive activities.

Toys for Twos. Toys for a two-year-old need to include a pounding board. Let him hit it when he is angry, or just when he needs to pound. He loves to take things apart, so blocks that stack inside of each other will interest him, as will things you may build out of interlocking blocks. He will do some building of his own with big wooden or plastic blocks. Usually by two, children are ready for books with one big picture to a page. Their vocabulary will grow by seeing the *A* for *apple* and *B* for *ball* pictures, though you will be weary of them. By two, some children can sit still for short stories.

TV for Twos. "Sesame Street" and other excellent children's TV programs will interest a two-year-old for a while. Spend some time watching with him and help him learn by talking with him about the program. Children may see life in bits and pieces, unless an adult helps those pieces of information to fit into the whole of life. And two-year-olds can understand those bits of knowledge. Our grandson and Grace were making a cake when he was only two and a half. As he "helped" her measure and stir, he said, "Grandma, that's cooperation!" His mother told me he had learned that big word on "Sesame Street," but it obviously made sense in the kitchen!

Importance of Praise. Be sure to praise your children from the first day you have them at home. Many parents are, by nature, critical, and there are times when you need to be so. You will find, however, that children respond far more to praise than to scolding. So begin early to develop your own habits of finding your child's good points, and tell both the child and another person about them. Honest praise to a child and to another adult about him, begins to reflect a positive self-image that will help him for a lifetime!

Between Three and Six

These children blossom in their imagination and creativity. They need play items that give them the opportunity to explore and develop these qualities. More nature hikes are great. Large crayons and blank paper, clay, or similar substances can lead to great artistic feats. Post these on the refrigerator or a bulletin board or send them to relatives. Children learn to believe they are worth something because the things they create are important to others! Tea parties and playing house are a source of great fun and a caricature of yourselves, Mom and Dad.

Stories. After three, stories become increasingly fun for children. Reading a library book or telling a story you've made up are equally delightful at this age. From three to seven, children are capable of vivid imaginations. Pretend friends, pets, and games are wonderful adventures to share. Just be sure the child and you both know you are pretending.

Building and Taking Apart. Both are possible in the late preschool years. Any old appliance can be a storehouse of fun. Be careful to teach your child how to dismantle the object, and do be careful of its safety. Any glass or sharp areas make it off limits. Be certain that your child understands which appliances are *old* and which are *new!*

Games Children Play

At Four and Five. These children often enjoy some of the board games with spinners and pegs. These can help them learn to recognize colors and numbers. They catch on early, however, to the thrill of winning. We believe in cheering when they win, and helping them learn to lose, as well. That obviously means that once in a while, you need to win (honestly), and then help the child to accept that—even grudgingly. It is wise to play one more game after you win, so the child has another chance to win. Don't be too tough a competitor until the child's skills grow to a point where he can handle it.

Starting School. Once your child starts school, he will enter the era of physical sports and school games. Usually he will prefer playing with friends to spending time with parents. You may be really useful if you will teach him how to do well in those sports his interest and physical skills are best suited for. But also teach skating, swimming (which may best be started in the preschool years), tennis, golf, or other games which offer social advantages.

At About Eight or Nine

Now you may want to explore "little league" sports for your child. For some athletically gifted children, these offer a chance to develop real skills and a team spirit. Our frank opinion, however, is against such sports for an average or unskilled child. We have watched the sad faces of the chronic bench warmers and have seen their growing embarrassment and depression. Maybe you can find teams whose coaches care about giving every child a chance to play, rather than having to win every game. This happens in less-organized competition, so choose a team that is good for your child.

Backyard Fun and Games

These still seem the most democratic and best suited to the healthy fun of childhood. Help your child learn how to give, take, and share in playing together. When children are under seven or eight, they enjoy adult participation in playing, if it isn't too controlling. This enables you to help your child (and even his friends) to develop good sportsmanship.

Family Night

We strongly urge every family to keep at least one evening every week as a family-fun night. As soon as children are able to do so, they may take turns choosing one of the games or activities that you, the parents, can offer. Everyone must be a good sport and enter into the fun. As you set the mood, your children will irresistibly be drawn into the fun. Sometimes you won't feel like doing this, but do it anyway!

Skipping only one time can spoil the ritual, and you will have a hard time recapturing it. It was our experience that we had to fight the school, church, and entire community to do this, but it was worth it.

Group Activities

Between the two of us, we have given nearly twenty years to serving as leaders or assistants to Scouts, Camp Fire Girls, and Sunday-school classes for our children. We wish we could do it all over again. Those groups have offered opportunities for personal growth and a healthy sense of belonging that have truly enriched the lives of many children over the years. Indian Guides and Indian Princess organizations have encouraged the involvement of dads with sons and daughters. Many other groups have depended more on mothers during the elementary-school years. We believe children need as strong a relationship with their dads as with mothers. Such groups are one means of developing that.

Try Togetherness at Work

Working together can be as enjoyable as play. While most children won't like leaving play to help with house or yard work, you can make those jobs so much fun that they really won't mind. We well recall the jokes, teasing, and laughter that went into planting gardens, spring housecleaning, and many otherwise tedious jobs. Your children will learn to work best if they learn by working with you, happily.

OUTSIDE ENTERTAINMENT

Movies

Entertainment outside the home needs to be discussed. Many Christians have strong scruples against movies, and when we read the advertisements of today's movies, we agree with them! Once in a while, however, a truly fine movie comes along. Such an event could be a special treat for your family. It could also support the production of better movies—if enough Christians responded to the really worthwhile ones.

Bad Movies. Do protect your children as long as you can from the frightening and crude movies that sound so exciting! Sooner or later, however, your teenager will attend a movie that is "gross," even in their opinion. We hope you will be on such good terms with her that she can come to you to discuss it. Being shocked or lecturing about such an event can only estrange your child. Ask her to describe the plot (if there was one!) and then, in a give-and-take discussion, help her discern what made that a negative experience. After we learned to stop overreacting and practice this way of dealing with such an issue, our children became closer to us, and they fairly quickly stopped seeing such movies.

Television

Television is another opportunity for some recreation with your children. Like movies, much television is worthless or damaging. But some programs are fun and an inexpensive means of entertainment.

About twenty-five years ago our family purchased our first television set. We were amazed with this invention, just as our parents had been intrigued with the radio, and our grandparents, the telephone. We gathered together to watch funny and sometimes poignant programs, crying and laughing together.

A Memory. I [Dr. Grace] recall vividly the sad tears of one of my first psychiatric patients. The girl of thirteen was estranged from her mother and was hurting over this. When I asked her how she thought things could become better at home, she sobbed out, "If Mom would even come and watch TV with us, we could talk about *it,* at least." And she was right! Television offers an outside topic of conversation that restores some communication between estranged family members.

A Dividing Element. Things have changed, however, since those days. Most American families now have two or more television sets. Many children have their own television and stereo sets in their rooms. Rather than serving as a family magnet, TV has now added to our isolation or has created battlegrounds.

A Change for the Worse. Programming also has changed. The comedy violence of "The Three Stooges" has given way to a series of cops-and-robbers episodes that teach violence in an intensive short course. Studies have revealed a high coincidence of major crime in a few days following a major TV showing of comparable crimes. The violence on television surely depicts the violence in our world, but it is also fed and worsened by the programs, according to many studies. As protests have grown against violence, sex has increasingly replaced it as an audience attractor.

Superthriller Movies. These capitalize on natural disasters to make entertainment. These have, in turn, been displaced by supernatural horror films, depicting demonic powers in a fashion that turns the sleep of many children into nightmares.

Children, addicted to the sophisticated, intense thrills of television, often have trouble finding significance in arithmetic or reading. Their own imaginations and creativity are stifled by the spoon-fed intensity of television.

Ban It? Should we, then, get rid of all of our television sets? Some people advocate that. Personally, we doubt that is the answer, but here are some suggestions:

1. *Schedule some TV time with your entire family.* Help them choose a program that can be understood on some level by everyone. Discuss the production. Think about its truth and error and point these out to each other. This process can be a marvelous tool for teaching logic and values to your children. We used to plan a weekend evening meal in front of the television for such a purpose, and we still find those memories of warmth and closeness as a family to be treasured.

2. *Monitor all of the programs your children watch.* If you find them offensive, take time to sit down and point out

such issues. Encourage your children to discuss these with you, and help them find a better program. With God's wisdom and help, do this in a way that will teach your child and not antagonize him. Being abrupt and negative may prompt more rebellion than learning!

3. *Write to your local television station if you especially like or disapprove of a program.* According to a friend who works for a local TV station, as few as one hundred letters may influence a change in a given program. Be logical and clear about your objections, and make suggestions regarding better ideas. Be constructive!

4. *Write to the companies that sponsor various programs.* Make them aware of your approval and disapproval. Again, be clear and fair in your reasoning. However sad it may be, money speaks. Without the advertisers, television in America would not exist as it now does. If enough people object, the economic factors will motivate the sponsors to influence the producers to present better programs.

5. *Encourage your friends to write their own opinions, as well.*

Suggestions on Family Level. Now on a family interaction level, here are some observations and suggestions. Once we saw a father enter his living room, where the children were watching a program. Automatically, he switched the channel to something he wanted to see. The children's faces reflected their frustration first, and soon their voices joined that expression of anger at his abrupt and thoughtless action. While television can unify a family, it can divide the members, as well.

Dad works hard for the family and deserves some rewards for that. As the head of the Christian family, the dad should be shown the respect of having some rights to at least see his favorite news or sports events on TV. But children need to learn respect, and to do so, they need to be respected.

In this case, television can become a fine channel—not for viewing, but for modeling courtesy, kindness, and respect. How nice it could be for that father to join the children in watching their program, enjoy it with them, and discuss its philosophy simply with them. When that event is over, he could remind the children that he has worked hard and needs some time to watch the news and relax. Perhaps, with coaching, they would even bring him a drink of iced tea and join him in watching his program. This will enable them to feel good about their giving something in return for their dad's work for them. Sharing television, deciding with reasons and fairness about who chooses what programs, and learning more about consideration for and sensitivity to one another's needs and feelings—all can come with using television constructively.

As an Escape. There are many ways in which one may escape today's tensions and stress. Television is one of them. After a week full of intense experiences with real-life dramas, we both can relax on a weekend evening over a television drama. Rarely, if ever, do we allow ourselves to take this sort of program seriously, but such an escape seems recreative and healthy.

Sometimes, however, it happens that people not only escape from their professional fatigue, but also from each other. The wife and mother who becomes addicted to soap operas may be avoiding dealing with relationships and communication with the real-life people with whom she lives. The father and husband may play the same game using a sports theme, and children certainly may add their version with cartoons or reruns.

If you have fallen into this habit, do take a look at breaking it. Such habits demolish the sort of congeniality, openness, and intimacy that should define a home.

Guarding Against TV Hazards. You need to guard against such hazards by helping your young child select appropriate programs. You will usually do better with an older child to discuss programs with him, and help him understand the good and bad aspects. You, as parents, need to watch your own use and example regarding TV. Television is in the world to stay. Use it with the wisdom and guidance of God's spirit.

Rock Concerts

Rock and other popular-music concerts have come to be common social events for young people. Few of these have any value for your children, and many are so vulgar and crude that it is difficult to understand how even adolescents could tolerate them. In our city, most such concerts involve marijuana smoking and the free flow of many drugs and alcohol. We strongly discourage such concerts for most teenagers. If you feel a rare one may be harmless, go with your children, even if you don't sit with them, and find out exactly what sort of influence this concert could have. Later, over a soft drink, discuss your re-actions calmly, and come to some decision about any future events.

Community Events

Most communities have sports events, plays, and some good concerts that may offer special family fun, if you can afford such an expense now and then.

One-on-One Entertainment

If you parents are as busy as we have been, you may consider another social event. In order to keep our communications open and our relationships alive, we took turns taking each child out for a treat now and then. A surprise trip for lunch to the nearest hamburger stand made an ordinary day a celebration. And an evening trip to the ice-cream parlor was a special date. Talking and laughing together in such a social setting can strengthen the bonds of love between you and your children, and may open up topics of conversation that need discussing.

Parents, you will often need to sacrifice some of your time with each other and for your own wishes. I hope you are willing to forego that time for these years. They may seem long, and you will be tempted to resent the sacrifices and wish this time to be gone, but using these years to build healthy children will pay great dividends later. (And there will be more time than you can use later on.)

Time Alone. Do, however, keep in touch with each other along the way. An evening out now and then, or meeting for lunch, can keep you in touch in a romantic way. One plan we put into effect for a long time helped us. As soon as we arrived home, greeted our children, and shared their days, we went to our room, closed the door, and spent half an hour simply talking to each other. The children were not impaired for life or even for the evening! I think they liked the security of our togetherness. At any rate, we liked it and it did keep us communicating through those hectic, busy days.

OTHER FAMILY RECREATIONAL ACTIVITIES

Reading Aloud to One Another

This can encourage a child's interest in books. If you have a flair for drama, assign each child a character, and have him read that person's conversation; or take turns reading a paragraph or a page. You will need to select books that fit your children's abilities, of course.

Hobbies

Sharing a hobby can be a marvelous experience. Hobbies are a wonderful escape from the stresses of a job, and they may be creative (and even a means of investing some money). Stamp and coin collections have become extremely valuable. Painting, carpentering, sewing of all kinds, playing a musical instrument, collecting insects and leaves, and many more ideas you can think of—all are interests that can last for a lifetime. Some of these involve no expense, and others have costs that can be kept to a minimum.

Hiking and Camping

Many families have learned to enjoy *hiking and camping* together. Such vacations may save money, and can develop creative and resourceful talents in each member of the family. We suggest you find and read some books before setting out on such adventures. Learn about poisonous plants, snakes, and other hazards; be sure you know something about first aid, and by all means, take plenty of insect repellent!

Pets

Sharing family pets can be a special experience. Both of us, as children, had dogs that were treasured friends and companions. There's no risk whatsoever in telling your pet all of your troubles, and even how mad you are at your brother. The pet will never tell, and it can relieve a great deal of tension to discuss such issues.

Summing Up

Playing together is an attitude as well as a planned function. If you will find and share some humor with each other, plan and structure some activities just for fun and for companionship, we believe your family will weather many hard times successfully.

15
The Seesaw World
of the Adolescent

The major emphasis of this book is on the prevention and handling of the problems of younger children. But the unique situations of adolescence as well as the seriousness of their import demand some attention.

In few other areas of life is our motto EXPLORE, DON'T EXPECT! so useful as it is in adolescence. Teenagers are in a major transition zone between childhood and adulthood. Many times neither you nor your teenager knows in which state he is! So keep your mind open to surprises on both extremes. Keep believing in the ultimately successful outcome, and your adolescent will be more likely to measure up to it.

PHYSICAL ASPECTS OF ADOLESCENCE

Rapid Growth

In the teen years, with spurts and lags, your child will grow faster than he has since the first two years of life. If your teen is fairly active, the amount of food he consumes can be budget breaking; clothes are rarely worn out before they are outgrown; and many physical changes tumble over one another in quick succession (just as the legs of teenagers do). This is the time to trade clothes and use hand-me-downs from friends and relatives, if your budget is tight. With creativity and a casual attitude, your teenager needn't feel embarrassed about wearing someone else's clothes.

Nutrition Neglect

While adolescents endure their greatest physical stresses, they often resort to the worst nutritional patterns. We went through considerable research about the eating habits of teens. One study revealed that in a large Canadian city, the majority of teenagers consumed two to three "junk foods" daily. *Junk foods* are those with plenty of calories but few of the basic nutrients the body needs. Over half of those young people skipped or skimped on breakfast. One may be sure that such practices are at least as bad in the United States.

Girls the Worst Nutritionally. Teenage girls are, as a group, the worst risk nutritionally. They become highly weight conscious, so they alternate between feast and famine. All too often, as they gain weight on those empty calories, their general health suffers. Due to their menstrual blood loss, teenage girls need twenty milligrams of iron daily, while boys only need fifteen.

In case you need to know, parents, adolescent girls need from 2,400 to 2,700 calories a day, depending on their metabolism, and how active they are. Boys' needs vary from 3,100 to 3,600 calories daily, since their bodies are usually larger.

Caffeine Overindulgence. A major dietary problem with teens is the unusual amount of caffeine they take in. Many young people are unaware of the fact that colas, chocolate, and tea all contain caffeine, as well as coffee. Caffeine has the effect of stimulating many of the body's systems, and may make young people feel jittery—and even irritable.

Nutrition Balance Important. Vitamins, proteins, fats, and carbohydrates all need to be present in proper balance to keep your adolescent healthy. He needs calcium, phosphorus, and fluoride for strong bones and teeth, as well as the iron for good blood. Check with your dentist or your local medical society to find out if the water in your area contains fluoride. It is as important not to get *too much* of the various vitamins and minerals as too little.

Just be careful that you do not set up skirmishes over food. During these tumultuous years, save your ammunition for the necessary battles. Those will deal with personal self-esteem, integrity, and helping your teenager stay away from drugs, alcohol, and rebelling. (More of that in a little bit.)

Guidelines for Good Nutrition

Here are some guidelines for good nutrition in adolescence.

1. *Find out from your physician what your specific child's calorie needs are.* He can tell you if your child is in a growth spurt, where he needs more protein, or is burning up energy in activities that require more starches or sugar—or both. Be sure to tell him the actual facts about your child's eating habits, and see if you need to give him or her supplemental vitamins or minerals.

2. *Discuss the nutritional needs of your son or daughter with the teenager, calmly and without scolding.* Ask your doctor or his nurse to talk with your young person, if you have already tried this in vain.

3. *Plan meals your teen likes, but add the nutritional elements that he needs.* For example, pizza with chopped pepper, tomatoes, meat, and cheese provides most of the basic foods—especially when you consider the quantities that are eaten! The same applies to tacos and hamburgers. Even hot dogs are not bad, if you add a tossed salad or fruit.

4. *Milk with fruit flavoring can replace chocolate, and carbonated drinks (not colas) with real fruit juice added are usually guzzled by teens.*

5. *A little imagination can make breakfast appealing, even for the girl who has lots of grooming to do.* A grapefruit half with half a cherry in the center to make it attractive is low in calories and invites a bite of breakfast. Often with this appetizer, a bit of sausage, bacon, or toast can be added without too much nagging. Don't fix a big meal and then feel hurt when she doesn't eat it. Just offer something along with your best "Have a good day" presence. She'll respond sooner or later, and you will be modeling the good mothering she will recall when she has her own teens someday.

When your adolescent needs to lose weight, plan lower-calorie menus with leafy vegetables, proteins, and fewer starches. Have attractive vegetable snacks with a low-calorie dip for after school and bedtime. Keep the special sweet treat for a surprise on those desperate days when your dieter is about to give up. Encourage your child to find a friend to join in the dieting, or join yourself, if you can do it. Help her stop eating just before she feels full, to shrink the stomach. And help her to get plenty of exercise. Eating slowly, and leaving the table to cut down the temptation to take seconds, also are useful habits to develop.

Above all else, avoid lectures, scolding, and put-downs. Any treatment or attitude that increases the stress in your child's life is likely to increase the nervous habit of eating. Usually significant overweight in teenagers is due to anxiety, depression, or loneliness. Try encouragement, listening, loving, and helping your adolescent look ahead.

The Underweight Teen. Occasionally, a teenager has difficulty gaining weight. For such a person, reverse the course described. Add more carbohydrates to this diet. At bedtime, a milk shake made with ice cream will tend to tip the calorie balance. Encourage this young person to eat just beyond a sense of being full, in order to stretch the stomach. Have a medical examination to be sure there is nothing wrong with the child's thyroid, blood count, or gastrointestinal tract, and then help the thin young person to live with that. Usually people who are underweight are healthier than those who are even slightly overweight.

Physical Problems of Teenagers

By adolescence, most young people have had the childhood diseases or their immunizations. They have given up the sniffles, except for a rare cold that warrants a day off now and then. They are growing rapidly and developing sexually, and that takes most of their energy.

There are a few problems unique to the teen years, however, that need your attention.

The Skin and Hair. Oily hair and acne are major teenage problems. Washing their hair nearly every day becomes a nuisance, but it is necessary for some teens. Parents, help your child plan a daily schedule that will include time for good grooming. Help each one pick the best time for such processes, and protect that time. Also help them select good shampoos, soap, deodorants, and cosmetics.

Acne is discussed in chapter 10. Try to understand how disfigured your child feels. Help cover the bumps and encourage him to remember that someday these will disappear.

When girls gain weight too rapidly, in the hips and breasts especially, the skin stretches so, it leaves *stretch marks* like those on the abdomen during pregnancy. Most girls are horribly embarrassed by these, but unfortunately, there is nothing that can be done about them. Even plastic surgery is of no help unless there is a great excess of skin from losing a lot of weight. Boys may have this, too, but in our experience, they are rarely, if ever, bothered by it.

Young people sometimes get body *lice* from public toilets or head lice from other young people at school. They are usually more embarrassed than young children, but they get rid of them just as well. (*See* chapter 10 on Illnesses—Skin Diseases.) Be reassuring! They (and you) will survive!

The Bones and Muscles. Teenagers are the victims of accidents more than they are of any other physical problems. (*See* chapter 10 on Illnesses—Accidents and Injuries.) In addition to those, they may have a recurrence of the "growing pains" of earlier years. And they sometimes develop *Osgood-Schlatter's disease.* This is a condition with pain and swelling in the bone, just below the kneecap. Apparently it is caused by stress from strenuous activity, because it is more common in athletes. It is not serious but does require limiting activity, and usually a splint to keep it from becoming a more serious problem.

Due to their rapid growth rate, many young people experience some *awkwardness.* They are extremely embarrassed by their falls, bumps, and spills, and they certainly do not need attention drawn to it. Avoid teasing, and ignore it (or casually comment on your own memories and how you outlived those difficult moments).

Special Illness. Rarely are there any special illnesses of the respiratory tract, or the stomach and intestinal tract. A truly worried or anxious young person may, however, develop stomach ulcers, or even ulcerative colitis. Any chronic pain in the upper abdomen should be checked by your doctor. Colitis is evidenced by alternating bouts of constipation and diarrhea. If the diarrhea becomes severe or contains mucus and blood, you do need to seek medical attention. This should include a psychiatric evaluation to help your child understand the interaction of emotional stress and physical reactions. He needs to learn to control both.

The Urinary and Genital Tracts. In teens any symptom involving these physical areas deserves your doctor's attention. No matter how good your child may be, there is the possibility of a rare indiscretion that could result in venereal disease or pregnancy. As physicians, we often are the ones who have to tell parents a daughter is pregnant or a son has gonorrhea. If there is any question, find out. If one of these is the diagnosis, don't rage and rant. That is the time for treatment and support. After the immediate medical condition is under control, find out what the needs and problems may be that motivated the sexual activities. You and your young person may need counsel to work out those needs!

Heart and Blood Vessels. This is rarely a part of the body that causes trouble in adolescence. Strep infections, if untreated, may affect the heart valves. A number of years ago this was commonly the cause of rheumatic heart disease. Thanks to antibiotics, this is now an extremely rare disease.

Neurological System (Brain and Nerves). Other than an extremely rare case of meningitis, or encephalitis, or serious accident, there are few problems that affect teenagers' nervous systems. Years ago we would see an occasional case of "St. Vitus's dance." This was the inability to control various muscles, and was apparently due to certain poisons that accompanied strep-throat infections. Just as rheumatic fever has nearly disappeared with good treatment of strep infections, so has St. Vitus's dance.

Eyes, Ears, Nose, and Throat. Eyes need to be checked yearly for any visual problems, and care should be provided as your doctor advises. There are sometimes infections of the ear. A swimmer's ear is common in warm, moist conditions and needs prompt medical attention, as does an earache or infection in the middle ear. (*See* chapter 10 on illnesses.)

Contact Lenses. Many parents wonder about the advisability of contact lenses for their adolescents. We believe these offer a great boost to a teenager's sense of well-being. This is especially true when glasses are very thick and could attract unhappy attention and teasing. If your teen has plenty of self-confidence and doesn't mind wearing glasses, they will meet the needs of good vision adequately and with less expense. For severe visual defects or severe self-consciousness, contact lenses can be worth their cost, if you can afford them.

We believe the soft lenses are more durable, more comfortable, and have much less danger of breaking and injuring the eye, in case of an accident. Allow your own eye doctor to advise you. Have your child learn good hygiene and teach responsible care of those lenses. There are some fairly reasonable insurance policies that can help with replacements of lost or damaged lenses. Ask your doctor.

Allergies or chronic infections of the *nose and throat* can be miserable and need medical care. Repeated infections may require the surgical removal of tonsils and adenoids. Your doctor is now trained to be very cautious about suggesting such a procedure. So if he does not recommend it, take him seriously.

Teach your teenager good health care and habits. Help him know how to avoid anxiety over his body, and the opposite extreme of ignoring or neglecting it. Pain is God's gift to you. Listen to it, and if it does not go away in a reasonable time or becomes severe, go to your physician for diagnosis and cure. *And teach this to your adolescent.* He will soon need to assume the responsibility for his own health maintenance. An annual physical with a minimum of laboratory tests will help anyone stay well, or get well quickly through an early diagnosis.

SOCIAL NEEDS OF THE ADOLESCENT

Your teenager's social fears and problems are probably matched only by yours as parents for him. Letting go of an adolescent is hard, and every difficulty he experiences will tend to create or exaggerate the fear that you have failed as a parent. You will feel sure at one time that your child will become a hopeless addict, and equally positive, at other times, that he is bound for the White House. Please accept both of these feelings as normal, and be sure that rarely does either happen.

Universal Needs of Teenagers

Here are some universal needs of teenagers. Understanding them will help you as you carefully guide them.

1. *Peer approval.* While your opinions and support will always be important, the approval of their own age group becomes temporarily of paramount importance. The big job of a teenager is to find out who he is, and become that person. To do

that, he has to separate himself from his family, and that means losing a lot of his dependency. To shore up his often sagging personal foundations, he will substitute various questionable friends. Usually that is temporary, but it can hurt and worry you while it lasts.

Know His Friends. Your teenager needs you to know and like his friends. Hard as that is sometimes, try it. Invite them into your home and get to know them. If they are truly a dangerous influence that you can't overcome, you may be able to help your child understand the risks and help him voluntarily break that relationship. Many times, listening to a young person discuss his friends opens an opportunity to point out certain signs in a casual way that will help your child see the risks.

Defense of a Bad Friend. Nothing, as a rule, sets up the stubborn defense of a really bad friend like parental attacks. Once that gets started, you may as well forget it. Anything you say will make your child come to the rescue of that friend, and even the most gross flaws will be flatly denied. At such a point, call a truce. Try to befriend the friend and help him in every way. Pray for guidance, love, and real healing of your relationship with your own child. Only in such a climate can your child discover that friend's defects for himself. Help your child stay active in a church or other Christian youth group. Keep him busy, and keep your own relationship with him open and loving. Waiting and praying through these treacherous waters is truly difficult.

2. *Developing personal identity.* During adolescence, you will usually be dismayed at your child's disagreement with your ideas and values. You will think you have totally failed as Christian parents. But you haven't. It's another way teenagers have of finding their own beliefs. Discuss issues, and question your teen's thinking. Share your methods of arriving at your beliefs more than the beliefs, per se. This can teach your child how to arrive at really honest decisions and values himself.

You will also be appalled at the language, music, dress, and all sorts of behavior of your child. Call a halt when you must, but in general such far-out behavior will be short-lived, unless you challenge them to the point of starting a power struggle. Do keep your own standards clear and steady. We have seen parents invade the life-style of their teens. Believe us, they do not need or want that!

3. *Independence.* You will help your teen and avoid rebellion, if you give him all the room he can handle. Instead of waiting for his pushing and challenging, ask him what decisions he is now ready to make. Check out his sense of responsibility and good judgment, and give him enough opportunities and freedom to explore—but not enough to make serious mistakes. If you keep a good balance in your availability and his independence, there will be times in which he will signal to you for help. Be there to offer it, and let him know you respect his asking. Even as parents you need advice at times, and it is wise to let your young people know that.

4. *Social skills.* They are extremely important to teenagers. Being able to swim, skate, play tennis, hike, bike ride, and take part in sports, open many doors to activities for sharing with friends. The more healthy, energy-burning activities young people do, the less likely they are to be bored and restless. It is in the latter social vacuum that drug abuse and sexual acting out so readily slip in.

Teach your teens how to adapt courtesy and good manners to the teen culture. Without being "goody," any young person can be kind and considerate. And even among teens these qualities are welcome!

Avoiding Questionable Events. Many teenagers could avoid questionable social events if they knew how to create better fun. Be creative, parents! Help your teens to become leaders in real fun rather than followers in so-called fun that ends in tragedy. A teenage friend of ours tells us that many of her schoolmates have almost no memories of their weekends. They are so "high" or so "hung over" that events blur into nothing. Life is a growing collection of memories, and it is sad to think of these lives that will be full of blank spots instead.

CAREER COUNSELING

The high-school years are crucial ones in preparing for jobs or professions. Do not let your child's teens slip by without helping him discover the unique interests and abilities that point toward his life's work. These need cultivating now.

God's Plan

One of the best components of my [Grace's] parents' legacy to me was the firm conviction that God has a very special purpose and plan for my life. It was most frustrating to me that God didn't write that entire plan in stone when I was born. In obedience to my parents' teaching, however, I have consistently prayed for guidance and made the best choices I knew how to make along the way. None of those choices was easy, and living them out has been most challenging. Nevertheless, as I look back, I can see the plan and know that it has been very good.

A sense of mission brings significance and meaning to lives. Very few young people whom we know seem to understand or even search for a divine plan and purpose for them as individuals. Be sure to teach this concept to your children. Sharing examples of God's direction in your own lives is one way to teach this.

Aptitude Tests

There are many well-devised aptitude tests that can help your young person to begin the exploring of his future. These are general enough to avoid undue limitations, but specific enough to point him in some special direction. You and your child's school counselor need to help him in choosing a course of study that will prepare him for more specific training.

Watch for Special Talents

Watching your child grow up, if you have paid attention, will give you insights about his interests and special gifts. One young man we know always had a keen sense of color. He now has a highly skilled position with a large paint firm that uses this unique skill. Don't force your child into a certain profession, but do talk with him about your observations and offer suggestions.

Showing Interest

One of the foundation stones of healthy self-esteem is a sense of personal worth and significance. You and your child's teachers need to show an interest in his future and respect for his potential. Go to his school events and meet his teachers. Find out what they think about your child and tell them some of your hopes and concerns. This may help the teachers to feel more personal concern for your child and bring to him an even greater sense of this personal worth.

Christ's Philosophy

Surely the greatest proof of individual value lies in the philosophy of Jesus Christ. He made it very clear that the entire world is of less value than one soul. Keep your family aware of God's special love for each one, and live out that love as their parents.

DISCIPLINE OF THE ADOLESCENT

Coming of Age

The historic Jewish rites of transition from child to adult status have much to teach us Christians. After months of study and work, a Jewish boy or girl celebrates coming of age in the religious ceremony and traditions of their faith. This is called the *Bar or Bas Mitzvah ceremony,* and is a serious and profound (as well as a joyous) time for the families of the celebrants. The ritual of this important occasion focuses child and parents alike on the change of his status.

No Gateway to Adulthood. Baptisms and *confirmations* are solemn and meaningful occasions in the Christian faith. But we have no special gateway through which youth pass into adulthood in all of our rituals and sacraments. It might be easier if we had. We are left with the need to struggle individually with our fears and our children's confusion regarding their responsibilities and our discipline.

Junior-High School

By the time a young person in the American culture reaches junior-high school, he has a great deal of freedom and responsibility thrust upon him. He is in even larger class groups than in elementary school. The impersonal climate has worsened, and it is largely up to him how he behaves and what sort of work he does. Occasionally, there are teachers who reach out in devoted concern, but by and large, school achievement is motivated mainly by the child and his parents during adolescence. You need to reinforce your child's power to choose wisely in school behavior and achievement.

Guidelines for Disciplining Adolescents

This power to choose quickly carries over into an adolescent's social and personal life, so an extreme quality and quantity of rebellion are possible. In the reality of such a climate, parents must operate with great wisdom and guidance.

Here are some specific guidelines we hope will help.

1.   Encourage self-discipline.

Since your child can and does make many of his own decisions, mentally give him that responsibility and tell him about it. Sit down together and discuss the rules you will maintain, and those he must now make and keep for himself. Ask him how much help he will need from you to keep proper study, sleep, eating, and recreational habits. Talk about curfews and places to go that are off limits. Let him know the problems, as well as the pleasures, of peer pressure and help him consider how he will handle that. Let him know what you absolutely will not tolerate, and tell him that you will be glad to stand by with a refusal when it's too hard for him to make right choices. It's easier for you to be "square" at this age than it is for him.

2.   Determine to treat your adolescent like an adult.

You may conduct your own private Bar or Bas Mitzvah ceremony, and remember the adult status of your child. Believe me, that will be difficult when he acts like a two-year-old instead of fifteen! The more you treat him like and expect him to be an adult, however, the more quickly he will return to that state. We often tell a teen to act like a grown-up, but treat him like a child. This unwittingly encourages him to keep acting like a child. He doesn't know at times what he wants, so if you must decide, choose the positive answer for him.

3. Set regular times for communicating with your teenager.

Do not wait for a crisis to make you talk together. Some families have—at least once a week—a family conference. They set up an agenda almost like a business meeting, but it includes the chance to compliment and appreciate each other, discuss the current state of family policies, any problems with household duties, borrowing practices and abuses, money issues, and so on. In the family of a dear friend, the nine-year-old (youngest) daughter called such a meeting. With all the dignity she could muster, she said, "We haven't had a meeting for a long time, and I just got lonesome for one." We can't think of a better reason. It is such sessions, conducted with warmth and logic, that can prevent serious problems. Issues can be settled by reasoning better than by angry arguments.

4. When you must discipline your adolescent, try doing so ceremoniously.

Usually this needs to be between parents and the offender— and not the entire family. Do not conduct such a meeting during a meal!

a. First, *get the information* correctly stated—all of it. Many times we have panicked at a report about our children's mischief, only to find we had but half the facts.

b. *Keep an open mind* to all the facts. You may tend to believe the worst, or want to believe the best, and either extreme will cloud the real truth for you. It may take time to check out the truth, and it is usually worth doing that (but not in too much detail).

c. *Find out how your son or daughter really feels about the problem.* They may hide deep anguish under a mask of indifference or anger, so don't be deceived by that. Above all, don't react unkindly.

d. *Be honest about your sadness, worry, and deep love.* Many parents cover these tender feelings with their own anger or indifference, and thus block honest communication.

e. *Do not take the misbehavior as an affront to you personally.* Given a day at a time, we know parents do the best job they can of raising their children. Whatever the issue, the choice of behavior belongs to your child—not you. So don't overreact, and try to recapitulate your whole parenting job at once. You need to help your child understand what he did that was wrong; what he must learn from that; and how to avoid repeating the error. *Also, he needs to be forgiven.*

f. *Often an action is wrong but the motive is right.* While many young people don't know why they did a certain thing, you may guess why. Perhaps they need to be noticed so they "clown" a bit in class. The clowning is disruptive, but the need for attention is normal. Help your child understand that and find a better way to gain attention.

g. *Agree on the consequences.* Without serious doubt, most young people want to be fine, respected and successful, just as you do. Believe that, and let them know you do. Then ask what, from this situation, your teenager thinks will help him learn to be that person. Perhaps the event itself includes the lesson. Often it implies the need to break old habits and form better ones. Structured study times, additional driving lessons, or grounding may offer the needed help. In any situation, be creative, but be firmly loving and keep the ultimate goal in mind. Be sure your teen pays the monetary cost of any irresponsibility. One girl told us she was never allowed to drive the family car until she had paid for any speeding ticket or repairs that were incurred by her carelessness.

h. *Avoid rescues.* Out of love or pity (or our own guilt feelings), it is easy to do too much for our children. A high-school son of one of our acquaintances was arrested for driving over eighty miles an hour on a highway. His father had the fine reduced, and even paid it for his son. That was not a deterrent to such dangerously reckless driving. The young man himself was embarrassed that his father protected him in that fashion.

i. *Do not use physical punishment.* Rarely, if ever, does this work for an adolescent. It is belittling, and spanking often involves sexual feelings because of the undressing that is part of the process. It is common that an attempt to paddle an adolescent includes a physical struggle, and one or both of you may be hurt or bruised in the process.

Useful methods of discipline include the loss of privileges, the reduction of an allowance, extra work, and grounding.

j. *Once you have agreed upon and set a consequence, do not relent.* Even if your child begs, apologizes, makes all sorts of promises or bargains, follow through. Do not allow pity or empathy to move you! Children almost always see this as softness on your part, and they tend to lose respect. Next time, it becomes even harder for them to believe you and easier for you to give in.

WHY TEENAGERS REBEL

There are three common reasons for rebellious behavior in teenagers.

Reasons for Rebellion

1. *Their parents are too rigid.* When you hold the reins too tightly or too long, a horse with real spirit will run anyway—and so will a child. With awareness, confidence, and love, such rebellion can be cured. It takes time and—often—outside help. Talk to each other as parents, with competent relatives, or a counselor, in order to see what your mistakes have been. But do get clear on these before you talk with your child. Then honestly describe your mistakes, form a plan for change that will include help from him, and put that plan into action. Allow for backsliding on both of your parts, but do not let that deter you.

2. *Their parents are too lenient or inconsistent.* Adolescents have some qualities similar to young horses. Colts will run wildly until they reach a fence. Unless they are taught to do so, they rarely jump a fence. But they become wild without fences. If you have been too lenient, be sure that both of you parents get together and put in some fences. At this time they dare not be too small, but they must be clearly marked and sturdy. Discuss this with your child, so he understands that you are doing this out of love and for his protection. You must expect him to test out both you and the fence. But once he can believe you, he will settle down to securely finish his growing up. Counseling may be needed to reestablish communication and work through the adjustments this requires.

3. *Teenage curiosity and exploration.* No matter how strict,

lenient, or perfect you may be, some young people simply have to try life for themselves. Like that incredibly energetic but foolish prodigal son, they must investigate a "far country." They skip school now and then, usually try smoking, beer, marijuana, and occasionally worse drugs. Like that son, they usually find out they really don't like it, and finally they return. (We are not telling you to excuse them—or to ignore their waywardness!) We know you won't do that. Just be sure to keep waiting and looking for them to come back, and be ready to celebrate, for they'll be ready to settle down. The "return" is usually an emotional one, though sometimes it is a physical return, because many kids do run away.

Reconsider Your Own Life-style

There is one last point to discuss in teenage rebellion. Many young people have rebelled against their parents' life-style. You may be too busy, too bent on establishing material security for them, or too involved in other events, even in the church. Whatever you may be doing that says to your child, "This is more important in my time allotment than you are," may be expected to cause some rebelling. When young people reach their teens, it is possible to believe they are ready for independence. It may be tempting to let go of them too completely in order to get on with your own interests. *Your children will always need you.* Keep that in mind, and avoid any hint of rearranging the children's place on your priority list.

THE PROBLEM OF RUNAWAYS
Grace H. Ketterman

Running away from home and family has involved literally millions of youths and is going into the third decade. Running has, in fact, become so common that it is nearly impossible to get anyone to assist in the search for lost boys and girls.

There truly is little that is new under the sun, and since the Pied Piper and Peter Pan, children have been easily enticed into adventures. The tragic aspects of today's runner, however, are the reasons for their running away, the places to which they run, and the damaging results of running.

Causes of Running Away

In the sixties, many young people left home as a sort of protest over their interpretation of their parents' materialism and relative unavailability to them as young people. Parents were enjoying an affluence that was relatively new in its quantity—following in the wake of the global tragedy of World War II and the economic depression preceding that.

One of my patients in the latter part of the 1960s was a handsome, freckled, teenage boy. He had been involved in some serious behavioral problems. Dan's father traveled a great deal, leaving him prematurely the man of the house. His mother needed his support and help and felt she dare not risk antagonizing him with any discipline. Dan sadly said one day, "My dad's never here when I need him. He says, 'Son, I'll be at the Sheraton Hotel in New York this week. Be sure to call me if you need anything.' But I can't talk long-distance about my girl friend!" Dan was right. Long-distance fathering could not meet his needs—or those of any child.

After a while, Dan could no longer tolerate the angry permissiveness of his mother or the absence of his dad. He left home and traveled for months about the country. So do many other Dans and Debs.

Many of the runaways of the sixties joined the Civil Rights movement, demonstrated against the war in Vietnam, and tried to find a cause big enough to believe in and fight for. They challenged their schools, the police, the courts, and authority in general. I believe they were disappointed at finding so few people who were stronger than they were.

Gradually there developed a reversal of the historic parent-child roles within the family. Instead of parents giving the alternatives of obedience or discipline, young people were threatening, "Give me my way, or I'll leave." When parents dared to hold fast to rules, children left.

The world in which we live (knowingly or unwittingly), encourages their leaving. Hitchhiking youngsters are quickly picked up by travelers. One teenage girl was secluded in the basement of her next-door neighbor's home while her parents desperately searched the community for her, fearing she had been killed.

As years roll by, there are few young people who lack an example by a friend who ran or who would at least encourage them to do so. An easy though superficial camaraderie flows among youth that allows them to come and go with little obligation and no deep attachments.

Some left (and evidence mounts that this number is increasing) because of real *abuse at home.* Young women and boys are facing sexual and other abuse from their own relatives. Children of a growing number of alcohol- and even drug-addicted parents feel safer anywhere than at home.

The Destinations

In my own personal search for a runaway child of a friend, I saw sights that indelibly told a story I can't forget. In an insect-infested basement was a group of runaway teens. A rusty bed spring on the floor was covered with a dirty, torn, but once-expensive blanket. A dirty, bent pan of watery bean soup was simmering on a tiny gas heater. There was filth and utter deprivation, yet each person there could have returned to comfort and even luxury.

Some of them eventually went, like the prodigal sons and daughters they were, back home. Some, however, stayed to prove they could make it or because they would not give up their power struggle.

And sadly, many parents are giving up and angrily rejecting their own children. A priest in a large rescue project in a large eastern city said that over 60 percent of the parents whom he calls about runaways refuse to send money for their return or even accept them back home. This priest sees these youngsters living out the worst consequences of the runaway's life. They literally *live on the streets.* They steal, work as prostitutes, escape through drugs, and many die of the diseases and deprivation of their life-style. A tragically destructive vicious cycle of hurting and being hurt builds to the explosive point that may have no return.

Paradoxically, many runaways search for and set up among themselves new families. Many runners join cults such as the Moon organization or other pseudoreligious groups. Many of them find a type of acceptance, a sense of belonging and security that they have never before experienced. Many of them especially seem to yearn for a father image, as reported among the followers of Jim Jones.

Tragically, some runners never return due to the ultimate "escape" of suicide or accidental overdosing with drugs. The second leading cause of death among adolescents is suicide. (The first is accidents.)

The Cure

There is, fortunately, great hope for the family of a runaway as well as for that person himself. The essence of the cure of a runner is this:

1. Determine which of the above causes (or any other) applies to your child. Do not settle for glib, superficial reasons, but search out the deep inner longings and unmet needs that are the very core of the problem.

2. Keep your loving concern active. It is tempting to give up, become angry, and retaliate or reject a child who seems to be the source of a family's heartache.

3. Be aware that a troubled young person is part of a complex family system that has acted upon him (or her) before he reacted. Each person in the family needs to adjust or change in some way if the identified problem person is to be restored.

4. Stop the power struggles. By the time a child is old enough to run away, he can only rarely be outmaneuvered in such a battle. A period of confinement through a stay in a court-operated detention place or a hospital is almost the only way parents can win a power struggle with a habitual runaway. Sometimes this deliberate confinement can save a child's life, so don't be too reluctant to choose it.

5. In most situations involving a runaway child, outside counsel is essential. Please do not give in to the temptation to deny that help out of either shame or false pride. Feelings between you and your child can be so powerful and so destructive that almost no person alone can work through them. A counselor who can interpret and arbitrate may save the day and help heal the wounds of each of you.

6. In working at the healing, we find that honest, loving acceptance of the child is absolutely essential. Before that young person can even consider your rules and conditions

upon returning, he or she must believe that you love them and will forgive the past.

7.   Contrary to the angry demeanor of such young people, most of them feel horrible. They believe they are bad, even worthless. They feel hopeless and helpless and they usually feel guilty. They have little faith in an unseen God, but they sense the worry and rejection of their angry, hurting parents. It is difficult for them to understand *forgiveness* or *redemption* unless some person models these qualities for them.

8.   Once your child is restored to your love and experiences forgiveness, he usually finds a flicker of hope again. Be very sensitive during this time and do not extinguish that hope. Be very positive. Reward each effort to improve with your most honest appreciation and praise. Do not overdo this.

9.   After returning from an episode of running, a child will in a sense regress. He will feel and act younger than his years. Encourage this. Give as much nurturing and protection as your child can accept. Slowly and gently resume a more age-appropriate mode of relating, but do so with constant unconditional love.

10.   Help your child decide on his own goals and even his own way to reach them. You may be surprised to find that once those inner needs are met, the goals are not different from your own.

11.   In most affairs of teenagers, you will find that suggestions and guidelines used with respect and sincerity will work. Demands and threats rarely succeed in anything but more rebellion and repeated runs. Likewise, gradual neglect or indifference will cause some misbehaviors that will seek to regain attention.

12.   Be careful to avoid, due to your fear, a tendency to rescue your child. You will need clear, consistent firmness in keeping the rules and limits that you have established together. Your child's old friendships and habits are powerful (as are yours!), and you will need to help each other to break them.

13.   Find, if you can (or establish), a group of other parents who have had similar problems. The lessons they have learned can guide and support you in ways that will be invaluable. They cannot take the place of a trained counselor, but they will be a priceless supplement.

14.   Practice the presence of Christ. Ask His guidance, open your mind to conceptualize ways in which He would handle a situation, and follow that guidance. The prayer support of friends and clergy will do more than you may ever know to effect quiet miracles.

God loves both you and your child. He wants to heal all your hurts and restore His joy and peace and love to your hearts and family.

HOMOSEXUALITY

The confusion of sexual identity has come to be commonplace in our Western culture. Among all of the homosexuals whom we have known personally, there has been profound pain and a deep wish for congruence in physical and psychological sexuality. In a homosexual, these aspects are incongruent, that is, a person who has all the physical traits of one sex feels like a member of the opposite sex, and prefers the company of people of the same sex. A homosexual man prefers the company of another man and can be most readily (or even exclusively) sexually stimulated by a man. Likewise, a homosexual woman is attracted to another woman. Female homosexuals are called *lesbians*.

Causes of Homosexuality

The causes of homosexuality are not clearly demonstrable, but we do know some influential factors.

1.   A child psychiatrist who is a professor in a university medical school believes that the parents, especially the mother, unconsciously give to an infant what he calls the *core gender*. By that he means that the infant is treated like and considered the sex that parent unconsciously prefers. As the child grows, the toys, wearing apparel, and behavioral expectations fit the sexual preference of the parent. So the child comes to feel like the person he or she believes that parent desires.

2.   A potentially homosexual child commonly has a feeling that the parent of the opposite sex disapproves of most people of his or her gender. For example, one patient recalled his

mother's repeated comments that indicated, "All men are dumb and undesirable." Furthermore, he believed that his father demonstrated that to be true. He was inept, irritable, and withdrawn. Not wanting to gain such an identity, this boy learned to feel safe by copying his mother. The habits of femininity became entrenched and he found himself attracted to boys when dating time came.

3. Many homosexuals had, in childhood, violent episodes of forced sexual encounters by older homosexuals. One young boy was forced by threats to submit to such an experience by an older man who sponsored a camping group. Apparently such an episode leaves the child feeling "tainted" or trapped in an identity he does not really want.

4. A common problem among homosexuals is that of dominating and emotionally cold parents. One young woman had craved her mother's love and tenderness as long as she could recall. Later she became involved in a relationship with a lesbian. When she awoke in the morning after a sexual encounter, she would invariably recall a dream that she was finally being cradled in her mother's arms.

5. Many homosexuals are plagued by fear and anger. The roots of these two emotions are lost in their memories, but they are powerful. It is often difficult for them to really trust anyone's love, so their relationships are all too commonly brief encounters. Jealousy and rivalry are often extreme and can result in serious conflicts.

6. Various personal and cultural experiences seem to indicate that as homosexuality grows more open and common, those who practice it become more violent. Many avowed homosexuals do not fit that pattern and deny it, but growing evidence certainly shows the possibility that this aggression can become dominant.

7. A group in the United States has been formed for the purpose of helping homosexuals who wish to leave that lifestyle and become heterosexual. It is called Exodus and its headquarters are located at P.O. Box 5439, Seattle, Washington, 98105.

What to Teach

As Christian parents, what should you teach your children about homosexuality? We believe that you need to explain the above facts to your older children. You should be prepared to discuss such issues when your children become aware of them. We have known of five- and six-year-olds who seem to have remarkably accurate information about "gay" people. Do not tell them more than they can handle, but please be certain that you know more than they. Keep them comfortable enough to return to you for more information when they are ready for it.

In discussing homosexuality, we hope you can find a way to express your disapproval of that life-style without condemning the persons who follow it. It is most comforting to leave the judging up to God. We can understand and love people of many kinds, without approving of specific behaviors.

Seeking Help

If you have fears about your young child's sexuality, check out your personal feelings about his or her sex. If you discover some deep resentments or anger, work those through. If you need a counselor to help you, do not be afraid to seek out one who can help you. If you aren't certain of your feelings but have old injuries from someone close to you, we strongly recommend at least a consultation with a trained counselor. You can almost certainly prevent the full-blown homosexual life-style from developing.

We know some of you will have suffered the heartache of a child who chooses this life-style due to various influences. No doubt you know the anger, guilt, and grief that attends such a discovery. Please do not reject that young person. Seek counsel to salvage a loving relationship and to heal the grief. Perhaps your child will be able to leave the gay world with help, prayers, and support. You must leave that to him or her and to God. We never knew such a person to be redeemed by either anger and rejection, or by pampering and "rescuing." But by support, honesty, and the healing of unintended hurts and mistaken attitudes, some have been restored to well-adjusted, heterosexual lives.

Part V

Helping a Troubled Child

16
Handling Difficulties and Suffering

"NO PAIN" PHILOSOPHY

In America there has been a growing belief in the philosophy that people should avoid pain at all costs and clutch at whatever pleasure they can find. This idea has influenced all ages and levels of society, and it certainly has affected our children. Many times parents with troubled children have said, "I only wanted her to be happy!" That childhood should be a golden time of carefreeness and joy is a common concern, and one with which one would not argue unless he faced more deeply the ultimate reality of life.

The Roots and Fruits of This Philosophy

We feel certain that this focus came about as an aftermath of the widespread deprivation of the depression in the 1930s, and the even more widespread tragedy of the war of the 1940s. No one wanted to endure any more heartaches, and perhaps we tried too hard to enjoy many of the things we had missed. Certainly we wanted a better life for our children.

The unfortunate aspect of this philosophy is the energy parents have invested in making life easy and happy for their children. They have showered them with material things and carried their responsibilities for them, in order to allow them the freedom the parents missed. On the other hand, mothers and fa-

431

thers have been angry at their children's lack of appreciation, their irresponsibility, and their utter lack of motivation. It must be confusing to a child to try to feel thankful for things he didn't really want—or even ask for. He must struggle with a search for qualities his parents have not taught him, but expect him to develop automatically.

GRIEF

This avoidance of pain is unrealistic and damaging to your children. In order to cope with a real world, children need to experience denial of their wishes. They can survive losses and need to learn early in life the process of grieving over such losses, large and small. So much has been written on grief that we do not need to duplicate it here. But briefly, these are the usual stages of grief.

Stages of Grief

1. *Denial.* This is an instinctive recoiling from the pain of a loss or disappointment, and wishing or pretending that it had not happened. A common example of this is the loss of freedom through the assignment of homework. Many children literally deny to themselves that such expectations are real. They simply do not do it.

2. *Anger.* It is always one way of protecting one's self from pain. When there is not enough love to bring comfort and security, anger becomes that security. If you remember this, a child's behavior during grief is understandable. A friend told us this story: As a child he was especially close to the minister of his church, and often played in his home. He was deeply grieved when he learned that this trusted friend had to move. After learning of this, he visited in his home, took one of the prized toys he had enjoyed and hit it against a tree, breaking it. Instead of scolding him, that rare and beautiful pastor picked the child up and held him in his lap. He shared the intense sense of pain with his young friend, and helped him talk and cry about it. The anger was only a cover-up.

3. *Sadness and preoccupation with the problem or loss.* When you catch a sad child unaware, he will often look sad. At other times, however, he may confuse you completely by being extrabusy or "hyper," or he will be occupied with

friends or TV. This is his way of trying to avoid the pain, and perhaps to help you to stop feeling upset about him. In loss and grief that affect adults, children often are unwittingly abandoned. When you try to protect a child from finding out about a death or other serious problem, you may end up only puzzling him. Children sense when something is wrong, and they usually imagine causes that are even worse than reality. But they need adults to invite them to discuss the issues and share their feelings.

4. *Feelings of guilt, self-blame or fear.* In times of loss adults, as well as children, feel that somehow they are responsible for this bad thing. When I was a child my [Grace's] mother was ill a great deal, and I recall fearing that my childish misbehaviors had been such a worry to her that they had made her sick.

When handled with common sense and honesty, there is *healing and a return to happiness* after these processes of grief. In small issues, this may happen in a matter of hours, while larger issues will take a year or more.

Guilt and Grief

The concepts about guilt, as it is involved with grief, deserve a more complete elaboration.

Early Years. Most children develop a sense of omnipotence during their early months. Their slightest cries, or even irregular breathing, attract adults like honey attracts flies. That may be well and good then, but in times of grief, this unconscious sense of omnipotence can cause the child (and many adults as well) to feel that they are the reason for the situation of grief and loss.

Furthermore, children from four to seven or older have many fantasies. When they are angry, those fantasies may be quite destructive. If some dreadful event overtakes the object of such fantasies, it is easy to see how a child might blame himself. But a child rarely talks about such guilty feelings or the fears they arouse.

Handling Guilt/Grief Feelings

Handling guilt feelings like these in children is extremely important, lest they become buried in the unconscious and forgotten. Many adult phobias are based on childish guilt. To prevent such problems, here are some suggestions:

1.   *Put into words what you suspect the child is feeling.* Ask him if it is possible that he feels he is to blame for the situation. In any way you can, encourage him to talk about his thoughts and feelings.

2.   *Even if he denies any feelings at all, take time to explain how the event really happened, and do so in a way that makes it very clear that he had nothing to do with its happening.*

3.   *Tell the child he need not feel guilty or afraid, but if he does, encourage him to come to you and talk about it.*

4.   *Remind him of the good things he does, and point out that he is a good person created in God's own image.* While it is normal to feel angry, sad, and even guilty, he need not continue to feel that way forever. If he is at fault, he needs to understand, to confess, and receive forgiveness. (We will discuss that later.)

5.   *Share similar feelings of your own with the child so he will not feel so alone or different.*

Kinds of Loss and Grief

Parents often fail to think about the wide range of grief and losses that are experienced in childhood. Now don't go on a witch-hunt and focus your daily attention on grief. But don't overlook significant happenings, either.

1.   One of the earliest losses a child knows is the *loss of his freedom.* This begins by one year of age, when he has to stay out of dangerous or off-limits areas. It continues with toilet training, learning to feed himself, starting school, sharing toys, and many other experiences. Wanting a new toy and not getting it is a small grief.

2.   *The loss of relationships* is a common grief for today's child. If the average American family moves fourteen times, as has been reported, think how many children have to lose—re-

peatedly—friends, as well as homes and neighborhoods! No wonder people today become "calloused."

3.   Memories of *the loss of pets,* broken toys, or other favorite items in childhood have often lingered on into adult life. Many times elderly patients have shared such pain with us for the first time. They recall how difficult it was to understand why Mother threw away a battered but dearly loved doll or teddy bear.

4.   As children grow older, *lost hopes* must be added to the list. Contests that were lost, games that didn't get to be played, school events that excluded a hopeful participant—all are examples of real pain and grief. Girls who are not invited to the senior prom always seem especially tragic, for the excitement of that special event can never be recaptured!

Dealing With Grief in Childhood

It helps to deal better with a child's grief when you, the parent, have learned to handle your own. Here are some suggestions, however, that should be helpful:

1.   *Accept the fact that it is normal to grieve, that your child is no exception, and that he will recover.* This philosophy will help you to avoid too much sympathy. Your child needs care and understanding, but pity can teach him to feel sorry for himself.

2.   *Do not yield to the temptation to replace a lost pet or toy at once, or in any other way to minimize the pain or grief itself.* Such a thing prevents the completion of the grief process and makes the child feel he has to get excited at once over the new item. He can't do both at once! You parents who have tried this may be upset, because your child did not seem to appreciate the new item or pet. You can now understand why that was true— he had not finished the grief process over that loss.

3.   *Talk with the child about his loss and sadness.* Help him find the words for grief and help him coordinate his anger and fear with the sadness.

4.   *Hold him while he cries, if both of you feel comfortable with that.* Sometimes just sitting with him in silence is helpful. We find a short story from our lives that relates to the situation at hand may help the person realize he, too, will survive and be restored to peace of mind.

5.   *Invite him to come to you for a repeat of some or all of the above steps whenever he likes.*

6. *Go to him once in a while and offer your presence as comfort.* Many children need an invitation to open up and to talk about painful feelings.

7. *When you see the child is ready, drop the event, unless for some very special reason one of you needs to refer to it.*

Guilt Over a Deliberate Misdeed or Careless Accident

With the rise in crime, more and more families will keep guns or other weapons at home. It is to be expected that some of these weapons will be used by children in play or, rarely, in real anger. One such child of seven, accidentally shot and killed his sister. It was sad and frustrating to try to reach the feelings in that boy. Within even two weeks of the accident, he had so tightly locked away or denied that event that he would not discuss it at all.

It is extremely important that a parent or other trusted adult talk with a child in such a situation at once. There is no use justifying or condoning it. The evidence is there, and the child is guilty. Let us now discuss much more common examples of real guilt, such as broken treasures or an injured playmate.

Dealing With Real Guilt

1. *Deal first with your own emotional reaction.* Put into words your anger, fear, or worry, and say why you feel them.

2. You will now be more ready to *notice and verbalize your child's emotions.* Even if you don't approve of those feelings, say the words, and help the child express them as he experiences them. Perhaps he is still angry over a fight, while you believe he should feel sorry for hurting his friend. Moralize later, but help your child be honest first. Listen to his anger, understand it, and get that out of the way. Then bring him back to facing the fact of his responsibility for hurting that friend. For example, he needs to find better ways to work out disagreements than by fighting.

3. *Get your child to help set things right.* He can help pick up broken pieces or bring you a sweeper, if he has broken a special toy. Perhaps he can help mend it. If he broke the property of someone else, he especially needs to fix it or earn the money with which he can replace it.

4. *After you are back in control of yourself and your feelings,*

arrange a time to talk with your child. Don't say, "I told you so," but do help a child grow in a sense of responsibility by using such a disaster to teach him a lesson in logic as well as obedience. Listen to his side of the situation. While his reasons will not justify the carelessness, stating them may save a little of his dignity and can help you to teach him how to manage better the next time.

5. *If possible, help your child "pay a penalty."* That is a way of making up for his misdoing. Working to pay for a broken glass or a friend's broken toy will teach him responsibility, and will help relieve his guilt. Adjust the job and the pay to the child's ability and the lesson that needs to be learned.

6. Sometimes a spanking or being sent to his room may impress on a child the lesson that needs to be learned. Often, however, the above procedure is quite enough. We believe the punishment should be of the least severity that will actually teach the needed lesson.

An Extreme Situation. In the rare event, as above, of a child's seriously injuring or even killing someone, you should follow as many of the above steps as you can. Be sure one of you parents or an adult he loves stays with him, while the other gets help for the victim. In such a time, he will need to be reassured that he did not mean to do it, and that he is still loved. Be sure to avoid ongoing blame and resentment, once the grief is over. Children see violence on one TV show, then see the victims up and about on another show. Few children understand the real cause and effect in death or injuries. Remembering this can enable you to forgive and help him.

Professional counsel may be needed in an extreme situation. Be sure to find someone who really understands family interactions. Then follow through with his recommendations until the problem is resolved.

Spiritual Concepts and Grief in Children

While we know, as adults, that God's plan and will are ultimately for our good, that is not so believable to a child. He may believe God is mean for letting a relative die or a friend move. Children sometimes become afraid that someone else, or they, themselves, may be next to die or to leave.

Explaining Death. Explaining the death of an older or seriously ill person is one thing. A child may conceive of this as merciful and kind—a release from pain. The death, however, of a friend, a parent, or someone to whom he feels close, is quite another.

When you've explained all you can, and even quoted Scripture in your attempt to comfort a child, you may have to get more honest and to the point. Admit that you don't have all the answers, and tell him you feel angry and sad, too. Go ahead and cry together.

Then remind yourself and your child that life isn't supposed to be all happiness. Tell him honestly that you don't like that, but you intend to learn from it. You can learn to care about his and others' pain, because you know how it feels. You're learning to survive and be stronger than the pain is. Be sure to tell the child you will stick with him and help him through this, too.

Grief and Anger

Accept the anger fraction of grief. Use the story about the boy and his minister from this chapter, or remember a scene from your own childhood. This is the time for helping your child to feel understood and supported by the experiences you both are enduring. Your sharing can draw you close in a bond that nothing can ever duplicate.

After the anger is over, the real sadness can be expressed. This is the time to hold, rock, or simply be with a child. He may even want to be alone for a while. Suggest some options and let him choose. Alternate silence with such soothing sounds or words as come to you. Grace's grandmother's Pennsylvania Dutch "Oi! Oi!" still comforts her memory.

Creative Release

If the child can or will, help him draw, color, or write about his grief. Doing something relieves the dreadful sense of helplessness we all feel in the wake of loss. Words are sometimes empty, but creatively expressing emotions can release the pressure of buried feelings.

As often and as long as he needs to, invite the child to repeat this process with you or another friend who can help him through it.

Getting Over Acute Grief

After the acute grief of a death is over, you may want to talk again about God's part in all of this. His giving you each other, helping you to get over the pain, His allowing you special memories, and someone to await you in heaven, all have comforted us at times and restored an enlarged concept of a loving God who can trust us with pain. As you cry out for guidance in talking with your child, God's Spirit will provide that.

The usual time for acute grief to subside is a few weeks. It does recur, however, like shock waves, at intervals. These become slowly less intense and further apart. Special anniversaries and holidays are painful for a year or two, but finally even those days become bittersweet memories and the grief is over.

Help your child avoid using his sadness as an attention-getter. If you are alert to such a possibility, you will pick up the clues. They usually involve drawing out the experience for fringe benefits, such as extra attention at bedtime, or as an excuse for some mistake. We hear occasionally of a schoolchild, who has been reprimanded, saying, "Mrs. Jones, you're too hard on me. After all, I'm a foster child!"

PHYSICAL PAIN

Sooner or later every child will experience physical pain. Usually the first pain of any consequence is the burning of a finger when a young child discovers what *hot* means. Another source of pain is the punishment of disciplinary action. It is instinctive for living creatures to withdraw from pain.

Dealing With Pain

Teaching a child to understand and cope with pain is, therefore, a complex process. Here are some suggestions for dealing with physical pain in your child.

1. *Touch or kiss the painful area lovingly,* when it is possible.
2. *Apply medication or a Band-Aid when these are appropriate.* Band-Aids are almost symbolic of love in these

days. One depressed teenager stated that she could never re-call her mother applying a Band-Aid to a scrape or blister in all her childhood!

3. *When the child is comforted a bit, explain whatever you can to him about the injury or illness.* It need not be ac-curate scientifically, but it will help him understand the situa-tion, and not see it as punishing or fearsome.

An earache, for example, is caused by swelling and stretching of the eardrum. A child can stretch his fingers or hand to the point of mild discomfort, and realize something about that ear-ache. Avoid blaming him for the earache. If he was careless about clothing or swimming, teach him, but try to do so without anger or condemnation.

4. *Allow your child to cry and discuss his pain, but teach him to express these feelings with control.* Hysteria is over-doing it and may hamper necessary medical care or other at-tention.

5. *Tell your child to be brave and to cooperate even though he hurts.* And show him how to do that by your own attitude.

FEARS IN CHILDHOOD

Children are born with a fear of loud noises and the fear of falling. When they encounter either of these, even as newborns, they jerk, their faces look surprised, and they usually cry. From this inborn fear, branch all of the vulnerable emotions—worry, anxiety, loneliness, and panic are some common examples.

Reacting to Fears

There are three reactions to his fear that a child needs: 1) comfort to calm the emotional response; 2) information about the frightening experience; 3) protection to restore a sense of safety and security. Sometimes parents are worried lest their child become a coward, and they scold or punish him for being afraid. Such a reaction is damaging to the child; while it may stop the display of those vulnerable feelings, it will either drive them underground or cover them with the child's anger. You may be unconsciously teaching your child emotional dishonesty. Fear may be lifesaving, and it needs to be permitted, with thoughtfulness.

Here are some responses to fear that we have found successful both in relieving it and teaching the child to understand and control fear on his own.

1. Find out the cause of a child's fear.

When he was three, our son came to our room in terror, night after night. A night-light, comfort, a better bedtime routine, all failed to stop the child's obvious fear. When all else fails, ask! When we finally asked him why he was afraid, he pointed to an alphabet poster with animal pictures on it that hung by his bed. He pointed a chubby finger at it and said, "Dem tigers!" Down came the poster and the night terrors stopped. It's not always that easy, but thoughtfulness and tenacity can find the answers.

2. Get calm and be reassuring.

A child's fears can worry any parent. And a worried parent will not seem strong to a frightened child. Remember you are smarter and braver than your child. You can handle this. Believe it.

3. Verbalize those feelings.

Put into words the emotions you see reflected on your child's face, and teach him to verbalize those feelings. It is hard to explain, but simply putting almost any feeling into words, makes it easier to deal with.

4. Don't ridicule or shame your child for his fears.

Go with him to show him there are no ghosts or burglars in his closet. Explain the mysterious noises of the night, so he won't imagine they are robbers. He will outgrow these fears more readily if you explain and protect, rather than if you scold or laugh.

5.   A night-light may help unless it makes weird shadows.

Having his very own flashlight sometimes is very comforting, and we knew a boy who felt extrasafe when his baseball bat was under his bed at night. Help your child formulate a plan of reacting to any fear he may experience. (Part of the plan needs to include adult availability.)

6.   Remind your child of God's presence.

Read some promises of His care and protection such as "What time I am afraid, I will trust in thee" (Psalms 56:3). Pray aloud, thanking God for His promise to take care of us.

7.   Your courage and strength will teach your child to be brave and will help him believe in God's protection even more.

8.   Be proud of every evidence of your child's courage.

His willingness to explore dark shadows with you takes some courage. Tell him that. Comment on the other aspects of your child's bravery, and even his honesty about his fears. Remember, courage is the effort to overcome fear, not the absence of it! It takes some moral courage even to admit one's fear!

9.   Remember, "Perfect love casts out fear" (see 1 John 4:18) and God's special love will guide you.

Love will work much more effectively to relieve fear than will anger or punishment.

Children may be afraid of very interesting things, so don't be surprised by anything to which your child responds in fear. Wind, lightning, thunder, or other loud noises are the same fear with which he was born. Animals, even some dogs and cats, may scare a child by a sudden approach or by making loud noises. Imaginary fears become common between three and six, due to the rich fantasies of creative children in those years. Fear of falling is another of the inborn fears and may make some children afraid of climbing, or other activities. Fear of parents' anger and of strangers may be irritating to you, the parents. Whatever the fear, the treatment is to be found in one or more of the principles above.

Phobias

At times, fears may become an emotional illness. We call them *phobias*. If a child has lost control of his rage and has seriously hurt someone, or even believes he has, he may combine guilt with his fear and develop serious symptoms. Sometimes these symptoms are a sense of anxiety or worry. At times, to overcome this intense anxiety, a child may develop rituals. Washing his hands again and again or other repetitive habits may help a child temporarily to feel a bit less guilty or fearful. Such a condition is called an *obsessive-compulsive neurosis*. It requires intensive psychiatric help for your child, and lots of guidance for you, as parents, as well.

CHILDREN AND DIVORCE

Divorce, directly or indirectly, now affects the majority of American homes. Many schools report at least half of their students live in families that have suffered the pain of broken marriages. We know of very few families in which some close relative has not suffered a divorce. This pain is especially hard on children. They are part of both parents, and usually love each one of them.

Reactions of Children of Divorce

These youngsters experience a range of profound emotional reactions:

1. *Fear* is one of the first feelings to hit a child. He is afraid of losing his security in the absence of one parent. Perhaps the other may leave, or maybe he will have to go away. A fear of being abandoned is almost instinctive.

2. *Helplessness* is one of the worst emotions we know. By its very nature it entraps its victim. Certainly children are powerless through the struggles that precede and are a part of any divorce.

3. *Guilt* is described by most of the children of divorce

with whom we have worked. Due to their early sense of omnipotence, as well as their being the focus of many of their parents' quarrels, children feel they are to blame for their parents' problems and divorce.

4. *Confusion* is easy to understand in divorce. Even the husband and wife who are involved have mixed feelings. Most divorcing couples we know stay strongly emotionally involved with each other, though in a negative way. Being a step removed from the conflicts, a child will often sense the caring each spouse feels for the other, and yet he sees them hurting each other. It really doesn't make sense!

5. *Grief* with all its denial, anger, and deep sadness is every child's legacy from a divorce. Too often there is no one to help the child get through his grief because his parents are involved with their own pain. Near friends or relatives can be most helpful at such a point.

Younger Children's Reactions. Children act out these feelings in many ways, but rarely directly. They have bad dreams and awaken with fears. They may regress to wetting or soiling, if they are fairly close to toilet training. Many younger children become hyperactive and "naughty." This serves two purposes:

1. *It focuses the parents' attention on the child instead of on each other's anger.*
2. *It usually results in some punishment that helps relieve his guilt feelings.*

Can't Communicate. Children may withdraw and isolate themselves emotionally and physically in their sadness and anger. They may need some privacy, but sooner or later, they need even more to talk out their feelings.

Children of divorce often feel that they cannot express themselves to either parent about the other, or about the entire situation. One seven-year-old boy was misbehaving in school, refusing to do his work, and was angry at home. He clearly said that he just needed to talk about missing his father, but when he even mentioned his dad, his mother would cry or be irritated. The child could only act out the confused feelings he had.

Practical Problems of Divorce

Preventing Problems. It looks as though divorce is here to stay for a while, so you need to understand some of the issues at stake. You can help prevent some of the worst problems, or alleviate those affecting your child or the child of people you love. Here are some ideas that can help you.

Do not criticize each other to the child. In fact, each parent and other friends need to point out the good qualities of both parents. True enough, he may wonder why two such "good" people can't get along, and that is an opportunity to help him learn from your (or their) mistakes. Explain, as well as you can, why the divorce was necessary. You can do this honestly and without insulting anyone.

Do not use the child as a go-between. It is tempting for divorced parents or other relatives to be curious about the life of the absent spouse. The child who spends time with each one can be the source of such information. Most children sense this at once and resent it.

If you must be divorced, *get an emotional divorce* even more quickly and completely than a legal one! Freeing yourself, as a divorced parent, from resentments, blame, and preoccupation with the whole situation, will solve many of the problems. You may even become friends with your ex-spouse and work together constructively for your children. We are seeing a number of divorced spouses forego their anger with each other in order to help their troubled child.

Avoid competition for your child's loyalty. Many divorced parents resort to buying the children's favor. Out of guilt or sadness, the absent parent may make visits a party time, or load a child with gifts he neither needs nor wants. The other parents will often react in anger, or will try to carry out an even bigger buying binge.

Another expression of this is in the competition for being *strict or permissive.* One parent inevitably feels like the ogre, the other an angel. Children quickly learn to take advantage of such situations to manipulate them to their selfish (and destructive) advantage.

Avoid pitying the child. In marriage or divorce, many bad habits of parenting are prompted by pity. Feeling sorry for a child promotes pampering; teaches him self-pity with its paralyzing helplessness; and allows you to rescue him from healthy reality.

Be slow and cautious in reaching out for dating relationships. Both divorcing parents and their children experience grief. Prompt replacements of the absent spouse with a girl or boyfriend is a form of denial. It stops the grief process and often is a form of retaliation against each other. Worst of all, it allows for a major decision that may lead to a new marriage, to be made in the worst of emotional circumstances.

Remarriage?

Take one step at a time. First, *finish grieving.* Next, *reestablish your own self and your new life-style and grow from the mistakes of the past. Then* consider remarriage. A child who has just lost a parent does not want to lose the other to a new spouse. He will resent the new person from the start, and will feel hurt, afraid, and resentful. At best, this is a risky climate in which to consider establishing a new family. Many Christians feel it is wrong to remarry after a divorce. We suggest you counsel with your minister regarding such a major decision.

Summary

Parents, *get an emotional divorce before a legal one.* Work through your hurts and anger. Be aware of your child's range of needs and feelings and encourage a loving relationship with the other parent and relatives.

1. *Allow him to talk, cry, and be angry; comfort him.*
2. *Explain the reasons for the divorce without blame or condemnation of each other.*
3. *Encourage the child to feel loving toward both parents and their relatives.*
4. *Plan for plenty of time with both parents and make that time as nearly like "normal" family living as possible.*
5. *Parents, stay in charge. Do not let a child threaten to go to the other parent when he is angry with one, or for his selfish advantages. To avoid this game of Ping-Pong takes the efforts of both of you.*
6. *Help your child keep respect for both men and women.*

Avoid any implications that all men are mean or all women are selfish, and so forth.

HEALTHY SEXUALITY DEVELOPMENT IN THE CHILD OF DIVORCE

At this time in our American culture, mothers are still given custody of the children in most divorce cases. Men are beginning to be more involved with their children, and some are now gaining legal custody. In order to establish their own personal and sexual identity, children need both male and female role models.

Role Model

If you are a single parent and the absent spouse cannot fulfill this need, find such a role model for the children. Help your children to love, trust, and respect adults of both sexes as close friends. Grandparents, uncles, and aunts can often be such backup people. So can teachers or neighbors. Do not hesitate to ask an appropriate person for special help in clearly defined ways. No one person can do everything a child needs, but you can build a support system of several people who can supply most of those needs without being burdened.

Finding a Male Role Model. It seems especially hard to find men who are able and willing to give themselves to little children. Encourage your church and schools to use more men as teachers or youth leaders for young children. Try your local Big Brothers Club. They are wonderful men, dedicated to this very service to little children, especially boys. In our city, however, this group has had hundreds more of requests than they have volunteers. This area of service is a gold mine for the outreach ministry of the church.

Parents, you need to find ways to teach your children sexual roles. Pay special attention to their dress, activities, and their concepts of manliness and femininity. In today's world, each of you must define these qualities individually, but do that—and then be proud of the qualities your children develop, and let them feel your approval.

While divorce, like death and other losses, brings pain to a child, you can turn that pain into a strengthening experience—

for yourself as well as your child. . . . "weeping may endure for a night, but joy cometh in the morning" (Psalms 30:5).

CHILD ABUSE

With almost daily headlines revealing the tragedy of child abuse, we think it is a new phenomenon. It has, however, always existed, and seems to be a part of the condition of mankind. It is not easy to define child abuse because a practice some people believe to be good discipline is the very thing others see as abuse.

Definition of Child Abuse

A definition we personally find helpful is this: "Child abuse is any treatment of a child that threatens his safety, or leaves physical or emotional scars." If your methods of punishment leave such marks on your child, please commit yourself to changing.

Description of a Child Abuser

There are several *common denominators of people who abuse their children:*

1. *They are lonely* and usually emotionally or physically far from their families. They are often afraid or suspicious of people, so they become "stuck" in their isolation.
2. *There often is conflict* in their marriages, or they are divorced.
3. *They are people who live under great stress,* such as financial, job-related pressure, trouble with neighbors, or housing.
4. They are *parents who were abused* by their own parents in childhood.

One abusive mother recently told us about the cruelty of her own mother. She said, "But, you know, I wish I could go back to her even now, I miss her so much!" She was explaining, a little bit, how it is that being abused creates habits of abusing. When this mother abuses her children, she is unconsciously being like her mother, and can momentarily feel the old closeness.

Strangely enough, the abusive parent really loves his child. More often than not, we have seen abused children preferring their own parents to the safest of foster care. Partly this is due to the love—strangely as it is expressed—of those parents. Abusive parents also generally are energetic people, and children tend to be attracted to people of high energy.

Qualities of the Abusive Parent

On a personal level, there are several qualities of the abusive parent that we feel need to be understood.

1. *Lack of self-control.* Abusive adults often act like spoiled children. They actually have a temper tantrum, and at that moment they feel powerful.
2. *Lack of self-confidence.* Parents who do not know their true wisdom and strength go to great lengths to try to prove themselves. Such people overreact to fairly normal situations with extreme rage.
3. *Lack of trust in their parents.* While they usually loved their parents, they were also put down by those parents. They usually felt either extremely intimidated by, or extremely powerful with, their parents.
4. *Seeing in the child some negative quality* that was present in their parents, in each other, or themselves. Unconsciously, such parents take out, on the helpless child, vengeful feelings that really belong elsewhere.
5. *Lack of sense of self-worth.* Because they basically feel so unworthy, abusive parents find it impossible to ask for help. They don't want anyone to know how bad they are, and feel if anyone knew, they would be even more rejected.
6. *Child learns to fit into the pattern.* Children quickly learn how to get a parent's attention. They may even sense that they are meeting a need in that parent by evoking the abuse. So the child forms the very habits that fit into the vicious cycle.

Treatment of Child Abuse

Obviously the best treatment of child abuse is the prevention of it. The following ideas will help in that prevention as well as contribute to a cure.

First of all, if you even suspect that you are an abusive parent, do something! Do not wait for the next explosive episode to happen. It could be the time when you might lose control and seriously hurt your child. Talk with your minister, some trusted friend, or a professional counselor.

If you can't bring yourself to talk to someone you know, *call your local child-welfare agency.* You need not identify yourself until you feel more comfortable. Ask for any help you need.

Find a "Parents' Anonymous" group. They are parents who are or have been abusive themselves, and they will fully understand your feelings. The national headquarters are:

> Parents Anonymous
> 2930 West Imperial Highway
> Suite 332
> Inglewood, California   90303
> *or*
> Parents Anonymous
> 250 West 57th Street, Rm. 1901
> New York, NY   10019

They will help you find or organize a group in your own vicinity.

Reread the above paragraphs and *try to identify your deep needs and feelings.* By knowing them and admitting them, you are well on your way to finding real solutions.

Dealing With Potentially Abusive Situations

In dealing with such situations, try one or more of these suggestions:

1. *Get in touch with your earliest feelings of desperation and rage—before they take your self-control away from you.*
2. *Remove yourself from your child and that explosive situation at once!*
3. *Talk with Jesus Christ. Close your eyes and imagine He is present with you—as He said He is. Tell Him how you feel and ask Him for whatever you need—love, guidance, tenderness, or whatever.*

4. *Call a friend, if you can. Talk over your problem and ask specifically for what you need. Plan together how you can safely discipline this child, or handle a touchy situation.*
5. *With courage and caution, go to the waiting child and put your disciplinary plan into effect.*
6. *Remember your own childhood. By recapturing your experiences of fear and anger, you may understand your child and learn to treat him better.*
7. *Learn to love yourself and treat yourself kindly, even in your deepest emotional being.*

If you have ever been an abusive parent, you probably should religiously avoid all physical punishment of a child. Just as one drink can revive an alcoholic's old habits, one such punishment can trigger a chain reaction of abuse. *Avoid it like the plague!* Chapter 13 on Discipline will help you with better ways to discipline.

Counseling

For some people, the best answer to child abuse is professional counseling. If you are an abusive parent, swallow your pride and go for it! It may save your child's life. It will certainly improve yours. You may learn how to understand and accept yourself as a whole person, as well as how to deal with your child. As you discover your strengths and weaknesses, you may find they balance out better than you feared. Learning to truly love yourself will inevitably teach you how to love others—including your child.

17
Solving Their Behavioral Problems

This chapter is a compilation of the major concerns parents share with us about their children's behavior. Some are serious; others are transient, and will go away with time. All of them need your understanding. Their listing here is alphabetical and has nothing to do with the seriousness of their effects.

In dealing with behaviors that create problems for you as parents, your children, or those with whom they relate, there is a need for special caution. It is tempting to believe that a good, sound spanking will drive the behavior out of them. And at times it will, just as touching a hot stove produces pain enough to keep a child from touching it again.

The older a child becomes, however, the more complex will his life and all of its branchings become. The way people treat a child teaches him a way of responding—gently and reasonably, or aggressively and impulsively. Furthermore, the reasons for specific behaviors become increasingly more relevant than the behaviors themselves.

In discussing these problem behaviors, therefore, please bear with the explanations. We are not against discipline, or even spankings. The biblical commands for this are clear and correct. But we do ask that you understand the deep needs and feelings that prompt a child's problem behaviors. You may well change his behaviors by punishment alone. But if his feelings are unrecognized and his needs unmet, other problem behaviors will crop up. Leaves from a bindweed root may be chopped off daily, but more will grow until the root is killed.

452

FACING THEIR BEHAVIOR PROBLEMS

A child's problems are often due to a root of bitterness and unlovingness in the heart of his parents, as well as to the foolishness of his own young life. So please think deeply and circumspectly about each issue that may involve your child *before* you plan a way of overcoming it.

Babyishness

This is acting like a baby or a child considerably younger than the child really is. The symptoms include crying with little provocation, acting more helpless than the child actually is, tattling, and otherwise seeking adult intervention; or regression to earlier patterns of thumb sucking, wetting, or soiling.

Causes of Babyishness

The *causes* of such behavior are:

1.   Being treated like a baby by a parent who is overprotective and anxious, or by grandparents or others.

2.   Feeling pushed to grow up too soon before a child's baby needs have been met. The arrival of a new baby may cause this temporarily as does the start of kindergarten and first grade.

3.   Grief or anxiety in a child may be manifested in babyish behavior. This is especially true if divorce is threatened. A child may hope his parents will see how much he needs them.

4.   Certain illnesses may cause some of these behaviors. Allergies, anemias, and some chronic toxic illnesses such as mild lead poisoning are examples.

Treatment of Babyishness

Be sure your child has a thorough physical checkup before you decide that babyishness is just a behavioral problem.

Do an inventory of your child's present life-style.

1.   *Has there been a big change in his accustomed amount or kind of attention?*

2. *Has he been around someone who has treated him like a baby? Have you done more babying than you realized?*

3. *Has there been a change in the family, such as Dad's changing jobs, Mom's going to work, or a death in the family?*

4. *Has there been extra worry or arguing between you parents? Little ears hear and sense many things you may not realize.*

5. *If your child is in school, is there a problem with a teacher or other children?*

The precise way of dealing with this problem must be related to the cause. Try matching these suggestions to the results of your inventory.

1. Get medical care, if that is indicated.

2. Explain your understanding of the problem to your child. Even when he can't talk, he will understand more than you think, and you will be developing the habit of fairness and reasonableness.

3. Make it clear to the child that both he and you will be making some changes, and describe those simply.

4. Explain these changes clearly and emphatically to older children, and any adults who will be dealing with your child, and request their help. This will provide consistency.

5. Decide on a proper response to the behavior: ignore it; put him in his room; or time-out (spanking usually prompts more crying and babyish reactions, so it is not a very effective tool for this problem).

6. Be careful to lavish positive attention and love on your child when he is not acting like a baby. Let him know your pride and respect for his efforts to control such behavior.

7. Be persistent. Too often, parents give up just short of success and try something else. Inconsistency causes confusion and defeat.

Bed-Wetting (Enuresis)

This is the continuation of, or the return to, nighttime wetting after daytime bladder control has been mastered. It may occur at any time during the night, and it may take place once or more often. Do not be concerned if your child is three or under. Many children do not stop nighttime wetting until they are four or five.

Causes of Bed-Wetting

The *causes* of enuresis are one or more of these:

1. Slower neurological development makes bladder control later and more difficult for some children.
2. The size of the urinary bladder is too small to hold a night's quantity of urine.
3. Excessive fluid intake in the late evening, especially those liquids containing caffeine, such as chocolate milk, colas, or tea. Caffeine strongly stimulates urinary output by the kidneys.
4. Profound sleep, so deep that the discomfort of a full bladder does not awaken the child.
5. Dreams in which the child goes to the bathroom—in bed!
6. Extreme dependence on the parents' help or reminders, instead of assuming personal responsibility.
7. Emotional distress including grief, anxiety, and anger.

In considering emotional distress, several events may trigger bed-wetting. *The birth of a new baby,* with the loss of a child's secure position in the family, often causes temporary regression or return to earlier habits. This is especially likely if the older child is just getting bladder control.

Beginning of a new life-style that is frightening to a child, such as moving, the divorce of parents, starting school, or being placed with a new baby-sitter.

Overly harsh punishment of a child or a brother or sister may sometimes result in wetting.

Treatment of Bed-Wetting

How can you handle bed-wetting so it will stop, without emotionally damaging your child? Both physically and emotionally, bladder and bowel control are difficult for children. They must give up their carefree state and take on new responsibilities. It's easy to forget the new habit or to prefer the old, easy life of wetting whenever he feels like it. So be thoughtful of your child while you are helping him to form or regain his control.

First, *have a thorough physical evaluation* and *remedy any problems that can be treated.* In many cases a prescription may relieve bed-wetting.

Next, *evaluate your child's toilet habits during the daytime.* If he empties his bladder every hour or so, it will not stretch enough to hold a full night's quantity. Help your child wait a few minutes longer than he thinks he can during the day, when he needs to void. When he can hold a cup and a half, he should be ready to stop wetting. Sometimes measuring the amount of urine can involve the child in the process of gaining control.

Notice how many liquids your child is drinking after the evening meal. Limit his drinks, for the last two hours before bedtime, to a single drink just before retiring. Avoid coffee, tea, or any caffeine drinks.

Be sure the child completely empties his bladder just before going to sleep.

Take stock of the emotional stresses that are affecting your child.

Taking Stock of Your Child's Emotions

Encourage the child to talk about any and all of his worries and feelings. When he has trouble doing so, start talking about such feelings yourself, but wait for long enough periods to allow him to open up.

Throughout the day, as you see emotions registered on your child's face, remember them. Try to get him to verbalize these feelings, and help him find the words to do it. Even if he must be angry or cry to get such feelings out, allow that, and help him to do it appropriately.

Give plenty of love and attention. Rocking and cuddling even an older child may give enough security to enable him to stop wetting. Sometimes growing up implies the loss of such loving attention. A child may prefer staying "little," and bed-wetting, because of his need for babylike attention.

Help the child find answers to his needs and problems. In listening, asking, and suggesting, you will help him know he and his needs are important, and that he can learn, with your help, to take care of them.

After you have a better understanding of your child's emotions, try these measures:

1. *If possible, have the sound sleeper take a short nap, or retire earlier, so he won't be quite so tired.*

2. *Get the child up and to the bathroom before he wets.* If he has a usual time this works, but often it does not. If you get him up, be sure he awakens, so he can get into the habit of awakening himself.

3. *Stop any anger and punishment for wetting.* Your very anger produces fear and resentment in your child, which may unconsciously affect his wetting, which produces, anger in you, which makes him more afraid—a vicious cycle indeed! Sometimes parents' anger sets up an unconscious power struggle. Your best maneuver, if this is your problem, is to give up. Strange as that may sound at first, it may give to a child the sense of power he needs. He's been using his power to resist; by stopping the fight, he may decide to use it to control.

4. *We do not recommend bribing a child for controlling a biological function.* Some parents have, however, found that it works!

5. Once in a while, we have found that *telling a child firmly and positively to quit wetting the bed has worked wonders.* The child must believe that you mean it and that he can do it.

6. While it is annoying to parents, *remember it is the child's problem.* Give it to him. When he is old enough, teach him to change and wash his own linens and rejoice when he stays dry!

7. Take heart. *Your tenacity will win out!* We rarely see a college student wet the bed.

Cheating

This is the practice of deception or fraud. It usually involves taking advantage of another person. In preschoolers, cheating begins when a child secretly refuses to play by the rules or take turns. As a child grows older, he may cheat in sports and in classwork, as well as in games.

Reasons for Cheating

The *reasons* for cheating are numerous. These are the most common ones and should help you to understand and deal with this issue:

1. Some children are just naturally aggressive. They have an inordinate need to win. If it takes cheating, then they may even do that.

2. A younger child may see an older or more manipulative child cheat, and may believe it pays. He cannot see far enough ahead to realize the ultimate problems that cheating involves.

3. A child may feel so compelled to measure up to an adult's expectations that he will do anything for the approval that involves. (Parents who demand *A*'s from a child who is truly not capable of *A* work may unwittingly tempt him to cheat. Parents who expect sports or other achievements of which a child is truly incapable may prompt cheating. Finally, severe disapproval or punishment for falling short may cause rebellion or fear that cause a child to cheat.)

4. By failure to recognize or admit that a child is cheating, parents unwittingly give their consent to it. (We find that to be all too common!)

5. Most children have a natural laziness—they prefer to find an easy way. Cheating may seem to offer that.

6. Being too trusting of a child who is struggling with problems can allow him to get by with cheating until it becomes a habit.

How to Deal With Cheating

This, of course, depends on the reasons for doing it.

Be Aware of Temptation. For all children, be aware of their being tempted to dishonesty. No one is above it, even adults. Be clear about your values and God's law regarding honesty: "Thou shalt not bear false witness."

Your Expectations. Take a look at your expectations and demands of your child. 1) *Are you expecting more in behavior, performance, and grades than your child realistically can do?* 2) *Are you so harsh in your discipline that you make your child afraid?* 3) *Are you too lenient, allowing your child to get by with cheating without your knowledge?* 4) *Are you in touch with your child's teacher, coach, or youth counselor enough to know whether he cheats with them?*

Changes in Your Behavior. Once you are aware of a mistake or imbalance in your expectations or discipline, plan for changes.

Rearrange your priorities. Honesty means more than the recognition of top grades or winning.

Talk with your child about his cheating and your mistakes, and make both clear. Your mistakes do not justify his!

Make it quite clear that cheating will not be tolerated and set up some consequences if it happens again. We suggest that those be directly related to the event. For example, cheating in a game means *no more playing today.* Cheating in school may demand *extra schoolwork or taking an* F. Don't be too easy if you expect your child to take you seriously. We feel that repeating a course in school, or even a year, may be a small price to pay for acquiring the trait of honesty.

Make it equally clear that you will be fairer, less angry and demanding, or whatever you need to do to create a secure environment for your child. Whether or not to cheat is each child's choice, but whatever you can do to make this environment fair and encouraging will help him to choose honestly.

Once your plan is made, *follow through!* Habits are hard to break, and you or your child may slip back into old ways. If that happens, don't give up. Just get going again.

Be sure to praise your child for his efforts to reform. And encourage each other as parents, likewise.

Childhood or Adolescent "Crushes"

These are usually strong, dependent feelings toward another person. While it often seems like love, such a relationship is almost always based on needs, and may become a serious problem when the other person either rejects your child, or becomes overly attached to him or her.

Crushes, when they exist, usually begin at about eleven or twelve years of age. They may involve another child of the same or opposite sex, or an older person, such as a teacher. While many such relationships are platonic, they may develop into sexual ones rather suddenly. We once believed that before puberty, children did not have sexual feelings. That is not true, and we now know children develop strong emotional and sexual feelings rather early.

Causes for Crushes

The reasons for such crushes are not always clear, but we do know the child sees in that other person certain powers and attributes that are meaningful to him. These qualities may not be real, and they are often imagined, or at least exaggerated. Knowingly or not, the other person fits into the relationship in a powerful way. The person who is the focus of the crush may have the positive traits of parents or other relatives, with few of the negative qualities. At any rate, he meets a deep craving by the child for security, significance, and seeming love. Some people see this as normal, but we see it as risky at best, and it may be downright dangerous.

Often such a relationship takes place just when a child is struggling toward independence. The other person may seem to be the gateway to that independent state, but actually he more often becomes a prison—a confusing blend of friend, good parents, and sweetheart.

The Characteristics of a Crush

These may vary some but you will recognize them clearly.

How They Start. Crushes usually start with respect, admiration, and trust. Usually there is a lighthearted fun side to the relationship as well.

Desperate Preoccupation. As the relationship grows, one usually gives the other too much power over his feelings, and there creeps into the friendship a desperate preoccupation with one another.

1. Your child may talk or seem to think of no one else but this friend.
2. He worries about the other's safety, activities, or friendship. He seems afraid of "losing" the person. There is none of the carefree joy of a truly trusting friendship.
3. A child neglects other friends and activities, mopes about the house, becomes moody, and seems happy only when he is with this special person.
4. Such a relationship carries the risk of sending a child

back into a "symbiotic" life-style, such as he knew with his mother as a tiny baby. He depends excessively for his emotional existence on someone else.

How to Handle a Crush

This is not an easy question to answer, so first of all slow yourself down and *do nothing,* until you have evaluated the entire situation. It may be the situation is only temporary and will flicker out promptly. Often the other person is not even aware of the child's feelings, and this will cause it to burn out with no trouble. When such is not the case, however, consider these steps.

Get acquainted with the person who is the other end of the relationship. You can soon tell whether this is someone who will fit into a good friendship or develop into a dangerous one.

Take a close look at your child's unmet needs, and see where these may be feeding a problem. Meeting a child's emotional needs demands a balance in affection, approval, consistency, and enjoyment. If there is too little of one of these qualities in your relationship with your child, correct that!

Rarely, you may need to call off the relationship abruptly and completely to protect your child or the other person. Usually, however, it is better to move slowly, help your child see the dangers, and choose to get out himself.

Sometimes there are good aspects to crush-type relationships. A shy child may become more outgoing through the other's example, or one who is bored with school may become motivated to learn through sharing the friend's interests.

Positive Features. When there are such positive and healthy features in the relationship, try these steps:

1. *Pray for guidance and wisdom.*
2. *Sit down calmly with your child—and, if possible, the friend.* Explain the risks and problems in the relationship as you see it: the exclusion of others, the loss of personal freedom, the moodiness and worry, and the risk of getting tired of one another.
3. *Point out the positive factors of sharing interests, feelings, and experiences.*
4. *Try to gain their cooperation in "cooling it."* Once they

understand these issues, many children are relieved to have someone help them do this.

5. *Together, outline a plan that will limit their time alone,* include some other friends, cut down on phone calls, and replace their parenting need with you, Mom and Dad, again.

6. *You will need to enforce the plan because most children won't have the willpower or maturity to follow through alone.*

You'll be glad you accomplished this difficult task! It can save some real heartaches for all of you.

Fire Setting

This is the habit of playing with matches, cigarette lighters, or other incendiary materials, or using them to start fires, large or small. Throughout history, people have been fascinated by fires, and children are no exception. They simply are not ready to handle fires, however, and the ultimate problem becomes the serious risk of destruction and death through arson or pyromania.

Reasons for Setting Fires

Most fire setters begin out of curiosity. They excitedly follow a fire truck on their bikes, or are intrigued with the flames in a fireplace or trash burner. They may discover, however, that such excitement can be duplicated through building their own fires. The more angrily a parent tries to stop this, the more secretive a firebug may become. At such a point, obviously, danger sets in. Secret fire settings all too often get out of control by accident, and become seriously destructive.

When children set fires it is often because of emotional problems, such as loneliness, a need for parents' attention, or a need for respect from their friends.

Fire-setting children often see their parents as threatening and angry people. Sometimes there are severe arguments in their families.

Children who become confirmed or stubborn in their fire-setting patterns, have been shown to have strong but confused sexual feelings. They sometimes hear their parents argue or fight in their bedrooms, and may believe that sexual issues are at stake in those troublesome problems. Somehow they confuse the excitement of a dangerous fire with sexual feelings. A person who finds such sexual arousal through fire setting is called a *pyromaniac*, and is a dangerous person.

Dealing With a Fire Setter

This is urgent and needs real caution to avoid sending the habit underground.

1. *Keep all fire-starting materials away from a child.* Small children can be cured by this simple process.
2. If you can see that your child is simply fascinated with the mystique of the flames, *schedule some times for a bonfire and a wiener roast, or a fire in a fireplace.* Teach him how to build a fire and control it. Tell him the extreme danger of fires that are out of control. Let him see pictures of a devastating forest fire. Be with your child at all times around a fire, until you are sure he is old enough and responsible enough to care for it properly.
3. *Look for emotional problems or symptoms that could result in fire setting.*

Along with exploring and working on these issues, remember this: *Tell your child to stop setting fires!* Let him know you simply will not tolerate it. Then go ahead with the more involved processes below.

Possible Emotional Problems. Are there *angry* arguments between you and your spouse that could frighten your child and make him angry, as well? If so, control those and keep them totally out of your child's hearing. You can argue and discuss issues successfully without being loud or explosive.

Are you *too angry* with your child? He may be angry with you but afraid to tell you. *Control your anger* and learn to be reasonable and fair by dealing with issues early, before you get to the boiling point. Encourage your child to tell his feelings, even anger, rather than to act them out.

There is evidence that serious fire setters have *strong sexual feelings* that they do not understand. With sensitivity, check this out. Keep your own sexual issues more private, but teach your child wholesome attitudes toward sex so it will not trouble him. (*See How to Teach Your Child About Sex,* Revell, 1981.)

Sometimes a child has too much or too little freedom or power. He may need more supervision or, on the other hand, you may be too controlling with him. Try to balance these issues in proportion to your child's sense of responsibility.

Discuss your child's feelings as you see them expressed in his eyes and on his face. Help him understand and talk about his loneliness, fears, angers, or any unhappy emotions. Help find the answers for his needs through your protection and love.

Seek Professional Help. If you need to, seek professional help. Some of these issues that read rather simply can be most complex. It is never a shame to need help. Ask your doctor or pastor for a counselor who is experienced in child and family problems.

BEHAVIORS THAT WORRY PARENTS

Hyperactivity

This has come to be a household diagnosis. Most children, however, who are *called* hyperactive are not truly that. The genuinely hyperactive child is best described as "driven." He is a wall climber, never still for even five minutes, constantly moving, making noises, and into everything. Even sleep may be interrupted and brief. It is difficult to believe the energy such a child consumes—and puts out. It is hard or impossible to cuddle, play games, watch television, or read with a truly hyperactive child.

Such a driven child needs to be seen by a pediatrician, a neurologist, and a child psychiatrist. Sometimes this is a sign of *severe allergies, slight brain damage, or infantile autism.* If none of those is diagnosed, you may be quite sure your child will outgrow this, but you will not be as sure that you will live through it!

Causes of Hyperactivity

Brain Damage. If there is brain damage in a hyperactive child, it is of a type that is very difficult to diagnose, and probably brain damage as a cause is quite rare.

Allergic Factors. These are also hard to diagnose (or to rule out, for that matter). A special diet that eliminates the coloring matter and additives that prevent spoiling, most carbohydrates, and certain fruits has been widely recommended. This is called the *Feingold Diet.* Some people believe it is a miracle worker, and others have had no improvement. That may be due to the fact that some hyperactivity is due to biochemical factors in food and some is not. If you believe your child has an allergy, have your doctor check that out, and follow any recommendations he makes.

Sensitive Nervous·Systems. Some children are born with extra-sensitive nervous systems. They see, hear, taste, smell, and feel much more sharply than other children do. It is possible that these children also react more intensively and are more active.

Lack of Communicative Ability. We know that children who cannot hear or speak are frustrated by their inability to communicate. Helen Keller is a classic example of a child whose wild behavior changed rapidly when she began to learn language. Perhaps some bright, young children are frustrated by their lack of words to say what they want to say. And certainly they must be checked for *hearing problems.*

Form of Manic-Depressiveness. There are some significant studies going on that suggest hyperactive children may have a mild form of manic-depressive illness or its equivalent. Some of them improve on lithium, a very successful medication for such a problem. A doctor especially trained in child psychiatry can help you find out whether this may be your child's problem.

Depressed Child. Sometimes a grief-stricken or depressed child may cover his tender feelings with wild activity. We have seen children act this way after a death or a divorce.

Need for Firmer Guidance. Evidence is building that strongly implies the need for firmer and more consistent guidance from parents. In an effort to show respect and consideration for so-called children's rights, parents give them illogical choices, and then may disapprove of a child's decision. An example of this is the experience we shared in which a young mother gently asked her two-year-old, "Susan, wouldn't it be nice if you put away your toys and took a nap now?" Susan, not thinking it at all nice, angrily threw the toys all over the room, and then ran about the house to avoid the nap!

Varied Treatment of Hyperactivity

Complete Medical Evaluation. This is absolutely necessary. Many doctors recommend a trial on certain medications. If your child's problem is severe, we recommend you try it at least long enough to see if it helps. If so, use it long enough to help your child form new habits. Then try him without it if your doctor is willing. We do not like children to become dependent on medicines, but there are cases in which such medication works.

Allergy Tests. Have any possible allergies tested by your child's doctor or an allergy specialist. The results of those tests will tell you whether you need to put your child on a special diet or have other allergy treatments.

Handling All Hyperactive Children

Be firm, gentle, and very certain in your training and discipline. If you are indecisive or inconsistent in your rules and consequences, your child is bound to feel anxious and act out that anxiety in hyperactive behavior.

Tell your child exactly what you want him to do and make him do it, if it is important. The soft approach, "Mark, don't you want to go to bed now? Mother wants you to," just won't work with a hyper child. Mark usually doesn't want to stop playing, even though he wants to please Mother. How can he decide that? Don't give him such choices. "Mark, in five minutes the timer will go off. That's your bedtime signal, so be ready for your snack and story" (or whatever your bedtime ritual is). He can feel safe and secure in your better judgment and healthy authority. If there are realistic choices, limit them and help him learn to choose.

Keep the environment calmer for a hyperactive child. Rock him slowly, sing and speak softly, have lower lights, and softer music. Even colors in his room should be subdued, if you have a choice.

Limit and carefully supervise television for the hyperactive child. Violence, loud noises, and the sudden scene changes can add to his nervousness.

If you have a truly hyperactive or "driven" child, get professional help. In addition, line up a collection of relatives and

friends who will give you an hour's relief now and then. It will
save your sanity and won't hurt the child.

Be sure to have a trade-off of Dad's and Mom's time. Sometimes one will be able to quiet a child more than the other. The
more quiet moments such a child finds, the sooner he will settle
down.

Lying

This is a deliberate denial or misrepresentation of the truth.
Sometimes it involves withholding part or all of the truth in a
misleading way.

The Causes of Lying

These are similar to those of cheating.

   1. In childhood, there also is a period of "yarn spinning"
or fantasy creation that is not lying. It may, however, lead to
lies later on because a child learns to get attention in this way.
The boundary between the real and the pretend may be
harder for some children to find.
   2. Lying often begins with its usefulness in getting a child
out of some punishment or responsibility.
   3. Boasting may become lying, and is always due to a
child's need for a sense of importance.

Treatment of Lying

Stop the Payoff. When you have figured out the reasons for
your child's lying, sit down ceremoniously and tell him these
benefits have stopped paying off. Let him know that you will no
longer tolerate dishonesty from him for any reason. He will no
longer get out of jobs, discipline, or the responsibilities of his life
by lying. This is to include school responsibilities as well as
those at home. Furthermore, if he does lie, tell him there will be
a consequence. Decide whether that will be a spanking, an additional job, or some other fitting discipline. Ask your child
what will help him most in breaking the habit of lying.

Cooperation of Others Necessary. Get the cooperation of all the
adults or older siblings who are involved with your child in

making this regimen work. Consistency and a united front will make the cure work much faster.

Follow Through. Be sure someone is assigned to follow through with this plan. One of you parents needs to check regularly to see if the lying has stopped completely. If not, has someone failed to carry out the discipline? Or is it just the backsliding of anyone who has to break a longtime habit?

More Recognition. If your child needs more recognition or less severe punishment, provide that. His importance to you as parents is paramount, so be certain he knows it. You can punish him when he needs it without devastating him.

Getting Rid of the Guilt. Help your child get rid of his guilt over past lies. Teach him why it is wrong—because it takes away trust, hurts others and himself, and lets him be irresponsible. Lead him privately in a prayer of confession, and share with him some of God's many promises of forgiveness as in First John. Help your child to ask forgiveness of those to whom he has been dishonest, if possible, and then bury the past.

Slipups. Begin a new era with a clean slate. But remember, old habits are hard to break, so don't feel all is lost if there is an occasional slipup!

Masturbation

This is the touching or fondling of genital areas for pleasure or sexual orgasm.

The Causes of Masturbation

These vary with the age of the child and with the way parents treat sexual matters.

In the Infant. Masturbation is the simple discovery of the anatomy, which also includes the ears, nose, fingers, toes, and navel. Touching the penis or clitoris may cause an erection, which is a pleasurable feeling. Some infants learn to repeat such touching, just as others suck their thumbs—because it feels good.

Preschoolers. These youngsters sometimes masturbate at bedtime, after they are out of diapers. It is a comfort to them and helps them relax and go to sleep. This is usually a transient habit and is commonly outgrown. When there is too much punishment for this (as for other misdeeds), it may become secretive, willful, and guilt producing. It may become a habit that is complicated by setting up a power struggle, making it very hard to break, and producing serious emotional problems.

Curiosity About Others. A by-product of masturbating may be a natural curiosity about the genitals of playmates. It is quite common for such inquisitive children to have exploring parties. Usually this is remarkably innocent and purely curious. They take down their pants and look at each other's genital areas. When you act shocked, or punish and shame a child for doing this, you may unwittingly heighten his curiosity and again drive him to secrecy. On the other hand, this practice invades an important area of privacy and can lead to excessive interest in sexual matters, prematurely.

We suggest that you deal with sexual curiosity by calmly getting the children's clothes back on, and then conducting an impromptu sex-education class, touching briefly on these ideas:

1.   *Let them know that curiosity is normal and healthy.*

2.   Tell them that taking off clothes and exploring each other's bodies is not the best way to learn about such questions at this time in their lives (or really until they are ready for marriage). Tell them not to do that again.

3.   The best way to find out about most things is to ask their parents. Suggest that they talk with their parents that day.

4.   With your own children, find out their questions and then, with the help of books or in your own words, explain the differences in boys and girls. In the context of the specific functions of male and female, help them understand that differences are logical and that they are an evidence of God's great wisdom in creating us.

5.   Assure your children that they may come to you at any time for further information. (*See How to Teach Your Child About Sex* by Grace H. Ketterman for your own resources.)

School-Age Children. Boys and girls of school age generally discontinue masturbating because their interests and energy become directed to areas beyond their own bodies. They may practice this briefly during bathing or at bedtime, but it is rarely significant.

If a child does masturbate habitually at school or become preoccupied and withdrawn, it usually is a sign of serious emotional problems. *These problems, however, cause the practice of masturbation and not vice versa!*

In Late Grade-School Years. Now masturbation may be a sign of too much sexual stimulation from TV, magazines at the local drugstore, or from classmates. You need to give your child healthy sexual attitudes and a good sex education. Be open, calm, and wise in discussing sexual issues with your children.

Adolescent Masturbation. This may become a problem, but it needn't. When a child reaches puberty, he will be capable of ejaculation and she, of orgasm in a more adult fashion. This may be so exciting that young people may try to reproduce it again and again. They may worry when they can't reach the climax and can become exhausted both physically and emotionally. They may resort to sophisticated fantasies that can produce guilt, or invite the acting out of those fantasies in premature sexual experimentation.

During Dating. Sometimes a young person may become sexually aroused. For some such adolescents, masturbation is an effort to avoid sexual intercourse and to protect themselves and each other from ill-advised sexual intercourse.

Sign of Loneliness. In some adolescents, as in some younger children, masturbation is a desperate attempt to find some sensual pleasure and self-love in a world that, to them, is unbearably lonely.

Treatment of Masturbation

This depends on the age, the causes, and the quality of the habit.

Infants and Young Children. These youngsters do not merit your worry. Do nothing about it, because it will stop as soon as the diaper goes on. Do be sure your baby has plenty of colorful toys, sights, and sounds to keep his interests focused mainly on areas other than any part of his body. Do not punish an infant for discovering the genital area, and do not treat it any differently from his discovery of the rest of his body.

Preschoolers. They need to have their energy and time devoted to exploring the big world outside their bodies. Keep toys, activities, and your involvement such that they will forget themselves and their bodies most of the time. When a preschooler does masturbate, watch to see if it is brief and casual. If so, we strongly recommend ignoring it. If it is intense and habitual, causing frustration to the child, we suggest you help him stop by the following means:

Explain to the child that such frustration and effort must be tiring and even painful to him or her. Ask him to stop doing it. Then find out if he feels he can stop by himself or needs help. Some ways of helping are:

1. *Allow him to stay up until he is tired enough to sleep readily.*
2. *Give him a sleep toy to fondle.*
3. *Read to him until he falls asleep.*
4. *Give him plenty of parental affection and encourage social interaction with friends during the day.*

On a daily basis, do anything you can to get his interests transferred to the world outside of himself. This is a gradual process of education and training toward *external* more than personal preoccupations.

Grade-School Children. Those who are having problems with masturbating will sometimes be reported by school staff or neighbors. Sexual behaviors are private and it is understandable that others may be troubled by such behavior. Please do not allow their anxiety to upset you, or make you be rude to your child or them. Here are some suggestions to help you in such a situation:

Explain to your child, if he needs it, that others are uncomfortable with such behavior, and tell him you expect him to stop playing with his body, especially in front of other people.

If he is a nervous child, and expresses this through genital touching, *help him find a better way* to communicate his needs and feelings. Teach him to draw little designs on scratch paper. Give him a "pet rock" or "worry stone." Children as well as adults do feel nervous and need some outlet for tension.

Find out why your child is so nervous, and help him find relief from the concerns that are causing this.

Find out if the child is depressed, lonely, or worried, and deal with whatever is troubling him in a loving way.

By developing wholesome sexual attitudes yourself, you can become so comfortable that your child will talk with you. He can then satisfy his curiosity from your teaching, relieve his fears by your protection, and can put most sexual matters aside until he is ready to deal with them.

Adolescents. Due to their sensitivity and the awakening of their adult sexuality, deal with them wisely and gently about masturbation. Explain to them all you can about their developing bodies and sexual feelings. Teach them that these are natural functions, made for a loving marriage, and that it is best to avoid stimulation of their sexual organs. Wet dreams in boys will take care of any buildup of seminal fluid, so they may relax and not worry!

As in young children, look for social loneliness and isolation. Encourage physical activities and help your teenager find friends. For all of us, centering attention on any area of ourselves is confining, while directing interests outward is rewarding and enriching.

At All Ages. In every case, avoid fostering guilt upon a child who masturbates. This can cripple a successful sexual life in marriage later on. Helping a child understand his feelings and needs can do the most to stop wrong and harmful habits and replace them with good and healthy ones!

Confession and Forgiveness. When your child feels guilty, help him determine whether he has done harm to himself or someone else. If so, he needs to make it as right as he can. If not, he needs to stop blaming himself. The ancient practice of confession, forgiveness, and restoration can relieve all guilt! Be sure your child knows God as a forgiving, healing Being, who will help him in every struggle.

Hair Pulling

This is a common manifestation of nervous tension in children.

Causes and Treatment of Hair Pulling

Pulling Her Own Hair. This is usually an outgrowth of the infant's tendency to rub her hair while nursing or sucking her thumb. She likes its soft feel. As she grows old enough to coordinate her movements, she may begin, accidentally at first, to pull her own hair when angry or frustrated. This can become a habit, and children may actually produce bald spots from pulling out their hair. This is not dangerous, and the hair will grow again. The frustration, however, needs some healthier outlet.

Eating Hair. Once in a while, a child will eat the hair that she pulls out. Now hair is not digestible, so it may collect in a child's stomach to the point that it has to be removed surgically. Such a habit is quite rare, but since its consequences are fairly drastic (surgery), we'd rather you prevented it. Just watch your child, and if you see her pulling hair out, distract her. Give her a doll, a blanket, or some soft, stuffed toy that she can stroke or even pull on.

If a young child swallows her hair, you may need to give her a pacifier, or some other means of biting and chewing. Especially look for signs of needing more holding and gentle nurturing. Hair pulling is an aggressive and angry act, and angry children need both discipline and gentle attention.

Substitute. Give a young child a soft doll or toy to hold and caress. The doll should have short hair, so the child is less likely to pull and swallow it. A doll's short hair is less likely to form a hairball in his stomach than his own longer hair. Since hair pulling is most common at bedtime, hold and rock the child until he is nearly asleep, so he won't have time to pull out his own hair before he sleeps.

Pulling Other Children's Hair. This is an outward expression of aggression. It is common in two-year-olds who are not ready to play with other children yet, but are put in the midst of others. Usually the pulling of a playmate's hair occurs as part of a struggle over a toy or a turn at playing. While most children lay aside such childish practices as they mature, some people carry the habit into older years. They punish their children, a spouse, or another person by grabbing a handful of hair.

Treatment. Treat this habit early by stopping such behavior in your child *as soon as it begins.* Supervise his interactions with other children, and help him learn to share and take turns. Teach him how to stand up against other children's selfishness, as well, without hurting them.

Nail Biting

This is another manifestation of nervous tension. It is the habit of biting off bits of one's own fingernails. It may start from a need to smooth a rough spot, but it often becomes a prolonged habit, extending even into adult life. Nail biters are nervous people. They really are upset or angry with someone else, but they are too controlled and considerate to hurt others, so they bite their own nails. They often do this to the point of biting nails off to the "quick." Nail biting, like hair pulling, is always a sign of stress.

Usual Causes of Nail Biting

1.   Too many demands or too high expectations at home or at school.
2.   Discipline that is more punishment than teaching, and is done with too much harshness or anger.
3.   A child may have had to grow up too soon, and may need more nurturing, cuddling, and affection such as he had when he was little.
4.   There usually is too little laughter in the life of a nail-biting child. He takes life seriously and reacts with frustration.

Your child's stress may be from one or all of these factors. If you are a conscientious parent, you may overreact and blame yourself for all of them. Or you may discount all of these reasons, and even the whole problem. So that you can more objectively see the whole picture, ask a trusted relative or friend to share his point of view about you as well as your child.

Treatment of Nail Biting

Eliminate or Reduce. Once you see the stress point, plan to eliminate or reduce it. You may not be able to entirely remove the pressure, but you may be more encouraging and support-ive—and less critical or angry about situations. Do avoid going to the opposite extreme of permissiveness or pampering.

Care of Nails. We suggest filing or trimming the nails daily to keep them smooth. A soothing, undelicious cream rubbed into the cuticle will help heal irritated fingertips, and will discourage the habitual biter. Nail polish can make the nails so smooth it will be harder to bite them.

Sugarless Gum. This can help satisfy a child's need to bite something and help break the habit of chewing nails or hair. We suggest using gum for the *shortest* time possible during the *hardest part of breaking an old habit.* It can become a habit it-self!

Child's Cooperation. Ask the child to stop. Seek his coopera-tion. This is last because it is so important. All of the above measures will fail *unless your child puts some willpower into deciding to stop and then doing it.*

Biting Playmates

Biting other children is another obnoxious habit, and one that will bring down upon you the wrath of the victim's parents, as well as that of their child.

Causes of Biting Others

Starts at Teething. We believe biting starts at the time of teething. It feels good to bite on something then, and many par-ents encourage it. They even allow an infant to bite on their own fingers in order to soothe those aching gums.

To our knowledge, no one has officially studied this, but it is very likely that two-year-olds who bite are those who "bit" or "gummed" someone while they were teething. When a child suffers the pain of frustration or anger, it will help him feel better to bite. It makes sense to bite the one who causes the pain.

Treatment. This cannot, of course, be tolerated, so you need to stop your child's biting. To do that, one of you needs to plan a day or two during which you focus on this problem. When you see an angry storm building up, take the child out of the situation, calm him down, and teach him an acceptable way to let out the normal frustrations he will feel. A pounding board, or yelling, will be better than biting.

Biting Back. If he does bite you, another child, or himself, it is a good idea to firmly but lovingly swat him or allow the other child to bite him back. Sometimes knowing how it feels to be bitten will help a child stop. This does not *always* work. If you physically punish him, be sure you do not do so in a childish, getting-even fashion. That will only make the situation worse, and he will feel even more like biting. Be firm, take charge, and simply do not allow the biting. Punishment will rarely be necessary if you do this well.

Selfishness (Also "Bullying")

Definition. Selfishness is the habit of being too concerned with one's own desires and welfare, and showing too little interest in others. In our experience, selfishness is a symptom of emotional hunger, and often covers very low self-esteem. It evidences a lack of trust in others to care about or share with one.

Grabby Twos. In normal two-year-olds, there is an intense struggle to define some sense of personal power. Twos become very grabby, and seem selfish in their attempts to test out their own versus someone else's power. Usually they give up such practices when they resolve the power issues, and we do not consider them truly selfish—simply two.

Causes

Other reasons for selfishness are these:

1. A child is spoiled by being given his own way too much. He can quickly come to expect it and demand it in selfish ways.
2. Giving in to a demanding child by an adult is almost al-

ways done out of frustration and fatigue, rather than love. Hence the quality of the enjoyment of getting what he wanted is tainted but not destroyed. He, therefore, will often continue his demanding ways, getting a little satisfaction and searching for more.

3.   There may be too little adult supervision, so a demanding child is able to continue bullying habits of getting his own way.

4.   Sometimes adults see these ways as strong, and feel the child is exerting leadership. They, therefore, may even encourage selfish, bullyish behavior through their misinterpretation.

5.   No one has taken time to teach a child to share, give in, or take turns. Few children do so naturally.

Treatment of Selfishness

This gets harder the older the child becomes. So start as early as possible.

Talk to Him. Talk with your child about selfishness, and how much it hurts other people. Tell him you will be watching for signs of it in order to help him understand and correct the bad habit. Seek his cooperation to overcome this trait.

Remove Him. When you see your child being selfish, remove him kindly from the presence of other children, and explain what he did and how it hurt the playmates. Tell him what to do instead, and then go back with him and help him do it. If he is around six or seven, he probably can and will do it without your help—so don't embarrass him needlessly. Embarrassing a child is more likely to cause rebellion than cooperation.

Disciplinary Action. If this direct and positive approach does not take care of the problem, establish some meaningful disciplinary action (with your child's input), and enforce it consistently. This may be temporarily removing him from playing with friends when he is selfish. It may be requiring him to give up a possession for a time, so he can learn how others feel when he grabs their things.

Watch for Unselfish Acts. Watch just as carefully for any *un*selfish act and let your child know your respect and pride in his efforts to change. It may help to make your child aware that he even *feels* better when he is unselfish than when he gets his way—at the cost of angering or even losing friends. (While one must do the right thing because it is right—and not because of how one feels—good feelings do help!)

Takes Time. Forming new habits takes several weeks in children. Stay close by to help your child really finish the job of forming new habits of generosity.

Your Example. Your example of sharing, taking turns, and putting your child or spouse first can be a marvelous teaching-learning experience.

His Own Turf. Each child needs some territory and certain things that are his very own. It's easier to be generous with most things when a child is allowed to protect these few things.

In teaching about any problem behavior, try to help the child see its importance in all of his life. It is easy to allow life to be a series of disconnected, senseless episodes, unless you take time to help your child put them into a meaningful perspective.

Sibling Rivalry

This involves excessive competition, fighting, and jealousy. While almost all children do normally struggle over possessions, power, and position, it is only when the normal rivalry gets out-of-bounds that you need be concerned. When real hatred or revenge becomes apparent, you need to step in to reestablish the peace and harmony of your home.

Causes of Sibling Rivalry

These range from healthy to dangerous factors.

Competition for Its Own Sake. This becomes fun in many families. It may even be a motivating force for successes in life.

Unusual Giftedness. A special talent of one child may cause the others to feel inferior. This may not be the fault of parents, but often a gifted child gets rewards of a sort that are so apparent, other children feel resentful and left out.

Emphasis on Special Ability. Most families have areas in life that are especially important to them. A child who happens to do well in such areas is often unconsciously praised more than children who do not. Such values range from appearance to superior intelligence or sports activities.

Relatives. They may be partial to one child over another and, occasionally, so are parents. You may be certain that the one who is left out will feel resentful and will try to get even by hurting the special child.

Unfair Disciplinary Practices. These often cause jealousy among siblings. Some examples of these are:

1.   One child may learn how to act so well before the parents that he can get by with major mischief behind the parents' backs. Other children hate this and resent the favored child.

2.   Due to a problem or handicap in one area of life, parents may pity a child, and let him behave badly in other areas of his life.

3.   A youngest child is often "excused" because he is "so little," or parents are just tired of rearing children, so they let misbehaviors go unchallenged.

4.   Like the proverbial "squeaking wheel," some children just demand more attention and get it, while more passive children want it but don't ask. Yet they feel hurt and angry due to the relative neglect this represents.

Arrival of a New Baby. This nearly always causes resentment and jealousy for a while. It may not show up at first, but watch for it, because it will happen. (*See* Preparing the Older Child in chapter 2.)

The Treatment of Sibling Rivalry

This is usually most rewarding.

Stay Out of It. In the case of normal, healthy competition, stay out of it. We understand that you may need more peace and quiet, and maybe you can teach your children to argue quietly. But they will more quickly establish their own lines of respect if you don't interfere.

Formulate Rules. Help them, however, to formulate some rules for fighting fairly.

1. *No hitting of each other, and no breaking or damaging of things.*
2. *Be able to win without "lording it over" each other, and to lose without pouting.*
3. *Sometimes having each child write out his "case" against the other and present it formally can stop tattling, or side taking on your part.*

Each Has Special Gifts. In the case of a gifted child, help the other children see their own special gifts, and try to avoid any judgments that value one over the other.

Search for personal areas of strengths. For example, a child who can smile genuinely or find laughter in life, may benefit people around him more than a scientific genius. Make it clear to your children that in God's sight, we are equally important.

Help each child use and develop his special gifts. Their value will be easier to believe if you spend some energy making that happen. Many highly successful people had parents who required and helped them to practice and to excel.

Praise and encourage your child. When you praise him, give simple, straightforward comments that are honest and believable. Never confuse such praise with a "but" and criticism. Look at your child when you compliment him, and let him see the pride in your eyes!

Check out your own and each other's attitudes and values to uncover any subconscious partiality.

1. Start with family resemblances. A child who looks like a relative you liked (or didn't) may be unknowingly favored by you (or disfavored).

2. As you think back over a child's life, were there times of special tenderness or antagonism that might create partiality or resentments now?

3. Does a child reflect good or bad qualities of your own or your spouse? How do you feel about those? These factors influence how you treat a given child, and how his brothers and sisters feel about him.

Take stock of the treatment each of your children receives from relatives. If Grandpa is partial to the oldest, make him aware that the others need him, too. You can turn that into a compliment of Grandpa, rather than a criticism. Help your children understand, however, that relatives will not always be impartial, but that does not mean the child is inferior.

Evaluate the children's behaviors, and how you handle each of these situations:

1. Watch closely for the sly child who starts an exciting fight, and then sits back safely while the others get punished.

2. When a child tells you that you are unfair, he's probably just trying to get you to back down. But once in a while he's right. Take a look at yourself.

3. If you have a handicapped child, or one who has special needs of any kind, be careful that you do not neglect the other children. They may all be drawn into the special care; or you may need to get relatives to help out, so you have a little free time for each child. Even handicapped children can and should give in to the needs of others.

Once in a while, parents may reject a certain child for a variety of subconscious reasons. They often feel so guilty about their bad feelings that they overcompensate and spoil such a child.

When a new baby is expected, plan carefully to avoid crowding out an older child. If possible, space your children so that the older one is able to understand and feel good about a new baby. Then include him in the care of the child as much as possible. (*See* Preparing the Older Child in chapter 2.)

Stealing

This is taking something by force or secrecy and claiming it for your own.

Reasons for Stealing

Some of these are similar to those for cheating, discussed above. But here are some specific aspects you need to understand.

In Younger Children. Especially in younger children, stealing is an aggressive way of getting an object a child wants. He may not realize that such an act is stealing.

Attention Getter. We have seen children steal in order to get attention from parents or teachers.

In Older Children. Stealing is commonly a way of gaining favor with other misbehaving young people. One girl proudly said that she was the "best shoplifter" in her crowd. Unfortunately, stealing has become a way of getting money for drugs or alcohol for many addicted young people.

Kleptomania. This is a special kind of compulsive stealing. It often is a means of getting attention, or expresses the need for being loved by some important person.

Treatment for Stealing

The *treatment* for stealing is *urgent,* and as with most other troublesome habits, it is easier to prevent than cure.

In a Young Child. Be sure that he understands the *mine* and *not mine* boundaries in life. If a young child starts to take an item from a store, you need to teach him the concept of purchasing things, instead of taking them. Help him select a small, inexpensive item and go through the entire process of purchasing it. Make it clear that this process is the only way to take anything out of a store. (Do not think that you have to buy something every time your child wants or grabs it. Just be certain that he knows that is the *only way to get something from a store.)*

Children may similarly pick up toys or other items from homes in which they may visit. We always found this policy helpful regarding items from another home: *We did not allow our children to borrow or accept as a gift anything from friends' homes.* If a gift was purchased for the child, of course, it could be a happy treat—but to take any other item home was forbidden. That saved a great deal of trouble in deciding whether a toy had been given, "borrowed," or stolen. Anything that did show up in a pocket was promptly returned.

Just as we expect each child to respect others' property, we need to respect his. Give him some space and things that he need not share. Require other children to respect that, too.

Unmet Needs. See if your child may have some needs that are not being met. Such needs may make stealing a temptation. This investigation is not to excuse the stealing, but to make the cure more thorough.

1.   In the busy whirl of providing materially for your child, you may have inadvertently robbed *him*—of the time and love he needs with you.

2.   Does your child feel so inadequate that he may have settled for friends who think stealing is brave or smart?

3.   Have other young people threatened him, to make him steal for them? There are many "bullies" in your child's world.

4.   Is your child using stolen things to "buy" friends? Every child wants to be liked and to have friends. It can be deceptively easy to be popular by giving gifts. You will need to tell your child how frail such relationships are, but he may have to find that out the hard way. Do help your child develop skills that promote healthy friendships.

5.   Check out your child's social contacts. Even in the fifth and sixth grades, there are children who are addicted to drugs and alcohol. In junior- and senior-high school this is rampant. Be sure your child is not stealing to support such a habit—for himself or his friends.

Treatment of Kleptomania

This is a serious psychological problem. Discipline and understanding alone will rarely cure it. *Do seek qualified counseling. This should involve you parents as well as your child.*

Importance of Child's Cooperation. Get your child's cooperation in breaking a habit of stealing. In the final analysis, you cannot make him stop (short of locking him up) without that willingness.

1.   *Establish the fact of his stealing—either by reliable witnesses or by the child's own admission.* Try to keep an open mind, without prejudice, regarding possible guilt or innocence, until the facts are clear.

2.   *Tell the child you will do whatever is necessary to help him stop stealing, and ask what he feels he needs to do so.* Do

not ask him at first *why* he stole, because he probably won't know. The stealing must stop while you and he are working out the basic problems.

3. *Let your child know you still love him and that God loves him.* You will forgive him, and so will God, but he must forgive himself. Let him know how hard that will be until he can understand himself. At this point, help him start to explore why he stole.

4. *If you and your child cannot discover why he began stealing, seek outside counsel.* This is such a serious problem that it could land your child in prison when he is older. Do not take a chance that it will pass.

5. *It is tempting to believe that a sound thrashing will cure stealing.* Perhaps in a very small child, it will. In older children, however, we have seen physical punishment cause estrangement and more rebellion. So if you do try it, be prepared to get other help if it fails.

Wrong Friends. If your child is involved with friends who are a bad influence on him (or he on them!), you will need to help him break off those relationships. This, also, demands your child's understanding and cooperation. Help him see the dangers to himself and his future. Your child deserves more from life than the consequences of a habit of stealing. If he is lonely or feels inferior, help him to begin to succeed, and teach him how to make better friends. Unfortunately, this takes time, and all too often parents of "good kids" are afraid to let them associate with a child who has had problems. Teach your child to be patient, steady, and to earn back the respect of others.

Be a Friend. Develop a friendship with your child. He still needs you as parents, but he also needs your love and support through the struggles of changing. Have some good times, keep him busy with a job, and proudly remind him of his successes.

Small Allowance. Be sure your child has a little money of his own—not so much that he can buy things he ought not have, but not so little he'll be tempted to steal things he could have.

Soiling (Encopresis)

This is the habit of having a bowel movement in his pants *after* a child has been well trained to the use of the toilet. This distasteful habit, in our experience, is always related to emotional stress that makes a child wish he were a baby again.

The Causes of Soiling

Severe Discipline. Discipline that is too severe and expectations that are too high—from the child's-eye view—may contribute to this problem. And there, of course, is where a child must live—on his own level! Worry, fear, and resentment, triggered by such treatment, may understandably create some reactions and the wish to be little again is likely to be part of that response.

New Baby. The birth of a new baby may threaten an older child's security. One way to be sure of some personal attention is to mess himself. True enough, it's bad attention, but to a child it is better than none.

Change in Life-style. From the age of four to six, a major change in life-style may trigger this regression—starting school, a family move, or a divorce may result in this habit.

Anger Reactions. A child may begin soiling from fear or worry, but when parents react in anger, a child may react to the parents' anger with more anger, compounding the problem. It is our experience that soilers do not express their anger or their fears directly. They need to be helped to do so honestly but also appropriately. You, as parents, will also understandably be angry at a soiler sometimes, but be sure to build a loving, positive relationship in all the other areas of his life.

Physical Reasons. There are, rarely, physical reasons for soiling:

1. Discomfort from constipation, diarrhea, rectal gas, or rectal irritation may all cause soiling at times. This is usually temporary, unless you overreact to it and unwittingly produce soiling from emotional causes.

2. Irregular toilet habits and poor hygiene, such as failure to wipe after a bowel movement or careless bathing, can create the personal odor and offensiveness of soiling.

3. Any birth defects that may cause soiling will show up earlier, usually within the first year or two of age.

The Treatment of Soiling

This is demanding and may go against all of your instincts.

Checkup. Have a good physical checkup and follow through with any medical recommendations.

Review Past. Think back thoroughly to the time the soiling began.

1. *Was there any big event in the family, such as a new baby, a move, a big argument, a job change, or Mother's starting to work?*
2. *Did your child start school, get a new baby-sitter, suffer an illness, or experience a great fear?*
3. *Is your child going through any other problem that involves severe discipline or fear of rejection?*
4. *Are the disciplinary measures you or a teacher are using too harsh or unfair to this special child?*

Communicaton. Does this child talk about his problem or his feelings? In our experience, most children who soil keep such feelings strictly inside. A child needs a healthy outlet for anger, fear, and worry—as well as love. Teach your child the language of feelings and give him permission to use it properly. This does not mean that he is to be impudent or rude.

Dealing With Stress. Teach positive ways of dealing with stress:

Give extra play and cuddling time to the child without commenting on the soiling. Let him know he is secure in your love.

If necessary, with a child under five or six, use diapers again. It's easier in the long run, and may help the child know he can regress if he needs to. Often paradoxically, the need subsides with the permission.

Any child who is capable should be taught to clean his clothing and himself, and be required to do this. It's best to be matter-of-fact, rather than shaming.

Cut down on stress by trying a little less responsibility; less severe discipline; giving more encouragement; talking about school adjustments; and giving lots of chances to discuss any family changes.

Believe (and you can!) and tell your child that you know he has a need to be little for a while. Tell him that he may be little by asking you to hold or spoil him, and that he need not mess his pants to be little. Tell him that as soon as he is ready, he is to use the toilet again. If this is a problem at all, it must be apparent that he is not going to do it until he is ready. He may realize your wisdom from such a statement.

Be certain that the child has permission to use the toilet as needed. At school this can be a problem for a five- or six-year-old. He may need someone to reassure him about the high-pressure water system at school. He could fear being flushed away!

It has been our experience that shaming or spanking, by their very nature, increase the stress and actually aggravate the soiling.

Every time your child uses the toilet instead of his pants, quietly compliment him.

It takes great willpower and effort for a child to overcome soiling or wetting. You may justifiably be proud of your child's improvement, and if you have weathered it, we are proud of you!

Stubbornness

This is the refusal to obey, yield, or comply with another's commands or wishes. Synonyms are *obstinate, determined, doggedly resisting,* and this trait can be extremely difficult to live with!

Causes of Stubbornness

Some of the causes of stubbornness can be outlined as follows:

Power Struggle. Stubborn children often are bright, energetic, and inquisitive. When such a child happens to be born to critical, unbending parents, he can start out in life with an ongoing power struggle that is intrinsically a part of stubbornness. It takes two parties (parent and child in this case) to keep such struggles alive.

Disciplinary Problems. Some of these increase stubbornness:

1.   Failure to start early in teaching obedience.

As soon as a child is able to move about on his own, he will invade areas or touch objects that are dangerous to him. It is *then* that you need to set limits and enforce them. Waiting for the child to get older will allow habits to form that reinforce his power and stubbornness, so they will be even more difficult to change.

2.   Failure to follow through sets the stage for a complication of this already tough struggle.

When a child is told to do something but finds out he really doesn't have to do it, he becomes confused. Usually, he will learn to test out the situation, and this testing out feeds into the struggle even more.

It is essential that you understand the difference in testing-out behaviors and rebellion. In the first, the child needs you to be firmer, more consistent, and to follow through on your requirements to the finish. In rebellion, parents are too rigid and harsh, so the child feels imprisoned. In this case, he needs more flexibility.

3.   Expectations are unrealistic.

Asking more of a child than he can do, or expecting less than his abilities indicate, are both frustrating to him. He needs to be understood and challenged.

4.   Discipline through emotional explosions can set up a parent-to-child combat that no one wins.

Or your child may even win (thereby losing!) by being stubborn.

5.   Power struggles are the building blocks of stubbornness.

The more of these you allow to develop, and the more in which you give in, the more likely it is that you will have a stubborn child.

The Treatment of Stubbornness

It is obviously based on stopping those damaging power struggles. Now that does not mean you should go to the other extreme and allow your child total freedom to become a little dictator! Take these steps:

First decide between yourselves, Dad and Mom, whether you are willing to be in charge. That requires time, energy, and real commitment. Being in charge automatically rules out childish arguments and fights, and sets up clear authority.

Expect your child to test out your authority and do not allow that to stop your plan. He needs you to stay in charge.

Lay aside past failures, fears, and resentments caused by your child's resistance. This will avoid the angry sort of unconscious retaliation that feeds power struggles and stubbornness.

Select one issue at a time, and work only on that issue. It may be picking up a messy room, or doing homework, but set up a plan. Ask your child what he is willing to do in order to stop fighting, and take care of that problem. Have some ideas about what you will do. (It may help you to know that your child really doesn't like the fights, either.)

State clearly what the goal is; how you will stop the old defeating habits; and how you plan to establish new patterns. Give your child the respect of recognizing his importance by seeking his help and ideas. Use them in formulating your plan.

Think often of your child's good qualities, and tell him about these. Let him know how much you love him in positive ways, as well as in discipline.

For a strong-willed child, a reason or explanation is helpful, but beware lest he trap you into the old habit of arguing.

Wait it out. This is the most difficult but most important part of the plan. Giving in is difficult for a stubborn child, and he won't be able to do it quickly. If you will firmly hold to your plan and be patient, you both will make it.

Carefully balance consistency (avoid being rigid) *and flexibility* (but do not be permissive).

Remember, your child wants you to be stronger than he is! Many of the things he does are a test of your strength.

Use Jesus' promise: "My grace is sufficient for thee: for my strength is made perfect in weakness . . ." (2 Corinthians 12:9).

Swearing

This is the use of crude or downright profane words as exclamations or in routine speech. It never occurs until the child hears and can repeat such language from another person.

Causes of Swearing

Hearing Others Swear. This may intrigue your child. Friends, especially older ones, may swear in a childish effort to prove their "toughness." This can be done with such a show of strength and energy that it invites duplicating.

Need for Peer Approval. This may prompt your child to adopt the coarse talk and other habits, too, of "tough" young people. If your child seems to need the approval of such friends, you need to explore his own self-concept. He may feel very weak and inadequate. Tough associates can seem to offer safety and power to such a child.

Need to Rebel. If you have been too strict and perfectionistic, your child may feel he has to do something drastic to break away from your hold over him.

Oftentimes, a child's swearing is a passing whim, started by fascination with the swagger of the one who teaches him. Give it some careful ignoring and a chance to die a natural death. If your child does not stop by himself, however, do pay attention.

Dealing With Swearing

Discuss the issue, person-to-person, with your child. Explain your values and your reasons for wanting him to stop using bad words.

See if your child, himself, can figure out why he is swearing, and recognize the reasons as being unworthy of his own values. If he can't explain the reasons, give him some ideas, and ask him to think them over. Allow your child time to think through the values that are at stake here. These concepts are usually involved and profound. The more he can really comprehend them, the more likely he will be to truly adopt them as his own.

If he is feeling weak or inferior, think out a plan to make him aware of his strength, so he can believe it. Be aware that telling this to a child never really convinces him. He has to see it for himself in his own behavior and successes. The best way we know to teach a child his capabilities is for you to indicate clearly to him the good qualities he demonstrates and the achievements he has made.

Help him set up a plan for breaking the swearing habit. Fining him a nickel or a dime, and having him work at a special job to pay that off, sometimes works. (Children often have very respectable ideas for discipline that work for them.)

Help your child find some acceptable word he can use to express strong feelings. Everyone needs some means of expression.

I know some of you will say, "Just whip him and make him stop." Perhaps that will work for you. We never argue with success. *But we can show you countless young people who have been driven by angry whippings into severe rebellion.* Spankings may work for smaller children, but in older ones, the loving, logical, but firm approach works far better and more often.

Help your child see for himself, then, the crudeness of bad language and how quickly its use becomes a habit. Remind him of God's special commands against taking His name in vain. Tell him clearly but kindly that you want him to stop, and then work out the plan for doing that.

Tattling

Tattling is the practice some children develop of telling the misbehaviors of another child to an adult who is in charge. It has, as its aim, the often-unconscious wish to make one's self look good at the expense of the other person. It involves a desire to get that other person in trouble, in order to get even for some reason or other. Eventually, a tattler ends up alone and miserable.

The Causes of Tattling

These relate to the child's sense of insecurity.

1. *He needs a great deal of adult attention and protection, and feels anxious or afraid when he is on his own.*

2. *Many times a tattler has been treated unfairly by an adult who may be partial to another child, but does pay attention to* him *under duress.*

3. *Since he has been hurt, he may feel a bit avenged and powerful by hurting someone else.*

4. *The tattler is a timid child, who discovers how to be aggressive in a passive way, and protects himself with the adult to whom he goes. As with any bad habit, tattling has some benefits to the child who does it.*

Dealing With a Tattler

This rarely requires professional help.

Pay attention to him and find out why he is tattling, or if, in fact, he is tattling at all. Sometimes a child is truly mature enough to see another child getting into a dangerous spot and really reacts from caring and protection.

Stop the payoff for tattling. Even if the victim deserves a punishment, make that become secondary to the act of dealing with tattling. Tell your tattler that you will not hear any more such reporting.

Observe closely your child's interactions with playmates. If they need supervision, step in quietly before the child feels a need to tell.

If one child is trying to get another one in trouble, because of a need to get even, find out how he was hurt. People almost never hurt someone unless they have been hurt first. It is an instinct to lash out when we have suffered pain.

Help the child talk about his feelings and explain the situation, if possible. Comfort him and then help him see how his habit of getting even in this passive way hurts the other person, who will hurt him even more. The eventual rejection of a tattler is painful to see, but in itself, this may cure him, if you refuse to pity or rescue him.

Teach him how to forgive, understand, and turn his hurts into a strong effort to stop pain, rather than inflicting more. You may show him how many acorns can grow from one. And help him understand that he must choose whether his anger will produce lots more anger or, instead, will be used to stop the fight and produce fun.

If the child tattles because of a need for attention, help him see that such attention costs too much. He will lose friends and will even lose his own self-respect. Find the time to supply his needs for attention in a satisfying way.

Tell your child there are three things he may do instead of tattling:

1. **Handle the situation himself by helping the other children do the right thing.**
2. **Trust an adult to handle the problem in his own way and time.**
3. **Let others make their own mistakes and learn from them—unless this involves real danger. If a truly risky situation arises, the child needs to report it. Be watchful lest in stopping tattling, you inadvertently destroy your child's healthy concern about the misbehaviors of his friends.**

Temper Tantrums or Breath-holding Spells

These are quite common in the two-year-old world. Sometimes such tantrums begin earlier than two and *extend on into early school years.* (In fact, you have probably seen some adults having tantrums!)

Symptoms

Tantrums are uncontrolled expressions of rage and frustration. They are expressed by screaming, kicking, hitting, head banging, and throwing things. Sometimes the child holds his breath in this fit, and may do so to the point of a brief convulsion and loss of consciousness. Such a spell rarely lasts more than two or three minutes, and is self-limiting. As soon as the waste gas (carbon dioxide) builds up in the bloodstream, it serves as a powerful stimulant to breathing. The child quickly revives and is fine. So do not panic about such an attack.

Causes of Tantrums

Reflex Action. Children's fits begin almost as a *reflex reaction* to fatigue, pain, or the inability to make something "do right." Blocks that will not stay stacked, or the stopping of play (which a child likes) for a nap (which he abhors) may be enough to precipitate the throwing of a fit. Other children may work for a long time on a special project with great patience, but then some relatively minor frustration will, like the proverbial straw that broke the camel's back, cause a fit.

Not Fatigue. Fatigue does not cause a tantrum, but it may shorten a child's "fuse," and make him more likely to explode. (It is tempting to excuse a child's problem behavior on the basis of his being tired and not teach him the controls that will stop it.)

Manipulative. While the original tantrums truly are beyond a child's control, he will quickly recognize the "fringe benefits" involved with them. Few expressions get the rapid response of adults that these fits do, and these childish tantrums then become manipulative trickery, which is much harder to eliminate.

Treatment

This should include the prevention of habitual "fit pitching," as well as curing it.

When a young child is tired, and has had an obviously hard time that results in a tantrum, we believe in holding, soothing, and protecting him. Our son had an especially short "fuse" and would go into an agony of frustration when something he was doing wouldn't work. Spanking him only enraged him more intensely. Ignoring him was impossible. We learned, by trial and error, to pick him up and wrap our arms gently and firmly around his body and our legs around his (to avoid bruises). We would quietly rock him, still crying and squirming, saying something reassuring. In a very few minutes he would relax, cry instead of yell, and we could both comfort and reason with him. Many two-year-olds just need the strength of the parent's physical control.

When a child throws a fit just for attention (and it is not hard to recognize that), it is best to ignore it. Even if you have to call on someone else for your courage, do not give in to a manipulative fit. Giving a child his way in order to stop a fit reinforces this behavior so well, that it will become extremely difficult to break. Do not let this type of fit gain any benefits for a child. In such a case, put the child in his bed or on a rug, so he cannot seriously hurt himself. Tell him firmly that you are not going to talk with him until he calms himself down. Then firmly walk away. Do not look back, or he will probably redouble his efforts. When he is calm, take time to hold him and talk over the issue at stake, and find the answers.

In breath holding, lay the child down, so the head is on its side and slightly forward. This prevents the tongue from falling back and choking him. If he does not start breathing in a minute or two, do not hesitate to go with him to an emergency room. You certainly would not be the first parent to do so for this reason. You may even use artificial respiration or mouth-to-mouth resuscitation, but we have not seen this become necessary, except for the parents' peace of mind.

Prevention of Tantrums

This can often be accomplished by the following measures:

Whenever you feel your child is becoming exceptionally tired or irritable, gently try to stop his activity or sit and help him with it until the difficult part is worked out.

When it is time to change one activity for another, give your child a forewarning. Rather than calling to him from another room, go to him and help him "shift gears," until he learns to change from one to another activity independently. We see this as teaching him and not spoiling him. You will not need to do this very many times before he will be able to handle transitions in his day all by himself.

When a child is under three, help him adjust to other children. Before that age, a child may have extreme difficulty in sharing, taking turns, or playing in general with another child. After three, children do this fairly automatically.

As your child grows older, you may need to speak very sternly to him, telling him fits are not to be tolerated. Decide then if he is to go to his room, be spanked, or lose some privilege. Be sure to carry out your plan *consistently,* and do not give up too soon. It is tempting to feel that a particular plan is not working, and stop just short of success.

Help your little fit thrower to find an acceptable way to get his understandable frustrations out. A pounding board, crying, or—best of all—talking about whatever is wrong, will give him something constructive to do with his pent-up feelings. The goal

in dealing with tantrums is to help your child to become aware
of his feelings and needs, to express them appropriately, and ask
for the help he needs to take care of the situations that produce
such problems.

Thumb Sucking

This is a big worry for parents of small children—and sometimes older ones. It is common in infants, but many of them give
up the habit in favor of the increasing number of external interests that take their attention away from their own bodies. It is
only in children older than two or three that most parents worry
about thumb sucking. A child may become attached to a pacifier, as well as to his thumb or fingers, and many parents dislike
the use of such a gadget because of the picture it presents of an
overgrown baby.

Causes of Thumb Sucking

Sucking Reflex. Babies start sucking their fingers or thumb in a
reflex manner. They accidentally discover that this brings some
of the pleasure that sucking on a nipple brings. Since babies
can't cry and suck at the same time, many parents are all too
happy for them to suck their thumbs at first. Only later do they
(the parents) discover that habitual thumb sucking is a problem, and even an embarrassment to them.

Oral Needs. We know that babies have strong oral needs. That
means that they need to have something in their mouths to feel
content. When babies nurse slowly enough, the satisfaction of
their sucking needs should be about the same as the satisfaction
of the hunger needs in their tummies. When they eat too fast,
however, they may get full before their mouths are satisfied. For
such babies, thumb sucking meets that need.

Comforting Habit. As a child gets older, the sucking becomes a
habit that is associated with sleeping, the relief of boredom, or
comfort. The more parents try to force him to stop, the more
unhappy the child becomes, the more comfort he needs, and the
more automatic is his habit of thumb sucking for comfort.

While parents worry about the deformity of teeth by thumb
sucking, some dentists tell us this rarely is a danger. Only if a

child persists in sucking with strong pressure against the gums while he is cutting permanent teeth is there likely to be a problem.

Treatment of Thumb Sucking

Prevention First. Once again, prevention is better than the treatment of thumb sucking. Allow plenty of time for sucking during feeding time, from birth on. Stop the baby briefly, if you are nursing, to prolong the feeding process a bit. Be certain the nipple holes on the bottle, if you are using bottles, are not too large. A slow, steady drip from an inverted bottle usually means the flow will be about right. Stronger babies, however, may need slower flow, and weaker ones a faster or easier flow.

Cover Hands. Keep the baby's hands and fingers away from his mouth at first. There are baby shirts with long sleeves that have cuffs. Your baby's hands may be tucked inside that sleeve like a mitten, so the fingers or thumb can't get into the mouth. Be assured that this does not seriously inhibit your baby's motions. He can move those fingers as much as he wishes inside those sleeves. After only a couple of weeks, the hands may come out.

Pacifier. If your baby seems to have a need to suck, we believe a pacifier is permissible. In fact, it may be a blessing. The newest ones are especially designed to avoid pressure on the developing gums, and they do not extend far enough back to gag a child, as the old kinds sometimes did. When your child no longer needs the pacifier, it can conveniently be lost—a thumb cannot!

Some people object to a pacifier on the grounds that they are unsanitary and they look bad. Frankly, we feel they look no worse than a thumb. You may keep several and have them disinfected, but after a few weeks, your child does not need a strictly sterile environment, anyway. You, of course, must decide whether to use this gadget or not.

Treating the Older Child

As a child grows older and is still sucking his thumb, you will need a different solution. Here are some useful ideas:

Give him plenty of cuddling, rocking, and happy physical contact, so he feels very safe. As you hold him, place a toy or your own hand in his to transfer its habitual position from the mouth to an external interest. To avoid boredom, babies need plenty of stimulation of all their bodies' senses.

Spend time with your baby in play to draw his attention outside of himself. Keep his hands busy doing active things—holding toys or teething biscuits. Using the hand to put edibles into the mouth can be a substitute for sucking the thumb.

When a child is about four, he can often successfully chew sugarless gum—without swallowing it. And this can give his mouth a real workout. He may not even want his thumb!

When our oldest child was four, we talked about the need for her to stop sucking her thumb in order to keep her teeth straight. She decided to work with us, and all by herself made up a game. She pretended to hide her thumb under her pillow at bedtime, so it wouldn't sneak into her mouth. It worked!

On the other hand, my [Grace's] little sister sucked her thumb. My parents made a real power struggle out of that. They used every known device to stop thumb sucking, and probably created a few! She outwitted them, and chose to quit sucking her own thumb only years later. This is another example of the destructive effect of power struggles and the effectiveness of the child's own decision to cooperate. Stay calm, firm, creative, and above all, *loving,* and you will work out the problem.

SPEECH PROBLEMS

Stuttering and Stammering

These are problems in speaking that involve involuntary pauses and the repetition or prolonging of sounds or syllables. It occurs much more commonly in boys, though no one knows why.

Causes of Stuttering

These are thought to be mostly emotional.

In Children Under Four. Stuttering is quite common at this age, and is usually due to a child's inability to think of the words to use. Along with his limited vocabulary, a child may have trouble keeping the attention of his listeners. Older children and adults commonly fail to see a younger child's conversation as important. They often give a child the brush-off, so he may try to keep their attention by continual talking. Being unable to think of enough to say or the right words to use may initiate stuttering, which becomes habitual.

Fearful Child. A child who is afraid of the anger or disapproval of his listener may stutter because of that anxiety.

Traumatic Experience. A serious loss, accident, or illness during the period of developing speech can result in stuttering; this is also related to fear.

Parental Anger. During this same time, a parent's intensely angry scolding and demanding of a child information such as a reason for misbehaving may result in stuttering.

Change in Handedness. There is still some belief that changing a child's handedness from left to right may result in stuttering.

Treating Stuttering

This is difficult because of the tension the problem creates on both sides. The listener inevitably will become tense, and will try to help the talker, who also is tense and embarrassed by his problem. Neither knows how to help his own nervousness, let alone the other's.

In Early Childhood. Simply ask the child to slow down in his talking. Give him your calm, undivided attention. If he seems to be groping for a word, supply it. Reassure him. Oftentimes he will stop stuttering in a surprisingly short time.

In an Older Child. Practice similar attention with a calm, reassuring manner. In addition, be careful to avoid scolding or irritation with this child. The more irritation he feels, the more nervous he will become, and the more he will stutter.

Discipline. In disciplining such a child, avoid intense anger. You can discipline him firmly but gently. Stutterers are exceptionally sensitive people, and usually will respond best to that approach.

Communication. Help your stutterer to admit and describe any fears, anger, or nervousness he feels. Avoid nagging, but remind him of your interest in his concerns. Then listen when he does talk.

Patience. While you need to help a young child find a word, this practice is not so good with older children. Just patiently give him time to find the word. He will need to do so to overcome this problem.

Don't Pity. It is very difficult, but try not to pity the stutterer. The more truly you can accept him, the more relaxed he can feel, and the less he will stutter.

Don't Change Handedness. Do not force a strongly left-handed child to become right-handed. As long as possible, offer a child his spoon, crayons, and other tools in his right hand. As he develops, however, and simply cannot use that right hand as well as his left, do not insist on the right hand.

Speech Therapist. Do not wait long to seek a speech therapist. If your own efforts have not relieved the stuttering in a few weeks, get help. The longer a child goes on stuttering, the more difficult it will be to break the habit. Practice patience, be deliberate and slow, and be encouraging with your stutterer. In such a warm, positive atmosphere, he will have the best chance to recover.

Delayed Speech

This is the refusal or inability to talk, well beyond the age when most children are talking. That time is hard to define because there are large variations in so-called normal times to start talking. Most people would not blame you, however, for seeking advice if your child has not done some talking by three or three and a half years of age.

Most children will say a few words by a year of age. They will use short sentences by two, and are able to talk a great deal by three.

The Causes of Delayed Speech

Physical Causes. These are a major worry and include:

1. *Brain damage to the speech area of the brain.*
2. *Most parents worry about mental retardation, and it certainly can slow down the development of speech.*
3. *Deafness also can slow down or prevent the learning of speech.*
4. *Being tongue-tied or having an abnormally shaped palate may delay speech, but these are more likely to cause abnormal sounds in talking.*

Nonphysical Causes. These include extremes of several kinds.

On one hand, *you may pressure your child so strongly to talk that he may rebel and stop.*

On the other hand, *you may not realize that you need to teach your child to talk,* and you may leave him too much to his own devices.

Sometimes a clever child can get whatever he wants without talking. He gestures, points, or in other ways makes clear what he wants. Older siblings are especially solicitious about waiting on a younger child. We find that third children are notoriously slow to talk due to this situation.

Sometimes parents do not spend enough time talking specifically with a child. Therefore, he has no incentive or opportunity to develop verbal skills. On the other hand, parents may talk too much, too fast, or in words the child cannot understand. To learn to talk, a child needs live language directed pointedly to him, listening and waiting for his response, as well as talking with him.

Treating Delayed Speech

This requires sensitivity and patience.

Consult a Physician. This is to be sure there is no physical defect. If there is, correct it.

Next, a Speech Pathologist. If the correction of physical problems does not cure the child, consult a speech pathologist and follow his recommendations.

Spend time with your child in these ways:

1. Start spending enjoyable time with your child and center this time on words. *ABC* books with attractive pictures of things your child likes are a good place to start.

2. Look for an item your child may get excited about. Show it to him, *say the word slowly and clearly and repeat it,* as you hand it to the child.

3. Ask the child to say the word with you, but do not act irritated if he won't. Be patient.

4. When you feel certain your child knows the word, require him to say it before you give him the item. If he won't say it, calmly put the item away, and tell the child when he is ready to say the word, he may have it.

5. Read stories, sing songs, and talk to your child. Someday he'll respond.

6. Be sure your child has time with other children. Very often they learn better from one another than from adults.

TV Helpful. Television may come in handy for the learning of words. "Sesame Street," "Mr. Rogers' Neighborhood," and "Captain Kangaroo" are excellent productions directed to a child's level. In your own location, you may also have some helpful programs. Watch such shows with your child, and say the words for various things, as both of you watch.

Avoid Punishment. Punishment for something you cannot really enforce is useless, and will only create a lifelong battle. Save it for situations that deserve it.

We had a patient who would not talk. His parents took him, at our recommendation, to every major speech-and-hearing clinic in the area. Each was, in its turn, futile. He would not talk. He functioned well in kindergarten—but he would not talk. Finally, in the first grade, he talked. He asked a question in a perfect fashion and has talked ever since. He now is a fine teenager in every respect.

"Be patient. Don't worry!" We suspect you will resent reading that again, but sometimes that's all there is to do.

Abnormal Speech

This is speech that is difficult to understand or is "different" from the usual sounds of a given language or dialect. Common sounds that give children trouble are *S, R,* and *L.*

Causes

The reasons may be physical, and these include being tongue-tied; having some weakness of the fine muscles used in speech; or some neurological "short-circuits" through which sounds are heard, interpreted, and reproduced. Partial deafness may also lead to abnormal speech sounds. More commonly, children are inadvertently taught or encouraged to use baby talk. Children's talk is uniquely charming, but such charm is lost when the baby talk continues after babyhood is over.

Treatment

This demands patient teaching. Many children who say *wabbit* instead of *rabbit* learn correct *R* sounds as they hear them and are required to practice talking properly.

Physical Problems. Correct any such problems your doctor thinks need help.

Teaching Him. When you are ready to devote some time to teaching, help your child to focus on his particular problem sounds one at a time. Exaggerate your own mouth, tongue, and teeth components in saying the sounds for him, and ask him to copy you. When he succeeds, praise him. When he doesn't, tell him, encouragingly, that he will be able to do so later on. Avoid nagging, ridicule, or punishment.

Be Consistent. Be careful to avoid a "double message" by thinking your child's baby talk is cute and yet expecting him to use adult talk on demand.

Encourage Playmates. Encourage your child to be around other children enough to learn from them.

Speech Therapist. If the problem really interferes with clear communication, and if the above methods are unsuccessful, consult a speech therapist.

Patience, prayer for guidance, and loving encouragement certainly create the best climate for correcting any problem!

TICS OR HABIT SPASMS

These are jerking movements of a muscle or set of muscles that start voluntarily as a reaction to a tense situation, but become beyond the control of the victim. They begin during an experience of intense fear or anxiety, but can become a habit with amazing rapidity.

Causes of Tics

Stress. To our knowledge, tics are always a sign of extreme intrapersonal stress. They are a child's involuntary reaction of fear to the pressure of intense anger, disapproval, or punishment. They usually begin after school age, and commonly are related to school and social problems, though they may involve a parent's reaction to these problems.

A Vicious Cycle. Adult reactions to tics unwittingly feed into the vicious cycle that keeps them active. Tics are so grotesque and annoying, that parents often react to them with irritation or even punishment. Remember that tics *originate* as a reaction to anger and punishment, and you will quickly see that more anger and punishment will inevitably make them worse. You must also understand that *these are truly beyond a child's control.* They are as automatic as blinking an eyelid to help remove an irritating grain of sand.

Treatment of Tics

This sounds simple, but it takes heroic self-control. We believe this will work in almost every case.

Avoid commenting about or reacting to this tic as you would avoid the plague. Do not respond to it!

Use your energy, instead, *to understand and empathize with your child. Find out what is hurting and frightening him and stop it.* Consider these possibilities:

1. *Perhaps a teacher or cruel child is making it too tough on him in school. Visit the principal, and seek his help in dealing with that.*

2. *Perhaps you have been too hard on your own child. Don't stop disciplining him, but tone down your anger. Real strength can be gentle!*

To help find the cause of your child's tic, *take note of when it happens.* After several times, you will begin to understand the specific stress that contributes to it and can reduce that or even remove it.

Teach your child to trust you with his troubles and to talk with you about them. The more he can discuss them, the more you can help find the answers to them—and the less those troublesome tics will happen.

It is not uncommon for adults to have some habit spasms such as a nervous cough, a grimace, or exaggerated blinking of the eyes, yet they function very well—so you need not be overly worried about your child. We say that because the less you worry, the calmer your child will feel. In this case, *the less you do, the better he will be.*

18
Learning From School Experiences

School problems have become newspaper headlines in the United States. Dropping achievement-test scores, as well as the failure to read and communicate with understanding, concern thoughtful educators in many places. Education has been invaded by political issues from the right and left extremes. Religious groups are concerned about the lack of teaching of values and morals. Yet recently a school system in our city tried to develop a series of classes on moral values. The local newspaper presented a front-page article on the opposition to this idea by a Christian group.

Both educators and parents are troubled about our schools. The costs of education continue to rise, while local budgets fall, and efforts to pass tax levies to avert financial crisis fail again and again.

This book certainly cannot answer these weighty questions, but we ask you to think with us about some issues that can be addressed.

PRESCHOOL EDUCATION

We are hearing about the need for early-childhood education and all-day kindergarten to help the children overcome educational lags or deficits. A few years ago it was fashionable to teach preschoolers to read, and recently a nationally syndicated television program demonstrated that infants can learn certain number concepts.

Why the Increase in Preschools

Preschools have popped up like mushrooms all over the United States. When such widespread developments take place, one can count on the fact that some unusual needs prompt them.

1. So many mothers have gone to work that the need for preschools or day-care centers is quite clear. Over 50 percent of married women are working today, which limits child-care resources in homes.

2. The availability of preschools tempts nonworking mothers to place their children in such a center, so they may enjoy more freedom.

3. Early-childhood education helps children prepare for the mental and social demands of school.

Advantages of Preschools

Any of the above reasons is valid for deciding to put your child in a preschool. But before you decide, sift through the specific needs you and your child have, and decide whether he should enter a preschool. If you are working, you must have child care, and a preschool may offer some advantages for your child. A chance to learn social skills in a warm, friendly environment can be especially useful to an only child, or the youngest one. Also, working mothers do not have the time to devote to many of the learning experiences of childhood, and a preschool can help you with teaching your child. Even if you are not a working mother, you may need some time for yourself or with younger children. Your child will benefit from social experiences with others, so you need not feel guilty if you do send your child to preschool. On the other hand, do not feel that your child will be deprived if you keep him at home.

Disadvantages of Preschools

The disadvantages of day-care centers and preschools are not many, but they are important. Although children do not mind having one or even two substitute mothers, adjusting to too many adults can be very hard on children. The confusion of a large number of other youngsters on a daily basis may be fatiguing. The expectations of preschool teachers may be too great or too little, and can add to a young child's confusion and stress.

In looking for a day-care center or a preschool, here are some useful guidelines:

Selecting a Preschool

1.　Seek a place where the staff is warm, consistent, and fair. If possible, drop in unexpectedly and observe the mood of the children who are there.

2.　You will want your child in a clean, pleasant environment. Bright colors, clean toys, and an organized physical plant are evidences of good care.

3.　Watch for an overly structured program. Children need time to just "be" as much as they need to do and learn. This balance in freedom and structure is vital.

4.　Observe the availability of attention by the staff to a child who is shy and quiet as well as the aggressive child. Sometimes a good child gets overlooked in attending to the "problem" children.

If your child shows signs of being upset after starting in preschool, check with the teacher to see if there is a problem. Often there is trouble in adjusting initially, but this works out with time. If you feel there is serious neglect or overly harsh discipline, consider another place. However, try to work out problems and avoid impulsive changes. You will not find a perfect place, and new adjustments are hard on children, too. Stick with your own priorities in child care, and stay with the place that best fits them.

Montessori Schools

Many people ask us how we feel about Montessori schools. These are based on the concepts of Maria Montessori, and were begun in Italy in 1906. They have become widespread in the United States. Her schools follow her fine beliefs. The philosophy of Montessori is based on encouraging each child's freedom and responsibility to explore and learn by natural consequences.

There is a great deal of adult time and attention in the teaching, which also includes a variety of materials and equipment. The value of Montessori schools depends on the training of the staff, their ways of relating to children, and to the child's specific needs. For the well-disciplined, bright, curious, and creative child, we have seen Montessori schools offer great opportunities for a child's development.

Children who have experienced the free and stimulating environment of such a school may be frustrated and bored in public schools. Some children who have less self-control, or who are hyperactive or anxiety-ridden, may be unable to function in the free setting of a Montessori school.

We suggest that you explore your community's resources. Your pediatrician or family doctor can advise you or will be able to help you find someone who can guide you in your choice of a preschool.

Keeping the Child Home

If you aren't working, and your child does not adjust well in preschool, keep him at home for a longer time and try again later. Trading child care with friends is another good answer to giving you some free time.

Children really do not play well with each other prior to the age of three. They play alone in the midst of others, but are so busy establishing their own rights and power, they make poor playmates. If you need care for a child under three, we suggest that you try a relative, friend, or neighbor. The personal attention such people can give in their homes, or even yours, and the chance to relate with only one person, will suit your younger child's needs better than a larger day-care center.

KINDERGARTEN

When to Start?

When should your child start school? Most schools will not accept a child in kindergarten unless he is five before the start of school in the fall. You may want to have your child wait an extra year, if the birth date is close to the borderline. This is especially true for boys. No one yet knows why, but boys are slower to develop in many areas of life than girls. We don't believe this means they are inferior—just different! In one school district, there were two-and-a-half times more boys than girls who were referred for special educational services. It is probable that some of that trouble might be avoided by waiting that extra year to allow the child an opportunity for greater maturation.

Is He Ready?

Here are some guidelines that may help you know *if your child is ready* for kindergarten:

1. *His attention span is long enough that he can sit still and do a required activity for at least twenty or thirty minutes at a stretch.*
2. *He is able to follow directions involving two or three steps. "Go and get that book; find your crayons; and color a picture."*
3. *He is able to respect and obey the rules and authority of the teacher.*
4. *He has reasonable ability to play and work with other children.*

If your child cannot measure up in at least three of these four common behaviors, he probably should wait until the next year. We have seen a number of children who were failing in some area before the end of the first semester in kindergarten. It is easier to build success than to overcome failure. It's no disgrace to wait!

EARLY SCHOOL DAYS

Many children go through several days of crying when they start school. Those who have become accustomed to preschool do less crying, or none at all. The start of school is the entryway into an entirely new era of life. When a child starts school, he loses more freedoms at one time than he will ever lose again. Understandably this will be sad, frightening, and even frustrating to him.

Rough Days at First

Expect your kindergartner (and your first-grader) to have some rough days at first. When our youngest sat down to dinner after the first whole day in first grade, she held her head in her hands and said dolefully, "Be nice to me, Mommy! I've had a hard day." And we knew she had, indeed. So we were "nice" to her, held her a while, and read her a long story at bedtime. Few children ask. Instead, many act out their needs in babyishness, petulance, and irritability. The underlying need is the same. "I've had a hard day; it looks like a rough year; *and I don't want to grow up!*" Parents, please hear that plea, and respond with gentleness and patience. In a few weeks, your child will accept the inevitable and will give up his babydom forever. Help him leave it gradually.

Get to Know the Teacher

Once your child is settled in school, get to know his teacher. That person will spend more waking time with your child than you will for the next nine months. Help her understand your child, his needs, and his interests. *Do not tell her how to do her job,* but be available to work with her, and then let go and trust her. Dr. Grace has worked extensively with several school systems, and has found that the overwhelming majority of teachers are dedicated and caring people who want your child to learn and succeed. In fact, their students' successes mirror their own achievements.

Parent-Teacher Problems

However, therein lies one of the most common problems we encounter in schools. When a child does not succeed, the teacher may fear she is failing. Not wanting to do that, she may unconsciously blame the parents or child. Now parents also want that child to succeed, for that will reflect their success at parenting. If the child fails, they will find it easy to blame the teacher, or the school system. This sort of blame, perhaps ever so subtle, can start a battleground that will see constant warfare throughout a child's school career.

Call a Truce. You, as parents, need to call a truce. Go *together* to your child's teacher if there are problems. Admit your own concerns about your child, and tell the teacher of your mistakes as well as your successes. Do not attack or accuse her, but ask her help and offer yours. In almost every situation where we have seen such an approach tried, the child settles down and begins to work for success.

An Incompetent Teacher. In the rare event of your child's placement with a truly incompetent teacher, go to the principal with good, solid information about that incompetence. There is a chance that your information is wrong, and you need an open mind to such a possibility. If, in fact, this teacher could be harmful to other children (as well as yours) and their educational processes are endangered, she may need help. You cannot realistically deal with her problem, but you could ask that your child be placed in another class.

Student-Teacher Problems

Sometimes there is no avoiding a serious student-teacher conflict. Do all you can to see to it that you and your child deal honestly and straightforwardly with such a problem. If no solution can be found that is to your liking, use the situation for your child's good. There are times throughout life that everyone has to work and deal with people who are difficult. You may use a "problem" teacher to help your child understand and learn how to work with someone who is difficult.

Beware Misrepresentations. Be very careful of a major danger in any problem your child may have at school! Most children learn early in life how to turn various situations to their own selfish advantage, even at the cost of honesty. School is a ready target for such manipulation. A child may misrepresent a person or an event to gain your sympathy or make you take sides against the teacher.

Do not be a part of such a trick. It will fix destructive habits firmly in your child's life. If you look closely, you may recognize that your child has done such things at home. He may be setting Mom against Dad more than you've realized, and that's a habit that needs breaking. So be sure you really listen to *all sides of an issue before you choose one.* Taking a child's side is not always in his best interest.

PRIVATE SCHOOLS

Know Your Public School

Many parents are concerned about what is being taught to their children. They worry about permissiveness in sex education, atheism, political liberalism, and the evolutionary theory of creation. We share your concerns about such teachings and others. They do exist, and they are probably more extensive in some parts of the country than in others. Parents need to know the climate of their local public-school system. This knowledge will be a good yardstick as to the type of education offered to their children.

These concerns of parents about their children's educations are philosophical and moral, as well as intellectual, and they are valid. There is little doubt that private and Christian schools offer special protection to your children during the years in which they are mentally vulnerable to error in teaching.

Selecting the Right School

If you can afford to send your child to a private school, think carefully about the range of needs of your child, as well as his unique personal gifts. Search for the school with the resources that best meet those needs. Here are some considerations to help you in selecting the right place for your child.

1. *Academic soundness* is vital to your child's learning now, as well as to his entire academic future. College work is very difficult when a child has poor foundations in broad knowledge or good learning skills, so be certain the school is not too easy.

2. *Ethical and moral values are of extreme importance in looking at private schools.* To find out about these areas, talk with several people, not just the headmaster. Visit chapel and sit in on classes that may help you grasp the tone of the whole school. Watch the students as they study and socialize together.

3. *Biblical and spiritual philosophies vary considerably*

among Christian schools. Ask frankly about the school's teachings concerning areas that are important to you. You probably won't find any one school that measures up to your desires in all areas, so be clear about the ones that are most significant.

4. *Clear thinking and intellectual honesty are fundamental to all learning.* Does the school teach your child how to think deeply about sensitive issues, weigh all sides, and come out with a logical as well as a spiritually sound point of view? Every child needs tools with which to think for himself and, in fact, these tools are more useful than memorized answers.

5. *Physical health is essential to a well-rounded life.* Does the school teach the importance of physical health and well-being? Your child needs to learn and practice good nutritional habits, the value of active exercise and physical education, and general health maintenance. Schools play an important role in supporting and furthering your own beliefs and teaching about these important health concepts.

6. *Creativity is a special gift of God to mankind.* What does the school offer in terms of helping your child discover, develop, and value his special creative gifts? As children develop academically, it is possible for these unique gifts to be neglected.

7. *Love and laughter are a balance to the serious affairs of learning.* What is the social climate of the school? Are there cliques and rivalry among the students? Or is there generally a sense of mutual respect and support for each other? Is there an appropriate encouragement of healthy good humor?

8. *Learning is caught as much as it is taught.* What is the attitude between students and faculty? Do authority issues or other divisive influences separate one from the other? Or do the faculty and administration relate with their students as friends and mentors?

9. *Good equipment helps open learning opportunities.* This is far less important, we feel, than other values. But today's world is a technical one, and being familiar with "gadgetry" can be a true advantage to your child.

10. *Practical living skills are important in your child's daily living.* Does this school emphasize homemaking, mechanical, and business courses as well as precollege courses?

If you can find a private school that rates high in most of these areas, make any reasonable sacrifice to get your child enrolled there! And it probably will be a sacrifice, because the cost of education has risen in proportion to the cost of living in general.

Disadvantages of Private Schools

There are a few problems with private schools that you need to consider:

It is not unusual for parents of a problem child to send him to a private school to correct those problems and "straighten him out." Your child will, therefore, be among certain young people who are not strong enough to be a good influence on him. Just be aware of this, and try to help your child be compassionate toward those who have difficulties. Help your son or daughter develop sound judgment and courage in issues of choosing right or wrong. They'll need those qualities forever.

Some private schools get out of balance in the issues listed above. They may be superb academically, but totally lacking in the encouragement of a healthy social climate. It is possible for athletic success to become more important than ethical and moral honesty. Rarely, a school may sacrifice academics for exclusive biblical teaching.

Jesus, we are told, grew in wisdom, and in stature, and in favor with God and man. That's a perfect balance in the wholeness of life. After all is said and done, this may be your very best guide!

PUBLIC SCHOOLS

For many Christian families, private schools are simply not an option. The extra cost may be prohibitive, no matter how sacrificial you are. In that case, you may do some very important things to help balance your child's learning and growing experiences in your public schools.

Become familiar with your child's textbooks and study materials. You do not have to master modern math or computer sciences—though you may. The teachers your child has will be skilled, as a rule, in the academic areas of life, but you can learn about their basic beliefs. Read enough of the science books to find out whether a balanced view regarding evolutionary theories is presented. Ridicule for biblical teachings needs to be recognized, if it is there, in order to protect your child from such biased attitudes.

Join a Cause? Many parents are banding together to fight such teachings and textbooks. If you feel led by God to join such a fight, do so. It has been our experience, however, that more harm than good can come out of some of these movements. Seek good counsel about whether to join a cause, or to quietly work on a one-to-one basis with your child, his friends, and their teachers or principal.

Get to know your child's teacher. Almost every school has an open house and a time for individual conferences with your child's teachers. *Be there!* Few things are more important than knowing those teachers, but do approach them with an open mind. "Explore—don't expect." Many teachers will share your deepest concerns, and will appreciate your support of spiritual and moral values. Even if your child's teacher disagrees with you, you need to treat him with respect and love if you are to influence him or her. By listening and discussing, you will learn much that will enable you to understand your child's school problems and help him to solve them.

Practice good reading habits. Read magazines and books of all kinds and think about their viewpoints on various issues. Discuss these with your children. By keeping a step or more ahead of the concepts your child is being taught, you can guide him. Use those priceless tools of logic and balanced, Spirit-led thinking that will help him find solid answers to confusion and doubts throughout life.

Keep your family in church and other Christian groups that will ground them in solid biblical teachings. Your children respect you, but they need the support of their peers in the day-to-day struggles in the classroom, so help your children find Christian friends who will be involved in their school activities as well as in church activities.

Keep the communication lines open and your relationships loving and respectful. Children will rarely discuss issues with parents who are angry or condemning. Learn to disagree agreeably and keep listening and talking.

No matter how hard you've tried, your children may seem to

abandon your teachings and adopt those of a more liberal nature. This is especially likely as they reach adolescence, with its
pressure to establish a sense of independence. You will be
tempted to try to force them into following your beliefs and
adopting your values. We urge you to resist this temptation. It's
likely that the issue itself is not even important! Teenagers have
to disagree with someone to prove their independence and the
more you push, the harder they feel they must push back. At
this age, listen to them, discuss ideas and issues as you would
with an adult friend, and don't be too troubled. Wait, pray, and
they, like the prodigal son, will come "home."

LEARNING DISABILITIES

Dyslexia

There are many children in schools today who have handicaps in specific areas of learning. For many, this problem is limited to reading and is called *dyslexia*. In others, it is related to
mathematics, and for many, it is spelling that seemingly defeats
them. In some cases, the reading and spelling problem is associated with a reversal of letter shapes. When *b* means *d* to a
child, *bad* becomes *dab* or vice versa. We can all agree that such
confusion would make it difficult to master spelling and writing,
as well as reading.

The Mechanism of Learning

Not only is there a problem with mastering the sounds and
shapes of letters, but there also are neurological factors that
enter into the learning process. As the eye sees a letter or word,
it sends a message to the visual center of the brain, which then
connects with the cortex (or outer layer) of the brain. Apparently it is there that the original object or word seen by the
eye is decoded into something we have seen or heard before, or
that seems new. People who study learning problems believe
that perhaps some short-circuit takes place in these complex
nerve tracts that interferes with the recognition of words or, in
similar ways, with sounds through the hearing devices.

Overcoming Learning Disabilities

While authorities are still studying the reasons for learning disabilities, educators are working hard to find ways to overcome them. Many schools have teachers who are especially trained and gifted in teaching such children to read, write, spell, and master arithmetic. If you believe your child has a special problem with learning, ask for him to be tested and placed with someone who can help him learn.

Even with a minimum amount of specialized help, many people seem to "outgrow" their learning disabilities. Usually by the seventh or eighth grade, these young people begin to develop enough successes to believe in themselves, and once they begin to do well, they can't be stopped.

Practical Considerations of Learning Disabilities

Lack of Concentration. Whatever obscure neurological or biochemical factors there may be, there are some practical issues involved in learning difficulties. When a child worries too much, when he has only partial information about family concerns, and when he has too few successes on which to build, he will have trouble concentrating. It's difficult to deal with multiplication tables when you're worried about your parents' reaction to your grade card, or you know your grandpa has had a heart attack. We see many children who are so preoccupied with television or even exciting plans for special coming events, that they are unable to focus on mundane topics like the Civil War or the people in Latin America.

How Parents Can Help. While it takes specially trained teachers to help a child learn proper letter and word formations, you, as parents, can help with the emotional blocks to learning. Let us suggest these steps for your consideration:

1. Consider and write down all the things about which your child could be worrying. Do this with your spouse or a person who knows your child well. Then ask your child about any worries he may have, and add them to your list.
2. Take one or two of these issues each day, and discuss them with your child. As much as possible, get the child to

talk about them and about his feelings regarding these problems.

3. Give him whatever information you can that will clear up those worries and really put them to rest.

4. Do not exaggerate or minimize your child's concern or feelings. Regardless of what they seem to you, they are real to him.

5. Help your child know that he may come to you with any worry he has at any time. Let him borrow your wisdom and strength.

6. Both you and your child may talk with the heavenly Father about any and all concerns and leave them with Him.

7. Be available to each child every day for the purpose of keeping that child's mind free of stored-up worries. If he doesn't come to you, go to him and ask if he needs to talk. Please avoid nagging, but simply be open. .

Stop Worrying. Try to leave the teaching of your child to his teacher. If she asks you to help him with some exercises or homework, do so. Avoid worrying, because unfortunately, rather than helping him, that will only convince him that he is a terrible problem. He already suspects that. There is a big difference between *having* a problem, for which you will eventually find the answer, and *being* a problem, for which there are no solutions. Help your child discover the areas in which he is successful, and let him know your honest pride in him. Don't overdo that, or he will think you are covering up your own worry or pity.

Relaxed Evenings. With the best intentions in the world, some parents keep a child plugging away at homework so much that he simply rebels. Dr. Grace's sister, who taught elementary school for over forty years, found that children did better in school when most of their evenings were times of fun and warmth within the family.

God's Plan for Your Child. Occasionally, tutors may help a child with a specific learning disability, and prevent the tension between you and your child that ends up defeating all of you. But again, *keep enough free time for your child to relax and be a child.* Almost always, children outgrow learning problems. If you don't allow those to be compounded by personality disorders or rebelling, he will compensate for them and forge ahead when he is ready. *Remember that God has a special plan for every child's life.* He will make that plan work, if you all work with Him.

THE GIFTED CHILD

Often we consider handicapped children the special ones, but gifted children are also "special." A child who learns quickly, and perceives deeply, may experience personal social problems. He cannot understand why other children are so slow, and they may resent the ease with which he learns or performs. Teachers and parents alike may enjoy the gifted child so much that they push him endlessly for ever-increasing successes. The child may feel like a whirling dervish who can't stop spinning, even for a moment's rest.

Needs of the Gifted Child

Actually, the needs of gifted children are similar to those of other children. They need loving acceptance, pride and approval, consistency, and joy in sharing their discoveries in life. No matter how capable they are, they need the security of your wisdom and experience. You will always be years ahead in those departments.

Gifted children need *discipline*. Teach your child the same respect and obedience as any other child learns. Keep him aware of his own and other's feelings, since superior intelligence can block the acceptance and expression of emotions. To be a whole person, your gifted child needs to be able to play, laugh, and cry, as well as learn and perform. He needs to develop a good conscience, since *responsibility in the wise and generous use of his giftedness must be taught.*

How to Avoid Egocentricity

Gifted people sometimes seem arrogant and ego centered. You may help your child avoid this obnoxious attitude. Begin the process of preventing conceit by keeping your own attitude healthy. Gratitude for gifts is appropriate, but taking the credit for a gift is not logical. God gives each of us certain abilities because He intends them to enrich our lives, and then to be used lovingly and creatively to improve our personal worlds. Teach your child such a concept, and he will learn to accept himself and his gifts with some balance in excitement and responsibility.

Special Programs

Schools sometimes ask that a gifted child be advanced a grade or be placed in special programs. Use your own judgment in such a question. Children do grow with greater challenges and expectations, but watch for signs that this may be creating either undue anxiety or conceit. A child may do better at the top of a good average class, than in the middle or lower portion of a program for gifted children. Most decisions are reversible, so you may choose to try such a program, but withdraw your child if any undesirable effects are seen.

"The Beginning of Knowledge"

There is so much to learn in today's scientifically advanced world. Keep your children motivated by your example and your encouragement of their natural curiosity. Support your schools in every way you can, but evaluate the risks and problems they pose, as well. Be especially aware of the fact that "the fear of the Lord is the beginning of knowledge . . ." (Proverbs 1:7).

19
Rearing Special Children

Every child is unique and special, right down to his footprints. But for some very significant reasons, some children are extra-special.

ADOPTIVE CHILDREN

This subject was discussed briefly in chapter 2, but we wish to address ourselves here especially to those who have experienced adoption, either as a parent or child.

For several years, I [Grace] worked closely with unmarried mothers and their babies. Most of them gave up those babies for placement in two-parent families, and I shared with them the pain of that experience. I wish every adopted person could know the selfless quality of the special love that prompted releasing that child for adoption.

Special Joy of Adoptive Parents

I also wish adopted people might know the special joy of their adoptive parents on the occasion of that adoption. Those couples who had so much love to give a child—and thought they might never find a child to receive it—were ecstatic over their new babies. They were carefully scrutinized and selected for their ability to be good parents.

A Painful Search

Today the media have dramatized certain reunions of adopted people and their biological parents. There has come to

be a great search for one's "roots" and ancestry. And that is understandable and natural—to a degree. Sometimes, however,
this search can unearth more pain than it does joy. I believe
some of that potential pain may be avoided by the following
ideas for adoptive parents.

Suggestions for Adoptive Parents

*Get Information. Find out as much as you can about your
adopted baby's parents.* Keep the positive information written
down, so you won't forget it, and *lose the rest.* Your child will
one day want and need to know: *the appearance of his biological parents; their special talents and interests; their medical
histories; and how much they loved that child.*

Your Search and Love for Him. As your child's ability to understand unfolds, *tell him something about his adoption.* The
facts regarding your search for him, and the love that you feel
for him, will help him be secure. You may want to refer occasionally to the gratitude and love you feel for the other parents
who gave him life. (Some adoptive parents feel unnecessarily
jealous or resentful of those biological parents. Such feelings
can only hurt your relationship with your adopted child.)

Clear but Casual. Keep the fact of your child's adoption clear
but *casual.* We have seen some adoptive parents celebrating
two birthdays—the biological one as well as the adoption day.
Perhaps that makes too big an issue of the adoption, and may
result in the child's feeling different rather than special.

How to Tell the Adoptive Child

The Story. How can you tell your baby he is adopted? and
when? One of the nicest ways to tell a child anything is in a
story. Our children, even as adults, like to hear about their
babyhood. So you may want to tell your tiny baby or older
child, almost as soon as you get him, the story of his birth.
Weave into that story your own part in looking for a baby to
love and share your home. Such a story becomes like an old
friend, and most children will want it repeated many times.
When they stop asking for it, lay it to rest.

The Maternity Home. It was not uncommon for parents to drop by the maternity home where their child had been born and ask me to talk with them for a while. Adoptive children are invariably pleased to hear about their birth, and the day their adoptive parents took them home. Driving by the hospital where your adopted child was born, or even showing him pictures, can establish his identity just a little bit more securely.

Lack of Available Children

The adoptive process itself is careful but relatively simple. It is *finding children available for adoption* that is now difficult. Since about 1970, legalized abortions, birth-control availability, and a liberalized public opinion about single parents keeping babies, has dramatically reduced the kind and number of babies who are adoptable. Private adoption is tempting when an available child comes to your attention. While private adoptions are legal, they are risky. There is a great deal of effort by qualified adoption agencies put into matching a baby and its adoptive family. Some adoptive parents simply may not be able to accept a baby with certain handicaps or familial traits. In a private adoption, such a situation is very difficult to handle, since there may be no other resources planned for the baby.

Go to a Recognized Agency

For these and other reasons, we strongly recommend, if you want to adopt a child, that you go to a *recognized* child-placement agency. Your minister or family doctor can help you locate such a place. They will work with you to discover just the sort of child whom you can honestly love and accept. And they will try to find such a child. Acceptance as an adoptive family by such an agency is not a pass-fail selection. It is a process of matching what you parents have to offer with the exact child who needs that—to the joy and fulfillment of both.

Today's Available Children

Children who are now available for adoption include those who are of mixed racial backgrounds; those who are older (from several months to several years); and some who may have various physical handicaps. Do not force yourself to accept a child about whom you can't feel truly good and loving. In your desperate wish for a child, it is tempting to accept any child at all, and then find you really cannot love him. That would be terribly unfair to both you and him. By waiting, the right child for you will come along if it is meant to be. The God who sees even a baby sparrow fall from its nest, surely knows and cares about every child. Trust Him to bring the right child and you together.

The Legalities

Be clear about the legal process of adoption. Most states issue a new birth certificate at the time of adoption, and seal the one on which the biological parents' names are inscribed. Such names are very difficult to obtain. Now there is a widespread movement to liberalize the release of information about biological parents. *Again, let me remind you that such information belongs to those other parents as well as the child, and it may not be wise or kind to dig into it.*

PREMATURE BABIES

With the increase in medical skill and the development of special equipment, many premature babies can now survive who once had no chance to live. A baby born much earlier than the seventh month, or twenty-eight weeks, is at great risk. Babies as small as two pounds and even less do survive, and babies as big as four pounds usually live.

Care of Premature Baby

Physical Needs. Any premature baby will probably be put in an incubator at least for a day or two. He will need to be checked carefully to be sure his heart, lungs, and other body functions are normal. If he is small or has any complications, he will need to stay in an incubator for a longer time. "Preemies" tend to be slow to regain their birth weight and to grow big and strong enough to be cared for in a regular crib. Often they must be fed through a stomach tube, and many of them need oxygen for several weeks or longer.

Emotional Needs. Hospitals now make heroic efforts to care for the emotional, as well as the physical needs, of preemies. They may be placed in a rocker which simulates the movement of a mother's body, and a tape or record of the sounds of a mother's heartbeat plays steadily to the tiny baby. Parents are allowed to scrub and gown, and handle their baby through the windows on the incubator.

Taking Her Home

If your preemie makes it, she should be as healthy as any child. Your doctor will not let you take her home until you are fairly comfortable with each other. So treat her as normally as you can. Follow your doctor's advice and enjoy your baby. Do remember, however, that she will develop in every way in relation to the birth date on which she should have been born, not the one on which she was born. Knowing this can help you to avoid worry that your child is retarded!

THE HANDICAPPED CHILD

There are many types of handicaps that may affect a special child. Much research and many millions of dollars have gone into understanding and preventing birth defects—but still they do happen. In today's ease-seeking world, it is tempting to try to avoid the birth of such a child.

Amniocentesis Findings

A procedure called *amniocentesis* is now used widely by obstetricians. A special needle is inserted into the water-filled sac in which a developing baby lives. By removing some of the fluid, it is possible to find enough cells from the baby's body to study the chromosomes. Certain birth defects, as well as the sex of the child, can be determined quite early in a pregnancy. A friend recently shared with us her anxiety about the results of such a test. If she were to learn that her expected baby would be born with Down's syndrome, for example, should she have an abortion? The legality of abortions is now established by the Supreme Court of the United States. Does that legality constitute permission for her to seek an abortion? And does it assume the responsibility for cutting short the unborn life of a child? We think not. However, these are questions each parent must answer for herself. Do not answer too hurriedly. Get all the information you can, and seek God's guidance.

Avoidance by Abortion

In considering the question of abortion, here are some issues to include:

Is the thought that motivates you to have an abortion a selfish one? Seeking pleasure and avoiding pain have come to be acceptable as a philosophy of life in today's world. Accepting the birth of a handicapped child, however, can be an opportunity for God to teach you some profound and beautiful lessons. *Refusing to accept that learning experience may be the same as setting up your judgment over God's.*

In considering the hardships of the life of a handicapped child, you may judge that preventing that child's birth is a truly unselfish act. Let us suggest that you think more deeply and explore further. Some of the most profoundly moving experiences of our lives have been those involving the unparalleled courage and compassion of severely handicapped children.

Sometimes an abortion is a tempting escape from financial burdens or a miserable marriage. Such an escape can remove the stress that may have driven you to a new depth in exploring God's loving power in your life.

Value of Pain

Taking into our human hands decisions regarding life and death is risky at best. Over a period of time, people can unconsciously become calloused to the prime issues of trust in God to apportion our pain and pleasures. The value of pain is easily forgotten, and it may be that we can make life so controlled that we forget we even need Him.

I [Dr. Grace] have worked in several capacities with parents of severely handicapped children. I have heard their anger and anguish, and have wept with them over the limitations of their children. Yet within the homes of most such children, I have seen the ultimate heroism. I have seen both parents and siblings grow in compassion, gentleness, and courage. These qualities have reached out to the pain of other families with similar problems in support and cooperation.

We believe in the healthy integration of all sorts of experiences into life—not just the pleasant ones. And we urge you to use any hardships life brings you to stimulate your creativity in finding solutions, as well as your trust in God's wisdom and power to help you.

Parents' Emotional Reactions

There are at least four major emotional reactions you may experience in dealing with a handicapped child.

1. Guilt

Many parents feel they have done something wrong and that they are being punished through their child's problem. Even when they know better intellectually, they feel guilty. Please throw that feeling out! Rarely, if ever, are birth defects anyone's fault. In any rare exception, if you may have been at fault, learn from the error, seek forgiveness, and *forgive yourself.* Guilt can prompt growth and change. It is good for nothing else, so lay it aside.

2. Anger

When you have to live with the aching hardships of a severely handicapped child, it is natural to feel angry. We believe that anger is normal. God Himself was angry, and Jesus was angry, as He drove the money changers out of the temple. God does not, we suspect, feel threatened by our anger, any more than we do when our little grandson gets angry. In fact, we once read that some of us begin to be honest with God only when we communicate our anger to Him. *Just don't let your anger separate you from Him.*

3. Blame

Anger directed at each other involves blame. Families with severely handicapped children have been studied by a colleague. He has seen more marital strife, and even divorce, among these families than in any other families. Much of this is due to one's focusing disproportionate time on the child, feeling resentful, and blaming the other, who blames the first for being such a "martyr."

4. Withdrawing

Instead of talking out the feelings above, many people try to hide them. In well-intended efforts to spare each other, they carry their burdens of sadness and anxiety alone. Please do not do that! You will find in sharing, a lightening of both loads, and even some creative answers of a practical sort to many problems. You needn't feel that it is weak to need each other as husband and wife, or to need the help of others.

Handling the Handicapped Child

How do you handle your handicapped child? Here are some practical suggestions.

1. Physically

Find and stay with a doctor who knows you and your child, and trust his medical guidance. He will tell you what specialists are needed and when. Be sure to follow his recommendations.

2. Emotionally

Finish your own grief. (*See* Grief in chapter 16.) Work to keep a realistic emotional balance yourself. Help your special child to understand himself and his limitations without pity. He will have times of frustration and grief. Accept these, and teach him how to get through them and to return to self-acceptance. Help him to balance courage with honest fear or resentment in times of special stress. Remember, it is normal to feel whatever you feel—but usually you can think and fight your way back to peace of mind and help your child to do so.

3. Behaviorally

Learn to know your child's limitations but also his capabilities. Be as firm and positive as you must to help him live up to his best, just as you would a child who is not handicapped. It is sometimes even more essential that a handicapped child learn obedience and cooperation than a "normal" child. Various treatments and procedures are easier and more effective when a child works with them.

4. Socially

The days of hiding a handicapped child in an upstairs room are, hopefully, over. If it is at all possible, help your child function to his maximum socially. Many special kinds of handicaps demand placement with others who have similar problems, for special schooling or therapy. Do find the courage to do this. Schools for the blind, deaf, retarded, and orthopedically handicapped are able to train and teach them much more effectively than most parents can do. Many times this demands a boarding school at an early age. As difficult as this is, we encourage it. This is not rejecting or dumping your child, but giving him the best opportunity to develop the potential he has. You will need to visit him, and learn along with him how to encourage maturation and maximum development.

5. Spiritually

You have the greatest of all assets in your trust in God. His power, love, and wisdom are promised to you. Call upon them and teach them to your child.

Other Children in the Family

Help other children in your family to accept the handicapped child comfortably. They usually will follow your example as parents. It is often necessary to spend inordinate amounts of time and energy with your special child. Take time to explain this to your other children. Include them in caring for their handicapped sibling, but avoid overburdening them. Find some time to spend with each child. One suggestion for finding extra time is by trading child care with parents who understand and share your special needs. Grandparents and other relatives also may help in some ways to free time for you to spend with the other children.

Time for Each Other

Especially, let us urge you to spend some time with each other as husband and wife. The strength of your good relationship is vital to your children's well-being. Each of you will also need some time entirely alone. Being free for even a short time will give you renewed energy for your heavy responsibilities. These times, far from being selfish, are necessary to keep yourselves in shape and enable you to keep going.

Institutional Placement

There may come a time when your special child becomes such a problem that you realistically cannot manage him for one reason or another. Seek all the advice you can medically, spiritually, and psychologically. *Do not confuse martyrdom with heroism.* If your child demands so much that everyone else in the family is suffering seriously, do not be afraid to accept institutional placement. That may serve your child's needs very adequately, perhaps even more effectively than you could do at home. You may fill the spot left empty by the loss of your child through helping other parents with similar problems, and certainly you can be of great service to the rest of your family.

A Final Word to Parents:
How to Regain Your Losses

By Grace H. Ketterman, M.D.

In the heart of every parent, there is a dream of being a truly great mother or father. The proof of that greatness, of course, is the ideal child who results from such parenting. Given a day at a time, most moms and dads do the best job they can possibly do, but mysteriously, things go wrong. Often no one knows just what happened, or when, that turned a child from an angel into a monster. At any rate, nearly all parents make mistakes and these need correcting.

As I followed my mother's coffin out of the church after her funeral service, many years ago, I recall thinking, "The next time I see Mother, we will understand each other!" In this life, we seemed to be at odds most of the time. I recall feeling responsible for her frequent physical aches and illnesses, and certainly she worried about my moodiness, and believed me to be rebellious.

Some years after Mother's death, I sat down one evening and in my imagination thought through a little dialogue with her. I said all the tender, yearning things I had wanted to say to her when she was alive, and somehow never could express. Then I struggled to imagine how she would have responded to me. Out of that deeply emotional experience, one fact emerged. My mother honestly loved me, and wanted the very best for me. Actually, I had not been aware of believing that she did not love me, but obviously I had felt that, for with the new awareness came a flood of relief! Almost instantly, I understood that I had not been a bad child, and she was not a bad mother. I could forgive her mistakes, and my own, and I learned some vital lessons.

PARENTAL MISTAKES

Most parents make either the same mistakes their parents made, or the opposite ones. My mother scolded us a great deal, so I rarely yelled at our children. Later, I realized I should perhaps have "yelled" more.

Looking back at your parents can be very helpful in understanding both mistakes and positive techniques. Please do not use such retrospection as an excuse for your own errors or to blame your parents! But do use it to help yourselves find the best possible balances in your attitudes and skills as parents.

Get Rid of Guilt Feelings

In correcting mistakes, you need to get rid of guilt and guilt feelings. These will, inevitably trip you up and cause you to compound one set of mistakes with still more. Guilt feelings, let us remind you, are a vague sense of having done wrong, without any clear ideas about what that wrong actually was. Discard such feelings, if you can, since they are not based on facts. They are remnants of unhappy childhood experiences, and are not valid for you as adults.

Amy's Memory. Amy had a particularly distressing childhood, and in her early teens tried repeatedly to work out those troubles through suicide gestures. I knew she was taking out a lot of anger, fear, and guilt on herself, but couldn't find out just what it was about. One day Amy remembered, and she panicked! As I sat with her, she trembled visibly under the impact of her memories. Brokenly, she described through her sobs repeated family scenes in which her mother and father argued with increasing intensity, until her father removed his belt and beat her mother into submission. It was Amy's belief, as a three-year-old child, that she should have made her father stop those beatings. She alone, she believed, could have protected her mother.

After hearing that story and quieting those wrenching sobs, Amy and I talked. As a young adult, she could understand the truth—no three-year-old had the power to stop an enraged man in such anger. She would likely have added to his fury and worsened matters. Self-forgiveness was possible only when Amy understood. When the false guilt was gone, Amy's suicidal attempts finally stopped, and she began to enjoy the security of knowing she had not been at fault.

Dealing With Real Guilt

Real guilt, of course, is knowing that you have broken a law, or have done something that has hurt someone else. For real guilt the answers are these:

1. *Admit that you have done the wrong.*
2. *Learn the best possible lessons from those errors, including why they were wrong and why you did them.*
3. *Decide upon a plan to correct your wrongdoing that includes confessing it, apologizing, and making it right in whatever way you can.*
4. *Ask God to forgive you, and then forgive yourself.*

Remember the incident only when you can use that memory to avoid repeating that same mistake.

Value of Hard Lessons. Remember, also, the value of the lessons you have learned from the hard times you lived through. Perhaps it was your parents' mistakes that taught you patience or sympathy and compassion for others. Just as "growing pains" are often a sign of physical maturation, so emotional pain is associated with personal development. This is not an excuse to be rude or careless about the way you treat your family, but it can help you to avoid being "bogged down" in despair.

When You Realize Your Mistakes

Discuss/Write Down. When you discover serious mistakes that you have made which hurt your child, *discuss them with another adult, or write them down,* so that you may clearly understand them, and then formulate a plan for changing.

Discuss With Your Child. Next, *find a quiet time in which to sit alone with your child and talk about the issues, and tell him about your sadness at the pain you unknowingly inflicted on him.* Briefly explain why you did those things, because usually the reason will be based on your deep caring for your child. And then make clear your commitment to change. Ask your child for help in breaking old habits and forming new ones. Be especially careful to follow through. Spouses can help each other, and so can other relatives or friends. Changing old habits is ever so difficult, and you will need encouragement and support.

You cannot go back and actually redo the things you've done wrong. But here are several creative ideas that you may use in trying to heal those hurts. You may think up your own ways to reparent your child.

Healing Old Hurts

One way to heal old hurts is to talk about them. We found that our teenagers enjoyed stories about their early childhood. At times, we have told about a particularly traumatic event, and then let them know that we shared the pain of that time. By getting them to discuss it, they have been able to release some of their resentments and find comfort. We try to understand where we made mistakes and admit our responsibilities for those mistakes. In doing this, however, *we do not absolve our children of their responsibilities.* They, too, have been at fault, and need to understand and correct that. We believe our example in owning up to our share, however, will enable them to admit their problems and work at changing them, even more successfully.

Show Your Affection

Try to find the time and some ways to show affection to your children. Older children usually do not like this in front of anyone else, especially their friends, but they do crave the warmth of your love. You may need to resolve much of the resentment between you, however, before your children will be willing to receive your love. In our experience, dropping by at bedtime can catch most young people in a vulnerable mood, and they are more likely to respond. If this does not happen at once, be patient and continue consistently.

Refusing Your Spiritual Values

Many Christian parents are deeply concerned and hurt when their children refuse to enter into family prayers, or even continue their own bedtime prayers. We have not found it possible to force young people into spiritual growth. It is likely, however, that when you mend your relationships with them, they will return to loving God in their own time. Whether or not your child enters into your prayers, continue your own intercession for them, but do so privately. Many children feel their parents are only trying to use religion to manipulate them into submission.

Listen, Laugh, Love

Be careful to listen more than you talk. Troubled young people do not open up quickly, and we have learned that patience has great rewards in the responsiveness it brings eventually.

Try to find laughter in your lives. When mistakes have left you with heartaches, life can become grim. It takes great effort to find humor in tension, but when you make that effort, the tension can often be broken. In Proverbs 17:22 we are told, "A merry heart doeth good like a medicine. . . ." With the cost of medicine what it is today, we may add that a merry heart is certainly less expensive!

Remember to compliment your child. Look at the positive attributes, not just the problems, and let him know how much you value them. Express the gratitude you feel for his life, and the good things it has brought to you.

Deliberately "spoil" a troubled child at times. Help your daughter with her hair or clothes. Surprise her with some makeup (if she is allowed to wear it), or a new set of hair ribbons when she least expects them. Take over your son's household job now and then, just to surprise him and say, "Son, I still love you!"

Communicate in deeds, words, and attitudes the sincere love you feel. When love is reestablished, forgiveness becomes easy, and finding new ways of living together and working out problems is possible.

Whatever your mistakes have been in the past, today is fresh and new. A wise man was inspired to write, "It is of the Lord's mercies that we are not consumed, because his compassions fail not. They are new every morning: great is thy faithfulness" (Lamentations 3:22, 23). You can count on that.

Bibliography

Armstrong, Julian. "Teenagers and Junk Food." *World Press* R27 (July 1980): 57.

A.M.A. American Dietetic Association, National Dairy Council, United Fresh Fruit and Vegetable Association. "What Part Does Nutrition Play in Fatigue?" *Current Health* 6 (February 1980): 16–18.

Beeson, Paul B., M.D., and McDermott, Walsh, M.D. *Cecil Textbook of Medicine.* Philadelphia: W. B. Saunders Co., 1979.

Berne, Eric, M.D. *Transactional Analysis.* New York: Ballantine Books, Inc., 1978.

Bettelheim, Bruno, Ph.D. *Love Is Not Enough.* New York: Avon Books, 1950.

Bloom, Benjamin S. *Human Characteristics and School Learning.* New York: McGraw-Hill Book Co., 1976.

Bowlby, John. *Child Care and the Growth of Love.* London: Whitefriars Press, Ltd., 1965.

Bremer, J. Lewis, M.D., and Weatherford, Harold L., M.D. *A Textbook of Histology.* Philadelphia: The Blakiston Co., 1975.

Campbell, D. Ross, M.D. *How to Really Love Your Child.* Wheaton, Ill.: Victor Books, 1977.

Caplan, Frank, ed. *Parents' Yellow Pages.* The Princeton Center for Infancy. Garden City, N.Y.: Doubleday & Co., Inc., 1978.

————. *The Parenting Advisor.* The Princeton Center for Infancy. Garden City, N.Y.: Doubleday & Co., Inc., 1977.

Chess, Stella, M.D.; Thomas, A., M.D.; and Birch, H. H., M.D. *Temperament and Behavior*. Garden City, N.Y.: Doubleday & Co., Inc., 1974.

Christophersen, Edward R., Ph.D. *Little People*. Lawrence, Kansas: H. & H. Enterprises, Inc., 1977.

Clarke, Jean I. *Self Esteem: A Family Affair*. Minneapolis: Winston Press, 1978.

Consumers Association of Canada. "Cola's Hidden Hazards." *World Press* R27 (May 1980): 57.

Coopersmith, Stanley. *Antecedents of Self Esteem*.

Dobson, James, Ph.D. *Hide or Seek*. Old Tappan, N.J.: Fleming H. Revell Co., 1974.

Dubos, Rene. "Nutritional Ambiguities" *Natural History* 89 (July 1980): 14.

Eden, Alvin N., M.D. *Handbook for New Parents*. New York: Berkeley Publishing Corp., 1979.

Editors of Consumer Guide. *The Complete Baby Book*. New York: Simon & Schuster, Inc., 1979.

Feinbloom, Richard I., M.D. *Child Health Encyclopedia*. The Boston Children's Medical Center. New York: Dell Publishing Co., Inc., 1978.

Fromme, Allan, Ph.D. *The ABC of Child Care*. New York: Pocket Books, Inc., 1977.

Gellis, Sydney S., M.D., and Kagan, Benjamin, M.D. *Current Pediatric Therapy Nine*. Philadelphia: W. B. Saunders Co., 1980.

Green, Morris, M. D., and Richmond, Julius B., M.D. *Pediatric Diagnosis*. Philadelphia: W. B. Saunders Co., 1954.

"Growing Furor Over Proper Foods for Kids." *U.S. News & World Report* 88 (March 24, 1980): 86.

Janss, Edmund. *How to Give Your Children Everything They Really Need*. Wheaton, Ill.: Tyndale House Publishers, Inc., 1979.

Kelly, Marguerite, and Parsons, Elias. *The Mothers' Almanac*. Garden City, N.Y.: Doubleday & Co., Inc., 1975.

LaHaye, Beverly. *How to Develop Your Child's Temperament*. Irvine, Calif.: Harvest House Publishers, 1977.

Pantell, Robert H., M.D.; Fries, James F., M.D.; and Vickery, Donald M., M.D. *Taking Care of Your Child: A Parents' Guide to Medical Care*. Reading, Mass.: Addison-Wesley Publishing Co., Inc., 1977.

Piaget, Jean, and Inhelder, Borbel. *The Psychology of the Child*. Translated by Helen Weaver. New York: Basic Books, Inc., 1969.

Smith, Lendon H., M.D. *The Encyclopedia of Baby and Child Care*. New York: Warner Books, Inc., 1980.

Spock, Benjamin. *Baby and Child Care,* rev. ed. New York: Pocket Books, Inc., 1976.

Swindoll, Charles. *You and Your Child*. Nashville: Thomas Nelson, Inc., 1977.

Vaughn, Victor C., M.D., and McKay, R. James, M.D. *Textbook of Pediatrics,* 10th ed. Waldo E. Nelson, M.D. and collaborators. Philadelphia: W. B. Saunders Co., 1975.

Young, Leontine. *Life Among the Giants*. New York: McGraw-Hill Book Co., 1966.

INDEX